AF789903

COST AND FEE ALLOCATION IN CIVIL PROCEDURE

IUS GENTIUM

COMPARATIVE PERSPECTIVES ON LAW AND JUSTICE

VOLUME 11

Series Editors

Mortimer Sellers
(University of Baltimore)
James Maxeiner
(University of Baltimore)

Board of Editors

Myroslava Antonovych (Kyiv-Mohyla Academy)
Nadia de Araujo (Pontifical Catholic University of Rio de Janeiro)
Jasna Bakšić-Muftić (University of Sarajevo)
David L. Carey Miller (University of Aberdeen)
Loussia P. Musse Felix (University of Brasília)
Emanuel Gross (University of Haifa)
James E. Hickey Jr. (Hofstra University)
Jan Klabbers (University of Helsinki)
Claudia Lima Marques (Federal University of Rio Grande do Sul)
Aniceto Masferrer (University of Valencia)
Eric Millard (Paris-Sud University)
Gabriël Moens (Murdoch University, Australia)
Raul C. Pangalangan (The University of the Philippines)
Ricardo Leite Pinto (Lusíada University of Lisbon)
Mizanur Rahman (University of Dhaka)
Keita Sato (Chuo University)
Poonam Saxena (University of New Delhi)
Gerry Simpson (London School of Economics)
Eduard Somers (University of Ghent)
Xinqiang Sun (Shandong University)
Tadeusz Tomaszewski (University of Warsaw)
Jaap W. de Zwaan (Netherlands Inst. of Intrntl. Relations, Clingendael)

COST AND FEE ALLOCATION IN CIVIL PROCEDURE

A COMPARATIVE STUDY

Edited by

MATHIAS REIMANN

Springer

Editor
Mathias Reimann
University of Michigan
Law School
625 South State Street
Ann Arbor
Michigan 48109-1215
USA

ISBN 978-94-007-2262-0 e-ISBN 978-94-007-2263-7
DOI 10.1007/978-94-007-2263-7
Springer Dordrecht Heidelberg London New York

Library of Congress Control Number: 2011940127

© Springer Science+Business Media B.V. 2012
Chapter 19 is published with kind permission of © Marco B.M. Loos 2012. All rights reserved.
No part of this work may be reproduced, stored in a retrieval system, or transmitted in any form or by any means, electronic, mechanical, photocopying, microfilming, recording or otherwise, without written permission from the Publisher, with the exception of any material supplied specifically for the purpose of being entered and executed on a computer system, for exclusive use by the purchaser of the work.

Printed on acid-free paper

Springer is part of Springer Science+Business Media (www.springer.com)

Preface

In the last five or so years, the costs of civil litigation and their allocation between the parties have become a major topic of discussion in many jurisdictions. Several countries have enacted new legislation liberalizing the market for legal services; international tribunals such as the European Court of Justice and the European Court of Human Rights have struggled with issues of access to justice; experts have been tasked with the writing of Reports on civil litigation costs to guide further reform; and scholars have published books and papers. Almost suddenly, it seems, lawmakers, legal practitioners, and academics have come to realize that few, if any, factors shape civil litigation as strongly and pervasively as who pays for what and how much.

This volume presents a thoroughly comparative approach to the topic. It contains a broad study on "Cost and Fee Allocation in Civil Procedure" drawing on data from almost 40 jurisdictions in six continents. This study is based on the General Report commissioned by the International Academy of Comparative Law and written for the XVIIIth World Congress of Comparative Law in Washington, DC, in the summer of 2010. The volume also presents 25 chapters on cost and fee allocation in particular systems around the globe, covering civil law, common law, and variously mixed jurisdictions in Europe, North and Latin America, Asia, and Australia. These chapters are derived from the National Reports presented at the XVIIIth World Congress but they were written specifically for inclusion in this book and with a view to highlighting the particular characteristics of the respective systems. Some National Reporters chose not to participate in this endeavor; all National Reports are accessible under http://www-personal.umich.edu/~purzel/national_reports/.

The picture that emerges is one of great complexity but it also shows several pervasive features and trends: an almost ubiquitous struggle with the high costs of civil litigation and often with problems of access to justice for most of the population; an increasing liberalization of the rules governing lawyer fees and a concomitant rise of success oriented modes of remuneration; and a growing reliance on methods of cost spreading through legal insurance, class actions, outside litigation financing, and other means. On the whole, the study suggests, the problems with high civil litigation costs and their allocation between the parties are more severe and pervasive in common law system than in civil law jurisdictions, and it proffers a few explanations for that observation.

I am grateful to all contributors to this volume most of whom had to put up with my repeated demands for revision, clarification, and amendment of their chapters, and I thank them for their cooperation and patience. I am also indebted to my research assistants Sarah Bullard and Alexander Fiedler who provided much background information. Finally, my secretary Cynthia Bever helped to keep track of the many contributions and to enforce the inevitable deadlines.

Ann Arbor Mathias Reimann
June 2011

Contents

Contributors

Neela Badami Senior Associate at Narasappa, Doraswamy and Raja, Bangalore, India; University of Michigan Law School, Ann Arbor, MI, USA, neela@narasappa.com

Alexandre Alcino de Barros Senior Associates ad L.O. Baptista Advogados Associados, Sao Paolo, Brazil

Nina Betetto Supreme Court of the Republic of Slovenia, Ljubljana, Slovenia, nina.betetto@sodisce.si

Camille Cameron Melbourne Law School, Melbourne, VIC, Australia, c.cameron@unimelb.edu.au

Nicolas Cayrol l'Université de Paris II (Panthéon-Assas), Paris, France, nicolas.cayrol@univ-tours.fr

Talia Fisher Buchmann Faculty of Law, Tel Aviv University, Tel Aviv, Israel; Harvard Law School, Cambridge, MA, UK, tafisher@post.tau.ac.il

Greg Gordon University of Aberdeen, Aberdeen, UK, law339@abdn.ac.uk

Burkhard Hess University of Heidelberg, Heidelberg, Germany, hess@ipr.uni-heidelberg.de

Rudolf Huebner University of Heidelberg, Heidelberg, Germany

Jan Hurdík Masaryk University, Brno, Czech Republic, jan.hurdik@law.muni.cz

Gyooho Lee Chung-Ang University School of Law, Seoul, Republic of Korea, ghlee@cau.ac.kr

Marco B.M. Loos University of Amsterdam, Amsterdam, The Netherlands, M.B.M.Loos@uva.nl

Alessandra De Luca Comparative Law, Faculty of Law, University of Florence, Florence, Italy, adeluca@unifi.it

Kalliopi Makridou Aristotle University of Thessaloniki, Thessaloniki, Greece, lioka2004@yahoo.gr

Jarkko Männistö University of Turku, Turku, Finland, jarkko@jarkkomannisto.fi

James R. Maxeiner Center for International and Comparative Law, University of Baltimore School of Law, Baltimore, MD, USA, jmaxeiner@ubalt.edu

Sílvia Julio Bueno de Miranda Senior Associates ad L.O. Baptista Advogados Associados, Sao Paolo, Brazil, sjbmiranda@gmail.com

Richard Moorhead Cardiff University, Wales, UK, moorheadr@cardiff.ac.uk

H. Patrick Glenn McGill University, Montreal, QC, Canada, patrick.glenn@mcgill.ca

Cândida da Silva Antunes Pires Faculty of Law, University of Macau, Taipei, China, csap@umac.mo

Mathias Reimann University of Michigan Law School, Ann Arbor, MI, USA

Issi Rosen-Zvi Buchmann Faculty of Law, Tel Aviv University, Tel Aviv, Israel, issirz@post.tau.ac.il

Marianne Roth Salzburg University, Salzburg, Austria, marianne.roth@sbg.ac.at

Vincent Sagaert University of Leuven, K.U.Leuven, Belgium; University of Antwerp, Antwerp, Belgium, Vincent.sagaert@law.kuleuven.be

Ilse Samoy Institute of the Law of Obligations, K.U.Leuven, Belgium; University of Hasselt, Hasselt, Belgium, ilse.samoy@law.kuleuven.be

Francisco López Símo University of the Balearic Islands, Balearic Islands, Spain, francisco.lopezsimo@uib.es

Martin Sunnqvist Faculty of Law, University of Lund, Lund, Sweden, martin.sunnqvist@jur.lu.se

José Ángel Torres Lana University of the Balearic Islands, Balearic Islands, Spain, torres.lana@uib.es

Manabu Wagatsuma Tokyo Metropolitan Law School, Tokyo, Japan, wagatsum@tmu.ac.jp

Alena Zaytseva Deputy Chief of the Private Law Department, Supreme Commercial Court of the Russian Federation, Moscow, Russia, 7746817@mail.ru

Caspar Zellweger Attorney-at-Law, Basel, Switzerland, zellweger@ballmer.ch

Part I
General Report

Chapter 1
Cost and Fee Allocation in Civil Procedure: A Synthesis

Mathias Reimann

1.1 Introduction: The Topic and Its Limits

This chapter provides a comparative study of the principles and rules governing costs and fees in civil litigation. It is based on the General Report written for the XVIIIth World Congress of Comparative Law held in Washington D.C. in the summer of 2010. It is thus draws heavily (albeit by no means exclusively, see infra Section 1.1.4) on the respective National Reports contributed to this Congress[1] Most, though not all, National Reporters also contributed chapters to this book.

Thanks to Sarah Bullard (J.D. University of Michigan 2010) and Alexander Fiedler (LL.M. University of Michigan 2011) for effective research assistance and to my colleagues Jody Kraus, Kyle Logue, and Mark West for helpful comments on an earlier draft.

[1] The General Report is published in Karen B. Brown and David Snyder (eds.), General Reports of the XVIIIth Congress of the International Academy of Comparative Law (2011). National Reports on Cost and Fee allocation in Civil Procedure were written by Camille Cameron (Australia), Marianne Roth (Austria), Ilse Samoy and Vincent Sagaert (Belgium), Silvia Julio Bueno de Miranda and Alexandre Alcino de Barros (Brasil), Patrick Glenn (Canada), Tang Xin and Xiao Jianguo (PR China), Jan Hurdik (Czech Republic), Richard Moorhead (England and Wales), Jarkko Männistö (Finland), Sophie Gjidara-Decaix (France), Burkhard Hess and Rudolf Hübner (Germany), Kalliopi Makridou (Greece), Thorgerdur Erlendsdottir and Sigridur Ingvarsdottir (Iceland), Neela Badami (India), Talia Fisher and Issi Rosen-Zvi (Israel), Alessandra Luca (Italy), Manabu Wagatsuma (Japan), Gyooho Lee (Korea), Candida Silva Autunes Pires (Macau SAR, PRC) Carlos Sanchez-Mejorada (Mexico), Marco Loos (Netherlands), Anna Nylund (Norway), Andrzej Jakubecki (Poland), Alena Zaytseva (Russian Federation), Greg Gordon (Scotland), Marko Knezevic (Serbia), Nina Betetto (Slovenia), HJ Erasmus (South Africa), José Angel Torres Lana and Francisco Lopez Simo (Spain), Martin Sunnqvist (Sweden), Caspar Zellweger (Switzerland), Fu-mei Sung and Taisan Chiu (Taiwan), Ayse Saadet Arikan (Turkey), James Maxeiner (United States), and José Tadeo Martinez (Venezuela).

M. Reimann (✉)
University of Michigan Law School, Ann Arbor, MI, USA

M. Reimann (ed.), *Cost and Fee Allocation in Civil Procedure*, Ius Gentium: Comparative Perspectives on Law and Justice 11, DOI 10.1007/978-94-007-2263-7_1, © Springer Science+Business Media B.V. 2012

1.1.1 The Significance of Cost and Fee Rules

The law of costs and fees is a major factor in the decision whether a dispute will result in litigation. In fact, in civil and commercial matters where money is usually the primary object, the financial burden of litigation may well be the single most important consideration in deciding whether to fight in court. Even if a matter is deemed important enough, and even if the chances of success are considered high, a party may not be able or willing to bear the cost of litigation.

In addition, the financial burdens of suing influence litigation strategy. In deciding exactly how to proceed, how much to invest, what risks to take, whether to appeal or not, etc., parties must take into account who will ultimately pay for it all. Thus, an understanding of the rules governing costs and fees is essential for an understanding of the dynamics of civil litigation.

Last, but certainly not least, financial costs and risks of litigation determine who has, and who is being denied, access to justice. Parties who cannot afford to sue (or to defend in court) are effectively excluded from the litigation system. They may well have valid substantive rights or viable defenses but cost barriers can render these rights and defenses practically useless. As we will see, this problem plagues many jurisdictions, albeit to varying degrees.[2]

1.1.2 The Importance of Comparative Perspectives

Practically speaking, understanding the rules governing litigation costs is most important at home. Yet, when transboundary litigation is growing fast, and when changes have been in the air in many systems, it is becoming increasingly important also to look beyond one's own jurisdiction. This is true for practitioners and lawmakers as well as for academics.

For legal counsel in transboundary cases, comparing rules on litigation costs is (or at least should be) an important element in choosing a forum (and sometimes the applicable law).[3] This is especially true when drafting a forum selection clause but it also matters more generally when deciding where to file (or whether actually to defend against) a lawsuit.[4] For legislators and policy makers, understanding how other systems deal with

[2] Infra Section 1.3.4.

[3] See Stefan Vogenauer, Perceptions of Civil Justice Systems in Europe and their Implications for Choice of Forum and Choice of Contract Law: an Empirical Analysis, in Stefan Vogenauer and Christopher Hodges (eds.), Civil Justice Systems in Europe: Implications for Choice of Forum and Choice of Contract Law (Oxford 2011, forthcoming).

[4] Assuming a choice, it would be an egregious mistake, for example, to file a clear winner in a jurisdiction where each party bears its own costs as opposed to a jurisdiction where the loser has to make the winner whole. In a similar vein, it would be a bad move to file

litigation costs is valuable when evaluating their own jurisdiction's regime. This is particularly salient if major reforms are being undertaken, as in most recently in Belgium (2007) and Portugal (2008) or considered, as is currently the case in the United Kingdom.[5] Finally, for legal scholars, especially those studying international civil litigation, the similarities and differences between the respective rules promise valuable insights. Comparison can indicate common problems (e.g., regarding certain claims), suggest a spectrum of solutions (e.g., ways to improve access to justice), and reveal worldwide trends (e.g., towards deregulation of lawyers' fees). It can even speak to the sense or non-sense of grouping legal systems into families or traditions (e.g. by looking at the degree of correlation between basic cost rules and membership in a particular legal family).

The purpose of this study is primarily to gather and organize data and to make sense of them by showing major commonalities and differences across jurisdictions. It is not to advocate concrete solutions to specific problems. While comparison includes pointing out pervasive questions and possible responses, how actually to resolve concrete issues usually involves political choices that comparatists are, contrary to what many of them believe, rarely competent to make.

1.1.3 From Obscurity to Prominence

For many years, there were precious few studies of cost and fee rules from a comparative (and foreign law) perspective[6] – a situation which actually provided the motivation for suggesting the topic to the International Academy of Comparative Law in 2007 for its 2010 Congress. In the meantime, that has changed. Today, there is a growing literature in this field.

Much of the initiative has come from European institutions. Most importantly, as part of the EU Civil Justice Project, a major comparative study of cost and fee rules has recently been undertaken at the University of Oxford.[7] In addition, the Council of Europe and the European Commission

---

a weak case (perhaps with a view of extracting a settlement) in a jurisdiction where the losing party pays all the costs rather than in system without cost shifting.

[5] See infra note 9.

[6] A major exception was Charles Platto, Economic Consequences of Litigation Worldwide (London: International Bar Association, The Hague, Boston 1999). The book provides valuable data about 20 systems (or regions) some of which were included in writing this General Report. The main problem with the book is that much of the information it provides has already become dated.

[7] Christopher Hodges, Stefan Vogenauer and Magdalena Tulibacka, Costs and Funding of Civil Litigation: A Comparative Perspective (Oxford and Portland/Oregon 2010) (hereafter cited as Oxford: Costs and Funding). While the book contains only 23 National

both solicited extensive studies related to this area in recent years.[8] Another, separate, impetus came from the current English reform debate which has resulted in a comprehensive review of the English system.[9] Finally, there are also quite a few recent publications in English addressing various key jurisdictions, such as England,[10] France,[11] Germany,[12] and Japan,[13] as well as occasional comparative studies on a limited scale.[14]

In addition, cost issues have increasingly occupied even international tribunals in recent years. Before the European Court of Human Rights as

Reports, the original Study conducted at the University of Oxford included 34 countries, see Christopher Hodges, Stefan Vogenauer and Magdalena Tulibacka, Costs and Funding of Civil Litigation: A Comparative Study, University of Oxford Legal Research Paper Series Paper No. 55/2009 (December 2009), available at http://ssrn.com/abstract=1511714 (hereafter cited as Oxford: Comparative Study). These countries overlap considerably with the jurisdictions covered in this chapter but each project also considers many jurisdictions not addressed by the other. The Oxford Study encompassed eleven systems not considered here: Bulgaria, Denmark, Estonia, Hong Kong, Hungary, Ireland, Latvia, Lithuania, Portugal, Romania, and Singapore; conversely, this General Report includes twelve systems not addressed by the Oxford Study: Brazil, Iceland, India, Israel, Korea, Macao, Mexico, Serbia, Slovenia, South Africa, Turkey, and Venezuela. Together the two projects thus draw on a total of 46 jurisdictions. The Oxford Study and the present chapter also overlap with regard to the questions they pursue but again, there is enough difference in coverage and thrust for one to complement the other. Overall, the focus of this General Report is somewhat narrower because it deals principally with the *allocation* of costs while the Oxford Study is concerned with *Costs and Funding of Civil Litigation* more broadly.

8 See especially European Commission for the Efficiency of Justice (CEPEJ), European Judicial Systems: Edition 2006 (2004 data) and European Judicial Systems: Edition 2008 (2006 data) – Efficiency and Quality of Justice (2008); and Jean Albert, Study on the Transparency of Costs of Civil Proceedings in the European Union: Final Report (2007).

9 Rupert Jackson, Review of Civil Litigation Costs, Final Report (Norwich 2010) (hereafter cited as Jackson Review).

10 Peter Gottwald (ed.), Litigation in England and Germany (Bielefeld 2010).

11 Dominique Menard, The Costs Battle: Cost Awards in France after the Enforcement Directive, Patent World 173 (2005) 13–15.

12 Gottwald, supra note. 10; Gerhard Wagner, Litigation Costs and Their Recovery: The German Experience, Civil Justice Quarterly 28 (2009) 367–366.

13 Matthew Wilson, Failed Attempt to Undermine the Third Wave: Attorney Fee Shifting Movement in Japan, Emory International Law Review 19 (2005) 1457–1488.

14 See Markus Jäger, Reimbursement for Attorney's Fees. A Comparative Study of the Laws of Switzerland, Germany, France, England and the United States of America; International Arbitration Rules and the United Nations Convention on Contracts for the International Sale of Goods (CISG) (2010); David Root, Attorney Fee-shifting in America: Comparing, Contrasting, and Combining the "American Rule" and "English Rule", Indiana International & Comparative Law Review 15 (2005) 583–617; see also Andrew Cannon, Designing Cost Policies to Provide Sufficient Access to Lower Courts. Australia/German/Netherlands/Northern Ireland/England, Civil Justice Quarterly 21 (2002) 198–253; Francesco Parisi, Rent-Seeking through Litigation: Adversarial and Inquisitorial Systems Compared, International Review of Law and Economics 22 (2002), 193–216.

well as the European Court of Justice, litigants have claimed – at times successfully – that high court costs or the denial of legal aid violated their fundamental rights under European law.[15] At least the member states of the European Union and of the Council of Europe thus operate under external constraints when regulating litigation costs, as well as, incidentally, public legal aid.[16]

1.1.4 The Database – The Developed Part of the World

As mentioned, this study is indebted to the National Reports from 35 jurisdictions.[17] It also draws – to a more limited extent – on the existing studies on costs and fees in civil litigation just mentioned.[18] Additional research provided occasional information on specific points.

The almost three dozen jurisdictions covered by the National Reports represent a substantial portion of the world's legal systems: they hail from all continents; represent civil law, common law, and Asian legal systems as well as various mixed regimes; and they include all major law exporting countries. They are also quite diverse: some are huge (like Russia), others tiny (like Macau); some are highly centralized (like France), others have a federal structure (like Canada); some are liberal and capitalist (like the United States), others authoritarian and socialist (like China). Together, they comprise over 60% of the world population and ca. 90% of the global GDP.

---

[15] Teltronic-CATV v. Poland (ECHR 10 Jan. 2006, Application no. 48140/00); DEB v. Germany (European Court of Justice, 22 Dec. 2010, C-279/09); see also Granos Organicos Nacionales v. Germany (European Court of Human Rights, Application 19508/07 – not decided on the merits), and Kottke v. Präsidial Anstalt and Seetly Stiftung (EFTA Court 17 Dec. 2010, E-5/10, concerning security for litigation costs before national courts).

[16] See infra Section 1.4.1.1.

[17] Australia, Austria, Belgium, Brazil, Canada, PR China, Czech Republic, England and Wales, Finland, France, Germany, Greece, Iceland, India, Israel, Italy, Japan, Korea, Macau (SAR PRC), Mexico, The Netherlands, Norway, Poland, Russian Federation, Scotland, Serbia, Slovenia, South Africa, Spain, Sweden, Switzerland, Taiwan, Turkey, United States of America, and Venezuela. These Reports are on file with the General Reporter; they are accessible, together with the Questionnaire, under http://www-personal.umich.edu/~purzel/national_reports/. With a few exceptions, this study does not provide pinpoint citations to the National Reports.

[18] Information on four additional jurisdictions, for which I had no National Report, was drawn from Platto, supra note 6, i.e., on Hong Kong, Denmark, New Zealand, Singapore. Since Portugal enacted major reforms in 2008, I also occasionally drew on the Portuguese Reports obtained by the Oxford group, supra note 7, from Barrocas Sarmento Neves, Sociedade de Advogados (Lisboa), available at http://www.csls.ox.ac.uk/documents/PORTUGAL.doc [cited as Oxford Portuguese Report/Barrocas] and from Henrique Sousa Antunes [cited as Oxford Portuguese Report/Antunes], available at http://www.csls.ox.ac.uk/documents/PORTUGALAC.doc. These additional five jurisdictions bring the number of systems considered to a total of 40.

Still, the systems included here do *not* represent the whole world. Serious gaps remain, largely as a result of institutional problems and resource limitations. Islamic systems are missing, Africa is severely underrepresented, and seriously poor countries are virtually absent.[19] In other words, the picture is by and large limited to the developed part of the globe.[20] To be sure, this is where most civil litigation takes place; it is also likely that most other systems in the world follow any of the major models included here, be it as a result of colonial imposition or post-independence borrowing. Still, it is important to keep in mind that the picture emerging from the present study shows mainly the situation in the rich and industrialized countries, and that it tells us very little, if anything, about the developing world.

1.1.5 Overview

Beyond this Introduction, this study consists of three main sections followed by a Conclusion. Section 1.2 deals with the issue of who pays; it outlines the basic approaches to cost shifting, considers the most important modifications and exceptions, and looks at the underlying policies. Section 1.3 turns to the question of how much?; it looks at the three major items – court costs, lawyer fees, and evidence expenses[21] – and conveys a sense of the overall financial burden of civil litigation. Section 1.4 then considers whose money actually pays for litigation costs; in particular, it surveys a variety of special mechanisms that distribute the financial risks of litigation, such as legal aid, litigation insurance, collective actions, success-oriented fees, and third party investment in lawsuits. The Conclusion suggests various groupings of legal systems with regard to cost and fee allocation in civil procedure.

1.2 Who Pays? The Basic Rules and Their Reasons

In looking at cost and fee allocation in civil procedure, the first question must be which of the parties has to bear which kinds of litigation expenses.[22] This depends primarily on the basic rules about cost shifting

[19] In terms of per capita GDP, no country covered belongs to the poorer half of the world.

[20] Other available studies do not remedy this problem because they suffer from exactly the same limitations.

[21] Throughout this study, these terms – costs, fees, and expenses – are used consistently to refer to courts, attorneys, and evidence taking respectively. They are not, however, fixed terms of art, and many National Reports and studies use them differently, e.g., in the sense of "court fees", "costs of evidence" or "expenses of legal representation".

[22] A separate question not pursued here is how much of the actual expenses are borne by the parties and how much is paid by the state (i.e., the taxpayer), but see infra Section

(infra Section 1.2.1). Yet, one must also consider the many exceptions and modifications to which these basic rules are often subject (Section 1.2.2). Beyond that, we will look at the avowed policies that underlie the various cost distribution regimes (Section 1.2.3).

1.2.1 The Basic Rule: To Shift or Not to Shift?

Comparative lawyers often think about cost and fee allocation in quasi Shakespearean terms: "to shift or not to shift?".[23] They then tend to divide the world into the systems that shift the winner's litigation costs to the loser – "the English rule" ("costs follow the event") – and the systems that make each side bear its own costs – "the American rule". This dichotomy indeed suggests itself if we look exclusively at the basic principles legal systems *proclaim*: the vast majority of countries claim to adhere to the "loser pays" principle while the United States does not.

Perhaps the most fundamental finding of this study is that such a dichotomy is hopelessly simplistic as well as virtually useless. It is hopelessly simplistic because the reality is much more complex: no system makes the winner completely whole (although some come very close), and even in the United States, some costs are shifted to the loser (although usually only a very small part); most jurisdictions operate somewhere in between. The usual dichotomy is virtually useless because what basic principle a legal system proclaims says little about which costs (and which amounts) are actually shifted to the loser: some jurisdictions announcing the "loser pays" rule arguably charge the loser for no more than in the United States.[24]

The world of cost and fee allocation in civil procedure is much better described as a broad spectrum. On one end are the systems that shift nearly all of the winner's litigation expenses to the loser; in the middle, we find many jurisdictions shifting substantial parts, but not nearly the whole; and at the other end, only a fraction of the winner's costs are recoverable. The exact line-up of the systems on this spectrum is debatable because it depends on the criteria employed. The following division is based on three primary considerations: First, what is the *basic principle* to which a jurisdiction subscribes – to shift or not to shift? Second, *what kinds of expenses* does a system impose on the losing party – all three major categories, i.e., court costs, attorney fees, and the expenses incurred by taking

1.3.1.3. This essay does not address cost and fee allocation in arbitration proceedings; for an analysis and discussion, see Jäger, supra note 14, 75–145.

[23] See, e.g., Jäger, supra note 14, at 1.

[24] "Arguably" because while they may also charge the loser only for court costs, these costs may be substantially higher than in the United States and constitute a larger percentage of the overall litigation expenses; see infra Section 1.3.1.2.

evidence, or only some of them (e.g., no attorney fees)? Third, does a system impose these amounts *in whole or in part* (especially full attorney fees or only a limited amount)?[25] For simplicity's sake, we will divide the systems covered here in three categories – major shifting, partial shifting, and minor shifting – and then proffer more fine-tuned distinctions within these groups where appropriate.

1.2.1.1 Major Shifting

I define systems as "major shifting" if the basic thrust of their rules is to make the winner, at least by and large, whole. In particular, these systems (1) claim to adhere to the "loser pays" principle, (2) shift in all three categories mentioned above (court costs, lawyer fees, and evidence expenses), and (3) impose either the full amounts or at least a sum considered close to it on the loser.[26] In other words, these systems not only proclaim the principle that the loser pays, they are also serious about it. The majority of the jurisdictions included in the present study fall into this category.

Contrary to widely shared assumptions, the poster child for the major shifters is not England – in fact, it is not even in this category (but rather in the next). Instead, the group consists overwhelmingly of members of the civil law tradition. Its hard core is a handful of "Germanic" jurisdictions in continental Europe: Austria, the Czech Republic, Germany, the Netherlands,[27] and Switzerland. But the club is actually much larger. It also comprises most other continental European systems, both in the East (Poland, Russia, Serbia, Slovenia) and the North (Denmark,[28] Finland, Norway, Sweden) as well as – heavily influenced by the Swiss and German tradition – Turkey. The group of major shifters also contains members clearly way beyond even a broadly defined "Germanic" family, both in Europe (Italy, Spain, after its recent reforms also Belgium and perhaps even Greece[29]) – and beyond (Brazil, Hong Kong,[30] Macau, Venezuela,

[25] It is a separate question, of course, whether these categories and impositions amount to a lot or relatively modest amounts of money, i.e., whether shifting costs the loser little or dearly. That depends on how high court costs, attorney fees, expenses of evidence taking, etc. are; see infra Section 1.3.

[26] Where the winning party (normally the plaintiff) has advanced these costs (such as filing fees), they must be reimbursed by the loser.

[27] The characterization of the Netherlands as a member of the "Germanic" family of European legal systems is debatable, of course.

[28] Platto, supra note 6, 144.

[29] The membership of Greece in this group is doubtful, see infra note 39 and text.

[30] Platto, supra note 6, 82–83.

and Mexico in civil cases[31]). Even the European Union has sometimes embraced a full cost-shifting rule.[32]

Yet, even the systems in this group do not necessarily guarantee the winner *full* compensation for *all* litigation expenses.[33] While they fully shift court costs and (as a rule) the expenses of judicially ordered evidence to the loser, they impose various limits on the recovery of the victorious party's attorney fees. In order to protect the loser from excessive claims, the winner can only charge what was necessary to conduct the litigation. In defining that, jurisdictions vary considerably in two regards: the mode of limitations they employ and the generosity they show to the winner.

There are three major modes of limiting the loser's liability for the winner's attorney fees. The most common continental European approach is to employ an official (often statutory) tariff for lawyers[34] (as in Austria, Belgium, the Czech Republic, Finland, Germany, Italy, Netherlands, Poland, Serbia, Turkey, and Switzerland). This tariff determines the amount the winner can recover from the loser, even if the winner and his counsel have agreed to a higher or lower rate.[35] The tariff approach is somewhat rigid but provides maximum predictability of the cost the parties are facing in case of defeat.[36] Another approach prevails in a group of Latin countries (Spain, Brazil, Mexico, and Venezuela): recoverable attorney fees are capped by varying percentages of the amount of the claim. This also makes the cost risk fairly foreseeable. Finally, some Nordic systems (Iceland, Norway, Sweden) as well as Russia use a more flexible means of control: the loser has to reimburse the victorious party's attorney fees (which are determined by the market) as long as they are necessary and reasonable. In case of dispute, the court determines what that means in the concrete case, often

[31] In Mexico, as a general matter, attorney fees are shifted to the loser in civil disputes, but not in commercial cases.

[32] Regulation (EC) No. 861/2007 of the European Parliament and of the Council of 11 July 2007 establishing a European Small Claims Procedure [2007] OJ L 199/1, Recital 29; the costs recoverable by the winner must, however, be "proportionate to the value of the claim" and "necessarily incurred", id.

[33] The results of the Oxford group research support this; see Oxford: Costs and Funding, supra note 7, [72], [20]; Oxford: Comparative Study, supra note 7, II.8, III.65 (regarding lawyers fees), III.81 (recoverability gaps in various systems).

[34] These tariffs are usually tied to the amount in controversy and then employ a multiplier reflecting various procedural acts or stages. As pointed out by the National Reporter for Italy in her comments on the Draft General Report, tying attorney fees to the procedural stage (as in Germany) instead of to concrete procedural acts (as in Italy) leads to greater predictability because the number of procedural acts within each state may vary from case to case.

[35] The tariff is usually degressive, i.e., a lower percentage for higher amounts.

[36] In some countries (e.g., Belgium, Italy, and Poland), the attorney fee schedule provides a (minimum-maximum) range within which the actual fee must be set, sometimes complemented by a standard fee (as in Belgium).

taking a variety of circumstances into account. This reflects a preference for ex post, judicial, case-by-case determination over an ex ante, legislative, one-size-fits-all solution (and is, in this regard, more in tune with the common law than the civil law tradition).

Certainly, even among the systems providing for major cost shifting, some are more generous to the winner than others. While the statutory tariffs in many countries fully cover the winner's attorney fees in routine cases, in others jurisdictions, the limits are much lower so that the winner usually chips in. Similarly, in some Latin countries, the percentage cap is set high enough not to create serious problems in most disputes (33% in Spain, 30% in Venezuela[37]) while in others, it is so low that it can render a substantial part of the winner's attorney fees non-recoverable (Brazil 10–20%).[38] Towards the bottom end of the generosity scale, cost shifting is decreasing to a point that is arguably no longer "major". In Greece, for example, while all cost items are shifted, the official tariff for (reimbursable) attorney fees is so low that "they do not cover, even in the slightest, the fee which the litigant in fact paid to his lawyer"[39]; the same must probably be said for Portugal.[40] In terms of practical outcome, these (and arguably other) jurisdictions thus could, and perhaps should, be classified as just partially shifting.

1.2.1.2 Partial Shifting

I define systems as "partially shifting" if their rules purport to compensate the winner for some of the litigation costs but have no ambition to make the victorious party routinely whole. These systems (1) still proclaim the basic principle that "the loser pays", but (2) either leave the amount of recovery to judicial discretion which normally results in merely partial shifting, or (3) shift only court costs and the expenses of evidence taking but not attorney fees. One can perhaps say that while these jurisdictions claim that the

---

[37] This, however, requires a "flawless victory" (on all counts) which is not easy to achieve in practice, Venezuelan Report I.1.

[38] In some jurisdictions, the victorious party even has a claim for its own work and other losses related to the litigation (Finland) while such items are not included in most other systems.

[39] Greek Report I.1. Yet, under the new statutory rules (2011), the official tariff applies only by default. If there is a written agreement between lawyer and client, it determines the fee that will be shifted, subject to reasonability control by the court.

[40] Portugal also limits the recoverable attorney fees to a percentage but pegs it to the "justice fee" (the official court, evidence, etc. costs). Article 41 sec. 1 of the 2008 Portuguese Legal Costs Act limits the shiftable attorney fees to between 10 and 25% of the "justice fee", leaving the precise determination to the discretion of the court, see Oxford Portuguese Report/Barrocas, Attachment I. Even if the "justice fee" is substantial, it is hard to imagine that such an amount would be anywhere close to the actual attorney fees in serious cases. This suggests that Portugal shifts only a very limited part of these fees to the loser and should thus not be considered a system with "major shifting".

loser pays, they do not fully mean it. Almost all jurisdictions not already in the "major shifting" category fall into this group. They form two subgroups to which we must add two – very significant – hybrids.

The first subgroup consists mainly of the British commonwealth tradition (primarily Australia, Canada, England and Wales, New Zealand,[41] and even Scotland as a mixed jurisdiction). This tradition is marked by three characteristic features. First, the "loser pays" principle is not a categorical (and often not a statutory) rule but rather a general guideline, basic expectation, and usual practical outcome. Second, the implementation of this principle is largely left to the discretion of the court, taking all the circumstances of the litigation into account; while this will normally result in cost shifting, the court may decide otherwise.[42] Third, in most cases, the exercise of judicial discretion will result in only partial cost shifting[43]; depending on the jurisdiction and the case, the successful party will thus often bear a considerable share of its own costs.[44] Three further jurisdictions from the (former) British orbit may be included here although they fit the picture only imperfectly because their basic rules do not commit to the loser pays principle. In Israel and South Africa cost allocation is left entirely in the discretion of the court in theory; in practice, however, winners are usually recovering at least part of their litigation expenses. In India, the statutory rule leaves cost allocation in the discretion of the court as well although it also indicates the expectation that normally, costs should "follow the event", i.e., be paid by the loser[45]; yet, in practice, Indian courts are very reluctant to shift costs in the majority of cases. In all these present

[41] Platto, supra note 6, 106.

[42] In England and Wales, Civil Procedure Rule 44.1 contains a long list of factors for courts to take into account. There are two kinds of cost shifting: on a "standard basis" which is subject to a proportionality test and usually results in merely partial allocation against the loser, and on an "indemnity basis" which usually amounts to (virtually) full reimbursement. The former is considered the rule, the latter the exception.

[43] In England, this is typical for cost shifting on a "standard cost" basis. The courts can hold the losing party fully responsible for the winner's costs but will do so only for special reasons, as under the English principle of "indemnity cost"; see Neil Andrews, Costs and Conditional Fee Agreements in English Civil Litigation, in Gottwald, supra note 10, 185 at 197–198.

[44] The Australian Report estimated that normally, only about 50–60% of the costs will be shifted to the loser in most Australian jurisdictions. The Oxford group mentions "recoverability gaps" of 30–45% for Australia, 25% for Canada, England and Wales, and 33–50% for Scotland (and Singapore), Oxford: Costs and Funding, supra note 7, [20]; Oxford: Comparative Study, supra note 7, III.81. Yet, these figures must also be understood as very rough approximations. Note, however, that the National Reporter for the United Kingdom commented that de facto, in England and Wales, cost shifting is normally total.

[45] Code of Civil Procedure sec. 35; see Neela Badami, Shifting Sands and Pyrrhic Victories (Section 13.3), Chapter 13, this volume.

and former commonwealth jurisdictions, the large role (if not complete predominance) of judicial discretion makes it difficult for the parties to gauge the financial risks of litigation.

The second subgroup consists of most of the East Asian countries covered here. They also proclaim the loser-pays principle but most of them (China, Japan, and Taiwan) apply it only to court costs and, except for China, the expenses of taking (court-ordered) evidence, thus excluding attorney fees. Yet, there are some variations and exceptions. To begin with, there are two important modifications in Japan: first, the (court) cost shifting rule is not much used in practice; second, in tort cases for personal injury, part of the attorney fee[46] is shifted from the successful plaintiff to the losing defendant – but not the other way around. Moreover, there is somewhat of an exception to the general approach when it comes to the fourth East Asian jurisdiction covered here: Korea extends the loser-pays principle to attorney fees as well although it also renders these fees only partially recoverable.[47]

Of the two hybrids, France presents the more curious case. Its cost allocation rules are highly complex.[48] Roughly speaking, they are based on a fundamental distinction between the legally inevitable costs of litigation on the one hand and further expenses on the other. The first category (*depens*) comprises the costs the parties (at the outset, usually the plaintiff) must pay as a matter of law in order to proceed with the case; they constitute a finite catalog, are regulated by statute, and consist mainly of a variety of fees which must be paid to the lawyer for filing the case (i.e., where representation by a lawyer is mandated by law) and to the court and its officials at various stages and for various purposes.[49] These costs are completely shifted to the losing party as a matter of law. By contrast, expenses not legally necessary – though perhaps practically inevitable – fall into another, open-ended category (*irrépetibles*). They include primarily the lion's share of further attorney fees (*honoraires*) which are determined by the market, but also other, incidental (e.g., travel) expenses. Whether, and to what extent, these costs are shifted to the loser is subject to (almost unfettered) judicial discretion. It thus depends on the circumstances of the case, including the economic situation of the parties, and, of course, the attitude of the judge, and it usually results in partial shifting at best. In a

[46] Usually 10% of the damages recovered, Japanese Report II.1.

[47] One could thus be tempted to group Korea with the British Commonwealth countries but that would overlook an important difference: contrary to the British tradition, Korea does not leave the amount of recoverable attorney fees to judicial discretion but rather determines it – very much in the civil law style – ex ante through an official tariff (setting an exact, and degressive, percentage).

[48] For a more detailed account, see Jäger, supra note 14, 29–37.

[49] Such as service of process, taking of evidence, translation of documents, etc. The basic court fees, i.e., the fees for just filing the case itself, are extremely low in France.

sense then, the French system is a hybrid between the civil law elements of statutory regulation and automatic shifting with regard to the official costs, and a quasi-English practice of discretion-based and partial shifting with regard to lawyer fees and other expenses.

The second hybrid of sorts is Mexico, and it is much simpler. As a general rule, in Mexico attorney fees are shifted in civil cases but not in commercial disputes.[50] Rather than putting Mexico in this middle category, one could thus also say that it belongs partially to the first group of complete shifters and partially to the last of minor (in fact, even non-) shifters.

1.2.1.3 Minor Shifting

The only country squarely in the "minor shifting" group is the United States. It (1) by and large rejects the loser pays principle, and it (2) by and large means it, although (3) cost shifting is not unknown.

The United States is distinct in part simply because it embraces a different ideology than almost all other systems in this study: it does *not proclaim* a loser pays principle.[51] The United States legal system by and large actually enforces the principle that each side bears its own litigation expenses. To be sure, court costs are routinely shifted to the loser,[52] but in practical (i.e., financial) terms, that hardly matters: the use of the courts is very cheap while lawyer time is very expensive. As a result, court costs usually constitute such a trivial fraction of the overall litigation expenses that their shifting is often overlooked altogether. It is also true that *some* evidence costs can be shifted to the losing party but, again, these usually involve rather insignificant amounts. What really matters in the United States is the general rule that the winner cannot recover lawyer fees which can be, and often are, enormous.[53]

---

[50] There are no court fees in Mexico because free access to justice is considered a constitutional right.

[51] The Oxford group concludes that this principle "is best explained by the critical role it plays in enabling the 'private enforcement' of law" in the interest of "wider public regulatory and observance goals", see Oxford: Costs and Funding, supra note 7, [79]; Oxford: Comparative Study, supra note 7, III.90. The US-American National Report solicited for this General Report does not support this explanation as a major factor, and it is doubtful indeed that this consideration is at the heart of the matter. In most areas in which "private attorney generals" play a significant role, such as antitrust, civil rights or environmental disputes, specific statutes *deviate* from the "American rule" and allow (one-way) cost shifting, see immediately infra.

[52] Still, the Oxford Study, supra note 7, perhaps overlooks court fee shifting when it states that the United States system "does not include cost shifting", at II.8.

[53] Of course, lawyer fees are in large part generated by the extensive discovery common in many cases in the United States, but evidence gathering also entails other expenses, e.g., for hiring expert witnesses, paying stenographers for depositions, or copying (and perhaps translating) massive amounts of documents.

Yet, even with regard to lawyer fees, there are significant (and usually overlooked) exceptions. Most importantly, a large variety of federal and state statutory rules (allegedly over 2000 altogether[54]) do provide for attorney fee shifting. Often, this is meant to encourage private lawsuits in the public interest; thus it works only in a one-way fashion, i.e., merely in favor of certain plaintiffs acting as "private attorney generals" – most famously in antitrust and civil rights cases but also under the Securities Laws, the Lanham Act (trademark) and the Copyright Act; some of this cost shifting is mandatory, elsewhere the court has discretion.[55] Furthermore, courts can and do shift attorney fees for a variety of special reasons, e.g., as a sanction for improper (especially bad faith) procedural action by one side (see infra Section 1.2.2.3). Finally, Alaska deviates from the lower forty-eight states altogether and generally subscribes to the loser pays principle, even for attorney fees.[56]

Still, cost and fee shifting in the United States is either minor (regarding court costs and some evidence expenses) or limited to special instances (regarding attorney fees). In general, the belief that in principle, each side is responsible for its own litigation expenses is deeply rooted, at least among lawyers. This combination of open rejection of the loser pays principle and actual refusal to shift the lion's share of litigation expenses in the vast majority of cases sets the United States apart from the rest of the systems covered here.

1.2.2 Exceptions and Modifications

While the vast majority of the legal systems covered here (and probably in the world) thus proclaim the loser pays principle, they all provide for exceptions and modifications of one sort or another. The variety of the respective rules is bewildering, and considering them in all their detail is unrewarding.[57] Still, there are some recurrent themes that are worth mentioning because they indicate certain underlying policies. Most exceptions and modifications can be grouped into four categories: modifications for special kinds of litigation, exceptions for particular parties, responses to split outcomes, and sanctions for causing unnecessary costs.

---

[54] United States Report II.A., citing John F. Vargo, The American Rule of Attorney Fee Allocation: The Injured Person's Access to Justice, American University Law Review 42 (1993) 1567, at 1629.

[55] For details, see Jäger, supra note 14, 51–60. Permitting "qualified one-way costs shifting" has recently also been proposed for England and Wales, see Jackson Review, supra note 9, xvii.

[56] Susanne diPietro and Teresa W. Carns, Alaska's English Rule: Attorney Fee Shifting in Civil Cases, Alaska Law Review 13 (1986) 33.

[57] For further details, see Jäger, supra note 14, 6–18.

1.2.2.1 Special Types of Litigation

To begin with, several jurisdictions, such as Australia, England and Wales, Norway, Scotland, and Turkey, forego or limit cost shifting in small claims cases which are sometimes heard in special courts and according to a simplified procedure. In such cases (and tribunals), court costs tend to be low and legal representation is often not required (and in fact sometimes prohibited, as in South Africa) so that the necessary expenses are likely to be small. Not shifting them imposes no great burden on either side, lowers the financial risks of suing, and thus facilitates access to justice.

A considerable number of jurisdictions make various exceptions from the loser pays principle in family law disputes – either generally (as in England, Norway, and Serbia) or in particular cases, such as divorce proceedings (as in Belgium, China, the Czech Republic, Finland France, and Sweden), child custody (Austria, Finland (with some exceptions), Sweden) or maintenance (Austria, Finland (again, with some exceptions), Greece), or in non-contentious (quasi-administrative) proceedings (Germany, Finland). And indeed, family disputes are special in at least two ways: they are not necessarily (and often not primarily) about money, and the parties are usually related to each other. As a result, making the "loser" pay for the "winner's" litigation expenses (e.g., in a child-custody proceeding) can look like adding insult to injury.

Many systems also exempt cases with a strong social element from cost shifting. This is especially true for labor disputes (England, Italy, Macau, Scotland, Sweden, etc.) but occasionally also for social security cases (e.g., in Italy and Belgium), and consumer litigation (e.g., Turkey, and in certain class actions, Brazil). Some jurisdictions privilege plaintiffs in public interest litigation by protecting them from cost liability if they lose their case (e.g., in Australia (at least sometimes), Brazil, England and Wales, and – in constitutional cases – sometimes Canada).[58]

Japan provides one-way shifting in personal injury cases in favor of victims so that the victorious plaintiff can recover his or her attorney fees from the defendant but not the other way around. The Jackson Review recently recommended the same approach for England and Wales.[59]

1.2.2.2 Party-Based Exceptions

When it comes to cost and fee allocation in *civil* procedure (i.e., in private and commercial litigation), one should think that all animals are equal; yet, in a surprising number of jurisdictions, some animals are clearly more

[58] In a similar vein, victorious plaintiffs acting in the public interest can sometimes recover their litigation expenses while other plaintiffs cannot, see supra Section 1.2.1.3.

[59] Jackson Review, supra note 9, 184–193

equal than others: while the system generally embraces the loser pays principle, certain parties are not liable for costs even if they lose. This is most understandable with regard to indigents or recipients of social security (as in Belgium, Brazil, Russia, Spain, and Turkey). It becomes a bit more questionable where the state protects itself from cost liability, either in whole (public attorneys in Spain) or in part (particularly limited cost recovery in Greece) or by granting cost immunity to parties affiliated with it (such as soldiers and diplomatic personnel in Turkey).

1.2.2.3 Sanctions for Causing Unnecessary Costs

The general cost shifting principles are frequently trumped by special sanctions for causing expenses without good reason.[60] Thus, even a winner cannot recoup litigation expenses when suing was unnecessary. Also, each party may be liable to the other for costs caused by certain acts, especially if such acts were procedurally improper.

1.2.2.4 Split Outcomes

A merely partial victory usually has a direct impact on the winner's cost claim against the loser. The systems covered here differ, however, in exactly how they react to such a situation.

Of course, the simplest reaction to a split outcome is to consider nobody a winner (or both parties losers) and thus to shift no costs at all. Indeed, many systems' first line response to split outcomes is to let each side bear its own expenses. This is true not only in the common law orbit where cost shifting has traditionally been regarded not so much as a matter of right but rather of judicial discretion. It is also the case in many civil law jurisdictions where cost shifting involves considerable judicial discretion, as in France.

Most systems, however, take into account by how much each side won or lost.[61] Exactly how they do so is substantially related to whether recoverable fees and costs are tariff-based or not. The jurisdictions determining costs and fees under a (quasi-) official schedule tend to split the costs fairly

---

[60] In civil law jurisdictions, these sanctions tend to be spelled out in statutory form (codes of civil procedure) while in common law systems, they are often a matter of judicial practice when exercising discretion with regard to cost shifting. In US federal courts, Federal Rule of Civil Procedure 11 also allows (cost and other sanctions) to be imposed upon both counsel and parties for improper procedural action.

[61] See also Oxford: Costs and Funding, supra note 7, [18]; Oxford: Comparative Study, supra note 7, III.75. Venezuela is an exception: cost shifting requires flawless victory. In other words, even losing a small part of the case completely bars any cost recovery in a manner reminiscent of the (now largely defunct) defense of contributory negligence in tort cases.

precisely. In systems entrusting cost shifting (vel non) primarily to judicial discretion, there is much greater play in the joints, and courts usually eyeball the cost distribution from a broader equity perspective.

1.2.2.5 Settlements

Similar to split-outcome judgments, settlements usually mean that each side prevails in part and thus calls for some kind of cost splitting. As a general rule, settling parties are free to allocate costs as they please, which in practice usually results in each side bearing its own cost. This is also the most common default rule.[62] In the absence of party agreement, several systems leave cost allocation to the courts (Australia, China, Finland, Iceland, Scotland, Switzerland, Turkey, England and Wales) dividing the burden according to a variety of criteria.

Note that in practice, settlements play a very significant role in most jurisdictions. In the common law orbit, settlement rates are so high that ending litigation by final judgment is clearly the exception[63]; as a result, cost allocation in common law (influenced) jurisdictions is – in reality – *normally* determined by the rules and practices governing settlements, not judgments. But also in the rest of the world, especially in continental Europe and on the Pacific Rim, settlement rates are often significant and can reach well over 50%[64]; thus even there, cost allocation in practice often by-passes the loser-pays principle and results in cost splitting. In other words, while the "American rule" is the *law* only in the United States, it is the prevailing *practice* in a great number of civil cases in the world today.

---

62 Some systems (Brazil, Greece, Macau) provide for equal division of costs which would imply that the party with the higher bill can claim part of its costs from the other side.

63 The National Reports for Australia, Canada, England and Wales, and the United States all indicate settlements rates of at least 90%; the Oxford group confirms that, see Oxford: Costs and Funding, supra note 7, [94–95]; Oxford: Comparative Study, supra note 7, IV.166. The situation in the mixed jurisdictions of Israel and Scotland is similar. The big exception in the common law orbit is India where settlement rates are apparently low. This may be due to the excessive delays in civil proceedings: if a decision cannot be expected for many years down the road, at least the party in the weaker position has little reason to give in by settling.

64 The information about settlement rates contained in the National Reports was generally patchy. Many Reports did not provide any data for lack of statistical information; some National Reporters proffered good faith estimates while a few others referred to hard data. In a few countries, such as Russia and Turkey, by far most cases go to final judgment. More typically, settlement rates of ca. 15–20% prevail, as in Austria, Germany, Iceland, Norway, or Serbia. Some National Reporters provided much higher numbers, as for China (50–70%), Japan (20–42%) or Switzerland (ca. 50% of all cases with a higher rate in commercial litigation). These numbers roughly match the data provided by the Oxford group, see Oxford: Costs and Funding, supra note 7, [94–95]; Oxford: Comparative Study, supra note 7, IV.165 (with the exception of Norway for which a settlement rate of 42% is reported).

1.2.3 Policies: Fairness or Instrumentalism?

The basic rules on cost and fee allocation, as well as the various exceptions and modifications, reflect certain underlying procedural policies. In the respective jurisdictions, these policies are rarely articulated with great clarity, not to mention sophistication, and one suspects that they are often not clearly understood either.[65] The National Reports thus often had to make informed guesses, stating as best they could what drives their system's approach. Still, the underlying policies can roughly be divided into two categories: considerations of fundamental fairness to the winner (infra Section 1.2.3.1) and instrumental goals of encouraging or discouraging litigation (Section 1.2.3.2). Of course, these policies are not mutually exclusive, and in fact, most systems covered here appear to pursue a mix of them. The United States, however, stands by and large apart in its almost completely instrumentalist position (Section 1.2.3.3).

1.2.3.1 Basic Fairness

As we have seen, the vast majority of systems embraces the loser-pays principle (supra Sections 1.2.1.1 and 1.2.1.2). In most of them, this principle reflects primarily an idea of basic fairness in the sense of substantive right: it seems just that the loser must compensate the winner.

1.2.3.2 Instrumentalist Considerations

Most jurisdictions covered here *also* base their cost shifting rules on instrumentalist grounds: these rules are meant to provide incentives for potential litigants to behave in a particular manner.[66] Here we have to distinguish two categories: discouragement of non-meritorious, and encouragement of meritorious, litigation.

In the majority of systems, the loser-pays rule is seen as a means to discourage non-meritorious claims.[67] The underlying logic seems simple enough: since the loser will pay twice (i.e., his or her own as well as the opponent's costs), someone with a dubious claim will also think twice before taking it to court. This study is not the place to discuss whether it really works that way. Suffice it to mention that a loser-pays rule also *encourages* parties to sue if they *expect* to win, and that over-optimism in

---

[65] The Oxford group reaches the same conclusion, see Oxford: Costs and Funding, supra note 7, [73]; Oxford: Comparative Study, supra note 7, IV.123.

[66] Only the Reports for Norway and South Africa disclaim such instrumentalist grounds. The Reports for India and Switzerland state that there is no unified or clearly articulated policy.

[67] This is reflected in the National Reports for Austria, Australia, Brazil, Canada, England and Wales, Germany, Greece, Israel, Japan, Korea, Macau, the Netherlands, Norway, Scotland, Sweden, and Venezuela; it is implicit in several others.

that regard is of course wide-spread.[68] In all likelihood, the deterrent effect of the loser-pays rule is not primarily due to the parties' perception of their respective position's merits. Instead, such deterrence is probably mainly the result of general risk averseness: by doubling the stakes, the loser-pays rule scares off parties who, like most, shy away from high downside-risks.

A few systems also see their loser-pays rule as an encouragement of meritorious lawsuits[69]: a party who is right should stand his or her ground even in court without fear of uncompensated litigation costs. To put it differently: access to justice should be free of charge for those with meritorious claims or defenses.[70] Apparently, these systems do not regard litigation as on balance socially undesirable and thus do not wish to discourage it in principle.

1.2.3.3 Pure Instrumentalism

In all this, the United States stands by and large apart: it is not only, as we have seen, the only system covered here which openly rejects the loser-pays principle (supra Section 1.2.1.3); it is also the only system that does not justify its basic rule (that each side bears its own expenses regardless of outcome) on fairness grounds – and it would be hard-pressed do so.[71] It is thus the only country predicating its basic cost rule purely on instrumentalist grounds.[72]

---

[68] All losing plaintiffs were (virtually by definition) over-optimistic and thus potentially encouraged, rather than discouraged, by the loser-pays role to file a suit which was then proven non-meritorious. Of course, the loser-pays rule will deter litigation if a party recognizes the weakness of the claim.

[69] This is mentioned in the National Report for Germany and intimated in several others emphasizing that the winner deserves to be fully compensated for the vindication of his or her rights.

[70] A few National Reports (especially for Austria, China, and Taiwan) also state that their cost rules are designed to encourage settlement. The loser-pays rule seems ill-designed to do that, except to the extent that it, again, appeals to the parties' risk-averseness. Systems can, and sometimes do, encourage settlement through special cost rules. Some punish a party that refuses to settle, e.g., by imposing the resultant litigation costs, as in Scotland under certain circumstances (if the defender lodges a judicial tender, offering to settle at a certain amount, and the pursuer continues the case and is ultimately awarded less than the defender offered). Others reward parties who do settle, e.g., by waiving part of the court fees, as in Portugal.

[71] That is not to say that it is impossible to make fairness arguments in defense of the "American rule". The most obvious such argument is that in many, if not most, cases, litigation outcomes are so unpredictable and luck-driven that both sides run a high risk of defeat which makes it fair for each side to bear its own cost. Another argument is that the American rule makes it each side's own business how much money to spend on the litigation. Whether these arguments are ultimately persuasive is of course a matter on which reasonable people can differ.

[72] In his comment on the Draft General Report, the National Reporter for the United States pointed out that "the instrumentalist view in the USA is an after-the-fact justification. It came into being only well-after the practice was established."

Moreover, US-American instrumentalism is one-sided: the basic cost rule is meant to lower the risk for the potential loser. This approach is defended primarily as facilitating access to justice, and that implies – at least de facto – encouragement of litigation.[73] Note, however, that the American rule encourages not only lawsuits the plaintiff is confident to win but also the ones the plaintiff thinks he or she may well lose (as long as the matter is not entirely hopeless). In fact, it is the latter effect – the implicit encouragement of weak lawsuits (often with the sole goal to force the defendant to settle) – that sets the rule in the United States apart from pretty much the rest of the world.

Whether the "American Rule" actually facilitates access to justice, and whether it does so in the right (i.e., meritorious) cases, is a question beyond the scope of the present study. The American National Report raises substantial doubts in this regard. It points out, inter alia, that the American rule can easily end up virtually prohibiting certain meritorious claims: since the plaintiff cannot recover his or her litigation expenses even in case of victory, the amount potentially won must be high enough at least to cover these expenses. Yet, given the high costs of litigation in US-American courts, this is rarely the case for small and even mid-size claims. As a result, these claims become financially impossible to litigate – ironically because of the very cost rule that is supposed to enhance access to justice.[74] In addition, if a case *is* actually litigated, the costs may be so high that even a *winning* plaintiff may pay more in expenses than he would pay as a loser elsewhere.[75]

1.3 How Much? The Financial Risks of Litigation

Whether a system shifts the winner's litigation costs to the loser (in whole or in part) tells only half the story. A realistic picture of what cost shifting means must include the sums at stake. *How much* money are we actually talking about? Only if we look at that question can we understand the actual impact of cost shifting vel non.

The answer we can give here, however, is neither complete nor precise. The data contained in the national reports in response to questions about actual litigation costs in certain types of cases are patchy. While reporters from systems calculating costs according to precise official schedules (such

---

[73] This fits with the usually very low court fees in the United States, see infra Section 1.3.1.2.

[74] Such cases are routinely settled; the impossibility of cost-effective litigation normally enhances the bargaining power of defendants and thus tends to lower the price of settlement.

[75] See the tables in the United States Report, VII.

as Germany or Switzerland) could provide exact figures, reporters from jurisdictions without such schedules could only give good faith estimates. A sizeable percentage of national reporters found it impossible to provide any reliable numbers at all because litigation costs in their systems depend entirely on the circumstances of the case so that generalizations are virtually impossible. Moreover, where actual numbers were provided, they had to be converted into a common currency (USD) according to fluctuating rates. Finally, all these numbers must be evaluated in light of the disparate purchasing power in the respective jurisdictions and, indeed, regions – $10,000 is a lot more money in rural China than in downtown London. As a result, the numbers given can only be rough approximations. Still, they show at minimum that among the systems covered, the actual financial impact of cost shifting (vel non) ranges from the truly trivial to the potentially prohibitive.

We will first separately look at the three major cost items in private litigation, i.e., court costs (infra Section 1.3.1), attorney fees (Section 1.3.2), and the expenses of taking evidence, e.g., for expert witnesses (Section 1.3.3). Then we will consider the total cost of litigation in order to get a sense of the overall financial burden involved (Section 1.3.4).

1.3.1 Court Costs: Trouble or Triviality?

As we have seen (supra Section 1.2.1), court costs are always shifted to the loser – even in the United States. Some jurisdictions, such as Mexico and Venezuela, charge no court costs in order to ease access to justice, others, like France and Sweden, keep them extremely low.[76]

1.3.1.1 Computation

Systems vary greatly as to how court costs are calculated. Most jurisdictions determine them under a schedule by amount in controversy (usually in a degressive fashion) while a few (notably the United States) usually charge a flat fee.[77] In some systems, like Germany, the basic court fee covers virtually the whole proceedings at the particular level, while in others, separate fees are charged at successive stages of the litigation or, as in France and Belgium, for various acts of officials, such as filing, service of process, stamping of documents, etc.; the individual items may look cheap but they tend to add up.

[76] See also Oxford: Costs and Funding, supra note 7, [13]; Oxford: Comparative Study, supra note 7, III.25.

[77] This has the effect, inter alia, that there is no penalty in terms of court costs for filing a grossly inflated claim which explains, in part, why US plaintiffs often file million dollar lawsuits where parties in other countries would be much more careful not to overstate their claim.

1.3.1.2 Differences in Size

Shifting court costs to the loser can mean vastly different things because the amounts involved vary enormously. For a $100,000 lawsuit, Canadian or US-American courts charge at most a few hundred dollars.[78] File the same action in a Brazilian, Greek or Russian court, and you come closer to paying $1,000. Take it to a Czech, German or Dutch tribunal, and you will need to put down $3,000–6,000. Bring the case in Switzerland, and court costs will amount to over $10,000.[79]

Substantial filing gees can constitute a serious barrier especially for plaintiffs. This can easily happen in cases involving large claims if court fees are tied to the amount in controversy, particularly where they constitute a fixed percentage, as in Poland. In 2006, the European Court of Human Rights decided that the required advance payment of court costs in Poland was so high that it violated the plaintiff's right of access to court under article 6 of the European Convention of Human Rights.[80]

1.3.1.3 Two Explanations

What explains the huge discrepancies among court fees? While multiple factors will be at play, two are worth at least brief consideration: the amount of work courts perform, and the underlying ideas as to who should pay for the civil justice system.

It is noticeable that common law systems often charge lower court costs than civil law countries. This may well reflect that common law judges by and large do less work per case than their civil law colleagues. As is well known, common law judges tend to play a more passive role while their civilian brethren are supposed to actively manage and resolve the dispute[81]; in addition, the settlement rate in the common law orbit is very high while civil law judges have to render a great number of final judgments in writing with reasoned opinions. The picture is far from perfect, however: for example, court fees are low in the United States and Canada but quite hefty in the England and Wales; in a similar fashion, they are quite high in Taiwan and in China[82] but surprisingly low in Korea and Japan (at least in small and midsize cases).

---

78 At least in the United States, it is often not worth the time and effort to try to collect the costs from the losing party.

79 Where court costs are substantial and tied to the amount claimed, parties sometimes save part of them by claiming only part of the amount really at issue, thus filing essentially a test case. This can also be done to save lawyer fees where they are determined by a schedule as well.

80 Teltronic-CATV v. Poland, ECHR 10 Jan. 2006 (Application no. 48140/99).

81 See the classic article by John Langbein, The German Advantage in Civil Procedure, 52 Chicago Law Review 823 (1985).

82 Again, this assumes that the respective approaches to calculation were truly equivalent. In their comment on the Draft General Report, the Chinese Reporters, for example,

Thus, other factors are at work as well. In particular, jurisdictions pursue different policies as to who should pay for the civil justice system. Many countries, such as Germany and Switzerland, but also England and Wales,[83] apparently expect mainly the litigants to pay for using the courts; these systems charge amounts that cover at least a significant part of the civil courts' operating budget – like they would for renting out a government-owned facility. The consequence of this approach is that court cost shifting matters substantially because it can easily involve a significant percentage of the sum in controversy and the equivalent of thousands of dollars. Other jurisdictions, such as Canada, the United States, Japan, and Korea, provide access to the civil courts essentially as a public (i.e., tax-funded) service; they charge merely a small entrance fee – as they would for a state museum or national park. Here, shifting court costs matters much less as it usually involves but a tiny fraction of the amount at stake and at most a few hundred dollars.[84]

1.3.2 Attorney Fees: The Lion's Share

As we have seen, the vast majority of systems covered here shifts attorney fees to the loser as well – in most cases either completely or at least a very significant share, although some jurisdictions may make the loser pay for only a small part.[85] At the end of the day, how much attorney fee shifting really matters also depends largely on their magnitude. That magnitude, however, is often very difficult to assess and largely impossible to generalize.

1.3.2.1 Computation

Determining the amount of lawyer fees is a complex business. Two principal approaches must be distinguished. In many systems, especially in

pointed out that they counted "nearly every cent that is spent by both parties during the first instance, second instance, and enforcement procedure."

83 See Oxford: Costs and Funding, supra note 7, [13]; Oxford: Comparative Study, supra note 7, III.26 (80% of court costs covered by user payments); John Peysner, Litigation Cost Recovery – Tariffs and Hourly Fees in England, in Gottwald, supra note 10, 138 fn. 4; the Jackson Review, supra note 9, recommends to abolish this policy and to fund the courts (largely) through taxpayer money so that the court fees can be lowered and access to justice facilitated, id., 50.

84 As the National Reporter for Japan pointed out in his comments on the Draft General Report, in cases with particularly large amounts at stake (such as some tort cases for environmental damage or HIV-infected blood products), Japanese court costs can rise to the level of a barrier to access to justice because they are tied to the amount in controversy.

85 Supra Sections 1.2.1.1 and 1.2.1.2.

continental Europe,[86] shiftable attorney fees are, as mentioned, set by an official schedule tied to the amount in controversy (and sometimes to the court in which the case proceeds) and providing either absolute amounts or a maximum-minimum range. Here, the amount of lawyer fees is set ex ante and thus fairly clear to both winner and loser. Other systems, however, leave the determination of attorney fees by and large to the market. There, lawyer fees vary greatly, depending on the mode of charging (by the hour,[87] flat fee, etc.), location, expertise and reputation of counsel, case complexity, and sometimes the client's resources; success fees often further complicate the picture.[88]

1.3.2.2 From Schedule to Market

The complexity of assessing lawyer fees is exacerbated by a general trend away from the former (schedule-based) approach and towards the latter (market-oriented) model. This trend manifests itself in two ways.

First, binding fee schedules are on the decline – several countries have lately departed from official tariffs, albeit to varying degrees. Some trend setting systems have abolished binding schedules altogether – Japan (2003), and Korea (2003) are prime examples. In other jurisdictions, these schedules were relegated to the status of a mere floor above which the parties can freely agree to a higher price, as has lately happened in Germany (2004), Greece (2011), and is beginning to happen in Switzerland.[89] Yet other countries rendered them non-binding as a floor but stuck to maximum limits, as in Italy (2006) or leave it to the attorney and his or her client whether to use the official tariff or a market rate, as in the Czech Republic and Poland.[90]

Second, prohibitions of success-oriented fees are on the decline[91] – many systems formerly opposed to giving lawyers a stake in the outcome of litigation are now permitting exactly that. England, once staunchly opposed to success-oriented fees, introduced conditional fees in 1990, expanded their use in 1998, and current reform proposals include the introduction of

---

[86] Note that this is not true for *all* of continental Europe because many jurisdictions there do not have an official attorney fee schedule, such as France, Spain, and the Scandinavian countries. On the other hand, there is apparently such a schedule in South Africa.

[87] For data on hourly fees in various jurisdictions, see Oxford: Comparative Study, supra note 7, Appendix III.

[88] See infra Section 1.3.4.

[89] See Swiss Report IV.2.

[90] There are signs of an incipient counter-trend in England: certain routine cases are handled under a fixed fee, and the recent reform proposals include the introduction of fixed costs in fast track litigation, i.e., cases of up to 25,000 pounds in which trial can be handled in one day, see Jackson Review, supra note 9, xviii, 146–168.

[91] See infra Section 1.4.4.

full-fledged contingency fees.[92] Perhaps the most dramatic change in that direction was the recent introduction of outright contingency fees (though only under certain conditions) in Italy (2006) and Germany (2008). Even conservative Switzerland, it seems, is moving in this direction.[93]

This dual trend towards deregulating lawyer fees has been the result of several factors. In some instances, binding schedules were simply deemed incompatible with the status of a free legal profession, as in France. In other jurisdictions, they were thought to violate competition (or antitrust) principles, as in Japan and Korea. In Europe, there were doubts whether such schedules violated the principle of freedom of services in the European Union, as in Italy.[94] In several jurisdictions, a policy of improving access to justice (especially for individual clients) drove price deregulation and triggered the permission of success-oriented fees,[95] in others, allowing such fees was meant to compensate for the restriction (or near-elimination) of public legal aid, i.e., constituted a way of privatizing litigation funding.[96] Deregulation was also a response to the increasing international competition from Anglo-American law firms whose prices were subject to precious few official restrictions. Last, but not least, liberating lawyer fees from binding tariffs and from prohibitions of success premiums fit the general trend toward deregulation and trust in market forces that has dominated most of the developed world, certainly until the onset of the financial crisis in 2008, and often beyond.

To be sure, not every jurisdiction covered here has joined the bandwagon, and not everybody involved is necessarily enthusiastic.[97] But the legal systems holding on to traditional regulations and prohibitions are now in the minority, and their number is shrinking. As the German Report put it, "the pressure to change the whole system is growing",[98] and change

---

[92] Jackson Review, supra note 9, xviii–xix, 131–133.

[93] See Swiss Report IV.3.

[94] The Italian deregulation came in part as a reaction to decisions rendered by the European Court of Justice, although the Court did *not* declare official fee schedules a per se violation of European law (see Case C-35/99 (*Arduino*) [2002] E.C.R. I-1529-1575; Joined Cases C-94-04 (*Cipolla*) and C-202/04 (*Macrino*), [2006] E.C.R. I-11421-11478). For a comment, see Martin Ilmer, Lawyers' Fees and Access to Justice – The Cipolla and Merino Judgment of the ECJ, 26 Civil Justice Quarterly 201 (2007).

[95] This was an important factor in Germany, Entscheidungen des Bundesverfassungsgerichts (BVerfGE) 117, 163–202 (2006).

[96] This was clearly the case in England, see United Kingdom, Lord Chancellor's Department, Access to Justice with Conditional Fees (1998); Neil Andrews, Cost and Conditional Fee Agreements in English Civil Litigation, in Gottwald, supra note 10, 185 at 187.

[97] The bar has not necessarily welcomed increased competition through deregulation, see Ilmer, id., at 308 (Italian bar protesting); as the National Reporter for Italy points out in her comments on the Draft General Report, there are efforts to reverse this trend by legislation, and it is conceivable that a more regulated regime will be restored.

[98] German Report, Conclusion.

points in the direction of free market prices for lawyer fees with few restrictions on success premiums. Since this has long been the situation in the United States, is tempting to speak of – yet another – "Americanization" of law in many parts of the world.[99]

Deregulating lawyer fees has its upsides,[100] but it does make it harder to predict them and it seriously complicates their allocation. Where such fees are fixed by an official schedule, shifting them to the loser is a fairly straightforward matter: the client pays the tariff, and if he wins the lawsuit, recoups from the loser what he owes his lawyer. Since both parties know the amount in advance, full fee shifting is no problem – the amount is fixed so that the winner (and his lawyer) cannot play with the loser's money, and the loser cannot claim unfair surprise. And since fee shifting normally involves few (or no) judgment calls, it can be handled on the clerical level and provides little opportunity for further fighting. By contrast, where the determination of lawyer fees is left to the market (and especially where success-fees are allowed), fee shifting becomes a lot more problematic: now, the winner can make arrangements with his lawyer potentially at the loser's expense, and the loser can often not predict how much he will have to pay. In order to protect the losing party, a legal system must now do one of two things. Either it limits the shiftable fee to a statutorily fixed amount, be it in form of a tariff or of a maximum sum or percentage of the amount in controversy; since that amount will usually be set on the low side, the winner will often not be made entirely whole; this is true in many jurisdictions, perhaps most dramatically in Greece.[101] Or a legal system must install an ex post reasonableness check on the winner's spending which also means that full reimbursement is not guaranteed; this is also true in many countries, especially in the Commonwealth group. Allowing success-fees of course exacerbates the problem. Shifting success premiums makes the loser liable for the reward the winner promised his lawyer; this adds insult to injury as the loser has to pay extra precisely for being defeated. Yet, not shifting success fees denies the winner full recovery of his litigation expenses. Finally, where the shiftable amount is no longer officially fixed ex ante (and especially where it includes some kind of success premium), the loser will often challenge the winner's reimbursement

[99] Cf. L'Américanisation du droit, Archives de philosophie du droit 45 (2001) 7.

[100] For an informative discussion of the advantages and disadvantages of strictly regulated lawyer fees, see Gerhard Wagner, Litigation Costs Recovery – Tariffs and Hourly Fees in Germany, in Gottwald, supra note 10, 149, at 174–184.

[101] See supra note 39 and text; note, again, however, that under the most recent statutory amendments (2011), a written agreement between lawyer and client can override the statutory tariff and also determine the fee to be shifted (within limits).

claim as unreasonable – which entails continued fighting even after the main case has been closed.[102]

In short, leaving lawyer fees entirely to the market, and especially allowing success premiums, entails three major costs: it is incompatible with routine full fee shifting because the winner's agreement with his lawyer cannot automatically determine what the loser owes; it creates predictability problems and thus fairness issues because the amount owed by the loser is not fixed in advance; and it invites second stage litigation because what should reasonably be reimbursed is often debatable.[103]

As a result of the current trends therefore, fewer and fewer legal systems will have fee shifting in the Austrian, German, or Swiss tradition: simple, quick, and usually uncontroversial; and more and more jurisdictions will have cost allocation as in Australia, England or Canada: complex, labor-intensive, and often contested.[104]

1.3.2.3 Absolute and Relative Size

While the computation of lawyer fees is plagued by complexities and uncertainties, especially in market-based systems, a look at the numbers presented in the national reports and culled from various other sources shows two things quite clearly.

First, on the whole, the sums involved in attorney fee shifting are very substantial. Even in jurisdictions with comparably moderate fees, the loser in a $100,000 lawsuit, for example, will owe the winner roughly between $5,000 and $10,000. In more generous jurisdictions, like Switzerland, the debt can easily be twice that amount. And in countries with truly high litigation costs, like Australia or Canada, the loser may owe even more, depending on the complexity of the case and on how much of the lawyer fees the court ultimately awards the winner. Again, generalization is difficult and perhaps not advisable. Suffice it to say that where attorney fees are shifted, it is not at all unusual for the defeated party in a mid-size case to

---

102 For England, see Martin Ilmer, Lawyer's Fees and Access to Justice, Civil Justice Quarterly 26 [2007] 201, at 207(with further references). Zuckerman on Civil Procedure (2nd ed. London 2006) par. 26.1 et seq.

103 In order to avoid these issues at least in part, England has introduced "fixed costs" for certain types of routine cases and for all fast track trials for under 15,000 pounds; see Oxford: Costs and Funding, supra note 7, [83 fn. 70]; Oxford: Comparative Study, supra fn. 7, IV.145 (incl. fn. 60).

104 Particularly in England, (second stage) litigation about costs is so notorious and widespread that insiders often speak of a veritable "cost war", see Richard Moorhead, Cost Wars in England and Wales: The Insurers Strike Back (Chapter 8, this volume); see also Andrews, supra note 90, at 204; Peysner, supra note 77, 140–141.

owe the winner 10% of the amount in controversy in lawyer fees alone.[105] Thus, potential liability for them is a very significant part of the overall litigation risk.

Second, in almost all systems, attorney fees invariably exceed court costs. In other words, lawyers are more expensive than courts.[106] This means that attorney fee shifting is practically more important than court cost shifting. How much more important depends on the jurisdiction involved. In this regard, there is a significant difference between continental civil law systems on the one hand and common law regimes on the other. In continental Europe, attorney fees typically exceed court costs by a fairly moderate ratio, typically ranging from just above 1:1 to around 1:6. In common law jurisdictions, attorney fees tend to exceed court fees much more dramatically. The reason for this difference is mainly that court costs are higher in civil law systems than in common law jurisdictions while the opposite tends to be true for lawyer fees.[107] As a result, the comparative importance of shifting court costs and allocating lawyer fees varies. In continental Europe, both elements often matter significantly (though lawyer fee shifting matters more) while in some common law jurisdictions, like Canada or the United States, court costs can constitute such a small item that lawyer fee shifting is all that really counts.

1.3.2.4 Avoiding Attorney Fees

Attorney fees are sometimes avoidable: the majority of legal systems covered in this report broadly permit self-representation, often at all levels; and even the minority of jurisdictions that require representation by a lawyer usually make exceptions for small claims (courts). Where litigants can – de jure and de facto – operate without legal counsel, the importance of attorney fee shifting is of course much diminished.

Yet, whether self-representation is a viable option in reality varies depending on the legal system and the nature of the case involved. In some systems, especially those with a civil law background, judges take a fairly active part in the proceedings and will usually help non-represented parties considerably, particularly in smaller and more routine cases. This is especially true in Asian countries[108]; but it is also the case in Latin America and

---

[105] This is of course on top of the fee owed to the loser's own lawyer, as well as on top of court costs (supra Section 1.3.1) and evidence expenses (infra Section 1.3.3) all of which can be very substantial.

[106] This is confirmed by the Oxford group, see Oxford: Costs and Funding, supra note 7, [107]; Oxford: Comparative Study, supra note 7, III.37. and 69.

[107] This is not because common lawyers are more expensive by the hour but because common law procedure is more party-driven and thus requires more lawyer time, see infra Section 1.5.2.

[108] This is expressly noted in the National Reports for China, Japan, and Korea.

even much of continental Europe. As a result, parties there often appear without lawyers, at least in the lower courts. In other jurisdictions, especially from the common law orbit, however, judges are traditionally much more passive and lawsuits are essentially party-driven; this, of course, makes it much harder for laypeople effectively to litigate pro se. And everywhere, large and complex cases are usually too difficult to handle without professional assistance.

1.3.3 The Expenses of Evidence: What Price Fact Gathering?

Almost all systems covered in this chapter in principle shift the expenses of evidence taking to the loser, most in whole, some at least in large part. Yet, again, this basic principle acquires real meaning only once we look more closely at what the expenses of evidence taking consist of and in particular, how substantial they are. In this regard, there are significant differences between three kinds of jurisdictions: civil law systems, common law countries in the British tradition, and, as the major exception to the rule of general evidence cost shifting, the United States.

1.3.3.1 Civil Law Systems

All civil law systems impose the costs of evidence taking on the loser. In most cases, however, the impact is relatively slight for two reasons.

First, since fact gathering is largely performed, or at least closely directed, by the judge, the court does most of the work, such as ordering documents, interviewing witnesses, inspecting sites, etc.; and this judicial work is already paid for in form of the – often very substantial – court costs. In other words, court cost shifting already includes much of the expenses of evidence taking.

Second, the *additional and separate* expenses of evidence are usually low because there is no common-law style discovery. In most cases, they only consist of fees and compensation for witnesses and perhaps the cost of copying documents. The amounts involved here are usually small and do not constitute a significant item in the overall litigation bill. The situation changes to some extent, however, if expert witnesses get involved. In civil law proceedings, expert witnesses are usually appointed by the court, and their fee will also ultimately be borne by the losing party. While expert witnesses are often paid according to an official schedule which remains below market rate, they can still be fairly expensive and thus have an impact on overall costs.

Still, all in all it is fair to say that in civil law systems, evidence expense shifting is usually secondary to both court costs and lawyer fees.

1.3.3.2 Common Law Jurisdictions

In common law jurisdictions in the English tradition, the expenses of evidence taking are borne by the loser as well, albeit often only in part. As in civil law proceedings, the impact of this rule is also softened by the fact that a large chunk of these expenses is already covered: now, fact gathering is largely performed by the parties' attorneys so that much of the expense of evidence taking is already included in the lawyer fees. Thus, lawyer fee shifting already includes much (if not most) of evidence cost shifting.

In practice, however, shifting the expenses incurred by evidence taking (be it in the form of lawyer fees or other items) is more important in the common law than in the civil law orbit simply because these expenses tend to be higher. This is so mainly for three reasons. First, evidence gathering by the parties' attorneys is more expensive since (common law) attorneys charge more than (civil law) judges. Second, during common law-style discovery, evidence is often taken by both sides (and thus twice) rather than only once by a (civil law) judge. Third, experts tend to cost more in common law jurisdictions because they are hired by the parties and thus at market rates, and because each side usually hires its own instead of relying on just one appointed by the court. As a result, the expenses incurred by evidence taking usually constitute a larger share of the total litigation bill in common law than in civil law systems – which makes shifting these expenses to the loser more crucial.[109]

1.3.3.3 The United States Approach

The United States approach to the expenses of evidence taking is sui generis for two reasons. First, the majority of fact gathering expenses are *not* shifted to the loser. These expenses consist of three major items: the attorney fees generated by the discovery process – which are (under the general US-American rule) borne by each party regardless of outcome; the costs of their expert witnesses – which are also not shifted; and "costs other than attorney fees"[110] – which *are* borne by the loser but comprise merely a variety of minor fees for (non-expert) witnesses, court stenographers, and copying.[111] Thus overall, only a very small, and in fact often trivial, part of the expenses of taking evidence are shifted. Second, as a result of a uniquely permissive discovery regime,[112] fact gathering in the United States is more

---

[109] This does not necessarily mean that the loser actually bears a greater amount of these costs than in a civil law court. Remember that most civil law courts routinely shift the total amount while common law judges often choose to shift only a part of the winner's litigation (including evidence taking) costs to the defeated party.

[110] See Federal Rule of Civil Procedure 54(d)(1).

[111] See 28 United States Code § 1920.

[112] Discovery is permissible not only with regard to evidence which is admissible at trial but also "if the discovery appears reasonably calculated to lead to the discovery

extensive – and thus more expensive – than anywhere else in the world. In most cases, the expenses of gathering evidence are – often by far – the largest item on the total litigation bill. Thus the practical impact of *not* shifting the lion's share of evidence costs (including expert witness fees) is tremendous: it entails a huge burden for the victor as well as a huge relief for the vanquished. In fact, not shifting the bulk of evidence costs is perhaps *the* defining feature that separates the United States from all other jurisdictions covered here. After all, like *all* other systems, the US-American regime makes the loser pay for court costs; like at least *some* other systems, it normally does not shift attorney fees; but like *no* other system, it makes each party pay for virtually all its own expenses of fact gathering regardless of outcome, and these expenses are normally very high.[113]

1.3.4 The Total Picture: Litigation Costs in Four Cases and Their Impact

If court costs (ranging from trivial to substantial), attorney fees (ranging from substantial to astronomical), and expenses of evidence taking (ranging from modest to crushing) are added together, it becomes clear that in most of the legal systems covered here, the overall financial burden of civil litigation is heavy, at least outside of small claims procedures. Unfortunately, it is almost impossible to obtain comparable figures for all these jurisdictions because overall litigation costs depend on a large number of variables including the nature and complexity of the case, the court in which a case is filed,[114] the computation and level of attorney fees, and the method of taking evidence. Still, in response to the General Reporter's request to indicate the total litigation costs for certain claims, most National Reports provided some useful figures.[115] While these figures also have to be taken with a very large grain of salt, they give us some idea of how much it may cost to litigate monetary claims on four levels.

---

of admissible evidence", Federal Rule of Civil Procedure 26(b)(1); this provision thus permits so-called "fishing expeditions".

[113] Under the discovery system in the United States, each side thus has the potential to inflict enormous costs on the other side which can usually not be shifted.

[114] In some systems, like France, Mexico, Serbia, and Russia, there are different courts, and sometimes different cost and cost allocation rules for private and commercial cases; in many other jurisdictions, such as Germany, Norway, and Sweden, family law disputes are subject to special rules and rates; and some systems, like Japan or the United States, treat cases for personal injury differently than, e.g., suits for breach of contract or injunctive relief.

[115] In schedule based-systems, these figures were usually fairly precise; in others, they were based on good faith estimates.

1.3.4.1 Small Claims

Litigating relatively small claims (e.g., roughly the equivalent of $1,000) is affordable where they are handled in special small claims courts with a simplified procedure and without legal counsel. This option exists in many systems and seems to generate few problems. Where such an option does not exist, however, and especially where the parties are (by legal requirement or choice) represented by lawyers, litigating small claims is at minimum disconcertingly expensive, often costing over 50% of the amount in controversy (as indicated by the figures for Belgium, China, the Czech Republic, Slovenia, and Switzerland) or outright prohibitive, i.e., costing *more* than the amount in controversy (as signaled by the numbers for Austria, Finland, Iceland, Italy, Spain, and Scotland, and possibly also in the Czech Republic, Germany, and the United States). In short, such small claims can usually not be efficiently handled in a regular (full-fledged) civil proceeding if lawyers are employed.

1.3.4.2 Small to Medium Cases

The litigation of small to medium claims (e.g., the equivalent of $10,000) raises similar concerns in many systems for which we have data. A few jurisdictions can apparently process such claims at fairly moderate cost, ranging from a few hundred to around two thousand dollars total (figures in that range are given for Belgium, Brazil, China, Greece, Iceland, Korea, Poland, Serbia and Taiwan). In most systems, however, the cost is in the thousands of dollars and thus represents a sizeable percentage of the amount in controversy. And in some jurisdictions, litigation costs closely approach or actually reach the claimed amount (Austria, Finland, Italy, Scotland, and Switzerland are in this category), making it, again, potentially inefficient to litigate such claims at all.

1.3.4.3 Medium to Large Disputes

In suits for medium to large disputes (involving the equivalent of $100,000), the absolute cost of litigation is even higher, but the relative cost goes down. While such litigation now often burns up tens of thousands of dollars, no system for which figures were provided exceeded 50% of the amount in controversy, and most ranged between roughly 10% and one third. The two main reasons for these more bearable ratios are the degressive scale of official court cost and lawyer fee schedules as well as more generally, the fact that lawyer time and evidence-taking typically do not increase in a linear fashion with the amount in controversy. Nonetheless, litigating these medium to large disputes is by no means cheap.

1.3.4.4 High-Value Litigation

Unsurprisingly, the litigation of large claims (e.g., $1,000,000) is most expensive in absolute terms and cheapest in relation to the amount at stake.

It may cost as little as around 1% (this is indicated by the figures given for Belgium, Greece, and, in commercial courts, Serbia) or as much as one third (as in Scotland) of the sum claimed.[116] The more typical ratios, however, range from about 5 to 15%. While this does not threaten to devour the claim, these percentages routinely translate into tens of thousands or dollars and can, in some systems, easily exceed six figures.

1.3.4.5 Litigation Costs and Access to Justice

On the whole, the magnitude of litigation costs in most systems creates three major problems. Not all of these problems occur in all jurisdictions, but most of them are pervasive in most systems.[117] First, outside of special courts with simplified procedures, small and perhaps even midsize claims can often not be efficiently handled because litigating them can easily cost more than their worth.[118] Second, litigating midsize and large claims is frequently so expensive that at least among private individuals, very few can afford to pay for it out of their own pocket. Third, in many systems litigation costs in large cases can be exorbitant (as well as highly unpredictable) so that the financial burden (or at least risk) is hard to bear even for deep pocket parties.[119]

Disproportionate costs constitute serious barriers for access to justice.[120] Mere cost-shifting from one side to the other cannot do much to solve this problem. It is true, of course, that under a loser-pays approach,

---

[116] While the National Reporters provided no figures for England and Wales nor for the United States, common experience suggests that in these systems, litigating a $1,000,000 claim could also cost hundreds of thousands of dollars although almost everything would depend on the kind and complexity of the case.

[117] The Oxford group also concluded "that in most states included in this study the costs of litigation are high in relation to the value of the case – sometimes they even exceed the value of the case," Oxford: Costs and Funding, supra note 7, [71]; Oxford: Comparative Study, supra note 7, III.70.

[118] Many National Reports flag this problem; see the Reports for Austria, Brazil, Switzerland, the Czech Republic, Italy, Japan, Mexico, South Africa (at least in unusual or novel cases), Spain (especially in consumer litigation), and Turkey.

[119] Interestingly, *all* National Reports from common law systems (Australia, Canada, England and Wales, and the United States) and mixed jurisdictions (Israel, Scotland, and South Africa) mention this problem. By contrast, only *some* of the civil law based countries report this concern. This indicates that systems with a strong common law element struggle more consistently with cost issues than jurisdictions with a civil law foundation. Given the more lawyer-centered nature of court proceedings in common law (influenced) countries, litigation costs there tend to be higher and, perhaps just as importantly, less predictable, see infra Section 1.5.2.

[120] Of course, access to justice is not only a matter of money but depends on a variety of other factors as well. Still, financial costs are an important hurdle for most potential litigants. In some systems, like Italy and India, the main problem is not cost but excessive delay. It is a common maxim in English that "justice delayed is justice denied", and if an injured party cannot enforce its claim through the legal process within a reasonable period of time, even free access to justice provides little help.

the winning party gets away free (or at least cheaply) – but only at the risk of being hit so much harder in case of defeat. It is also true that if the costs are not (or only partially) shifted, the burden on each side is lighter – but only at the price of having to pay (and often dearly) even when winning hands-down. In either case, rules on cost and fee shifting leave the financial burden of litigation on the parties to the litigation,[121] and these costs can be ruinous, sometimes even for winners.

1.4 Whose Money? Access to Justice Through Mechanisms of Risk Distribution

In reality, however, parties often do not pay for litigation costs with their own money. In response to the problems mentioned, most jurisdictions have developed mechanisms to distribute the financial risk of civil litigation among larger groups. Cost and fee allocation in civil procedure cannot be fully understood without taking these mechanisms into account. They range from traditional legal aid to modern models of litigation as an investment opportunity. Some distribute civil litigation costs more widely than others.[122]

1.4.1 Legal Aid: Assisting the Needy

All systems covered in this chapter provide some form of legal aid. This aid comes in three basic varieties which may be called public, semi-official, and pro bono. Depending on these forms, legal aid is subject to various conditions and limitations.

1.4.1.1 Public Legal Aid

Public legal aid directly funds the parties through state money – usually by waiving court fees, often (though not necessarily) by paying for lawyers,[123] and possibly even by covering the expenses of evidence taking. It thus distributes litigation costs extremely widely: these costs are ultimately borne by the taxpayers in the respective state entity (federation, state, province, etc.).

---

[121] Some are paid by the state, e.g., where court fees are so low that the judicial system must be heavily subsidized by tax payer money, as in the United States.

[122] We leave out here cost distribution by firms through the market to consumers of their services or products because this mechanism is used for virtually all firm costs and thus not particular to civil litigation expenses.

[123] In many systems, lawyers taking on public aid cases are paid only a (sometimes severely) reduced fee; it stands to reason that this will often affect the quality of legal representation.

Public legal aid is offered – at least in principle – in all systems included here, with the exception of the United States[124] and Russia.[125] In the European Union, there is now a right to legal aid under Article 47 sec. 3 of the Charter of Fundamental Rights.[126] In many jurisdictions, it is the only kind of legal aid systematically available[127]; in others, it operates in addition to various other forms of assistance (infra Sections 1.4.1.2 and 1.4.1.3).[128] Public legal aid is broadly conceived in that it can usually cover both plaintiffs and defendants.

Yet, public legal aid helps only a small segment of all litigants because it is subject to serious restrictions. Their severity and, as a result, the actual availability of legal aid, varies among the systems covered here. Most importantly, *all* jurisdictions impose two very significant limitations. First, only

---

124 There is some – very limited – federal funding in support of legal aid efforts but no general public legal aid system. The Oxford group's statement that such a system is not necessary in light of the availability of contingency fees (for indigent parties), is largely (though not completely) untrue, Oxford: Costs and Funding, supra note 7, [22]; Oxford: Comparative Study, supra note 7, III.100. First, contingency fee arrangements are usually available only to plaintiffs, and mainly in tort cases (i.e., not to defendants and not in all forms of litigation). Second, even for tort plaintiffs, a contingency fee arrangement is not viable in low value disputes, as the Oxford Study itself later points out, id. III.113; in fact, this can be true even in high value cases if in light of the necessary investment into litigation, they do not promise sufficient return. Thus the statement in the Oxford Study is true mainly only in the sense that because of the contingency fee system, *some* parties do not need legal aid.

125 In the United States, there is no generally available public legal aid for private litigation although there are – very limited – federal funds to support legal representation of indigents by lawyers. The federal government and the states do, however, subsidize litigation by providing use of the court system at very low (usually flat) rates (see supra Section 1.3.1.1). As long as parties act pro se (i.e., without a lawyer), they thus often face low financial access barriers to justice, especially in small claims courts and procedures. Where this is not a realistic option, the low court costs cannot make up for the high attorney fees common in the United States. In Russia, public legal aid is available only to a very limited extent in certain classes of civil litigation (as well as, more generally, in criminal cases). Bar associations sometimes provide legal aid as well, see infra Section 1.4.1.2.

126 Article 47 sec. 3 of the Charter of Fundamental Rights of the European Union provides:

> Legal aid shall be made available to those who lack sufficient resources in so far as such aid is necessary to ensure effective access to justice.

127 This is reported for many civil law countries, including Austria, Belgium, Finland, Germany, Greece, Italy, Korea, Mexico, Russia, Serbia, and Venezuela. In some of these countries, private legal aid is available by way of exception on an ad hoc basis.

128 This is reported for Brazil, Canada, the Czech Republic, England and Wales, Iceland, India, Israel, Japan, Macau, the Netherlands, Poland, Scotland, and Turkey, although the degree to which private forms of legal aid exist in these countries apparently varies a great deal.

indigent parties are eligible, i.e., parties who fall below a (sometimes statutorily defined) income or wealth threshold; that threshold is mostly so low that public legal aid is normally unavailable to the middle class.[129] Second, all systems require that the applicant's case pass a – variously defined – merits test; in other words, states do not fund long shot litigation. In addition, many systems impose various other kinds of restrictions, such as not covering liability of the other side's expenses in case of defeat, providing only partial or temporary help or excluding certain kinds of disputes.

In several systems, the availability of legal aid for civil litigants has been diminishing as public funds have been in ever shorter supply, especially since the 2008 financial crisis.[130] The French Report speaks of an outright "crise du système d'aide juridique".[131] This has increased the pressure to provide semi-official or private forms of legal aid – or to turn to alternative ways of litigation cost distribution altogether (infra Sections 1.4.2, 1.4.3, 1.4.4, and 1.4.5).

1.4.1.2 Semi-official Assistance

In several jurisdictions, needy parties can receive help from various public institutions, such as clinics operated by law faculties in Iceland, Israel, Mexico, Norway, and the United States; state bureaus in the Czech Republic; or public prosecutors in Poland. In other systems, like Belgium, Brazil, the Czech Republic or Russia, bar associations provide assistance. And help is sometimes available also from various non-governmental organizations, such as trade unions for labor and employment disputes, e.g., in Belgium, Italy, Germany, and the United States, or other non-profit groups, as reported for Israel, Macau, and Poland. This assistance may be limited to legal advice but sometimes also includes free representation in court. The cost of litigation (at least the part absorbed by these institutions) is thus distributed to all those who fund the respective programs through their time or their money.

1.4.1.3 Pro Bono Work

In a number of jurisdictions, legal aid is available in form of pro bono work performed by law firms: these firms provide free advice and representation to particular parties. In effect, pro bono work is funded by all paying clients of the firm.

---

[129] The same conclusion is reached by the Oxford group; see Oxford: Costs and Funding, supra note 7, [24]; Oxford: Comparative Study, supra note 7, III.103.

[130] This is confirmed by the Oxford group, see Oxford: Costs and Funding, supra note 7, [24]; Oxford: Comparative Study, supra note 7, III.102. For England, see Andrews, supra note 90, at 187.

[131] French Report IV.2.

Pro bono work is a fairly strong tradition in the United States where law firms are under at least a moral obligation to devote a certain percentage of total lawyer time free of charge to litigation in the public interest or to help parties who cannot afford to pay for professional services. Pro bono work is also known in Australia, Brazil, Canada, the Czech Republic, England and Wales, Scotland, Israel, Japan, Norway, Mexico, and, in nascent form, apparently in China; tender beginnings are reported from France as well. Yet, even where pro bono work has become an established practice, as in many common law countries, in terms of providing (free) access to justice for parties in need, it is but a drop in the bucket.

1.4.2 Litigation Insurance: Buying Protection

In most of the systems covered here, the market has responded to the limited availability of legal aid by offering insurance against litigation costs. This is particularly attractive to the middle class and smaller businesses, i.e., potential parties who are too wealthy to qualify for legal aid but not wealthy enough to absorb litigation costs in all but the smallest cases. Litigation insurance also comes in three basic forms which may be labeled package deal, free-standing, and (British) "after-the-event" policies.

1.4.2.1 Package-Deal Insurance

Litigation insurance is frequently part and parcel of policies covering other, standard, risks. It is most commonly included in automobile, home-owner's, and professional malpractice coverage. In some countries, like Finland and Switzerland, it can also be part of commercial liability protection.

Under such policies, the insurer absorbs not only the liability risk but also funds (in part of course in its own interest) litigation triggered by events covered by the policy.[132] In reality, such insurance applies almost exclusively to defendants in tort cases. It can actually cover not only the defendant's own litigation costs but also, where the defendant loses and costs are shifted, liability for the victorious plaintiff's bill.

Package-deal insurance distributes the litigation costs among all policy holders in the respective category and thus very widely. This keeps the price for coverage fairly low; after all, the number of actual lawsuits is relatively small compared to the number of policies written.

This kind of legal cost insurance is surprisingly common. It is available (in one form or another) in the majority of countries covered here and very popular in a number of them. In these jurisdictions, many middle-class members are thus protected against much of the financial risk of litigation

[132] This usually gives the insurer a say in the selection of the attorney, often also in the litigation strategy, and sometimes even in whether and how to settle a case.

inherent in everyday activities, such as driving a car, owning a home, or engaging in a profession or business.

1.4.2.2 Free-Standing Litigation Insurance

A less common but still fairly wide-spread form is free-standing insurance for litigation costs. In many countries, individuals[133] can buy policies protecting them specifically against the financial risk of a lawsuit. In particular, losers are insured both for their own bills and for having to pay the winner's. This coverage usually extends to both plaintiffs and defendants. Yet, it is typically limited in two ways. First, it usually covers only certain kinds of cases – normally the kinds of litigation in which private individuals typically get involved: consumer, landlord-tenant, tort litigation, etc.; family law disputes may or may not be included.[134] Second, the benefits are often capped at a certain amount.

Such free-standing litigation insurance also distributes the cost risk among all policy holders and thus very broadly. Since it also applies to plaintiffs, i.e., the parties who decide to go to court,[135] it implies a higher risk than the merely defendant-oriented package-deal insurance. It is therefore more expensive. Still, the premiums are affordable for most middle-class individuals.[136]

As a result, free-standing litigation insurance is enormously popular in parts of Western Europe, especially where full cost-shifting makes litigation financially dicey. In Germany, almost half of the population (43%)[137] enjoys such coverage. It is also common in France[138] and Iceland, a "widespread industry" in Switzerland, "increasingly popular" in the Netherlands, and known in Belgium,[139] and Sweden. Thus, in such countries, the costs of much routine civil litigation are not necessarily borne by middle class individuals in person but rather collectivized through the insurance

---

[133] This kind of insurance is not reported for businesses.

[134] In many systems, it covers not only civil litigation but also the costs of defending oneself against civil infraction and criminal charges (in practice most often for traffic violations).

[135] Under the respective policies, they usually have to clear that decision with the insurance company which will not provide coverage for bringing frivolous claims.

[136] This may be because the actual litigation rate is still relatively low. The French Report, e.g., states that despite great popularity of litigation insurance, only 2.4% of all new cases filed in 2007, and only ca. 2% of all civil litigation expenses, were actually covered by it, see French Report V.4.

[137] German Report V.4.; Gerhard Wagner, Litigation Costs Recovery – Tariffs and Hourly Fees in Germany, in Gottwald, supra note 10, at 171 fn. 69 cites 41.6% for 2007/2008.

[138] The French Report states that ca. 40% of all households are covered and that this percentage is growing fast, French Report V.4.

[139] Here, it is actually encouraged by tax breaks with a view to facilitate access to justice.

market.[140] Recent reform proposals encourage the introduction of such insurance for England and Wales as well.[141]

1.4.2.3 British After-the-Event Insurance

A very special form of insuring against litigation costs has developed in Britain. In sharp contrast to the more widespread kinds of litigation insurance (Sections 1.4.2.1 and 1.4.2.2) which is bought *before* anything bad happens (and certainly before litigation is underway), British-style "after-the-event insurance" (ATE) is purchased *after* a dispute has arisen and in fact often even after a lawsuit has been filed. It usually works in tandem with – and it is best understood as a complement to – a "no win, no fee" agreement with one's own lawyer (infra Section 1.4.4.2), creating a "unique and bizarre system".[142]

Lawsuits entail a particularly great financial risk in the British environment of high litigation expenses, low cost predictability, and substantial fee shifting. The parties thus have a strong interest in insuring against the consequences of losing the case in two particular regards: against having to pay their own counsel, and against having to reimburse (at least much of) the opponent's expenses. Regarding the fee of their own lawyer, parties can protect themselves through a "no win, no fee" agreement.[143] Regarding their liability for the other side's costs, they can protect themselves by buying ATE insurance to cover these costs (up to a certain amount). This insurance is typically bought (usually through their solicitor) at the outset of the litigation. The combination between a no-win-no-fee agreement and ATE insurance thus means that the losing party does not have to pay any attorney fees – its own lawyer receives none, and its opponent's are covered by ATE insurance.[144]

There is more good news, at least from the winner's side: if the case is won, the insured can usually shift the premium to the loser as part of the litigation expenses.[145] And if the case is lost, the insurance premium

[140] As the Oxford group points out, litigation cost insurance can lower the holder's willingness to settle and thus adversely affect settlement rates, Oxford: Costs and Funding, supra note 7, [276]; Oxford: Comparative Study, supra note 7, IV.167.

[141] Jackson Review, supra note 9, 79.

[142] Peysner, supra note 77, at 137.

[143] To counterbalance that risk, the lawyer usually receives a success premium on top of his or her usual fee in case of victory.

[144] This is just a rough outline. The details vary greatly because the market offers different models tailored to various kinds of litigation and to the needs of the parties involved.

[145] This is normally permitted in England and Wales, but not in Scotland.

does not have to be paid at all as the insurer absorbs that risk.[146] Thus, the insured party cannot lose on litigation expenses. This raises concerns regarding fairness to the other party and has led to vociferous debates in the United Kingdom.[147] The Jackson Review thus recommends to render ATE premiums as well as success fees irrecoverable from the loser.[148]

Of course, there is bad news as well: premiums are very high and can easily reach 25% of the amount of coverage. This is so for two fairly obvious reasons. First, after-the-event insurance comes into play often (though not always) when litigation is a certainty so that the risk of cost liability is very high. Second, ATE insurance distributes litigation costs only among real (not merely *potential*) litigants, and even here only among the subset buying such coverage. This pool is much smaller, of course, than for other litigation insurance so that each insured's share of the risk is much higher. In combination with conditional fees, ATE insurance has thus been "the major contributor to disproportionate costs in civil litigation in England and Wales".[149]

1.4.3 Collective Actions: Banding Together

Parties can spread litigation expenses also without resorting to public legal aid or private insurance, namely by banding together: they can pursue their interests collectively and thus share the costs. This occurs overwhelmingly on the plaintiff side. Collective actions come in many forms, shapes, and sizes, and the details vary greatly depending on the legal system involved.[150] Roughly speaking, however, they can be put into three major categories: class actions, group actions, and suits by organizations representing collective interests.

1.4.3.1 Class Actions

The (by now) classic form of the class action is its United States variety in which one or several named plaintiffs represent the interests of a large

---

146 In this regard, ATE insurance is highly similar to a contingency fee arrangement; the main difference is that the insurance company, rather than the plaintiff's lawyer, plays the role of litigation financer.

147 See Peysner, supra note 77, 137–138; Oxford: Costs and Funding, supra note 7, [22]; Oxford: Comparative Study, supra note 7, III.115.

148 Jackson Review, supra note 9, XVI, 87.

149 Jackson Review, supra note 9, XVI.

150 The situation in the United States is presented and compared with various European models by Samuel Issacharoff, Aggregating Private Claims, in Gottwald, supra note 10, 63–77. For an overview of the situation in Germany, see Astrid Stadler, Aggregate Litigation – Group/Class Actions in Germany, in Gottwald, supra note 10, 79–93.

number of similarly situated claimants who will all be bound by the final judgment or settlement unless they have opted out.[151] Similar class actions exist in Australia, Canada, Israel, and apparently also in Russia. In some other jurisdictions, class actions are available for very specific kinds of litigation, such as consumer rights in Brazil and Finland, securities actions in Korea, and actions by non-profit organizations in Sweden. In addition, there has lately been a lively discussion in the European Union and in many of its member states about introducing class actions in particular contexts, especially for consumer claims and antitrust violations.[152]

How exactly litigation costs and fees are allocated in class actions varies considerably across jurisdictions.[153] Under the United States approach and similar models, successful plaintiff attorneys receive (in some cases huge) legal fees which must, however, be approved by the court. These fees are usually charged on a contingency basis (see infra Section 1.4.4.1) and thus come out of the plaintiff's (collective) damage awards, in one form or another. This often results in wide cost distribution among a very large number of claimants. In fact, individual plaintiffs usually do not pay anything out of pocket.[154]

1.4.3.2 Group Actions

The variety of group actions across jurisdictions is even more bewildering than the various forms of class actions. They range from German investor dispute groups which approximate class actions in some regards, to the English *Group Litigation Order*, to Austrian procedures in which consumers assign their rights to the group, and the Greek model which is essentially still a form of joinder of actions. In a similar vein, cost rules vary considerably: in Germany, group members bear the costs according to the relative value of their claims; in the Netherlands, group actions are financed by membership fees; in England and Wales, group members are severally liable for litigations costs, etc.

Yet, all these models have in common that by joining a group, plaintiffs share litigation costs with the other members through one mechanism or another. This enables plaintiffs to litigate their claims more economically

[151] See especially Federal Rule of Civil Procedure 23.

[152] For an overview, see Matthias Casper, André Jansen, Petra Pohlmann and Reiner Schuler, Auf dem Weg zu einer europäischen Sammelklage (Munich 2009).

[153] In Finland, for example, they are borne by an ombudsman.

[154] As is widely known, in many US-style class actions, successful plaintiffs themselves also rarely gain much. In many cases, their individual claims are very small (so small that they could not be litigated individually); in others, the class action is really about going after a wrong-doer with little or no pay-out to the plaintiffs (as is typical in securities class actions). In some cases, however, individual plaintiffs may receive considerable benefit, e.g., in class actions for mass toxic torts.

than in an individual action. In fact, many such claims, especially in the consumer context, are too small to be pursued on an individual basis at all. In these cases, group actions work like class actions: by defraying litigation costs, they provide access to justice for holders of claims that could otherwise not be judicially enforced.

1.4.3.3 Organizations Pursuing Collective Interests

In a considerable number of jurisdictions, organizations can bring suits in the collective interest, especially to enforce rights of consumers. These suits are usually not for damages to the organization's members but rather pursue injunctive relief: prohibiting certain activities, remedying harmful situations, declaring standard contract clauses void, etc. The respective organizations are usually plaintiffs in their own right and, as such, subject to the general cost rules (i.e., potentially liable to the winner). In some jurisdictions, they are privileged, e.g., by not being liable for the defendant's expenses if they lose in Brazil, or by not having to pay court costs, as in Macau.

To be sure, the primary policy driving lawsuits by organizations acting in the public interest is to overcome the collective action problem. But these suits also spread the financial risks inherent in litigation among all those who finance the respective organizations, be they members or outside donors. Thus, such organization suits facilitate access to justice for claims that would not be brought if single (or a small group of) individuals had to bear the financial risks.

1.4.4 Success-Oriented Fees: Winners Pooling with Losers

By far most jurisdictions included here permit success-oriented lawyer fees in one form or another.[155] Such fees are mostly considered from an incentive perspective: if a lawyer's reward depends (in whole or in part) on the outcome of the case, the lawyer will work harder for the client because their interests align.[156] Sometimes, contingency fees in particular are also understood as a mechanism to provide access to justice: for better or worse, they allow suits by plaintiffs who could not pay for a lawyer if the fee were not taken out of the damages won. Beyond all that, however, success-oriented fees also facilitate access to justice more generally. In contrast to legal aid,

[155] See also the overview provided by the Oxford group, Oxford: Costs and Funding, supra note 7, [132–133]; Oxford: Comparative Study, supra note 7, Appendix VI.

[156] At least with regard to contingency fees in the United States that is not necessarily so, as is well known. Lawyers may actually have an incentive to sell-out their clients' interests, e.g., if a quick settlement reaps substantial awards whereas obtaining more money for the client beyond that point may involve so much time that is not cost-efficient for the lawyer; see Michael Horowitz, Making Ethics Real, Making Ethics Work: A Proposal for Contingency Fee Reform, 44 Emory Law Journal 173 (1995).

litigation insurance and class actions, they do so not by spreading costs to large numbers of potential or actual litigants but rather by shifting the financial burden to the party who can more easily bear it. Different versions of success-oriented fees accomplish this in slightly different forms.

1.4.4.1 Contingency Fees

Typically, a contingency fee has two characteristics: it is due only if the client wins (otherwise the lawyer gets nothing), and its size is tied to the amount won. Such *quota litis* arrangements are often considered a hallmark of the US-American litigation system (especially in tort cases); they have also been much disparaged especially in continental Europe because giving a lawyer a direct financial interest in the outcome of the litigation appears unethical to many observers on the continent and elsewhere.[157] Yet, contingency fee arrangements are surprisingly common in many parts of the world. Of the jurisdictions surveyed here, almost half (14 out of 35) allow them in one form or another,[158] and the Jackson Review recently recommended that they be allowed in England and Wales as well.[159]

Through a contingency fee arrangement, parties insure themselves against two particularly bad risks: most importantly against having to pay one's lawyer although nothing was gained (the case was lost), and perhaps less importantly, against having to pay one's lawyer a lot although little was gained (the case was won but the result was meager). Parties, in fact usually plaintiffs, insure themselves against these risks by agreeing to pay a lot in case of victory but nothing in case of defeat. This helps both winning and losing plaintiffs to handle the financial risks of litigation for a simple reason: it is much more bearable, both financially and emotionally, to part with a share of the spoils if one wins than it is to pay for one's lawyer's work if one returns from court empty-handed.

1.4.4.2 No-Win-No-Fee Agreements

No-win-no-fee agreements (also known as conditional fee agreements) also make the lawyer's remuneration contingent on the outcome of the case but they differ from the typical contingency fee in that the size of the fee is

---

[157] They thus remain prohibited in many jurisdictions, especially in Europe. See the long list of (more than a dozen) countries in Oxford: Costs and Funding, supra note 7, [25–26]; Oxford: Comparative Study, supra note 7, III.110.

[158] Canada (including, in practice, Quebec, even though Article 1783 of the Civil Code prohibits advocates from "acquiring litigious rights"), China, Finland (for special reasons only), Germany (as of recently and only as a last resort for access to justice), Greece, Iceland, Israel, Italy (as of recently), Japan, Korea, Mexico, Russia (at least in practice), Slovenia, Taiwan, and, of course, the United States. Oxford: Comparative Study, supra note 7, also reports them to be permitted in Estonia, Hungary, Lithuania, Slovakia, and Spain, id., III.110. Note that contingency fees are often capped by legislation (to a certain percentage) or judicially controlled under a reasonableness test.

[159] Jackson Review, supra note 9, 131–133.

not (at least not strictly) tied to the sum won (or saved).[160] No-win-no-fee agreements are also very common; they are allowed even in many jurisdictions that prohibit contingency fees, such as Australia, England, Wales, and Scotland, Serbia, South Africa, and Venezuela.[161]

In terms of risk sharing, no-win-no-fee agreements work much like contingency fees but they protect only against the first of the two downside risks mentioned before, i.e., having to pay one's lawyer even though the case was lost.[162] The insurance premium essentially consists of paying much upon winning,[163] the benefit lies in owing nothing upon losing. Again, winners and losers form a risk pool which is based on the (at least implicit) understanding that the lucky shield the unlucky from having to suffer insult in addition to injury.

1.4.4.3 Success Premiums (Uplifts)

Success premiums are the mildest form of success-oriented fees. They are permitted in the majority of the systems covered here (20 out of 35) and very popular in many of them. Jurisdictions often regulate them in various ways, e.g., by limiting them to a percentage of the overall fee.[164]

Success premium agreements are a mechanism of merely partial insurance against the downside risk of having to pay one's lawyer even in case of defeat. The insurance premium clients pay is lower than in the other cases (supra Sections 1.4.4.1 and 1.4.4.2) because it consists only of the additional success fee; the coverage is also more limited because the client still owes the basic (and thus lower) fee, win or lose. Even here, however, winners and losers pool the financial risk of litigation by paying extra for victory in order to buy some relief in case of defeat.

In summary, in the great majority of systems included here, success-oriented fees permit litigants (primarily plaintiffs) to shift the burden of having to pay their lawyers from losers to winners. This helps both sides because winners are more willing and able to bear this burden than losers.

---

160 In contrast to contingency fee agreements, no-win-no-fee arrangements are also more common on both the plaintiff and the defendant side.

161 At least in England, their introduction in 1990 and expansion in 1998 was an attempt by the government to compensate for the drastic cuts in public legal aid, i.e., a result of privatizing litigation funding, see Andrews, supra note 90, at 187.

162 In other words, they do not protect against the risk of having to pay one's lawyer a lot although the gains were small. At least in theory, a client could still owe fees that render the victory pyrrhic.

163 Since lawyers have to be paid for their work by someone, they must of course charge more (if they win half their cases, double) under a no-win-no-fee arrangement than otherwise.

164 The Oxford group reports such caps for Australia, the Czech Republic, and England and Wales, Oxford: Costs and Funding, supra note 7, [25]; Oxford: Comparative Study, supra note 7, III.106.

In all this, lawyers are, so to speak, the brokers for a system of insurance that protects against a major downside risk of litigation. With this protection, parties can face proceedings with somewhat greater equanimity and often gain access to justice they could otherwise not afford.

1.4.5 Outside Investment in Litigation: Sharing the Spoils

A final way of alleviating the financial risks of litigation is to let outside investors take over the case in return for a reward if the plaintiff wins. While there are various strategies and several hybrids between them, two basic forms can be distinguished: assignment of claims and outside litigation funding.

1.4.5.1 Assignment of Claims

The more traditional strategy is to sell and assign a plaintiff's claim to another party which then pursues it in court. In this case, a new creditor replaces the old one and then sues in his own right. Jurisdictions vary with regard to whether, and to what extent, this is allowed. The civil law tradition has not had a problem with such assignments in principle,[165] although many countries forbid the sale of claims to an attorney.[166] The common law tradition, by contrast, long outlawed the assignment of claims, at least for litigation purposes.[167] Today, common law systems tend to allow the practice but usually continue to consider it illegal with regard to tort claims for personal injury (to the body, feelings, reputation, etc.) – here, only the victim him- or herself can sue. The law is similar in Israel and South Africa.[168] Legal systems worldwide also vary with regard to whether the sale and assignment of claims (as far as they are allowed) is common or rare.

The sale of a claim for litigation (or collection) purposes transfers the risks of a lawsuit from the assignor to the assignee. Of course, this is not free: the assignee purchases the claim only at a discount. In other words, the old creditor avoids the financial risks of litigation by transferring the difference between par value and discounted price to the new creditor.

---

[165] See Wagner, supra note 130, at 172. Some civil law jurisdictions, however, apparently, forbid it, e.g., Korea, Norway, Serbia, Taiwan, and Turkey.

[166] This is indicated in the National Reports for Austria, Italy, Macau, Slovenia, Sweden, Switzerland, and Venezuela. The Reports for China and Switzerland also point out that the sale of just the right to sue is not allowed.

[167] See, for the development and current situation in the United States, the detailed analysis by Tony Sebok, The Unauthentic Claim, 64 Vanderbilt Law Review 61 (2011).

[168] Apparently not in Scotland, however.

This usually amounts to a cost distribution scheme among former creditors. The reason is that purchasers of claims (for litigation or collection purposes) normally buy them en masse knowing that they will win some and lose some, and that they charge the discount rate reflecting the average risk of success to all sellers. To put it differently, the risk is being collectivized among all sellers via the discount rate.

1.4.5.2 Outside Litigation Funding

A more recent strategy is to have the original creditor pursue the claim against the debtor but to bring in a third party to fund the litigation in return for a share in case of success.[169] While, from an enforcement perspective, an assignment strategy makes most sense for a large number of small claims (supra Section 1.4.5.1), outside funding is primarily suited for large and complex claims, i.e., for litigation that threatens to be costly but also promises to be rewarding. Such outside litigation funding began in Australia in the 1990s and then spread rapidly, first to other common law jurisdictions, such as Canada, England and Wales, and the United States; later, it also came to several civil law countries as well, such as the Netherlands, Austria, and Germany.[170] Especially in Australia and England, it has grown into an industry of impressive proportions.

Jurisdictions differ, once again, as to whether (and under which circumstances) outside litigation funding is permitted. The civil law tradition apparently has no problem with the phenomenon – perhaps simply because it has not much dealt with it, at least until recently.[171] The common law,

[169] In recent years, the literature on third-party litigation funding has become a deluge; see, e.g., Michael Abramowitz, On the Alienability of Legal Claims, 114 Yale Law Journal 697 (2004); Isaac M. Marcushammer, Selling Your Torts, 33 Hofstra Law Review 1543 (2009); Marco de Marpurgo, A Comparative Legal and Economic Approach to Third-Party Litigation Funding, 19 Cardozo Journal of International and Comparative Law 343 (2011); Jonathan T. Molot, A Market in Litigation Risk, 76 University of Chicago Law Review 367 (2009); M.J. Shukaitis, A Market in Personal Injury Tort Claims, 16 Journal of Legal Studies 329 (1987); US Chamber Institute for Legal Reform, Selling Lawsuits, Buying Trouble: Third Party Litigation Funding in the United States (2009).

[170] This is confirmed by the Oxford group, Oxford: Costs and Funding, supra note 7; Oxford: Comparative Study, supra note 7, III.116. For an overview, see de Marpurgo, supra note 162 (ch. III.B.).

[171] The National Reports from the civil law jurisdictions either indicate that such funding is allowed or contain no response to this particular question; in France, the question is apparently being debated and no final conclusion has been reached; for an overview, see also de Marpurgo, supra note 162 (ch. V.B.). As Gerhard Wagner, supra note 130, at 172, remarked: "It is one of the enigmas of comparative civil procedure that the civil law with its hostility towards contingency fees, has no qualms with the assignment of claims and the funding of litigation through a third party whereas the common law allows contingency fees or at least success fees which involve the personal economic interest of the lawyer in the outcome of the litigation while it bans the promotion of litigation

by contrast, has traditionally prohibited "maintenance", i.e., third-party help provided for litigants. In most jurisdictions, this prohibition has been greatly relaxed, at least if the third party has a bona fide reason for getting involved. Still, "champerty", the subcategory of "maintenance" in which the third party aids the litigation in return for a share of the spoils in case of success, remains more contested. While some common law systems (e.g., several US states) continue to prohibit it,[172] there has recently been a liberalizing trend. Important signals came from England and Australia when courts overcame the categorical prohibition of "champerty" and allowed outside litigation funding in principle.[173] On the whole, there is little uniformity and much confusion about exactly what kinds of outside involvement in litigation is permitted in common law jurisdictions.[174]

Funding of litigation by outsiders is essentially an equity investment and works much like a contingency fee arrangement: in case of victory, the investor receives a percentage of the spoils, in case of defeat, the plaintiff pays nothing (and will usually be covered regarding his liability for the defendant's costs as well). Outside funding differs from a traditional contingency fee approach mainly in that the investor is not the plaintiff's lawyer but a separate commercial enterprise. This helps to make litigation funding tolerable for jurisdictions which are opposed to letting the litigants' attorneys have a direct financial (*quota litis*) stake in the case.

Like a contingency fee arrangement, outside litigation funding benefits plaintiffs in two principal ways: in return for sharing the prize, it insures them against having to pay potentially huge litigation costs even though the case was lost. And it provides access to justice for parties who cannot themselves fund, or stomach the financial risks of, large-scale, high-stakes litigation.

Outside litigation funding raises a lot of questions to which answers are still in short supply.[175] Whether it will establish itself as a more common and popular response to the high financial risks of complex civil litigation remains to be seen. Future trends will depend largely on whether an

---

by third parties. It seems that the funding of litigation through outside investors is much more harmless, in terms of public policy, than to allow a lawyer to act, at the same time, as counsel and as entrepeneur operating with a portfolio of claims."

172 Many (but not all) common law jurisdictions have made an exception for contingency fee agreements between parties and their lawyers.

173 Giles v. Thompson [1994] a AC 142 (England); Campbells Cash and Carry Pty. Ltd. v. Fostif Pty. Ltd., [2006] HCA 41; (2006) ALR 58 (2006) (Australia). For a detailed argument that the traditional common law restrictions have become dysfunctional and should thus be lifted, see Sebok, supra note 160.

174 For an overview of the – highly fragmented – situation in the United States, see Sebok, supra note 160.

175 Some of these questions are outlined in Oxford: Costs and Funding, supra note 7, [98–99]; Oxford: Comparative Study, supra note 7, III.118.–121.

international market for such funding continues to develop, what alternative mechanisms will become available (e.g., class actions in continental Europe), and how regulators and courts will react.[176]

1.5 In Conclusion: Grouping Cost and Fee Allocation Systems

One of the major dimensions of comparative law has long been to organize legal systems into groups, families or traditions. As is well known, such classifications are fraught with danger because they tends to oversimplify reality and are often biased in favor of traditional categories.[177] Still, grouping legal systems can be a valuable heuristic device as it can bring similarities and differences into sharper relief and thus provide a sense of how legal systems in the world relate to each other. This is particularly true if such groupings are undertaken in specific contexts, such as cost and fee rules, rather than in an all-encompassing fashion. It is therefore tempting to ask whether the jurisdictions surveyed here can be classified in a plausible manner from a cost allocation perspective.

1.5.1 Regional and Cultural Clusters?

One can indeed identify several regional or cultural clusters. Yet, it requires some temerity and is far from a perfect game. Some clusters are more plausible than others and some conceivable ones don't work out at all.

Perhaps the most plausible cluster consists of a large number of legal systems in Western and Central Europe which are centered around what Zweigert and Kötz labelled "The Germanic Legal Family"[178]: the German-speaking jurisdictions (Germany, Austria, Switzerland), the Netherlands in the West, the Scandinavian systems in the North, and the Central European countries in the East and South East; though geographically distant, Turkey is also part of this cluster. As far as they are covered here, these systems all embrace the loser-pays principle, shift both court costs and attorney fees (more or less completely), and assign judicial discretion a relatively weak role. It is not, however, a perfectly "Germanic" group because some countries clearly from outside of this tradition fulfill the same criteria (e.g., as of recently, Belgium).

---

[176] The Jackson Review, supra note 9, takes a favorable view, see id., 117–124.

[177] See Hein Kötz, Abschied von der Rechtskreislehre? Zeitschrift für europäisches Privatrecht 3 (1998) 493.

[178] Konrad Zweigert and Hein Kötz, An Introduction to Comparative Law (Tony Weir transl., 3rd ed., Oxford, New York 1998) 132.

By contrast, it is *not* plausible to speak of a "Romanistic Legal Family"[179] in cost and fee allocation matters. The differences among the members of this family are just too fundamental. In France, only the official (court, etc.) costs of civil procedure are allocated to the loser as a matter of law (other costs, especially attorney fees, are left to the judge's discretion); in Italy and Belgium, all costs are routinely shifted (as in the "Germanic" group, supra); in Spain, fee shifting is subject to a cap of 33% of the amount in controversy; etc. Here, diversity triumphs over similarity.

Beyond Europe, there are three other groups that are plausible according to the criteria employed here.

The first group consists of the members of the British Commonwealth tradition, i.e., England and Wales, Australia, and Canada (except Quebec) as well as the mixed jurisdictions of Israel, Scotland, and South Africa: by and large, the loser-pays principle prevails, both court costs and attorney fees are usually shifted, but judicial discretion plays a major role. It is not, however, a perfect line-up either. Some jurisdictions, like Israel and South Africa, leave cost allocation entirely in the discretion of the courts in theory although they shift at least part to the loser in practice. Also, India does not fit the picture well because the statutory presumption in favor of cost shifting is largely ignored in practice.

The second category comprises the East Asian legal systems of China, Japan, and Taiwan. They subscribe to the loser-pays rule; but they normally shift only court costs (i.e., not attorney fees); since statutory rules prevail, judicial discretion is fairly weak. Yet, the concept of an Asian legal systems group is somewhat problematic: while Korea fits in some regards, it differs from the other countries in that cost shifting includes attorney fees as well, albeit it only within statutorily defined limits.

Finally, there is, arguably, something that may be called an "Iberian tradition", encompassing Spain, Portugal, and many jurisdictions in Latin America. Here, the loser pays (in principle) all, i.e., both court costs and attorney fees; the latter, however, tend to be shifted only in part as they are often limited by varying percentages of the amount at stake or of the official (court) fees. And while there are statutory rules, judicial discretion plays a considerable role in the individual case. Yet, there are also some significant variations among the countries in this group[180] which may well cast into doubt whether it makes sense to conceive of such an "Iberian tradition."

If these groupings are at least plausible hypotheses, they should eventually be tested by considering jurisdictions not covered here: e.g., the Baltic States and Hungary in continental Europe, Hong Kong and New Zealand in the British Commonwealth orbit, Vietnam and Cambodia in East Asia, as

[179] Id., 74.

[180] For example, in Mexico, there is no cost and fee shifting in commercial cases at all, and in Venezuela, cost shifting requires a perfect victory.

well as Argentina and Chile in Latin America.[181] If cost and fee allocation in these jurisdictions confirms the existence of the suggested groupings, search for explanations of the intra-group similarities would be in order. It would have to consider the historical connections, look for transplants from major exporting systems within the respective groups (Germany, England, Japan, Spain), and it should consider social, economic, and cultural factors. Such a search for explanations, however, requires a study in its own right and is beyond the scope of this chapter.

1.5.2 *Civil Law v. Common Law?*

While dividing the world into a civil and a common law tradition was a staple of comparative law for most of the twentieth century, this approach has recently been much disparaged.[182] Today, it is almost generally accepted that such a wholesale division is too crude, too private law centered, too tied to outdated views of legal sources, and too blind to the prevalence of variously composed hybrid legal cultures, to serve as a *general* criterion for classifying the world's legal systems. The traditional dichotomy remains useful, however, within several more narrowly defined contexts. One such context is civil procedure. Here, the respective models continue to differ in their basic structures: on the civil law side, a sequential proceeding actively administered by a quasi civil-servant magistrate with the cooperation of the parties; in the common law tradition, a trial-oriented battle fought by the litigants in occasional interaction with a more passive, umpire-like judge. Despite many reforms on both sides, these traditions continue to cast a long shadow.[183]

---

[181] A preliminary look at data available in Platto, supra note 6, and various national reports solicited by the authors of the Oxford Study, supra note 7, suggest that at least the first and third groupings envisaged here make sense. With regard to a Central and Eastern continental European group, Bulgaria, Denmark, Estonia, Hungary, Latvia and Romania all embrace the loser-pays principle and shift both court costs and attorney fees; yet, it appears that in some of these jurisdictions, especially in Denmark and Hungary, judicial discretion does play a fairly significant role. In a similar vein, the information available about further (former) British commonwealth members Hong Kong, New Zealand, Singapore, and also Ireland is compatible with such a grouping; again, however, the role of judicial discretion is apparently weaker in some of these jurisdictions (such as Hong Kong) than in others (such as Ireland). With regard to the second group, one could also conclude that the denial of attorney fee shifting in the Philippines and Indonesia reported by Jäger, supra note 14, at 1 (fn. 1) put these countries in line with the most of the other East Asian jurisdictions covered in this essay, i.e., Japan, Taiwan, and China.

[182] For a search for an alternative approach, see Ugo Mattei, Three Patterns of Law: Taxonomy and Change in the World's Legal Systems, American Journal of Comparative Law 45 (1997) 5.

[183] Even though the major reform of the English civil justice system in 1998 has shifted much control over the course of litigation from the parties (and their counsel) to the

Cost and fee allocation is an element of civil procedure. It is thus worth asking whether one can meaningfully distinguish a civil and a common law approach to this area. Note that in pursuing that question, what counts as a "civil" or a "common law" jurisdiction must be determined by looking at the respective systems' procedural structures.[184] In that sense, the majority of the jurisdictions covered here, i.e., the continental European, East Asian, and Latin American systems, belong to the civil law tradition; by contrast, the (former) British Commonwealth countries (Australia, Canada, England and Wales, India) and the United States form a common law group to which the mixed jurisdictions of Israel, Scotland, and South Africa can perhaps be added. So, do the similarities and differences in cost and fee allocation we have recorded reflect such a grouping?

From most of the perspectives considered in this Report, the answer is no. Certainly, the acceptance (vel non) of the loser-pays principle does not depend on membership in this or that group: it is true that all civil law systems embrace a loser-pays rule, but so do the clear majority of common law jurisdictions (i.e., all except the United States).[185] Certainly, whether only court costs or also attorney fees are shifted has nothing to do with the traditional categories: most civil law systems shift both but some do not (China, Japan, Taiwan, and, in a sense, France), and the same is true on the common law side (cf. the United States). Nor does the role of judicial discretion necessarily turn on a jurisdiction's membership in the civil or common law group: while judicial discretion is more pervasive in common law systems, its role is also strong in France, i.e., at the very heart of the civil law culture, and it is a considerable factor in several Latin countries. One cannot even say that the degree of compensation (full v. partial) distinguishes the two groups: to be sure, in many common law and mixed jurisdictions, cost shifting is often incomplete, but that is also true for quite a few civil law systems, such as France or Portugal; in fact, a winner is likely to fare much better in Britain, where in practice most costs are allocated to the loser, than in Greece, where the shiftable amounts of attorney fees are woefully low.

court, the impact of the reform on the ground has apparently been fairly limited; in particular, it has done little to bring the costs of litigation under control, see Adrian Zuckerman, Court Case Management in England and the Civil Procedure Rules 1998, in Gottwald, supra note 10, 1–13; Peysner, supra note 77, 146–147.

184 In other words, it does not matter for present purposes what other, traditional criteria suggest, such as the influence of Roman (private) law, the role of codification (and statutes) versus case law, or the emphasis on a more theoretical versus a more practice-oriented legal education.

185 It is true, however, that given the large role of judicial discretion in the commonwealth tradition, its members' commitment to it is sometimes dubious, as in the cases of Israel and India, see supra Section 1.2.1.2.

Yet, there are two features that do distinguish civil law systems on the one hand from common law jurisdictions on the other – at least in the sense of general tendencies: the absolute amount of lawyer fees, and their predictability. Since, as we have seen,[186] lawyer fees usually constitute the lion's share of the litigation bill, these are matters of considerable practical importance.

First, it appears that lawyer fees for litigation are, on the whole, higher in the common law than in the civil law systems.[187] This is not because common lawyers charge more per hour than their civilian colleagues[188] but because they do more work when litigating a case – for a more general and a more particular reason.[189] In general, in the more lawyer-driven common law procedure, attorneys have to do a lot of the driving that is performed by the judge in a civil law court. In particular, the different approaches to fact-gathering tend to generate more billable hours in a common law than in the civil law proceeding: not only is common-law style discovery operated by counsel rather than by the judge, it is also by its very nature much more labor-intensive than civil law-style evidence taking[190] – and thus a lot costlier.[191] Small wonder then that complaints about disproportionate lawyer fees are more frequently heard in the common law than in the civil law camp.[192]

---

186 Supra Section 1.3.2.2.

187 Ilmer, supra note 96, at 307, confirms this with regard to England, though without further references.

188 Hourly rates range widely across both civil and common law jurisdictions, see Oxford: Comparative Study, supra note 7, Appendix III.

189 As the National Reporter for the United States pointed out in his comments on the Draft General Report, there is – at least arguably – an additional reason, i.e., the different degrees of legal certainty in civil and common law systems: where the law is less certain, it takes more work to decide cases. The hypothesis of significantly differing legal certainty between civil and common law, however, is difficult to generalize and even more difficult to verify. It is true though that in the United States, the high degree of private law fragmentation in the federal system (where most private law is left under the legislative and judicial jurisdiction of the states) diminishes the degree of legal certainty and often increases the legal complexity of disputes.

190 See supra Section 1.3.3.2; Langbein, supra note 75. To be sure, the extent of permissible discovery varies hugely among common law systems with the United States presenting an extreme case. Yet, even under more restrictive approaches, as in the England and Wales, fact-gathering is usually more labor-intensive than in civil law jurisdictions.

191 In his comment on the Draft General Report, the National Reporter for the United States proffered an additional argument: in common law countries, the bar tends to have greater control over the litigation system than in civil law countries where the state is more directly involved; the bar thus serves its own interests with less restraint in the former than in the latter.

192 Supra note 142 and text; see also Jackson Review, supra note 9, 36–39 ("proportionate costs"); Zuckerman, supra note 183, at 14; Andrews, supra note 90, 188–189; Peysner, supra note 77, 145–146.

Second, the amount of lawyer fees generated by litigation is more predictable in civil law jurisdictions than in common law systems. With regard to about half of the civil law countries surveyed here, this is straightforward: these countries determine (at least the shiftable amount of) lawyer fees under an official schedule (usually tied to the amount in controversy); as a result, one can predict the amount imposed upon the loser with fair accuracy. By contrast, the common law systems included here *all* leave the pricing of lawyer services to the market and then control fee shifting (if any) by judicial discretion; as a result, predicting the how much the loser will have to pay is inevitably a matter of more or less informed guessing.[193] But even in civil law jurisdictions without an official schedule, lawyer fees may well be more predictable than in the common law world. The reason is that in the civil law, the amount of ultimate lawyer fees is less dependent on how a case evolves than in the common law – and thus more predictable. This is, again, due to the fact that lawyers are less involved in a civil law proceeding than in a common law litigation. If a case drags on or becomes complex in a civil law court, much of the resultant work will be done by the judge, and that work is already paid for in form of the predetermined court fee[194]; in addition, fact gathering will normally stay within comparatively narrow limits and thus entail fairly moderate cost. By contrast, if a case drags on or becomes complex in a common law court, the lawyers will have to do almost all the resultant work which will translate into fast-growing fees; in particular, discovery can become very time-consuming and thus drive the lawyers' bills to dizzying heights. In short, the chance that lawyer fees spiral out of control as a case evolves is much smaller in a civil law proceeding than in a common law litigation. That keeps the ultimate amount of lawyer fees – at least somewhat – more predictable in Brazil, China or Spain than in Australia, England or the United States.[195]

---

[193] There are exceptions. In England and Wales, for example, certain cases are handled under a fixed fee, see supra 103; US-style contingency arrangements also make the fee quite predictable, albeit only in terms of a percentage of the amount eventually won (if any).

[194] Court fees do not present a predictability issue because virtually everywhere, they are determined by law in precise amounts tied to the amount at controversy and/or the stage reached by the case.

[195] The greater predictability of lawyer fees in the civil law world is also indicated by the willingness of the various National Reporters to predict the litigation bill in certain kinds of cases. While a clear majority of Reporters from civil law jurisdictions provided numbers, a clear majority of Reporters from common law systems refused to do so because the uncertainty was just too great. Of course, one must not overrate these reactions because much depends on the individual Reporters' willingness to venture a guess (several Reporters from civil law jurisdictions also refused to provide a good faith estimate because too much depends on the circumstances of the case). Still, it is noteworthy that Reporters even from civil law jurisdictions without official fee schedules apparently felt by and large more comfortable to provide good faith estimates than their common law

The magnitude and predictability of attorney fees matter when it comes to allocating them between the parties. Shifting higher fees to the loser is a bigger deal and thus requires more deliberation and circumspection; and the higher the fee, the greater the temptation to shift it only in part. Shifting unpredictable fees raises serious fairness concerns because predictability is one of the hallmarks of due process[196]; and the greater the unpredictability, the greater the need for ex post judicial control. As a result, systems that generate higher attorney fees at lower predictability must struggle harder with shifting them from winner to loser.

To end on a provocative note, one can perhaps say that at least among the common law jurisdictions, the United States has got it right after all: if lawyer fees are unregulated, unpredictable, and high, shifting them to the loser is so fraught with problems that it is better not to undertake it at all.[197]

colleagues. If attorney fees are by and large *considered* more predictable in the civil law systems, this may well reflect that they actually are.

[196] See Burger King Corp. v. Rudzewicz, 471 U.S. 462, 471–472 (1985); World-Wide Volkswagen Corp. v. Woodson, 444 U.S. 286, 297 (1980).

[197] See Oelrichs v. Spain, 82 U.S. 211, 231 (1872).

Part II
National Reports

Chapter 2
The Price of Access to the Civil Courts in Australia – Old Problems, New Solutions: A Commercial Litigation Funding Case Study

Camille Cameron

2.1 Introduction

Like many of the jurisdictions considered in this volume, Australia struggles with how best to manage and control the cost of civil litigation. The purpose of this chapter is to explore the connections between the cost of litigation and Australia's cost and fee allocation rules. Section 2.2 provides a broad overview of those rules and related practices. Only the key features are mentioned; readers can refer to the "Country Report" for additional details.[1] In Section 2.3 the rise of commercial litigation funding in Australia is discussed. The prominent place it has assumed in the litigation landscape in a relatively short period of time is attributable to key features of Australia's cost and fee allocation rules. It is therefore a window through which we can get a clear view of those rules. Section 2.4 offers some final analysis and conclusions.

---

[1] *See* http://www-personal.umich.edu/~purzel/national_reports/. The focus in this chapter is on litigation in the superior courts. There are small claims courts and tribunals that deal with minor civil disputes. Some features of those tribunals include restrictions on legal representation and rules that the parties should bear their own costs. Many of the costs and funding issues considered in this paper would therefore not be relevant in those courts and tribunals.

C. Cameron (✉)
Melbourne Law School, Melbourne, VIC, Australia
e-mail: c.cameron@unimelb.edu.au

M. Reimann (ed.), *Cost and Fee Allocation in Civil Procedure*, 59
Ius Gentium: Comparative Perspectives on Law and Justice 11,
DOI 10.1007/978-94-007-2263-7_2, © Springer Science+Business Media B.V. 2012

2.2 Overview of Litigation Funding and Costs in Australia[2]

The costs-shifting ("loser pays") rule applies in Australia. Successful litigants can expect an order for reasonable costs, called party and party costs.[3] This is not, however, a complete recovery. There will in most cases be a substantial gap between the costs expended by successful parties and the costs they can recover. The irrecoverable portion of the successful party's costs is estimated to be in the range of 40–50%. Anecdotal evidence suggests that this figure may vary depending on whether a particular jurisdiction has prescribed scales of costs.[4]

It is possible in some cases to get an order that costs will be paid on an indemnity basis. This is virtually a full recovery, but such orders are not easy to obtain. There must be some special or unusual feature in a case to justify an order for indemnity costs, such as delay or non-compliance on the part of the losing party. There are also provisions in the procedural rules relating to formal settlement offers that provide for an indemnity costs order where a defendant refused a reasonable settlement offer.[5]

There is a particular view of fairness informing some of the justifications for the loser pays rule – it would be unfair for a successful plaintiff whose claims have been vindicated or for a successful defendant who had no real choice but to incur the cost of defending the claim, to have to absorb the litigation costs. But of course the fairness arguments cut both ways. Costs shifting has also been described as "a crude exclusion device the burden of which falls disproportionately on individuals and community groups which do not have the same deep pockets as governments and corporations."[6] In its 1995 report on costs shifting the Australian Law Reform Commission

---

[2] Some of the content in this Section is adapted from Camille Cameron, ch 6, *Australia*, in C. Hodges et al, eds, *The Costs and Funding of Civil Litigation, A Comparative Perspective*, Hart, November 2010.

[3] Exceptions to the loser pays rule include costs penalties for refusing a reasonable settlement offer, tribunals and small claims jurisdictions in which the norm is no costs shifting, costs orders where a party has had mixed success, and the willingness of courts in an appropriate case to exercise their costs discretion in favour of an unsuccessful public interest litigant.

[4] Scales of costs are prescribed amounts for court fees and other expenditures, usually contained in schedules or appendices to Rules of Court. In the State of New South Wales, where there are no such scale costs, estimates are that successful parties will recover 65–85% of their actual costs: Lord Justice Jackson, *Review of Civil Litigation Costs, Preliminary Report*, May 2009.

[5] In the State of Victoria, for example, if a defendant in a personal injury case rejects the plaintiff's settlement offer, and the plaintiff does as well or better at trial than the offer, the usual order will be for costs to the plaintiff on an indemnity basis. *Supreme Court General Civil Procedure Rules 2005*, Rule 26.08(2).

[6] Victorian Environmental Defender's Office, quoted in Victorian Law Reform Commission, *Civil Justice Review, Report, 2008* (VLRC Civil Justice Review 2008).

stated that submissions made during the consultation process indicated that the costs shifting rule is most likely to deter "people who may suffer substantial hardship, such as the loss of their home, car or livelihood, if required to pay the other party's costs, and people or organisations involved in public interest litigation who have little or no personal interest in the matter."[7] This view is shaped less by ideas of adversarial contest, reward and vindication and more by ideas of access to justice and to the courts. Whatever its justifications, the cost shifting rule is an entrenched feature of civil procedure in Australia and not likely to be easily displaced. Almost all major reviews of civil justice in Australia have favoured its retention.[8]

All Australian courts charge fees prescribed by statute.[9] Typical charges are for filing documents in court, issuing a subpoena, using court mediation services, and daily fees for court hearings. Australia does not have a true user pays system. The fees charged for these and similar services fall well below the actual cost of maintaining courts. For example, the Commonwealth of Australia reported in 2009[10] that court fees charged by the Federal Court amounted to 9.3% of total Commonwealth expenditure on that court.[11]

The costs between lawyers and their clients consist of the lawyers' fees and disbursements. The primary method of charging clients is by time billing based on an hourly rate. There are some exceptions to the hourly rate approach, however, and these may be increasing. Fixed fee agreements for specific services or discrete tasks, such as preparing a will or a contract, are common. Some commercial clients use their market power to demand alternatives to hourly billing, and law firms have responded to this market demand by bidding for legal services. This can be in the form of an agreed amount for a project or for parts of (or events within) a project.

Another common billing arrangement is the conditional fee (also called "no win-no fee"). Lawyers using this model agree not to bill the client until the case is resolved. If the client is successful, then the lawyer will be paid his fees, either calculated on an hourly basis or at an amount agreed

---

7 Australian Law Reform Commission, *Cost Shifting – Who Pays for Litigation in Australia?* 1995 (*Cost Shifting 1995*) at [4.14].

8 In *ALRC Cost Shifting 1995*, the Australian Law Reform Commission endorsed the loser pays rule but recommended that courts should be able to depart from the rule if "a party's ability to present his or her case properly or to negotiate a fair settlement is materially and adversely affected by the risk of an adverse costs order." [12.40] This proposal has not been adopted.

9 See for example *Federal Court of Australia Act 1976 (Cth)*, s. 60 and *Federal Court of Australia Regulations 2004 (Cth)*, Schedule 1.

10 *Commonwealth Access to Justice Report 2009*.

11 *Commonwealth Access to Justice Report 2009*, ch 3, p 45, quoting the Productivity Commission, *Report on Government Services*, 2009. The percentage of recovery varies across federal courts.

in advance between the lawyer and the client (but not as a percentage of the damages awarded). If the client is unsuccessful, the lawyer will not be paid. The risk of an adverse costs order, always a factor in a system with costs shifting, remains with the client.[12] These conditional fee agreements often include a term that the lawyer will in the event of a successful outcome charge a premium, also known as an uplift (success fee). This fee is a matter between the lawyer and her own client; it is not recoverable from the opposing party. The maximum uplift fee permitted in Victoria and New South Wales is 25%.[13] There is some evidence to indicate that in personal injury cases in Victoria, claimants receive 80–85% of their damages, after deduction of the success fee.[14]

2.3 Commercial Litigation Funding

Commercial litigation funders have a significant and growing presence in Australia. The need for commercial litigation funders exists primarily because of gaps in the market created by the costs shifting rule and the prohibition against lawyers charging contingency fees.

The role of litigation funding companies in Australia in litigation other than insolvency cases was, until recently, uncertain. Their legitimacy was challenged on the basis of maintenance (improperly encouraging litigation), champerty (funding a third party's litigation for profit) and abuse of process, and there were conflicting judicial decisions.[15] In 2006 the High Court of Australia resolved the conflict by endorsing the role of institutional litigation funders.[16] The trial judge had accepted arguments that the litigation funding agreement was invalid because it amounted to "trafficking in litigation". The Court of Appeal reversed the trial judge's decision and described a need for a change in attitudes about litigation funding. In the Court of Appeal, Mason P stated:

> These changes in attitude to funders have been influenced by concerns about access to justice and heightened awareness of the costs of litigation. Governments have promoted the legislative changes in response to the spiralling costs of legal aid. Courts have recognised these trends and the matters driving them. 'Ambulance chasing' still has negative connotations in many quarters, but it is now

[12] Unlike England, there is no market for "After the Event (ATE)" insurance in Australia to cover the adverse costs risk.

[13] State practice varies. Recovering a success fee under a conditional fee arrangement is more common in Victoria than in New South Wales.

[14] Lord Justice Jackson, *Preliminary Report*, 2009 (n 28), ch 58, p 588.

[15] The key cases are discussed in *Fostif v. Campbells Cash and Carry Pty Ltd* [2005] NSWCA 83, [2005] 63 NSWLR 203.

[16] *Campbells Cash and Carry v. Fostif* [2006] HCA 41.

> widely recognised that there are some types of claims that will simply never get off the ground unless traditional attitudes are modified. These include cases involving complex scientific and legal issues. The largely factual account in the book and film *A Civil Action* has demonstrated the social utility of funded proceedings, the financial risks assumed by funders, and the potential conflicts of interest as between group members in mass tort claims propounding difficult actions against deep-pocketed and determined defendants.[17]

The High Court, without responding specifically to these comments, endorsed the legitimacy of the commercial litigation funding arrangement. The *Fostif* decision gave an already emerging litigation funding market a substantial boost.[18]

There are at least six litigation funding companies operating in Australia. Two of these companies, IMF (Australia) Ltd and Hillcrest Litigation Services Ltd are listed on the Australian Securities Exchange. Of these, IMF is the most visible. It began its litigation funding activities in insolvency cases, but has assumed a growing presence in large commercial cases and in securities class actions. When IMF expanded its litigation funding activities beyond insolvency cases to other commercial litigation and securities class actions, it was gambling that traditional views about maintenance and champerty would be displaced by acceptance of "the social utility of litigation funding."[19] Subsequent jurisprudence, culminating with the 2006 High Court decision in *Fostif*,[20] has vindicated this view. A review of IMF's business model and practices offers some insight into how the litigation funding market in Australia operates.

When it listed on the Australian Stock Exchange in 2001, IMF included in its investment protocol a minimum case size restriction of $2 million. It takes the view that funding smaller claims is commercially unviable. This decision was a response to its previous experience of cases in which too much of the settlement or judgment sum was taken by legal costs and the fees of lawyers and IMF.[21] It makes an exception for small claims that can be prosecuted as a group action; aggregation of many small claims converts single unviable claims into a commercially viable group action.

---

[17] *Fostif v. Campbells Cash and Carry* [2005] 63 NSWLR 203.

[18] Another factor contributing to the growth of commercial litigation funding has been the effort of plaintiff lawyers to prosecute class actions.

[19] John Walker, *Litigation Funding*, presentation to the AILA (Australian Insurance Law Association) National Conference, 2006, available at http://www.aila.com.au/speakersPapers/downloads/2006_Conference/06-11-01_John_Walker.pdf last accessed on 26 April 2011. These words were also used in 2005 by Mason P in *Fostif v. Campbells Cash and Carry*: see above note 16.

[20] *Campbells Cash and Carry Pty Limited v. Fostif Pty Ltd* [2006] HCA 41; (2006) 229 CLR 386.

[21] Ibid, and information provided by IMF to the author.

Other factors determining IMF's case choice, in addition to claim size, are:

- the likely investment is less than 10% of IMF's current assets or facilities;
- net return to the plaintiff must be greater than 60%;
- IMF's return on investment must be at least 300%; and
- cases must rely mainly on documentary rather than oral evidence.[22]

Assuming the case meets the factors listed above, IMF then conducts a rigorous analysis of the claim, defence, parties, and costs. The analysis includes estimates of the likely duration and cost of the entire litigation and of separate components of the case. The risks assumed by a litigation funder in exchange for a percentage of the settlement or judgment sum include paying any order for security for costs and paying the defendant's costs if the claim fails.

If a case passes these tests, the funded parties sign a funding agreement in which they agree that IMF will take a percentage of the settlement or judgment sum, in the range of 20–40%.[23] In return, IMF agrees to pay the claimant's legal fees and disbursements, to assume the risk of and to pay any adverse costs order, to pay security for costs if ordered, and generally to assist with project management. Information this author has obtained in connection with a related research project indicates that some funders take an active role in the management of cases but that this can vary as between funders, and even between claims managers working for the same funder.[24]

As few cases will meet IMF's investment protocols, it follows that commercial litigation funding will not provide access to justice for most claims. This is left to lawyers who are willing to take smaller or riskier cases on a no win, no fee basis. There is some anecdotal evidence, however, that the entry of commercial litigation funders into the civil litigation landscape has had a detrimental effect on the willingness of lawyers to run cases on a no win, no fee basis. If lawyers can choose cases that funders are willing to underwrite, they may be inclined to reduce their portfolio of no win, no fee cases.[25]

Commercial litigation funding exists and thrives in Australia because of certain conditions in the market for legal services. One of these is that

[22] Ibid.

[23] Hillcrest Litigation Services Limited declares a range of 25–45% in its 2010 *Annual Report*.

[24] *The Role of Institutional Litigation Funders in Australia*, made possible with funding provided by the Melbourne Law School. This variation among claims managers is one example of how the practice of litigation funders is akin to that of insurers.

[25] One experienced litigation solicitor interviewed in relation to other research the author is conducting (see above note 24) expressed the view that this shift is occurring.

Australian lawyers are prohibited from charging contingency fees. If that restriction were removed, plaintiff lawyers who presently depend on litigation funders might be more willing to accept the risk themselves. This is, however, subject to a substantial caveat. As long as costs shifting remains – and it will – there will be relatively few law firms with the resources to take on the added risk of an adverse costs order, at least in large commercial litigation and in many class actions. This may create a market for litigation insurance that caters for the risk of adverse costs. Unlike some of the other jurisdictions considered in this book, after-the-event and before-the-event litigation insurance have not yet flourished in Australia.

Commercial litigation funding is attractive for other reasons as well. The priority it accords to realistic case budgets appeals to many commercially-minded litigants intent on managing the risks created by the unpredictability of fees and costs. This feature of litigation funding has also been commented on favourably by Australian judges. In *QPSX*, for example, French J stated:

> Where [litigation funding agreements] involve the creation of budgets by funders knowledgeable in the costs of litigation it may inject a welcome element of commercial objectivity into the way in which such budgets are framed and the efficiency with which the litigation is conducted.[26]

A recent procedural reform in the State of Victoria picks up on this sentiment. Section 50 of the *Civil Procedure Act 2010* gives a court the power to order a lawyer to prepare a budget that states the estimated duration of a trial, the estimated costs and disbursements, and the estimated amount of any adverse costs order.

Canadian, American and European funders are becoming interested in the Australian market.[27] For example, International Litigation Funding Partners Pte Ltd, a Singapore-based company in which a Canadian law firm has a substantial interest, funded the *Multiplex* securities class action.[28] That case became the vehicle, over several years, for some major judicial

---

[26] *Civil Procedure Act 2010 (Vic)*.

[27] In 2006, it was estimated that 95% of the litigation funding business in Australia was done by 6 or 7 Australian litigation funding entities then operating. The gradual entry of non-Australian funders into the market in the intervening 4–5 years will have altered this estimate. The interest in foreign markets works both ways. In its *Annual Report* for 2010, at p 4, IMF refers to its "entry into offshore markets, including the United States and United Kingdom markets" (see also p 58). The report is available at http://www.imf.com.au/pdf/AnnualReport2010.pdf, last viewed on 26 April 2011.

[28] This was a class action by shareholders against Multiplex for damages for losses allegedly caused by the company's belated disclosure of cost problems related to the construction of the Wembley Stadium.

and policy clarifications of the proper role and limits of commercial litigation funding. Two outcomes of that case with significance for litigation funding deserve brief mention.[29]

Any expectation that it would be smooth sailing for litigation funders post-*Fostif* were dashed when the Full Court of the Federal Court ruled (2-1) in *Brookfield Multiplex*[30] that the arrangement in that case between the commercial litigation funder, the law firm representing the class, and the members of the class was a managed investment scheme as defined in the *Corporations Act*.[31] One ramification of that decision was that the arrangement should have been registered under the relevant provisions of the *Corporations Act*. Another was that the impact of the decision extended beyond the boundaries of the particular case. There were other funded class action proceedings underway that had not been registered as managed investment schemes. The Australian Securities and Investments Commission intervened to grant a temporary exemption for the class actions affected.[32] Discussions then began about how best to respond to the decision. One possible outcome was that the matter would go to the High Court of Australia. A more expeditious outcome was realized when the Federal Government introduced a regulation to reverse the effects of *Brookfield Multiplex* by excluding funded class actions from the definition of a managed investment scheme. This was the best outcome. The cost of a further appeal to the High Court was averted, and the new regulation clarified the confusion that *Brookfield Multiplex* had created. Most knowledgeable observers thought that classifying the funder/lawyer/class arrangement as a managed investment scheme was akin to trying to put a square peg into a round hole.[33]

---

[29] It is beyond the space constraints of this chapter to do anything other than a cursory overview of the case and its consequences. For additional information see: *Multiplex Funds Management Ltd. v P Dawson Nominees Pty Ltd* [2007] FCAFC 200 (appeal dismissed, *P Dawson Nominees Pty Ltd v. Multiplex Ltd* [2007] HCA 1); *Brookfield Multiplex Limited v. International Litigation Funding Partners Pte Ltd* (2009) 180 FCR 11; *Brookfield Multiplex Limited v. International Litigation Funding Partners Pte Ltd (No 2)* [2009] FCAFC 147.

[30] *Brookfield Multiplex Limited v. International Litigation Funding Partners Pte Ltd (No 2)* [2009] FCAFC 147. This is a representative proceeding (i.e., a class action) by shareholders against Brookfield Multiplex for damages for losses allegedly caused by the company's belated disclosure of cost problems related to the construction of the Wembley Stadium.

[31] *Corporations Act 2001* (*Cth*).

[32] See ASIC media release, November 2009, 09-218MR, *ASIC grants transitional relief from regulation for funded class action*, available at http://www.asic.gov.au/ (under Publications – Media Centre), last viewed on 26 April 2011.

[33] Information obtained by author in connection with research project referred to in note 24, above.

A second, very significant contribution of the *Multiplex* securities class action came with the decision of the Federal Court in *Multiplex Funds Management Ltd v. P. Dawson Nominees Pty Ltd.*[34] As a result of that decision, it is possible to have as one element of the definition of a class the requirement "and have signed a funding agreement with [Funder X]". The validity of this approach was challenged on the basis that it created an impermissible opt in requirement in what is an opt out system, because people were being asked to take the specific step of signing the funding agreement as a condition of being in the class. Initial judicial decisions in the Federal Court and the Supreme Court of Victoria were to the effect that these clauses were inconsistent with the opt out nature of the class action legislation. In this *Multipex* decision, however, the validity of such clauses was endorsed. The court found that the language of the legislation did not prohibit such an arrangement. It was relevant that people signed the funding agreement before the class action was commenced, which meant that when they signed there was not yet any class action into which a person could opt (thus avoiding the opt in criticism).

One result of this decision is that closed classes are permissible. There are good reasons for commercial litigation funders to prefer this approach. They take on a substantial risk when they fund a class action, including the obligation to pay the defendant's costs if the class action fails. The signed agreements with class members provide certainty and give them the assurance that they will be paid in the event of success.

Whatever one's view of these *Multiplex* decisions, they highlight the ad hoc way in which commercial litigation funding has been developing in Australia. In 2006, regulation of commercial litigation funders was explored by the Standing Committee of Attorneys General,[35] with no specific regulatory outcomes. Nothing has been done since that time to put in place any regulatory framework. It has been left primarily to the courts to define the proper scope and boundaries of commercial litigation funding. This is how regulation is happening, and views vary about whether this is sufficient. Some lawyers are of the view that no additional regulation is needed; where conflicts between lawyers and funders emerge, they say, lawyers will be robust enough to behave in the interests of their clients and, where necessary to stand up to the funders. Others decry the incongruous, or perverse, situation in which lawyers, who have a duty to the court, are prevented by law from charging contingency fees while litigation funders, who have no such duty, are able to do so. But apart from intervening to remedy the *Brookfield Multiplex* problem, it appears there is nothing, yet, about the

[34] [2007] FCAFC 200.

[35] *Litigation Funding in Australia*, Discussion Paper, Standing Committee of Attorneys General (SCAG Report 2006).

way litigation funding is operating to convince regulators that any further public regulatory intervention is required.

In addition to their role as key players in the "extraordinary" jurisprudential developments that occurred in *Multiplex*, litigation funders are increasingly prominent in more ordinary, run-of-the-mill decisions. This reflects the degree of control litigation funders have assumed in litigation – control made possible by the imprimatur given by the High Court in *Fostif* to their robust participation in the cases they fund. In *Pharm-a-Care Laboratories*,[36] for example, court approval of a class action included consideration of the fairness and reasonableness of the percentage of the settlement amount that would go to the litigation funder. And it is increasingly common to see discussions in cases about how much of the information disclosed by the defendant to the plaintiff will be available to the litigation funder.[37]

Civil justice reforms are reflecting the new reality of litigation funders who like the degree of control approved in *Fostif*, and who use it. In the State of Victoria, for example, new statutory obligations aimed at improving the conduct of civil litigation apply not only to parties and their lawyers but also to litigation funders and insurers.[38]

2.4 Conclusion

The rise of commercial litigation funding in Australia is a predictable result of the interaction of a variety of factors, including costs shifting, the prohibition on lawyers charging contingency fees, the hourly billing practices of lawyers, and the open-ended and unpredictable nature of civil litigation. Litigation is expensive, especially complex commercial litigation and class actions, and few Australian law firms have the resources to finance such cases themselves. Commercial litigation funders saw an opportunity to use the expertise they obtained in insolvency litigation in new categories of cases. Their efforts have been greatly assisted by favourable court decisions and the maturing of Australia's class action regimes.

---

[36] *Pharm-a-Care Laboratories Pty Ltd v. Commonwealth of Australia* (No 6) [2011] FCA 277.

[37] See for example *Cadence Asset Management Pty Ltd v. Concept Store Ltd* [2006] FCA 711; *QPSX Limited v. Ericsson Australia Ltd (No 5)* [2007] FCA 244; and *Kirby v. Centro Properties Limited* [2009] FCA 695.

[38] See for example s. 10, *Civil Procedure Act 2010 (Vic)*. This was one of the reforms that the Executive Director of IMF called for in his 2006 AILA presentation: see above note 19.

Chapter 3
Litigating in Austria – Are Costs and Fees Worth It?

Marianne Roth

3.1 Introduction

This article follows the structure of the General Report on "Cost and Fee Allocation in Civil Procedure" by addressing the three main questions of who has to pay, how much and whether the Austrian legal system facilitates access to justice through cost distribution.

The system of cost and fee allocation in Austrian civil procedure has proven reliable: it ensures a maximum of predictability of litigation costs and guarantees access to justice by providing legal aid. Nevertheless, the risk of losing the case, which is generally associated with high costs, may act as a deterrent for parties to commence civil proceedings.

3.2 Who Has to Bear the Costs?

3.2.1 "Major Shifting" as the Basic Rule in Austria

The basic rule of cost and fee allocation in Section 41(1) of the Austrian Code of Civil Procedure (*Zivilprozessordnung*) provides that the loser has to pay all costs – court fees, the fees of attorney and expert fees, and the costs of the parties – but only as far as these costs were reasonable and necessary. For example, costs for consulting an attorney or a detective are considered necessary, whereas costs arising from filing a lawsuit with a court lacking jurisdiction or for correcting a deficient written pleading are

Many thanks to Mag. Marianne Stegner for her valuable assistance in preparing this article.

M. Roth (✉)
Salzburg University, Salzburg, Austria
e-mail: marianne.roth@sbg.ac.at

M. Reimann (ed.), *Cost and Fee Allocation in Civil Procedure*,
Ius Gentium: Comparative Perspectives on Law and Justice 11,
DOI 10.1007/978-94-007-2263-7_3, © Springer Science+Business Media B.V. 2012

not.[1] The same is true for costs, which have been incurred due to excessive caution; they can also not be reimbursed.[2]

Under the loser-pays principle, the law treats court costs and attorney fees alike. The amount of these expenses, however, is regulated in two specific statutes and in distinct ways: according to the Court Fees Act (*Gerichtsgebührengesetz*), the court charge is a general fee depending on the amount in dispute. Under the Attorneys' Tariff Act (*Rechtsanwaltstarifgesetz*), by contrast, counsel has to be paid for each individual performance he or she makes in the course of the proceedings.

According to the basic rule that the loser pays all, the defeated party also has to bear the costs of experts and witnesses, together with all other costs of the litigation, at the end of the proceedings. Under Austrian law, every witness and expert can recover the necessary costs for travel and accommodation as well as loss of income. In the course of the proceedings, the party who proffers evidence of a witness or expert has to advance the respective costs if they are likely to exceed €200 (ca. $280).[3] If both parties proffer the evidence of the same witness or expert, each party has to advance half the costs.[4] Whether or not the costs for taking evidence are a significant factor in the overall litigation bill depends on the kind of evidence as well as on the particular case. Obtaining an expert opinion, e.g., can be expensive.

The rules of cost and fee allocation also apply for appeals in the courts of second instance and third instance, pursuant to Section 50 of the Austrian Code of Civil Procedure. Thus, the losing party in the court of last instance has to pay the entire legal costs, regardless of whether he or she has won below.

The primary justification for the basic rule can be seen in the fundamental principle that the winning party should not have to suffer any loss from the proceedings, i.e., that the party prevailing should not be burdened by any court costs or fees.[5]

The Austrian Code of Civil Procedure gives judges ample opportunity during the entire proceedings to promote a settlement, for example, in the preliminary hearing (*Vorbereitende Tagsatzung*), according to Section 258(1), subparagraph 4, of the Austrian Code of Civil Procedure. In case of settlement, the parties normally agree that each has to bear its own

---

[1] *Fucik* in *Rechberger (Ed.)*, Kommentar zur ZPO, 3rd edition, Springer Verlag 2006, § 41 marg. No 5.

[2] *Rechberger* and *Kodek* in *Blanpain, Colucci,* and *Taelman (Eds.)*, International Encyclopaedia of Laws. Civil Procedure. Austria, Kluwer Law International 2005, 66.

[3] Exchange rate at the time of data gathering: €1 = $1.4.

[4] Sections 40, 365, and 332 of the Austrian Code of Civil Procedure (cf *Obermaier*, Das Kostenhandbuch. Kostenersatz im Zivilprozess und im Verfahren außer Streit, 57 et seq.).

[5] *Chvosta*, Prozesskostenrecht, Manz 2001, 13 et seq.

expenses. Moreover, the parties frequently agree that as the plaintiff has to pay the entire court fees in advance, the defendant will reimburse half of these fees to the plaintiff on an amortized basis. If the parties to a settlement do not agree on an allocation of costs, Section 47(1), Sentence 2, of the Austrian Code of Civil Procedure sets forth that the entire be costs offset.[6]

3.2.2 *Exceptions and Modifications to the Basic Rule*

There are certain statutory exceptions to the basic rule that the loser has to pay, reflecting the idea that the party who is responsible for certain acts in court has to bear the costs associated with these acts, irrespective of the outcome of the proceedings, For example, the costs resulting from re-opening a case or from setting aside a default judgment have to be paid by the party responsible for creating the situation, regardless of fault (Sections 154, 397a(4) of the Austrian Code of Civil Procedure). In other cases, a party may be liable because he or she acted in a culpable manner: if the litigation becomes more costly because the party has filed an application or other brief missing a deadline, or because the party has protracted proceedings maliciously, he or she has to bear the resultant costs (*Kostenseparation*, Section 48 of the Austrian Code of Civil Procedure).[7] Finally, in cases where a defendant has not given reasonable cause for the action, and recognizes the plaintiff's claim on the first occasion in the proceedings, the plaintiff has to bear all costs even though he or she wins the case on the merits (Section 45 of the Austrian Code of Civil Procedure).[8]

Party agreements allocating costs and fees in case of litigation are not common in Austria. Even if such an agreement is reached, it is only valid between the parties, i.e., that it cannot bind the court. As a result, if one of the parties wants to enforce such an agreement, it will have to pursue a separate action after the proceedings on the merits of the main case.[9]

[6] *Roth* in *Verschraegen (Ed.)*, Austrian Law – An International Perspective: Selected Issues, Jan Sramek Verlag 2010, 135.

[7] *Deixler-Hübner* and *Roth*, Der Zivilprozess in der Praxis, 4th edition, LexisNexis ARD Orac 2006, 20.

[8] *Rechberger* and *Kodek* in *Blanpain, Colucci,* and *Taelman (Eds.)*, International Encyclopaedia of Laws. Civil Procedure. Austria, Kluwer Law International 2005, 66.

[9] *Deixler-Hübner* and *Roth*, Der Zivilprozess in der Praxis, 4th edition, LexisNexis ARD Orac 2006, 18 et seq.

3.3 The Calculation and Determination of Costs and Fees

In Austria, cost allocation rules have the function of preventing careless and unnecessary civil proceedings. The risk of losing a case has a deterrent effect – especially for the plaintiff – and can thus be seen as impeding access to justice. The likelihood of such deterrence increases with the amount in dispute: the higher the amount in controversy, the higher the legal costs-and the greater the impact of potential economic imbalance between the parties, especially between consumers and companies.[10]

Usually, each party has to bear its own costs for the time being during course of the proceedings, and the winning party can only subsequently claim compensation from the opponent.[11] In particular, upon filing a lawsuit, the plaintiff has to pay the court fees in advance. Paying attorney fees up front, especially a retainer, is not required by law but an attorney may demand that the client pay a certain amount prior to initiating the litigation.

3.3.1 *Court Costs*

Court costs consist of a general and comprehensive fee the size of which depends on the amount in dispute. They are regulated in the Court Fees Act (*Gerichtsgebührengesetz*). The Act stipulates that when the amount in dispute is under $490,000 (ca. €350,000) the fee is a lump sum. Above this amount, the fee is calculated at 1.2% of the value of the case, plus a fixed sum of $2,940 (ca. €2,100); in cases involving an amount of controversy of $490,000 (€350,000), this amounts to a fee of $8,820 (ca. €6,300).

3.3.2 *Attorney Fees*

Attorney fees are also determined by statute, i.e., the Attorneys' Tariff Act (*Rechtsanwaltstarifgesetz*). Under this law, the attorneys' fees also depend on the amount in controversy: the higher the amount, the higher the fees. Yet, attorney fees in Austria are not lump sums; rather, attorneys are paid for their various acts during the course of the litigation. Hence the ultimate sum depends, inter alia, on the number of written statements, and on the number and length of hearings.[12]

---

[10] *Wagner*, Rechtsprobleme der Fremdfinanzierung von Prozessen (I), Juristische Blätter 2001, 416.

[11] *Rechberger* and *Kodek* in *Blanpain, Colucci,* and *Taelman (Eds.)*, International Encyclopaedia of Laws. Civil Procedure. Austria, Kluwer Law International 2005, 66.

[12] *Heller* in *Colman (Ed.)*, Encyclopedia of International Commercial Arbitration. Austria, Wolters Kluwer 2009, A3.33.

The statutory tariff is always used to determine how much the losing party has to pay to the winner. Between themselves, attorneys and clients are free to enter into any form of fee arrangement that is not totally beyond the scope of what is customary; they can thereby increase or decrease the statutory rates by consent. In such negotiations, the main criteria for increasing or decreasing the rates are the rules of supply and demand, of business competition, and of the overall status of an attorney, i.e., such his or her reputation, seniority, and success rate in litigation. In order to protect inexperienced clients, the Austrian Bar Association exercises some control over such fee arrangements. If no arrangement has been made, reasonable fees may be charged.[13]

Representation by an attorney is not, however, required in all cases. Parties are free to represent themselves, e.g., in proceedings before the district (i.e., lower first instance) courts, if the value of the case does not exceed €5,000 (ca. $7,000). If the amount in controversy exceeds this sum, as well as in all cases before regional (i.e., higher first instance) courts, and in all appellate proceedings, including proceedings before the Austrian Supreme Court, representation by an attorney is mandatory (*absoluter Anwaltszwang*, Section 27(1) of the Austrian Code of Civil Procedure).[14] There are a few exceptions: an application for legal aid does not require representation by an attorney (Section 72(3) of the Austrian Code of Civil Procedure) nor does the conclusion of a settlement before the district court, if the amount in dispute exceeds €5,000 (Section 27(3) of the Austrian Code of Civil Procedure).[15]

In all the cases where the parties are free to represent themselves, they can either do so in person or appoint a non-professional representative, who is, however, not allowed to take a fee (Section 29(1), (3) of the Austrian Code of Civil Procedure).

Parties in proceedings before labor and social courts do not have to engage an attorney. Instead, they may opt for representation by an employee of the Chamber of Commerce (*Wirtschaftskammer*) or the Chamber of Employees (*Kammer für Arbeiter und Angestellte*) respectively (Section 40 of the Austrian Labor and Social Courts Act).[16]

---

[13] *Heller* in *Colman (Ed.)*, Encyclopedia of International Commercial Arbitration. Austria, Wolters Kluwer 2009, A3.30; *Roth* in *Verschraegen (Ed.)*, Austrian Law – An International Perspective: Selected Issues, Jan Sramek Verlag 2010, 141.

[14] Under Austrian law, in terms of representation by an attorney, there is no distinction made between barristers and solicitors. An Austrian attorney has the right to advise his/her clients in all legal matters and to represent them before any court or administrative authority within the country (*Heller* in *Colman (Ed.)*, Encyclopedia of International Commercial Arbitration. Austria, Wolters Kluwer 2009, A3.1 and A3.19).

[15] *Deixler-Hübner* and *Roth*, Der Zivilprozess in der Praxis, 4th edition, LexisNexis ARD Orac 2006, 4.

[16] *Heller* in *Colman (Ed.)*, Encyclopedia of International Commercial Arbitration. Austria, Wolters Kluwer 2009, A3.25.

In some other cases – particularly in cases pertaining to marriage and divorce – a party can choose to either represent himself or to be represented. If the party chooses to be represented, however, the representative has to be an attorney, provided that (at least) two attorneys are registered in the respective location (*relativer Anwaltszwang*, Section 29(1) of the Austrian Code of Civil Procedure).[17]

3.3.3 Who Determines the Amount?

The court finally determines the particular amount to be awarded to the parties. In order to obtain reimbursement, each party has to file a breakdown of its costs until the end of the oral proceedings (Sections 52 and 54(1) of the Austrian Code of Civil Procedure). If the counterparty does not accept the other party's statement, it has to file an objection within 14 days (Section 54(1a) of the Austrian Code of Civil Procedure). Based on this material, the court rules on the costs by means of an order (*Beschluss*).[18] This decision is an integral part of the final judgment (Section 52(1) of the Austrian Code of Civil Procedure). If the parties have to bear their own expenses regardless of the outcome of litigation, however, a separate court order will be made. The court has discretion as to what extent the costs were necessary, but it is bound by the tariff as to the amounts awarded.[19]

3.4 Instruments of Cost Distribution

3.4.1 Success-Oriented Fees

For the protection of clients, success-oriented fees such as contingency fees are basically forbidden according to Section 879(2)(2) of the General Austrian Civil Code (*quota litis*).[20] Yet, a success premium or a lump sum fee calculated as a percentage of the amount in dispute is allowed, as long as it is not calculated as a percentage of the sum won.[21]

[17] *Deixler-Hübner* and *Roth*, Der Zivilprozess in der Praxis, 4th edition, LexisNexis ARD Orac 2006, 4.

[18] *Rechberger* and *Kodek* in *Blanpain, Colucci,* and *Taelman (Eds.)*, International Encyclopaedia of Laws. Civil Procedure. Austria, Kluwer Law International 2005, 67.

[19] *Id.* at 66.

[20] *Apathy* and *Riedler* in *Schwimann*, Kommentar zum Allgemeinen Bürgerlichen Gesetzbuch, vol IV, 3rd edition, LexisNexis 2006, Section 879 of the General Austrian Civil Code, marg. No. 16; also refer to Section 16(1) of the Attorneys' Tariff Act.

[21] *Krejci* in *Rummel*, Kommentar zum Allgemeinen Bürgerlichen Gesetzbuch, 3rd edition, Manz 2000, Section 879 General Austrian Civil Code, marg. No. 209.

If the winning party has negotiated a special fee with the attorney (which may, as mentioned, be higher or lower than the statutory tariff), the losing party is not bound by such an arrangement but simply has to pay the tariff.

3.4.2 Sale of Claims

It is not permissible to sell claims for purposes of litigation to an attorney (Section 879(2)(2) of the General Austrian Civil Code). Private corporations, such as Advofin, however, do finance litigation and assume the financial risk. Such agreements are not considered *quota litis* arrangements and therefore legal under Austrian law since Section 879(2)(2) of the General Austrian Civil Code only addresses attorneys but not corporations financing litigation, such as Advofin.[22]

3.4.3 Litigation Insurance

Insurance against the overall costs of litigation is increasingly popular in Austria. According to statistics provided by the Austrian Underwriting Association (*Österreichischer Versicherungsverbund*), a total of 2,975,359 insurance contracts for litigation protection existed in 2008. This number includes policies held by businesses as well as private persons, but excludes legal protection in connection with automobile liability insurance. In most cases, plaintiffs filing a lawsuit carry legal cost insurance.[23]

Automobile insurance and homeowners insurance may cover legal assistance in litigation in that particular area. In most cases, one has to buy litigation cost coverage separately. In recent years though, a few companies providing automobile liability insurance include automatic legal protection.

In practice, the plaintiff or his or her attorney must notify the insurance company of the intended litigation. The insurer will then verify whether the case is covered by the respective policy and whether the total amount insured is exceeded. If all terms and conditions are fulfilled, the insurance company will provide a note of coverage to its client.[24]

---

[22] Refer to Judgment of 23 February 1999, Austrian Supreme Court, 5 Ob 28/99z; RS 0016814 T 2.

[23] *Hausmaninger*, The Austrian Legal System, 3rd edition, Manz 2003, 222.

[24] *Roth* in *Verschraegen (Ed.)*, Austrian Law – An International Perspective: Selected Issues, Jan Sramek Verlag 2010, 144; *Wandt*, Versicherungsrecht, 5th edition, Heymann 2010, para. 938.

3.4.4 Legal Aid

Legal aid is available to any natural person who is unable to bear the expenses of participation in legal proceedings without endangering his or her livelihood, regardless of whether the applicant is a plaintiff or defendant, national or alien (Sections 63(1) of the Austrian Code of Civil Procedure). An applicant for legal aid has to prove that his or her income is too low and that he or she does not own sufficient property to engage in civil proceedings without jeopardizing his or her basic maintenance. In these conditions are fulfilled, the judge has to grant legal aid, unless the party obviously cannot win the case.[25]

Since 1 July 2009, Section 63(1) of the Austrian Code of Civil Procedure was amended so that only natural persons, but no longer corporations or other legal persons, are entitled to apply for legal aid.[26] The European Court of Justice, however, recently held that according to Article 47(3) of the European Charter of Fundamental Rights, legal aid shall in principle be available to legal persons as well.[27] This ruling has provided strong support for the critics of the 2009 amendment of the Austrian Code of Civil Procedure.[28]

Legal aid consists mainly of a waiver of court fees by the state and – if required under the rules of representation (Sections 26 et seq. of the Austrian Code of Civil Procedure)[29] – of the appointment of an attorney by the Bar Association. Hence, legal aid is not offered by a special organization, but rather by each attorney free of charge. Every attorney is assigned between five and ten legal aid cases each year. The court decides whether or not, and in which form, legal aid should be granted. If the court grants free representation by an attorney, the Bar Association assigns counsel according to its internal distribution system. An attorney so assigned may not refuse to take the case without good cause. Hence, within the system of legal aid, Austrian attorneys have a legal obligation provide free legal assistance in a certain number of cases.[30]

---

[25] *Rechberger* and *Kodek* in *Blanpain, Colucci,* and *Taelman (Eds.)*, International Encyclopaedia of Laws. Civil Procedure. Austria, Kluwer Law International 2005, 152; *Heller* in *Colman (Ed.)*, Encyclopedia of International Commercial Arbitration. Austria, Wolters Kluwer 2009, A3.26.

[26] Until 1 July 2009, legal aid was available to natural and legal persons alike.

[27] European Court of Justice 22.12.2010, C-279/09, *DEB Deutsche Energieberatungsgesellschaft mbH/Bundesrepublik Deutschland*.

[28] *Slonina*, Verfahrenshilfe für juristische Personen: Ein Weihnachtsgeschenk des EuGH?, ecolex 2011, p. 410 et seq.

[29] See *supra* 3.2.

[30] *Heller* in *Colman (Ed.)*, Encyclopedia of International Commercial Arbitration. Austria, Wolters Kluwer 2009, A3.27; *Chvosta*, Prozesskostenrecht, Manz 2001, 14 et seq.

Irrespective of, and in addition to, legal aid available to persons in need, free legal advice is provided by the district courts (called *Amtstag,*) and the Bar Association on special days of the week.[31]

3.5 Conclusion

Austria belongs to the majority of countries whose systems can be defined as "major shifting". Accordingly, the Austrian Code of Civil Procedure follows the loser-pays principle, which has been embraced since the Code's enactment in 1895. The system is designed so that all three categories of costs – namely court costs, lawyer fees and evidence expenses – are shifted on to the loser with only few exceptions.

Like most countries in continental Europe, Austria has a statutory tariff for lawyers: the Attorneys' Tariff Act ensures predictability of costs and limits the losers' liability for the winners' attorney fees to the legal tariff. Moreover, the Court Fees Act provides predictability of litigation costs by stipulating general sums depending on the amount in dispute. Beyond a certain amount, a statutory percentage – using the value of the case as a calculation basis – has to be paid.

The risk of losing a case and thus being charged with the costs of litigation functions as a deterrent to commence civil proceedings in Austria and thus may be seen as impeding access to justice. The right to have common access to justice is supported, however, by various instruments of cost distribution, particularly by the rules on public legal aid.

In Austria, legal aid is granted in the form of a waiver of court fees as well as in the form of free advice and representation by lawyers. By providing legal aid to parties who lack the financial means to litigate, the Austrian Code of Civil Procedure pays attention to the due process requirements of equality before the law and of a fair trial as set forth in Article 6 of the European Convention on Human Rights.[32]

---

31 Article 1 Section 54 Bylaws for the Courts of I. and II. Instance; http://www.srak.at/service-informationen/service/1-anwaltl-auskunft.

32 *Chvosta*, Prozesskostenrecht, Manz 2001, 14 et seq.

Chapter 4
"Everything Costs Its Own Cost, and One of Our Best Virtues Is a Just Desire To Pay It." An Analysis of Belgian Law

Ilse Samoy and Vincent Sagaert

4.1 Introduction

This contribution summarizes the main features of the Belgian statutory rules on cost and fee allocation in civil procedure. The rules on judicial expenses and costs, and of their recoverability, are laid down in the Belgian Judicial Code of 1967 (hereafter: J.C.), specifically in Articles 1017–1024. Articles 1018–1019 and 1022 J.C. give an overview of the recoverable costs. Articles 1020–1021 J.C. deal with the payment of and the decision upon the allocation of procedural costs. Article 1023 J.C. introduces a prohibition of "increase clauses". Article 1024 J.C., finally, deals with the costs of enforcement. As it will emerge from this contribution, the current rules underwent a major statutory amendment in 2007, introducing a (fixed) recoverability of lawyers' fees.

4.2 The Basic Rules: Who Pays?

4.2.1 Starting Point

According to article 1017 J.C., each final judgment refers – even ex officio – to the expenses to be paid by the party found to be in error by the judgment (the losing party). In other words, the loser has to pay or reimburse the judicial costs to the winner. As the allocation of the procedural costs is

---

"Everything Costs Its Own Cost, and One of Our Best Virtues Is a Just Desire To Pay It." – John Ruskin, from: Letters of John Ruskin to Charles Eliot Norton Vol. 1 (Houghton Mifflin 1904) 243, digitized by the Internet Archive in 2011, *available at* http://www.archive.org/stream/lettersofjohnrus01rusk/lettersofjohnrus01rusk_djvu.txt

I. Samoy (✉)
Institute of the Law of Obligations, K.U.Leuven, Belgium

University of Hasselt, Hasselt, Belgium
e-mail: ilse.samoy@law.kuleuven.be

M. Reimann (ed.), *Cost and Fee Allocation in Civil Procedure*,
Ius Gentium: Comparative Perspectives on Law and Justice 11,
DOI 10.1007/978-94-007-2263-7_4, © Springer Science+Business Media B.V. 2012

a legal effect of the basic judgment on the substance of the dispute, the court or tribunal does not have to give specific reasons for its allocation of costs unless a party has expressly raised this point during the procedure (in which case the arguments must be answered).[1] The shifting of costs is not grounded in general civil liability rules.[2] It is based on the principles of procedural risk and policy: each party starting legal proceedings is subject to the risk that his claim or defense will be dismissed, and has to take that risk into account at the initiation of the case.[3]

Two requirements have to be met in order to shift costs to the losing party: (1) there must be a *final* judgment and (2) there must be a "forfeiting" (i.e., "*losing*") party. A *final* judgment is each judgment in which a court or tribunal exhausts its power to decide on an object of litigation, except for the means to appeal against this decision (Article 19, par. 1 J.C.). An intermediate judgment will adjourn the issue about the expenses until the final judgment. The losing party is the party that suffers an adverse final judgment in favor of the other party.[4] If the Public Prosecutor, which occasionally represents the State in civil matters, is the losing party, the judicial costs and expenses are borne by the State.[5]

4.2.2 General Overview of the Recoverable Judicial Expenses and Costs: Art. 1018 J.C.

Article 1018 J.C. enumerates the recoverable judicial expenses and costs:

1° the various court fees (*griffierechten/droit de greffe*) and registration duties (*registratierechten/droit de régistration*), as well as the stamp duties (*zegelrechten*) that had to be paid before the abolition of the Code on Stamp Duties[6];

2° the price, emoluments and wages for judicial acts;

---

[1] Belgian Supreme Court 11 May 1989, *Arresten van het Hof van Cassatie* 1988–89, 1059; Belgian Supreme Court 18 October 1985, *Arresten van het Hof van Cassatie* 1985–86, 228; J. LAENENS, K. BROECKX, D. SCHEERS & P. THIRIAR, *Handboek gerechtelijk recht*, Antwerp, Intersentia, 2008, 490; D. MAES, "Artikel 1017 Ger.W.", in X., *Artikelsgewijze commentaar: Gerechtelijk recht*, Mechelen, Kluwer, p. 103, n° 2.

[2] Belgian Supreme Court 15 May 1941, *Pasicrisie* 1941, I, 192; G. DE LEVAL, *Eléments de procédure civile*, Ghent, Larcier, 2005, 453.

[3] B. DE TEMMERMAN, "Rechtsvergelijkende variaties op een heikel thema", in F. EVERS & P. LEFRANC (eds.), *De verhaalbaarheid van de kosten van verdediging: en wat met de toegang tot de rechter?*, Bruges, Die Keure, 2005, 25 and 29.

[4] Belgian Supreme Court 26 September 1983, *Arresten Cassatie* 1983–84, 72; J. LAENENS, K. BROECKX, D. SCHEERS & P. THIRIAR, *Handboek gerechtelijk recht*, Antwerp, Intersentia, 2008, 490.

[5] Belgian Supreme Court 11 May 1922, *Pasicrisie* 1922, I, 285.

[6] The Code on Stamp Duties has been abolished by the Act of 19 December 2006, *Belgian Official Gazette* 29 December 2006, date of entry into force: 1st of January 2007.

3° the price for the authenticated copy (*uitgifte/expédition*) of the judgment;
4° the expenses concerning all evidentiary measures, including expenses for witnesses and experts;
5° the expenses for travelling and lodging of judges and clerks of the court (if any), and of the parties when their trip has been ordered by the judge, as well as the expenses of documents which have been drafted with regard to the legal proceedings;
6° the expenses of judicial procedure (*rechtsplegingsvergoeding/indemnité de procédure*), as stated in Article 1022 J.C.;
7° the fees, emoluments and costs of the mediator, nominated according to Article 1734 J.C., if parties decide to hire a mediator.

The enumeration in Article 1018 J.C. is not exhaustive.[7] As it emerges from parliamentary debate preceding the approval of the statutory amendment, the judge has a certain freedom to add costs not included in the list of Article 1018 J.C.[8] Additional costs can cover, for instance, the expenses made to obtain a certificate of the defendant's domicile or a copy of a criminal file (e.g., if such is needed to sustain a divorce claim).

4.2.3 The Expenses of Judicial Procedure (Lawyers' Fees): Art. 1022 J.C.

The enumeration of Article 1018 J.C. contains one category covering "the expenses of judicial procedure, as stated in Article 1022 J.C.". Article 1022 J.C., in turn, was recently radically amended by the Act of 21st April 2007, which introduced one of the most important innovations of the last decade in Belgian law.[9]

Before the 2007 amendment, Article 1022 J.C. only covered the costs of "material acts" accomplished by a lawyer. The amounts of the recoverable sums according to Article 1022 J.C. were fixed in the Royal decree of

---

[7] J. KERKHOFS, "Uitgaven en kosten", in G. VAN MELLAERT (ed.), *Praktijkboek gerechtelijk recht*, Bruges, Vanden Broele, 22; J. LAENENS, K. BROECKX, D. SCHEERS & P. THIRIAR, *Handboek gerechtelijk recht*, Antwerp, Intersentia, 2008, 484.

[8] F. MEERSSCHAUT, "Draaglast van de gedingkosten", *Jura Falconis* 1986–87, 277.

[9] Act of 21 April 2007 concerning the recoverability of fees and costs related to a lawyer's assistance, *Belgian Official Gazette* 31 May 2007. For a general overview: see I. SAMOY & V. SAGAERT, "De Wet van 21 april 2007 betreffende de verhaalbaarheid van kosten en erelonen van een advocaat", *Rechtskundig Weekblad* 2007–08, 674–698; J.F. VAN DROOGHENBROECK & B. DE CONINCK, "La loi du 21 avril 2007 sur la répétibilité des frais et honoraires d'avocat", *Journal des Tribunaux* 2008, 37–60.

30th November 1970 and were limited.[10] Pursuant to the French tradition, they did not include lawyers' fees.[11] Each party (the losing as well as the winning party) had to pay his own lawyer's fees, which were in principle irrecoverable regardless of the result of the litigation. Under the old regime, the amounts of the expenses depended upon (1) the court or tribunal before which the case was brought and (2) the value of the claim, but were generally rather limited. Additional expenses of judicial procedure could be awarded when additional judicial acts had to be accomplished, for instance personal appearance, reopening of debates, expert investigation, witness interrogation, etc. But in general, these sums were very limited and did not take the real costs of the litigation into account.

The 2007 amendment has greatly expanded the concept of expenses of judicial procedure. It now covers what was previously excluded: lawyers' fees. In this manner, Belgium has become a "major shifting system", as defined in the General Report, and it has thus joined the solution prevailing in the Germanic legal family. The new Article 1022 J.C. defines the expenses of judicial procedure as "a fixed compensation for the expenses and fees of the lawyer of the winning party". The term "fixed" demonstrates that the losing party does not have to compensate the actual fees paid by the winning party to his lawyers; instead, these fees are limited to a fixed amount, related to the size of the claim. The word "lawyer" shows that the winning party is only entitled to expenses of judicial procedure if he is assisted and/or represented by a lawyer. Hence, a party that defends her own legal interest during a judicial proceeding or who is assisted by another person (e.g. a trade union representative before the industrial courts, or a public servant in tax matters), is not entitled to these expenses. The Constitutional Court has decided on several occasions that this distinction does not violate the constitutional discrimination prohibition.[12] A lawyer acting *qualitate qua* as tutor ad hoc, provisional administrator or trustee in bankruptcy is not entitled to expenses of judicial procedure either, unless he is represented by another lawyer.[13]

The fixed amounts of the judicial expenses no longer depend on the court or tribunal before which the case is brought but are now contained in an

---

[10] Royal Decree 30 November 1970, *Belgian Official Gazette* 3 December 1970, erratum 12 February 1971.

[11] G. DE LEVAL, *Eléments de procédure civile*, Brussels, Larcier, 2003, 431; B. DE TEMMERMAN, "De verhaalbaarheid van kosten van juridische of technische bijstand", *Tijdschrift voor Privaatrecht* 2003, p. 1016, n° 2.

[12] Belgian Constitutional Court 5 May 2009, n° 73/2009, www.grondwettelijkhof.be, r.o. B.4.3; Belgian Constitutional Court n° 182/2008, 18 December 2008, *Belgian Official Gazette* 22 January 2009, *Rechtskundig Weekblad* 2008–09, 1217 and www.grondwettelijkhof.be.

[13] J. LAENENS, K. BROECKX, D. SCHEERS & P. THIRIAR, *Handboek gerechtelijk recht*, Antwerp, Intersentia, 2008, 488.

official schedule (see infra). The legislation provides that for special reasons, a judge can increase or diminish the basic amount at the request of one of the parties, where appropriate after questioning by the court, within the parameters of a fixed minimum and maximum. The judge has to take into account four criteria: the financial ability of the loser (in order to diminish the amount); the complexity of the litigation; any contractually agreed compensation between the winner and his lawyer and whether reimbursement of the regular amount would be manifestly unreasonable.

The King has, on the basis of these statutory rules, issued the Royal Decree of the 26th of October 2007, in which he has determined a basic, maximum and minimum amount of attorney fees as a function of the value of the litigation. These fees generally come to approximately 10% of the value of the litigated case but are set in a degressive fashion. For example, for a case up to €250, the basic amount is €150; if the amount in controversy is between €10,000 and €20,000, the basic amount is €1,100; for a claim between €100,000 and €250,000, the basic amount is €5,000; for a claim above €1,000,000, the basic amount is €15,000. The General Report indicates that in comparison to other countries, these amounts are rather small. If the winning party has paid a larger fee than the amount which he can recover, he will have to bear the difference (Article 1022 *in fine* J.C.). In addition, since the 2007 Act, any amount of the winning party's lawyers' fees that exceed fixed expenses can no longer be claimed against the losing party on any other ground, e.g. via the rules on contractual or extra-contractual liability. This is, however, still progress from the winner's perspective, as in the past he could normally not recover any fee or cost at all.

It remains questionable whether additional amounts paid to a lawyer can be recovered as damages for having to defend against a vexatious or completely non-meritorious claim, or in case of manifestly inadmissible or redundant proceeding. A proceeding is not only vexatious if a party has the intention to harm the other party, but also if the procedural behavior contravenes that of a prudent and careful person.[14] The victim of such a proceeding can not only claim damages on the ground of fault liability, but Article 780*bis* J.C.[15] allows the judge to award a civil penalty, both in the first instance and on appeal. Although many legal scholars have argued that

[14] Belgian Supreme Court 31 Oktober 2003, *Arresten van het Hof van Cassatie* 2003, 2011, *Journal des Tribunaux* 2004, 135, note J.-F. VAN DROOGHENBROECK.

[15] This provision has been introduced in the Judicial Code by Act 26 April 2007: "The party who manifestly uses judicial proceedings with delaying or illegal purposes can be condemned to pay a pecuniary offence from €15 up to €2,500, without prejudice to claimed damages (...)."

these damages and penalties cannot be added to judicial expenses,[16] the Constitutional Court has indicated the opposite view.[17]

Belgian law permits the use of success fee agreements in favor of the lawyer. Strict no-win, no-fee agreements are, however, prohibited. An agreement between a lawyer and a client that determines the fees *exclusively* in relation to the result of the litigation, is also prohibited (Article 446ter, par. 2 J.C.). In this way, the Belgian legislature aims to prevent the lawyer herself from becoming a party to the litigation. An inquiry organized by the professional Bar Association demonstrated that the large majority of lawyers apply an hourly fee (40,35%). In international relations, this percentage is even larger (55,58%).

4.2.4 Expenses for Experts: Act of 15th May 2007

Article 1018, 4° J.C. provides that the expenses for the taking of evidence, *e.g.* the expenses for witnesses and experts, are also recoverable costs.

The rules in the Judicial Code governing expert investigations have been amended by the Act of 15th May 2007. The expert's costs and fees are governed by Articles 987–991*bis* J.C., which provides for three elements: the retaining fee, the taxation after the end of the investigation, and the final settlement. An expert is only paid after the termination of the investigation. In order to secure effective payment and to protect the expert against the parties' insolvency, an advance to the expert's fee (prepayment) has to be provided at the clerk's service. The amount of the prepayment is fixed during the first meeting concerning the expert investigation (Article 972, second par. J.C.). According to Article 987 J.C., the judge can, if necessary, decide how the prepayment is to be apportioned between the parties, subject, however, to one restriction: if a party, according to Article 1017 J.C. cannot be charged to pay the judicial expenses and costs, the judge also cannot order this party to pay the expert's prepayment. In social security proceedings, for instance, the State will have to pay the expert's prepayment as it has to bear the judicial expenses and costs (cf. *infra*).

The fee is, as a general rule, taxed by the expert himself, with respect of Article 990 J.C. This provision obliges the expert to provide a detailed statement for taxation, mentioning separately: hourly wages, moving expenses, residence expenses, general expenses, amounts paid to third parties, and

[16] *Report of the Senate*, *Parliamenty Documents* 2006–07, n° 3-1686/5, p. 27; P. LEFRANC & F. EVERS, "Leidt de verhaalbaarheid van de advocatenkosten tot een meer toegankelijke justitie?", *Tijdschrift voor Mensenrechten* 2007, afl. 4, p. 9; J.F. VAN DROOGHENBROECK & B. DE CONINCK, "La loi du 21 avril 2007 sur la répétibilité des frais et honoraires d'avocat", *Journal des tribunaux* 2008, (37) nr. 5.

[17] Belgian Constitutional Court 18 December 2008, *Belgian Official Gazette* 22 January 2009, 3343 and www.grondwettelijkhof.be, B.10.2.

prepayments. There are no fixed legal tariffs for expert expenses. According to Article 991, second par., J.C., the taxation has to be based on three elements: the diligence with which the work has been carried out, the compliance with deadlines, and the quality of the investigation. The amount at stake is irrelevant.

The judge, when making his decision on the judicial expenses and costs in the final judgment, decides also on the allocation of the expert's costs. The winning party, which has made a prepayment of the expert fees, cannot claim interest on these expenses for the period preceding the final judgment.[18]

4.3 Exceptions and Modifications

4.3.1 Specific Rules (Article 1017, First par. J.C.)

The general rule of Article 1017 J.C. is subject to several exceptions. An interesting exception is made in case of divorce by permanent breakdown of marriage. Article 1285 J.C. states that the costs are divided between the parties where both parties seek divorce, unless the judge or the parties state otherwise. If only one party claims the divorce by permanent breakdown of marriage, the costs have to be borne by the claimant. The Constitutional Court has ruled that this distinction is discriminatory. As the legislature considers both cases instances of no-fault divorce, the measure in case of unilateral request cannot be considered as a financial penalty for the claimant.[19] More fundamentally, one can wonder whether the condition of Article 1017 J.C. to have a "losing party" is met in case of no-fault divorce.[20]

The Act of 21st February 2005 has introduced a new chapter in the Judicial Code that regulates judicial and extrajudicial mediation (Articles 1724–1737 J.C.) with the overall goal to encourage it. A mediator tries to settle the dispute by agreement. The costs of *judicial* mediation (in contrast to the costs of *extrajudicial* mediation) are part of the judicial expenses and costs enumerated in Article 1018 J.C. and are to be borne by the losing party. However, Article 1736 *juncto* 1731 J.C. seem to be considered *lex specialis* to Article 1017 J.C., making the latter inapplicable. Article 1736 J.C. on judicial mediation refers to and declares applicable Article

[18] Belgian Supreme Court 30 March 2001, *Rechtskundig Weekblad* 2001–02, 699; Belgian Supreme Court 24 September 1953, *Pasicrisie* 1954, I, 36.

[19] Belgian Constitutional Court 21 October 2008, *Rechtskundig Weekblad* 2008–09, 1341, comment F. SWENNEN & S. EGGERMONT.

[20] See also: F. SWENNEN & S. EGGERMONT, "Kosten en rechtsplegingsvergoeding bij de echtscheiding op grond van onherstelbare ontwrichting op basis van art. 229, § 3, B.W.", *Rechtskundig Weekblad* 2008–09, 1343–1344.

1731 J.C. on extrajudicial mediation, stating that both of the parties have to bear the costs of the mediation equally, unless they have agreed otherwise. Therefore, the costs of (unsuccessful) mediation have only to be borne exclusively by the loser if parties have agreed to that. Article 1731 J.C. states further on that the mediation protocol must clearly state the manner of taxation of the mediator's fees, the rates, and the payment conditions. The rules on legal aid are extended to judicial and extrajudicial mediation.

The most important *lex specialis* is Article 1382 Civil Code (the general rule on tort law). According to the Belgian Supreme Court, the rules on judicial expenses do not exclude the application of the rules on tort law.[21] According to the principles of tort law (Article 1382 Civil Code), a party can be charged to pay litigation costs, if the costs are caused by his wrongful act, even if he is the winning party.[22] In other words, expenses for redundant acts or useless expenses have to be borne by the party who has undertaken the act, even if this party is successful in its arguments afterwards.

4.3.2 Agreement Between the Parties (Article 1017, First par. J.C.)

According to Article 1017, first par. J.C., parties can enter into an agreement on the allocation of the judicial expenses and costs, which will be ratified by the judge. Parties can agree to waive any claim for judicial expenses and costs, to waive any derogation from the basic amount of the expenses of judicial procedure, or to impose some optional costs on the losing party, e.g. costs of a notice of default, moving expenses, etc.

Yet, article 1017, first par. J.C. has to be read together with Article 1023 J.C. According to this provision, all contractual stipulations providing that the amount of the claim will increase if the claim should be enforced in a law suit, are void. According to the Belgian Supreme Court, this provision is a matter of public policy,[23] meaning that any contractual derogation is void, can be contested at any stage of the law suit and should even be raised *ex officio* by the court or tribunal. The basis for the rule is the right of each party to defend itself. The possibility of contractually increasing the compensation would tend to make the defendant waive his right of defense, in order to avoid paying increasing amounts.[24]

---

[21] Belgian Supreme Court 15 May 1941, *Pasicrisie* 1941, I, 192.

[22] Belgian Supreme Court 14 May 2001, *Pasicrisie* 2001, 852; Belgian Supreme Court 24 April 1978, *Pasicrisie* 1978, I, 955.

[23] Belgian Supreme Court 7 April 1995, *Pasicrisie* 1995, I, 403.

[24] A. VAN OEVELEN, "De ongeldigheid van het beding tot verhoging van de schuldvordering ingeval deze in rechte wordt opgeëist en de toepassing ervan op de invordering

Historically, Article 1023 J.C. was inserted in the draft of the Judicial Code together with a possibility to recover the attorney fees. Although this latter possibility was abolished during the parliamentary debate, the prohibition of clauses increasing the amount in case of lawsuit in Article 1023 J.C. has been maintained. Therefore, this provision is often interpreted in the following manner: contractual clauses derogating from the statutory rules with regard to judicial expenses *before* a legal proceeding has been initiated are deemed to be (absolutely) void. Once a legal proceeding has been initiated however, such clause should be considered valid according to Article 1017, first par. J.C. The Belgian High Council of Justice also came out in favor of the possibility of contractually derogating from the statutory rules.[25]

4.3.3 Social Security Proceedings (Article 1017, Second par. J.C.)

A major exception, provided in article 1017, second par. J.C., applies to certain judicial proceedings with regard to social security. Here, the judicial expenses and costs (including costs of enforcement) are borne by the Belgian State, except, again, for vexatious or completely non-meritorious proceedings. The legislature deemed it desirable to open the possibility to initiate more cost-efficient proceedings with regard to social security issues, except if the private claimant is acting wrongfully in these proceedings. As the General Report indicates, Belgium finds itself in the company of several other legal systems with similar policies and rules.

4.3.4 Apportionment of Costs (Article 1017, Third par. J.C.) (omslaan van de kosten/répartition des coûts)

According to Article 1017, third par. J.C., a judge can – even *ex officio* – set off ("*divide*") the parties' judicial expenses and costs against each other in two cases: if both parties are considered losing (in part) or if they are spouses, family members in the ascending line, brothers or sisters, or family

van advocatenhonoraria", (case note of Belgian Supreme Court 7 April 1995), *Rechtskundig Weekblad* 1995–96, 190; E. WYMEERSCH, "Toetsing van verhogingsbedingen", *Rechtskundig Weekblad* 1976–77, 137–138.

[25] Hoge Raad voor de Justitie, http://www.hrj.be, 24. The High Council of Justice is an independent body which, apart from its task in the appointment and control of judges, also has the power to advise and give proposals with regard to the general functioning and organisation of the judicial system.

members in the same degree. In the latter case, the apportionment of the costs is merely optional.[26]

4.4 Conclusion

Belgium has lately radically amended the rules governing the allocation of civil litigation costs and fees. Belgian procedural law used to follow strictly the French law on cost shifting, not allowing the winner to recover attorney fees. Through statutory amendment in 2007, Belgian procedural law has deviated from the French model and opened the possibility to recover attorney fees according to an official schedule. In doing so, Belgian law has joined the European (civil law) mainstream. The official tariff operates by introducing fixed amounts of recoverable costs, depending on the value of the litigation. The amendment has, in the first years of its application, not only triggered many technical changes but also a new culture of litigation, which will be further developed in the upcoming years. Despite the lack of statistics at this moment, it is largely felt that the new Act has an impact on the ease with which litigation is initiated. Moreover, because attorneys have a professional duty to inform their clients of the costs of litigation – including the potential costs under the new schedule system – this may have a possible impact on how individuals deal with legal disputes.

---

[26] Belgian Supreme Court 17 March 1966, *Pasicrisie* 1966, I, 920.

Chapter 5
Major Shifting: The Brazilian Way

Alexandre Alcino de Barros and Sílvia Julio Bueno de Miranda

5.1 Basic Principle

As indicated in the General Report, Brazil is a member of the (majority) group of countries which can be characterized as "major shifting". The Brazilian loser-pays rule is based on the idea that the process should not result in loss to the party who had her right recognized in court.[1] Instead, it should put her in the same economic situation that she would be in if the object of the dispute had been fulfilled without the need of a lawsuit. Following that, Brazilian law imposes liability for costs on the losing party.

5.2 Costs Incurred in Civil Litigation in Brazil

5.2.1 Court Costs

Each Member of the Brazilian Federation has different laws regulating court costs. In spite of these differences, the general rule for both the Federal Court[2] and the majority of the states[3] is that the filing fees are determined

[1] THEODORO JUNIOR, Humberto, *Curso de Direito Processual Civil* – Rio de Janeiro: Forense, 2000, v. 1, p. 79 and ABREU, Frederico do Valle, *O Custo Financeiro do Processo in* Revista dos Tribunais, 2003, v. 818, p. 67.

[2] Federal court costs correspond to 1% of the amount of the dispute. Law N. 9.289/96 and Resolution 278/2007, Schedule of Costs I – Civil Actions, Item (a) Civil Litigation. Under this Schedule of Costs, the minimum amount to be paid as court costs in the Federal Courts currently corresponds to R$10.64 and the maximum corresponds to R$1,915.38.

[3] As an example, the general rule in the State of São Paulo is that prior to filing a civil action before such Court, the plaintiff shall pay initial costs corresponding to 1% of the amount of the dispute. See Article 4, I and § 1, São Paulo State Law N. 11.608/03. Under

A.A. de Barros (✉)
Senior Associates ad L.O. Baptista Advogados Associados, Sao Paolo, Brazil

M. Reimann (ed.), *Cost and Fee Allocation in Civil Procedure*,
Ius Gentium: Comparative Perspectives on Law and Justice 11,
DOI 10.1007/978-94-007-2263-7_5, © Springer Science+Business Media B.V. 2012

by the amount in controversy, with a cap – which is also true in most jurisdictions covered by the General Report. For that reason, the plaintiff shall always indicate the amount in controversy, even if the dispute has no immediate economic content.[4] If the defendant challenges the amount, the judge shall decide it.[5]

In case of appeal, parties shall pay the expenses incurred with the transportation of the physical process ("*porte de remessa e retorno*"), calculated based on the number of sheets contained in the files. These costs are usually insignificant when compared to the other court costs.

The law also authorizes the judge to impose fines for malicious abuse of process,[6] for presenting appeals that are clearly inadmissible or dilatory,[7] and for acts offensive to the dignity of justice,[8] among others.

5.2.2 Attorney's Fees

Brazil is part of a minority of systems under which representation by a lawyer is mandatory, except for small claims. In addition to this common exception, Brazilian law does not require legal representation when the party is an attorney duly enrolled at a Brazilian State Bar Association or if there is no attorney available to represent such party in the process.[9]

Attorneys and clients are free to contract the payment of the fees. The amount varies widely depending on the location, the area of practice and the expertise of the firm. Success-fees are allowed and quite common. The Bar Associations of each Brazilian state only establish floors for

---

these rules, the minimum amount to be paid as court costs currently corresponds to R$79.25 and the maximum corresponds to R$47,550.00. In order to appeal the party shall have paid costs of 2% of the amount in dispute, in the case of adjudication of a right (where there is no conviction of the losing party to pay a certain amount); or 2% of the monetary judgment, where the sentence has condemned the loser to pay a certain amount. See Article 4, § 2, São Paulo State Law N. 11.608/03. The minimum and maximum amounts to be paid as court costs for appeal are the same as the ones applicable to the initial costs. In addition to these costs, the party shall pay the costs related to the transportation of the process. See Article 4, § 4, São Paulo State Law N. 11.608/03.

[4] Article 258, Brazilian Code of Civil Procedure (Law N. 5.869/73).

[5] Articles 259 and 261, Brazilian Code of Civil Procedure (Law N. 5.869/73).

[6] Article 18, Brazilian Code of Civil Procedure (Law N. 5.869/73).

[7] Article 538, sole paragraph, and Article 557, § 2, Brazilian Code of Civil Procedure (Law N. 5.869/73).

[8] Article 601, Brazilian Code of Civil Procedure (Law N. 5.869/73).

[9] Articles 259 and 261, Brazilian Code of Civil Procedure (Law N. 5.869/73).

different services,[10] above which the parties are free to negotiate with their attorneys.

5.2.3 Evidence Expenses

The general rule is that the party requesting the evidence shall bear the corresponding costs of production, including expert fees, costs of travelling and hotels.[11] If such evidence is requested by the judge or by both parties, the claimant shall bear the costs. Parties are free to appoint a technical assistant to monitor the work carried out by the expert, and they usually do; in these cases, they also have to bear the fees and expenses related to such assistant.[12] The amount of these fees shall be established by the expert after his appointment in the procedure.

Costs related to the taking of evidence may represent a considerable amount, and may even be decisive in a plaintiff's decision to bring a case to court. In most cases, however, they do not represent a significant amount of the overall costs of litigation. When compared with the U.S., for example, they are usually minimal – as it happens in other civil law systems.

5.3 The Brazilian Meaning of Shifting

The Brazilian system imposes on the losing party all three major categories of expenses, i.e., court costs, lawyer, and evidence expenses. However, it does not entitle the winner to recover the full amount spent in litigation, as detailed below.

5.3.1 Court Costs

All court costs are subject to shifting.

---

[10] As an example, the Minimum Fee Schedule approved by the São Paulo Bar Association is available at http://www.oabsp.org.br/tabela-de-honorarios/tabela-de-honorarios-completa-nova. There is no immediate consequence if a lawyer charges less than those minimum amounts. However, the Bar Association Code of Ethics provides that lawyers must avoid degrading the value of their services, not charging an insignificant amount or less than those minimums, unless they have a justification for that. Article 41, Brazilian Bar Association Code of Ethics.

[11] Articles 19 and 20, § 2, Brazilian Code of Civil Procedure (Law N. 5.869/73).

[12] Articles 20, §§ 2 and 33, Brazilian Code of Civil Procedure (Law N. 5.869/73).

5.3.2 Attorney's Fees

Following the same approach as other Latin countries, recoverable attorney's fees[13] are capped. The exact percentage is awarded by the judge, and it may range from 10–20% of the monetary judgment[14] – a low percentage in comparison with other countries examined in the General Report. Where there is no monetary judgment, the judge shall determine these fees according to his equitable discretion.[15] In both cases, he shall take into account the attorney's degree of professional care, the place where the services were rendered, the nature and importance of the case, the work carried out by the attorney and the time required for rendering such services.[16]

This approach avoids a concern pointed out in the General Report that the free determination of lawyer fees and the availability of success-fees could lead the winner to make arrangements with his lawyer potentially at the loser's expense.

Any fees exceeding the amount set forth by the judge shall be borne by each party, in accordance with the services agreement executed by and between the party and her attorney.

5.3.3 Evidence Expenses

As pointed out in the General Report, all civil law systems impose these costs on the loser. The prevailing party may recover all the expenses incurred with the taking of evidence, provided that such expenses had been duly proved in the process (receipts, vouchers, etc).

5.4 Shifting Procedure

Prior to filing a civil action before a Federal Court, the plaintiff shall pay half of the court costs as initial costs.[17] Upon an appeal, the party appealing shall pay the other half.[18] If there is no appeal, the defeated party shall pay the other half only if she presents a defense in the enforcement proceeding or hinders its performance.[19] When an action is filed before a state court, the plaintiff shall pay all of the court costs as initial costs. Parties to a

[13] Article 20, *caput*, Brazilian Code of Civil Procedure (Law N. 5.869/73).
[14] Article 20, § 3, Brazilian Code of Civil Procedure (Law N. 5.869/73).
[15] Article 20, § 4, Brazilian Code of Civil Procedure (Law N. 5.869/73).
[16] Article 20, § 3, Brazilian Code of Civil Procedure (Law N. 5.869/73).
[17] Article 14, I, Law N. 9.289/96.
[18] Article 14, II, Law N. 9.289/96.
[19] Article 14, IV, Law N. 9.289/96.

contract may not agree on who should advance the payment of court costs, for example establishing that these costs shall be collected by the defaulting party. The rules governing the payment of such costs are mandatory and parties may not derogate from them.

During the proceedings – from the beginning of the lawsuit until the enforcement of the decision – each party shall advance payment of costs and expenses of the procedural steps that she carries out or requires,[20] such as experts' fees, witnesses' travel expenses, photocopies, etc. In addition, the plaintiff shall anticipate payment of costs related to procedural steps ordered by the judge ex officio or requested by the Public Prosecutors' Office.[21] The judge may prefer to have the parties sharing the costs of each of these steps, since the prevailing party will be reimbursed at the end of the proceedings. Whenever a party fails to comply with such a duty, the respective procedural step requested by such party will not be carried out. If the procedural step is requested by the judge ex officio or by the public prosecutor, and a party refuses to pay for that, the judge may determine that the payment only be made at the end of the proceedings, by the losing party.

At the end of the lawsuit, as determined in the final judgment, the loser must reimburse all costs and expenses paid up-front by the prevailing party over the course of the proceedings.

5.5 Exceptions to the Shifting Rule[22]

In line with other jurisdictions which exempt cases with a strong social element from cost shifting, Brazilian laws dealing with class actions aimed at the protection of collective, diffuse, and public rights set out specific rules in that regard.[23]

Public Civil Actions do not require that parties advance payment of court costs, attorney fees, expert fees, and any other court costs. In addition,

[20] Article 19, *caput*, Brazilian Code of Civil Procedure (Law N. 5.869/73).

[21] Article 19, § 2, Brazilian Code of Civil Procedure (Law N. 5.869/73). Please notice that it is very uncommon for judges or public prosecutors to request such procedural steps.

[22] As indicated in the General Report, some systems forego or limit cost shifting in small claims. Although such claims may be heard in Special Courts in Brazil, according to a simplified procedure, and self-representation is authorized is these cases, the cost shifting is also applicable here. Please note that Special Courts allow self-representation where the amount in dispute does not exceed twenty times the Brazilian minimum wage. Article 9, Law N. 9099/95. The minimum wage is currently R$465.00 (Law N. 11.944/ 2009). See Article 20, *caput*, Brazilian Code of Civil Procedure (Law N. 5.869/73).

[23] Some examples: public property, the environment, and the interests of consumers, people with disabilities, children and adolescents. Each of them is provided for in a specific law, such as the Public Civil Action (Article 18, Law N. 7347/85) and the Popular Action (Article 5, LXXIII, Brazilian Constitution).

associations acting as plaintiffs shall not be responsible for paying attorneys' fees and court costs in case they lose the case, unless there is proven bad faith.[24] This rule is justified by the public interest underlying these actions.

As to the Popular Action,[25] costs and initial court costs shall only be paid at the end of the proceedings.[26] In the event the case is upheld, defendants shall pay the costs and other expenses directly related to the process, either judicial or extrajudicial, as well as attorneys' fees.[27] If the claim is held malicious, the plaintiff shall pay the court costs multiplied by ten.[28]

In class actions aimed at protecting the interests of consumers, children and adolescents, claimants are not required to make an up-front payment of fees and court costs. Moreover, they are exempt from the payment of court costs and attorney's fees, except in cases of proven bad faith.[29]

5.6 Exceptions to the Rules Concerning Costs

5.6.1 Indigents

Brazil has a publicly funded legal aid system to serve the people who cannot afford the costs of litigation.[30] Parties are exempt from paying the courts' costs and expenses, as well as the attorneys' fees of the opposing party in the case they lose.[31]

The benefits of legal aid are available to those individuals who really cannot afford the costs of civil procedure without causing damages to themselves or to their family.[32] This condition must be proven during the procedure by means of a declaration included in the plaintiff's initial submission.[33] The judge may also determine that the individual submit tax

---

[24] Article 18, Law N. 7347/85.

[25] Popular Actions may be filed by any citizen to request the annulment or declaration of invalidity of acts detrimental to the assets of the Union, of the Federal District, of the States, of the Municipalities, of the Municipal Entities, etc. (Article 1, Law N. 4717/65).

[26] Article 10, Law N. 4717/65.

[27] Articles 12, Law N. 4717/65.

[28] Articles 13, Law N. 4717/65.

[29] Article 141 §§ 1 and 2, Law N. 8069/90; Article 87, Law N. 8078/90.

[30] Article 5, LXXIV, Brazilian Constitution and Article 2, sole paragraph, Law N. 1.060/50.

[31] Article 3, Law N. 1.060/50.

[32] Article 5, LXXIV, Brazilian Constitution and Article 2, sole paragraph, Law N. 1.060/50.

[33] Article 4, § 1, Law N. 1.060/50.

returns in the process. If it is proven that the plaintiff was not eligible for legal aid, he shall be condemned to pay ten times the courts costs.[34]

5.6.2 Split Outcomes

In line with most of the systems analyzed in the General Report, Brazilian rules handle the issue of split outcomes by examining how much each side won or lost. When the plaintiff's claim is partially rejected, the costs shall be proportionally divided between the parties.[35] If only a minimal part is rejected, the litigant who lost most shall bear the full payment of the court costs.[36]

5.6.3 Settlement

Parties settling disputes by agreement usually decide on the responsibility for court costs, attorney's fees and expenses. If they fail to do that, all costs shall be divided equally between them.[37]

If a party withdraws from her claim or recognizes the rights claimed by the other party, the costs shall be paid by the party withdrawing or recognizing the right. If the withdrawal or recognition is partial, the responsibility for costs and fees will be proportional to the amount that is withdrawn or recognized.[38]

Brazil has no statistics on the percentage of cases resolved by settlement, but practice indicates very low rates. Since it takes many years for a definitive decision to be obtained and enforced, the party in a weaker position often prefers to postpone it. There is an incipient movement to encourage settlement and disseminate the use of alternative dispute resolution in Brazil. In addition, many courts, such as the São Paulo State Court, have been organizing weeks called "National Conciliation Week", when judges across the country are committed to helping the parties to achieve settlements.[39]

---

[34] Article 4, § 1, Law N. 1.060/50.

[35] Article 21, Brazilian Code of Civil Procedure (Law N. 5.869/73).

[36] Article 21, sole paragraph, Brazilian Code of Civil Procedure (Law N. 5.869/73).

[37] Article 26 § 2, Brazilian Code of Civil Procedure (Law N. 5.869/73).

[38] Article 26, *caput* and § 1, Brazilian Code of Civil Procedure (Law N. 5.869/73).

[39] Information on the National Conciliation Week is available at São Paulo State Court's website (www.tj.sp.gov.br).

5.7 Distribution of Civil Litigation Costs

The same publicly funded legal aid system which exempts indigents from courts costs also gives them access to public defenders, i.e., in civil cases, an attorney representing them.[40] Lawyers and law firms also carry out pro bono work for indigent people.

Public-private funded help is also available, such as the program developed by the State of São Paulo with the Brazilian Bar Association. Lawyers interested in helping those in need may register to participate in this program, and the fees are paid by the State of São Paulo based on amounts previously established. Other programs exist throughout the country.

Finally, a party may transfer the right to collect an amount in dispute – together with the risks of the claim – to a third party as long as the assignment follows the legal requirements, including notifying the other party to the dispute, who must consent to the substitution.[41]

Although Brazilian law does not prevent the parties from insuring against the costs of litigation, including attorneys' fees, it is not common practice.

5.8 Conclusion

Costs and fees should not be considered as a serious or severe obstacle to filing an action, in view of the benefits of the publicly funded legal aid, the legal aid programs developed in partnerships between the government and private entities and the freedom of the parties to agree on the amount and form of payment of the attorney's fees. However, it should be noted that most of the people who are entitled to such benefits, especially in the case of natural persons, have no access to such information and therefore do not enjoy its benefits.

In practice, however, parties pursuing their rights before the Brazilian Courts still face many other difficulties, and the constitutional rule commanding access to justice for all still stands as a challenge and an objective to be reached. Brazil's Supreme Court is the most overburdened court in the world.[42] It takes many years for a definitive decision to be obtained and enforced, and sometimes such length is enough to hinder the access to justice. Also, most people who are entitled to the benefits of legal aid have no access to such information and therefore do not enjoy these benefits: lack of proper legal advice and lack of information also exclude several parties.

[40] Article 3, Law N. 1.060/50.

[41] Article 42, § 1, Brazilian Code of Civil Procedure (Law N. 5.869/73).

[42] When less is more; Brazil's supreme court. (Supreme Federal Tribunal), The Economist (US), May 23, 2009.

As to the future, a major reform of the Brazilian Code of Civil Procedure in underway,[43] aiming to reduce the volume of claims pending in the courts and the long duration of the proceedings. Up to now, no major amendments regarding the rules on cost and fee allocation have been presented. However, the Commission in charge of the reform project already stated that it intends to discourage frivolous claims that further increase the case load of the Brazilian courts, and changes to these rules are probably the easiest way to achieve this goal. Given the Commission's aim of improving the Brazilian legal system, it is an important moment to understand the rules governing litigation costs in other systems and analyze what particularities would better fit in the Brazilian system.

[43] The first version of the bill drafted by a commission of legal experts is available at the STJ's website: http://www.stj.gov.br/portal_stj/publicacao/download.wsp?tmp.arquivo=1541.

Chapter 6
The Irrelevance of Costs Rules to Litigation Rates: The Experience of Quebec and Common Law Canada

H. Patrick Glenn

The cost of litigation in Canada is now well beyond the financial means of the vast majority of the population, and Canada therefore joins those other common law jurisdictions in which the courts and the legal profession have been unable to control the inflationary tendencies of adversarial-style procedure. The public service which the courts are intended to provide has thus been rendered largely ineffective by the actors within the system.[1] In this, the Canadian experience is not unique, but the most interesting feature of the Canadian law of costs and fees results from the Quebec experience, which indicates that significant reform cannot be brought about by variation in, or manipulation of, the costs rules operative on conclusion of the litigation. More significant reforms appear called for, though there is no current movement towards the German model of fixed litigation fees (subject to explicit contractual variation). It remains a matter of conjecture whether the adoption of contingent fees and class actions, in all provinces, has provided an effective form of relief against the underlying problem of cost.

Civil procedure in Canada, including the law of costs and fees, is largely provincial in origin and therefore varies from province to province. The law of Quebec shares some basic rules with the common law provinces but is the most distinctive of the Canadian provinces. Since the beginning of the nineteenth century Quebec's civil procedure follows, however, an adversarial model.

1 See the recent criticism by the Chief Justice of Canada, Beverly McLachlin, reported in The Globe and Mail, February 10, 2011 ("If you're the only one who can provide a fundamental social need from which you benefit, I think it follows that you have to provide it").

H. Patrick Glenn (✉)
McGill University, Montreal, QC, Canada
e-mail: patrick.glenn@mcgill.ca

M. Reimann (ed.), *Cost and Fee Allocation in Civil Procedure*,
Ius Gentium: Comparative Perspectives on Law and Justice 11,
DOI 10.1007/978-94-007-2263-7_6, © Springer Science+Business Media B.V. 2012

6.1 The Basic Rule: Who Pays?

While each side in litigation is responsible in principle for the honorarium of their own lawyer, all Canadian jurisdictions follow the "world rule" that costs in principle are "in the cause". The loser pays the amount of costs which are allowable, though the loser's liability is subject to the discretion of the court in appreciating the conduct of the litigation.[2] The costs rule extends to both allowable attorney fees and court costs, though they are separately determined. The "loser pays" rule was received in Canada through reception of French and English law and rests on the traditional justification, that a successful party should not have to bear the cost of establishing their right against an unjust claim or defence. Some maintain that a further justification for the rule would be its deterrent effect on litigation, in the form of the down-side risk of having to cover costs of the other side in addition to one's own costs.

While the rule is that the loser pays, application of the rule varies considerably. In Quebec the loser pays very little, since the tariff of costs payable is maintained at a very low level, making the Quebec situation closer to the "American" rule that each side bears their own costs. This position may also reflect the historic French position that lawyer's fees are not recoverable (*"frais irrépétibles"*). In the common law provinces the winner will recover more than in Quebec, but the amount will vary depending on the level of costs fixed by the court, which may range from full through substantial to only partial indemnity, and by any further element affecting the discretion of the court, e.g., abusive procedure in a winning cause. Costs awards may therefore fill an important disciplinary function.

6.2 The Determination of Payable Costs

Court costs, in the narrow sense, are fixed by Regulation under the relevant statute of the court in question but they are not a significant factor of litigation expense, usually in amounts of only hundreds of dollars in superior court actions, e.g., for filing fees. Lawyers' fees, however, are subject to market forces and there is no statutory or regulatory control of them. Empirically fees vary according to province, rural or urban environment, and large or small firm size. A recent survey gave average hourly fees for a

[2] Art. 477, Quebec Code of Civil Procedure (CCP). The rule appears to be jurisprudential in the common law provinces, and thus constitutes judicial practice in the exercise of the court's discretion in awarding costs, stated statutorily in Ontario in s. 131 of the Ontario *Courts of Justice Act*, R.S.O. 1990, c. 43, as amended ("... the costs ... are in the discretion of the court, and the court may determine by whom and to what extent the costs shall be paid").

lawyer with 10 years' experience of $382 in Ontario and $467 in the western provinces.[3] In Ontario fees are said to range up to $900 per hour. In Quebec a recent survey showed that only 2% of the profession was charging more than $500 per hour, with a further 1% at more than $400.[4]

Costs which are to be shifted between the parties (including court costs, other allowable disbursements and counsel fees) may be fixed either by the presiding judge or by an assessment or "taxing" officer (variously named). Traditionally the presiding judge would give the appropriate costs order (on which, see below), and the taxing officer would hear representations of the parties and fix the actual amount based on proof of the work done, usually in reliance on a fixed tariff of costs which would set out allowable items and rates for them. In recent years, probably because of the size of costs awards, both the awarding and the fixing of costs may be done by the trial judge, at his or her discretion. Appeal is possible both from an order of an assessment officer or from a costs order of a presiding judge, depending on usual criteria for appeal.

It is with respect to the nature of the costs order and the general scale of its amount that the greatest differences exist amongst the provinces. In general three models are discernible.

The first model is that of Quebec, where there is an established tariff of recoverable costs and fees but which has been consciously and deliberately neglected, such that recoverable costs are very low. This removes much of the down-side risk of litigation, and there is a view that this is the main reason for the government's failure to revise the tariff. The Quebec Bar has officially and publicly protested against the lack of revision, but to no avail. Currently the *Tarif des honoraires judiciaires des avocats* allows, for example, for $1,000 in fees recoverable from the other side in the most expensive class of cases (over $50,000) for obtaining a contested judgment on the merits, without regard to the length of the trial. Fifty ($50) is allowed for each contested motion. Since recoverable fees are so low, there are a number of exceptions. Two are provided by the Tariff itself. Article 15 thus allows for a "special honorarium" in an "important" case. This provision has generated a large amount of case law but it is not the case that it has become a general means of subverting the low level of recoverable costs. In *J.T.I. MacDonald Corporation* c. *Procureur Général du Canada* [2009] R.J.Q. 261 Justice Nuss of the Quebec Court of Appeal stated that a requested sum of $90,000 "far exceeds any amount previously granted as a special fee.... This special fee is not meant to be a substitute for extra-judicial fees". A further exception provided by the Tariff itself is found in art. 42, which provides that in cases valued at over $100,000, a further honorarium of 1% on the amount exceeding $100,000 is recoverable. In a

[3] The Canadian Lawyer, June, 2009, p. 33.

[4] Le Journal du Barreau du Québec, May, 2009, p. 32.

case in which $1M is recovered this would provide a further amount in fees of $9,000. Given the obvious limits of the Tariff, efforts have been made to include lawyers' fees in recoverable damages but with only limited success. In *Viel c. Entreprises immobilières du terroir ltée* [2002] R. J. Q. 1262 it was decided that such damages could be awarded only for abuse of process and not as simple compensation for the cost of recovering damages.

The second model is the traditional common law model, which prevails in some provinces outside of Ontario. Here there is a tariff of costs or fees, as in Quebec, which bears a closer relationship to market amounts, and the costs order made by the court will be followed by taxation or verification of precise items before an assessor, a Master or a taxing officer. Depending on the frequency of revision of the Tariff, the recoverable costs here will be significant. They may be made even more significant if the presiding judge orders not simply "party and party" costs, as they are traditionally known, but "solicitor-client" costs which are still higher. Party and party costs are usually estimated at 50–60% of lawyers' actual fees; solicitor-client costs will cover up to 90% of such fees. There is even a further category of "solicitor-own client" fees which requires full compensation of the opposing side's counsel. The type of award varies on the presiding judge's appreciation of the conduct of the litigation. Solicitor-client costs are generally awarded only in cases of "scandalous" or "reprehensible" conduct on behalf of a party.

The final model is that of Ontario, which has recently abandoned the idea of a tariff or "grill" of costs in favour of the presiding judge ruling on costs, generally after submissions by the parties on the complexity of the case, time actually spent, hourly rates and other factors. The assessment may be made on a "partial indemnity", "substantial indemnity" or "full indemnity" basis, which largely corresponds to the prior distinction between party and party costs, solicitor-client costs, and solicitor-own client costs. Here a global amount will be fixed, though a judge may also order a "line-by-line" assessment to be undertaken by a taxing officer. Costs here may be very substantial and the deterrent effect of the common law costs rule is fully evident.

6.3 Taxation of Lawyer Fees

The above discussion relates to the shifting of costs and fees between the parties. It is also the case that the fees owed by a client to his own counsel are subject to some form of control other than through normal litigation. In the common law provinces there is a procedure of "taxation" or assessment of counsel fees, which is available to either client or counsel on simple motion within a case or on its completion. The assessment officer or taxation Master bases the fee award on a range of criteria which include market rates for counsel of similar standing and expertise, time spent on the case, importance of the case, success in the case, and so on. Case law thus develops which is the origin of the notion of "solicitor-client" costs, used when a costs order is made on this basis, in order to substantially compensate a party for their costs. In Quebec there is no procedure for taxation of fees by a court officer but the Quebec Bar offers an arbitration programme under which fee disputes may be resolved, a reflection of the traditional jurisdiction of the *batonnier* in France to resolve fee disputes.

A recent survey of fees charged by lawyers, based on responses given by them, gave as the lawyer's fee for one party for a two day trial in Ontario (with no indication of the amount in question) a minimum of $18,738 and a maximum of $90,404, with an average of $45,477. For both parties combined this would yield fees of:

Minimum: $37,476
Maximum: $180,808
Average: $90,954.

The significant factor appears therefore to be the length of trial as opposed to the amount in question, and the amounts indicated above would indicate a daily lawyer's fee to each party of approximately $22,738, this including preparation time but not disbursements, court costs or expert fees.

6.4 The Financial Burden of Litigation

Parties are allowed to represent themselves and because of the costs of litigation this has become a frequent occurrence, with estimates of up to 30% of cases now involving self-representing parties. This has become a concern of the judiciary given the adversarial nature of proceedings. Counsel is generally required only in cases of representation of a moral person or a person under a disability (see, e.g, CCP, art. 61, Ont. RCP 7).

Given the cost of litigation, parties may ask for provisional or interim costs orders to be made, to allow them to finance their litigation. This is exceptionally granted, e.g., where the plaintiff could not afford the litigation, appeared to have a meritorious claim, and raised issues of public importance; *British Columbia (Minister of Forests) v. Okanagan Indian Band* (2003) 43 C.P.C. (5th) 1. The Quebec Court of Appeal recently refused such an order, however, on the ground that an action against a doctor with respect to a child born prematurely does not raise questions of public interest; *St. Arnaud c. C.L.* [2009] R.J.Q. 239.

Given the financial burden of litigation there has been a significant shift to alternative methods of dispute resolution. Figures are not available for the entire country but the most striking statistics are those of Quebec, where there has been a significant decline in litigation rates, comparable to that which has occurred in the United Kingdom, and paralleling in some measure the phenomenon of the "vanishing trial" in the U.S.A. In Quebec the Superior Court, the high court of first instance, has seen its litigation rate decline from approximately 55,000 new cases per year in 1977 to only some 16,000 in 2007, a decline of some 70%. The decline in the intermediate court of first instance, the Quebec Court, has been nearly as severe, from 96,000 in 1977 to 49,000 in 2007, a decline of 49%.[5] This very sharp decline is the more striking since Quebec's costs rules have been deliberately allowed to move very close to those of the U.S.A., where the general rule that costs are not shifted has historically been justified as promoting litigation through the removal of down side risk. The Quebec experience indicates, however, that, at least where the expense of litigation reaches a certain level, such an accommodating costs rule has no effect in stimulating litigation. A shifting of allowable costs at the end of a court action has little effect in the overall assessment of the financial viability of a lawsuit. Concentration on costs rules in the reform of civil litigation appears ineffective.

6.5 Extraordinary Measures: Success-Oriented Fees, Sale of Claims, Class Actions

These devices have been adopted in all provinces as measures intended to facilitate access to courts.

(i) **Success-Oriented Fees.** Given the cost of litigation, and the fees charged by lawyers, a number of devices have been adopted in an attempt to alleviate the resultant problems. Historically, contingent fees based on a percentage of the amount recovered have been permitted in some provinces since the late nineteenth century and most provinces adopted them in the course of the twentieth century. Ontario was the last to do so in the early years of this century. Quebec has historically prohibited the *pactum in quota litis* for lawyers and this prohibition remains in the Civil Code (art. 1783) but is ignored in practice. Contingent fees are combined with no win-no fee arrangements and are thus properly designated as contingent fees and not conditional fees on the UK model. It is abusive to combine a contingent fee with an agreement to be compensated on a normal basis in the event of loss, though this has been attempted. Contingent fees are subject to restrictions in some provinces, e.g., in Quebec contingent fees have been declared by the courts to be unacceptable in family law cases. There are also caps on the use of contingent fees in certain types of cases, e.g., in British Columbia the maximum percentage in an automobile accident case is 33 1/3%; in other cases of personal injury or death it is 40%. Even where

[5] D. Jutras, "Culture et droit processuel: le cas du Québec" (2009) 54 McGill L. J. 273 at 279.

there are no caps on such fees, however, the client is entitled to taxation of the fee according to the procedure for general taxation of fees discussed above, so there is judicial control on the reasonableness of a contingent fee in the circumstances of the case. In *Walker* v. *Ritchie* [2006] 2 S.C.R. 428 the Supreme Court of Canada decided that a "risk premium" was not payable by the losing defendant when plaintiff's counsel was acting on a contingency basis.

Contingent fees are less frequent in Canada than in the United States, however. There are few if any civil juries in Canada (they are precluded in Quebec); medical costs are entirely covered by the public Canadian health care system; and there are few punitive damages awards. Some reluctance towards contingent fees may also be generated by the costs shifting rule. If counsel has agreed that the plaintiff client is to be free of all cost, and costs are awarded against the losing plaintiff, who is liable to pay those costs? Lawyers who have paid them have been allowed to deduct them as an expense for income tax purposes and this potential liability to the other side may deter some lawyer use of contingent fees. There appears to be no "after the event" insurance developed in Canada, as in the U.K., to cover the possibility of an adverse costs award in the case of a suit brought on a contingency fee basis.

(ii) **Sale of Claims.** Common law jurisdictions have been historically adverse to assignment of claims though as a matter of general law the more permissive attitude of equity came to prevail. French civil law in contrast has historically been very open. Where the assignment is for a litigious claim, however, there remain particular limitations which are those of champerty and maintenance in the common law provinces and the "*retrait litigieux*" (litigious redemption) in Quebec.

At common law it was tortious to maintain the lawsuit of another by providing financial assistance (maintenance) or by doing so and taking a part of the proceeds of the litigation (champerty). These torts are still alive today though they no longer apply to the lawyer acting on a contingent fee. They remain applicable to third persons, though it is now the case that maintenance and champerty can be justified if there is a valid business purpose to the assignment or the assignee has some pre-existing financial interest in the enforcement of the claim. A garage selling automobiles might thus sue for the damages of its clients when the warranty company which the garage has recommended fails to honour the terms of the warranty of the vehicles sold. In the absence of such an interest, however, a third-party stirring up litigation for its own profit may be guilty of champerty and may even be found liable for solicitor-client costs against a winning defendant; *Smith* v. *Canadian Tire Acceptance Ltd.* (1995) 36 C.P.C.(3d) 175. There are firms advertising their willingness to financially support litigation for a share of the proceeds (Lexfund, BridgePoint Financial Services) but the practice does not appear to be widespread in Canada. The shadow of maintenance and champerty falls across such practices, and ethical objections have been raised that third-party financing is inconsistent with the lawyer's ethical obligation being owed uniquely to the client.[6]

In Quebec there has historically been no objection to the sale of litigious rights (except in the case of sale to lawyers), reflecting the open attitude of French civil law. There are no torts of maintenance or champerty in Quebec. A remedy against Pothier's "*odieux acheteur de créances*" is found however in article 1748 of the Quebec Civil Code (the litigious redemption) which allows the debtor to discharge the debt by paying to the purchaser of the litigious right the amount of the sale plus any costs of the sale and interest. This in itself may deter third-party financers.

(iii) **Class Actions.** Class actions have brought about particular rules for their financing. All Canadian provinces now allow class actions but there is considerable diversity with respect to the costs and fees which they generate.

Quebec has been described as the "paradise" of class action funding, since the Quebec government established and annually funds a Class Action Fund for the purpose of financing class actions. The Fund was felt necessary because of the costs of litigation and the risk of losing class representatives being held liable for (even low) costs awards. In the result, a class representative (in reality the lawyer acting for such a representative) may apply for funding to cover court costs and lawyer and expert fees, while the Fund will assume liability for any eventual costs award in the event the class action is rejected. Ontario has also established a Class Action Fund but without government financing. The resources of the Fund are drawn from the interest on lawyers' trust accounts. The Ontario Fund does not cover lawyers' fees or eventual costs awards, and costs awards have been made against unsuccessful class representatives in Ontario.

Other provinces have provided no institutional means of funding of class actions and have either prohibited the awarding of costs in class actions, though subject always to the court's discretion (British Columbia) or simply allowed the usual costs rule to stand (Alberta). In the latter case in particular the costs rule may constitute a considerable deterrent to class actions.

6.6 Conclusion

It appears impossible to conclude that the extraordinary devices of contingent fees, sale of claims, class actions, and litigation insurance have compensated for the financial burden of litigation. These devices have been

[6] P. Fuchs, "Innovation or Interference? Third-party litigation funding offers access to justice – but is the ethical price too high?" The National, Oct–Nov 2008 at 49.

less widespread than in the U.S.A., for the reasons indicated above. In both the U.S.A. and Canada they have been considered necessary, and rejection of significant costs-shifting in the U.S.A. and Quebec has been unable to offset significant declines in litigation rates. It is paradoxical that such solutions to the costs of litigation have been ones which allow lawyers to charge still higher fees.

Chapter 7
The Double Face of Cost and Fee Allocation in the Czech Republic

Jan Hurdík

7.1 Access to Justice as the General Goal of the Legislator

Access to justice – in compliance with international and European conventions on human rights – is one of the basic rights guaranteed by the Czech constitutional order. Thus one might suppose that this basic right will be applied consistently in the legal order and also in practice, particularly in court practice. Yet, one of the key preconditions of equal access to justice is the ability to pay for participating in court proceedings (court costs) and effective representation (attorneys' fees). It does the Czech lawmakers credit that they strive persistently to ensure an equal access to justice, and that they view the reimbursement and payment of procedural costs as based on that fundamental right. But in their efforts they have come across opposing interests that appear in legislation as well as in civil courts that often make achieving meaningful access difficult. This results in inconsistency and in contradictory solutions, raising doubts whether access to justice is really equal and without substantial barriers due to financial means.

7.2 The Pre-Velvet Revolution Foundations of the Current Regime

The existing legal regulation of cost and fee allocation in civil cases in the Czech Republic is still based on a conception coming from the time before the Velvet Revolution, i.e., before 1989. Consequently, the legal framework of Czech regulation is significantly socially determined, and if reflects a time when lawsuits were low both in number and value. Historically, this small number of low-value cases corresponded with a relatively low amount

J. Hurdík (✉)
Masaryk University, Brno, Czech Republic
e-mail: jan.hurdik@law.muni.cz

M. Reimann (ed.), *Cost and Fee Allocation in Civil Procedure*,
Ius Gentium: Comparative Perspectives on Law and Justice 11,
DOI 10.1007/978-94-007-2263-7_7, © Springer Science+Business Media B.V. 2012

of up-front court costs. Advocates' services, too, were relatively affordable in relation to average wages in former Czechoslovakia. This was due in part to legally fixed advocates' tariffs and – in cities with courts – due to the local legal aid bureau's system of allocating cases. By contrast, the current situation of cost and fee allocation in the Czech Republic presents a different and more complicated picture: on the one hand we can see a socially determined striving for access to justice, and on the other hand, the practical application of principles and rules of cost and fee allocation reveal some aspects that conflict with this underlying policy.

7.3 General Rules on Cost and Fee Allocation

In Czech law, the court will order the unsuccessful party to reimburse the party that has fully succeeded for the costs needed to effectively enforce or defend his or her rights ("loser pays"). The court fee, as part of the parties' cash expenses, and the costs of legal representation (attorney fees and notary fees are determined by a special legal regulation) are integral parts of procedure costs, and must therefore be borne by the loser as well. As a result, the court returns to a successful plaintiff the costs he spent on an effective enforcement of his rights. In the case of a successful defendant, the court awards reimbursement of the costs she spent on her defense. As far as attorney fees are concerned, however, cost shifting is limited to the amount provided for by an official schedule which may be lower than the fee agreed upon between attorney and client.

This brings us to the question whether all of the winner's costs and fees are reimbursed or just a part of them (e.g. a reasonable amount). An unsuccessful party is obliged to pay the successful party reimbursement of the costs needed for a meaningful application or protection of law. The costs that can be awarded must thus meet the requirement of meaningfulness. If the party has only been partly successful the court proportionally divides reimbursement of the costs between the parties, or it may state that neither is entitled to reimbursement. However, even if the party has only succeeded partly, the court may award full reimbursement of his costs if he only failed in a minute part of the case or if the decision about the amount of payment depended on an expert opinion or was at the court's discretion.

Generally, the same rules apply to appeals, i.e., when making a cost determination on appeal, the court will use the same procedural regulations as the court of first instance. If the appellate court changes the decision of the court of first instance, it will include in the cost determination the costs of the appellate procedure as well. If the appellate court overturns the decision of the court of the first instance, returning the case to the lower court or referring the case to a court with proper subject-matter jurisdiction, then reimbursement of the costs of appeal will be newly decided by the court of first instance.

The cost of evidence, including the witness fee, is included in the procedure costs as well. The witness fee consists of reimbursement for the witness's cash expenses and loss of earnings. The interpreter's fee, the expert witness fee, and the witness fee are paid by the state immediately after they have been incurred. Depending on the result of the procedure, the state is entitled to reimbursement of the procedure costs it paid, provided the parties are not exempt from court costs. Costs of this type play a major part in the amount of procedure costs, especially as far as expert witness fees are concerned.

If the civil suit is settled, neither party is entitled to reimbursement of procedure costs unless the settlement agreement states otherwise. Therefore if the parties do not agree on reimbursement of procedure costs in their settlement, when approving the settlement, the court will decide that neither party is entitled to reimbursement of procedure costs. An appeal against that decision is admissible. We don't know the percentage of civil suits settled in this way because there are no official or unofficial data on that matter.

7.4 Legal Aid

There is a publicly funded legal aid system provided by Czech civil procedure.

In addition to attorneys, state-financed civic advisory bureaus give free legal aid to litigants. At present, the Czech Bar has also started a program of free legal aid provided by its members. As for procedure costs and exemptions, there are several relevant provisions in the most important civil procedure regulation, the Civil Procedure Code.

(1) Exemption from Court Fees.

At a party's motion, the presiding judge of the bench deciding the case may grant the party either a complete or a partial exemption from court costs, provided that it is justified by the party's situation and that the suit is not wanton or obviously non-meritorious. (Section 138, Civil Procedure Code). The Act on Court Fees then distinguishes material, personal, and individual exemptions. Material exemptions apply to an enumerated list of cases – e.g. those concerning guardianship, judicial care of minors, mutual maintenance duty of parents and children, probate proceedings in the first instance, etc. As for the court fee, there is a rule that if the plaintiff is exempt from the fee and the court thus grants the motion, it is the defendant who pays the fee or a portion of it. Of course, the defendant is only required to pay the fee if he himself is not exempt from the court fee and does not have any right to reimbursement of procedure costs against the plaintiff.

(2) Appointing a Legal Representative.

If a legal representative is appointed for a party that is exempt from court fees, the exemption includes cash expenses and the fee for representation to the extent of the exemption granted (Section 138, Para 3, Civil Procedure Code). Furthermore, the cash expenses and the fee for representation are paid by the state (and also reimbursement of the value added tax if needed). The state may also provide the attorney with an appropriate payment in advance if it is justified (Section 140, Para 2). If an attorney is appointed for a party, the person who is obliged to pay procedure costs will also have to reimburse the state for the attorney's cash expenses and representation fee.

Personal exemption is the exemption of certain entities – e.g. the Czech Republic and state funds, territorial self-governing units if the dispute concerns execution of the state administration, or the plaintiff in workers compensation proceedings. Courts grant exemption on a case-by-case basis upon the motion of a party, which may be submitted at the institution of the suit or anytime until judgment is final. If the plaintiff is exempt from the court fee, this fee or its proportional part is paid according to the result of the proceedings by the defendant unless he is entitled to reimbursement of procedure costs against the plaintiff or unless he is also exempt.

(3) Privately Organized Help.

There are of course various private organizations providing legal help which litigants may consult. First, there are attorneys or notaries that provide their services principally for payment – either on the basis of a contract with the client or according to the official attorneys' tariff. However, at present there is free legal consulting provided by attorneys registered with the Czech Bar as well. It is also possible for individuals to take advantage of various legal advisory bureaus. Free legal advice is available at the so-called free civic advisory bureaus, which are non-governmental organizations providing independent, impartial and free social advice. Their target group is mainly people in a difficult financial situation but in practice anyone may address these bureaus because they do not check an applicant's financial situation. Civic advisory bureaus also provide legal aid in the form of legal advice or they may help applicants draw up petitions, etc.

(4) General (Legal) Availability of Legal Aid to All Parties in Need.

Legal aid provided by free civic advisory bureaus seems to be generally available to everyone as explained above. As for reimbursement of civil procedure costs, as mentioned, the court may exempt a party from court fees if it is justified by his situation (mainly social and financial factors) and it is not a wanton or evidently unsuccessful lawsuit. The court may take into account a party's financial situation at its discretion, which enables individual consideration of all circumstances of the case. However, when deciding to exempt a party from paying court fees, the court must not simply take into account the financial situation of the applicant; it must also consider the reason for which the exemption is sought, i.e. in particular, the amount of the court fee or the amount of the expected procedure costs.

Section 150 of the Civil Procedure Code constitutes a potential corrective of the general rule of reimbursement of civil procedure costs. Pursuant to that section, the court may make an exception and not award partial or complete reimbursement of costs in specific circumstances. The court's decision that a given case is exceptional and that specific circumstances apply must be based on an examination of all aspects of a case. This is not as arbitrary as it may sound because it requires a careful consideration of all decisive factors. When examining specific reasons, the court takes into account financial, social, personal and other circumstances of all parties to the proceedings. It is necessary to consider not only the circumstances of the person who should pay procedure costs but also how such a decision would affect the injured party's financial situation in particular. It is also important to take into account the reasons why a claim has been asserted and even the conduct of the parties during the proceedings.

(5) Litigation costs and fees as barriers to access to justice.

The willingness to bear procedural costs – or the risk of bearing them – is an expression of a genuine intention to litigate. Court fees as well as attorney's fees are calculated based on the amount for which the suit is filed. Access to justice is available even to the poorest strata of the population due to the introduction of the previously mentioned provisions: exemption from court fees, appointment of counsel, reimbursement of representation costs and cash expenses by the state, and special exceptions to costs shifting even with regard to the winner's attorney fees. Nevertheless, litigation costs can be a barrier to bringing certain kinds of actions, e.g., because the amount in controversy is too low to make litigation economically feasible. It all depends, of course, on whether the petitioner is willing to pay the necessary costs of procedure resulting from the amount for which he is litigating. For example, if a party is litigating for performance with a monetary value of 2,000 CZK, the court fee is 600 CZK and the attorney's fee – if the party wants to be represented – is 6,000 CZK (without VAT). In such a situation, litigation appears to be economically utterly useless, especially if there is a serious risk of losing the case.

7.5 Law on the Books v. Law in Action

One can say that the Czech legal system by and large respects and realizes the constitutional principle of access to justice:

(a) There are two opportunities (pursuant to the Civil Procedure Code and the Bar Rules – see above) to obtain free legal aid in justified cases.
(b) The Czech legal order allows an exemption from court taxes (fees) in justified cases.
(c) The amount of the attorney's fees is basically determined by the Bar Rules.
(d) The final reimbursement of (all) costs is basically (with some exceptions) decided in favor of the winner.

This system is evidently oriented toward ensuring broad access to justice.

Yet, in real life, we witness a slightly different development that presents an obstacle to the realization of access to justice:

(a) In reality, the principle under which the loser always pays all costs is compromised by an insufficient degree of effectiveness and predictability of the functioning of the judiciary. The Czech legislature is presently developing private substantive law through a complete re-codification of the existing civil, family and commercial codes. In addition, the legislature has had to modify civil procedure law in reaction to the new forms of substantive law. At the same time, due to the "Europeanization" of court practice (among other things), the real practice of Czech courts changes when the existing standards of decision-making are changed. Such a situation diminishes the predictability and stability of judicial decision-making. The resulting uncertainty makes the loser-pays rule harder to justify and, more generally, weakens actual access to justice by discouraging people from litigating their rights.
(b) There is also an increasingly visible conflict between access to justice as a basic right as an object of the public interest (public policy) and its implementation through legal aid when it is carried out by private business. The influence of private business turns out to increase.
This development has some serious practical consequences. While court practice relating to the allocation of costs and fees basically continues without change, the behavior of private businesses is increasingly more influenced by economic liberalism – private lawyers try all the time to increase their profits. Consequently, application of cost and fee allocations rules is undergoing several changes:

- First, there has been a marked increase of the attorney fees charged in the contract between client and lawyer, especially in big cities.

Some attorneys charge clients thousands of Czech crowns, i.e., hundreds of US dollars, for a one-hour legal consultation. This amount cannot be compensated in the case of successful litigation because courts may award the winner reimbursement of the costs of the attorney's representation only up to the lump sum calculated on the basis of standard fees set forth in the attorney's tariff.

- Second, and as a result, there has been an increase in the disparity between contract attorneys' fees in big cities and in the country. In the country, a class of "meadow lawyers" (i.e., less affluent counsel) has reappeared, often because of the need for social aid. Legal aid provided by urban attorneys can be far more expensive than legal aid provided by their rural colleagues, i.e., "meadow lawyers". There is no corresponding difference in the quality of legal aid provided by these two groups.
- Third, there is a problem with some attorneys receiving double fees: when the court adjudicates reimbursement of costs to the winner, many attorneys consider the reimbursement to be their own bonus even if they have been already paid by their clients. Agreements between the attorney and client often lack a clear agreement preventing this problem.

(c) Recently, part of the adjudication process in civil cases has also been transferred to the area where both principles operate: private enterprise and public service. An example is transferring part of the judgment enforcement to the hands of private such as debt collection agencies which have their own economic interests or, pursuant to a special act (No 216/1994 Coll.), to arbitration procedures, which have been increasingly dominated by the private and special interests of the big players in the market.

These are only some examples illustrating the conflict between the public (legal) basis of the principle of access to justice and the private way of ensuring it. The Czech approach to civil litigation costs, and of access to justice, is thus Janus-faced.

7.6 Conclusions

Unfortunately, many of the facts mentioned in this paper cannot be sufficiently supported by a set of official statistical data. In Czech civil procedure, the possibility of collecting statistical data about payment and reimbursement of procedure costs is restricted because procedure costs and their reimbursement are decided independently by courts of the first and second instances and because an appeal of a reimbursement decision is not admissible. Thus the Supreme Court (where most statistical evaluations are made) does not have such data at its disposal. For this reason no complete statistics are available. In our view, the justice department's approach evidences a lack of interest in relevant knowledge of financial limits of access to justice or in a more consistent regulation of its functioning.

Chapter 8
Cost Wars in England and Wales: The Insurers Strike Back

Richard Moorhead

8.1 Introduction

Whilst characterised as a "loser pays" system, cost rules for litigation in England and Wales have, in recent years, become much more complicated than that. Separate from the other British systems in Scotland and Northern Ireland, which have their own characteristics, the last decade and a half has been the age of the Cost Wars, an end to which is not in sight.

In sketching this history, the chapter concentrates on personal injury claims as the predominant form of civil litigation and also the one over which most controversy has raged (other than libel litigation where the media has been adjutant in its own cause).

8.2 Pre-1995 Legal Aid, Hourly Fees and Subterranean "Speccing"

Up until the mid-90s, clients with personal injury claims had two main options for funding a lawyer if they were not members of a trade union. They could pay a lawyer themselves on an hourly fee basis or they could seek legal aid for their claims. It is worth dwelling for a moment on what legal aid meant for the lawyer and the client. This serves as a frame of reference for what has subsequently happened (with some of the reforms seeking to create a system of legal aid funded by insurers rather than by the State[1]). It is also important because, in broad terms, this system remains

[1] R. Moorhead, 'CFAs: A Weightless Reform of Legal Aid?', Northern Ireland Law Quarterly, 53 (2) (2002) 153–166.

R. Moorhead (✉)
Cardiff University, Wales, UK
e-mail: moorheadr@cardiff.ac.uk

M. Reimann (ed.), *Cost and Fee Allocation in Civil Procedure*, 117
Ius Gentium: Comparative Perspectives on Law and Justice 11,
DOI 10.1007/978-94-007-2263-7_8, © Springer Science+Business Media B.V. 2012

in place for about 50% of medical negligence claims (though current indications are that the Government will remove these cases from legal aid too).

Under the legal aid scheme, cases are (or were) assessed on their merits and also the client's income and capital. Clients might be asked to make a contribution out of income or capital but otherwise were protected from paying their own lawyer's costs. They would also, save in exceptional circumstances, be protected from having to pay their opponent's costs. That is, they were granted protection from the normal rule in personal injury litigation that the loser pay the winner's costs.

If the client's case was lost, the lawyer was paid by the legal aid fund, usually at the end of the case, on "legal aid rates". These were significantly below private practice rates (about a half to one third of private rates would give a broad indication of the difference). If the client won the case (at trial or through settlement), the lawyer could claim their costs from the opponent at private rates. This meant that for the lawyer, winning was significantly more profitable than losing. There was a degree of payment by results and costs were shifted one way, from claimant lawyer to defendant insurer.

Defendants (which usually meant insurers) tended to claim that legal aid was a blank cheque, which meant that the claimant was under no pressure to settle. Weak cases could be brought to extort nuisance settlements from defendants who would never get their costs back because of the protection provided against cost recovery by the legal aid certificate. There was the potential to claim against the legal aid fund, but this was possible only in rather limited circumstances and not much used. Similarly, because lawyers were getting paid anyway, and were being paid on an hourly basis under both schemes, they had every incentive (defendants said) to rack up as many hours as possible and the system, it was said, was too expensive as a result.[2]

In the late 1980s, legal aid had covered extensive sections of the community – as many as 75% of households – but by the mid-1900s, it had begun to decline towards covering about half the population. A debate about the needs of MINoLAs (middle-income no-access to legal aid) began. Similarly, the (then Conservative) Government began to express concern about the sustainability of the legal aid scheme. Those who did not qualify for legal aid had the unappetising prospect of paying privately on an hourly rate basis although it was widely reported that practitioners were willing to take cases on a "speculative" basis, particularly if those cases were racing certainties for success: solicitors would tell clients they did not need to worry about paying their fees if they lost, because they would not lose, and would claim the fees from their opponents if they won. Arguably in breach of

[2] Some support for the proposition was found here: G. Bevan, 'Has There Been Supplier-Induced Demand for Legal Aid?', Civil Justice Quarterly, 5 (1996) 98.

professional conduct rules, the practice became known as speccing (because the fee was a speculative one, dependent on winning). Yet, clients did not have the benefit of cost protection should they lose. Those who supported speccing were unperturbed by that.

8.3 1995–2000

After a quite turbulent debate, with particular resistance coming from barristers and the judiciary, the government reversed the legal system's longstanding hostility to contingent fee agreements. As a result, CFAs have been permitted since 1995 for personal injury, insolvency, and human rights cases, and since 2000 in most areas of litigation other than family and criminal. Partly to sidestep concerns about "the American problem", the introduced Conditional Fee Agreements (CFAs) were deliberately distinct from US-style damages-based agreements where a lawyer is paid a fee as a percentage of the client's damages.[3]

These "English" no win no fee agreements generally operate on the basis that lawyers get paid nothing if they lose but their normal fee (often called the base costs) plus a percentage of that same fee (the uplift or success fee) if they win. That "normal fee" would usually be calculated on an hourly basis (though lower value personal injury cases are increasingly falling under state-sponsored fixed fee regimes set after industry wide negotiation, see below).

Pre-2000 CFAs were introduced to supplement, not replace, legal aid. Lawyers were allowed to claim a success fee of up to 100% of their normal rate. If they won the case, the normal fee would be payable by the unsuccessful opponent. The success fee would be payable by the client out of their damages. That fee was subject to a voluntary cap, set by the Law Society, of 25% of the client's damages. If they lost the case, the lawyer would not be paid at all. The opponent, however, could then claim their costs from the unsuccessful claimant. To protect the claimant in such circumstances, after the event insurance (ATE) was developed. The premium for such insurance could be paid for by the client or their lawyer but it could not be claimed from the opponent.

8.4 Post 2000 to Date

The Access to Justice Act 1999 led to the current scheme of *recoverable* conditional fees. The background to the changes lay in the removal of most personal injury claims from the legal aid scheme. This was part of

[3] See, R. Moorhead, 'An American Future? Contingency Fees, Claims Explosions and Evidence from Employment Tribunals', Modern Law Review, 73 (5) (2010) 752–784.

a package seeking to contain legal aid budgets. Estimates varied but around £30–50m was spent supporting personal injury claims per annum.[4] One of the reasons the reform proposals were criticised was that this sum of money supported a much larger body of casework (because winning cases were funded by opponents, the £30–50 million was only spent on the losing cases but enabled the winning cases to be brought). A second reason was that the (then) Labour government was reneging on the previous Government's promise that CFAs were not a replacement for legal aid. A third reason was the view that asking the kinds of poorer clients, who would originally have been funded under legal aid, to pay insurance premiums either up front or out of their damages was untenable or inequitable. Similarly, to ask them to fund success fees out of their damages was in breach of the principle of full compensation. This principle had, of course, been breached in fact already by the 1995 reform, but the breach was given extra weight by the importance of every pound of compensation to low income claimants. The result of all this debate was that in 1999, significant changes were made to the CFA regime, apparently in some haste.[5] Most importantly, in order alleviate concerns about undercompensation of claimants, both success fees and the ATE insurance premiums became recoverable from unsuccessful opponents.

For claimants, and their lawyers, the impact of these reforms was positive. Insurance companies developed ATE insurance products where the insurance premium was only payable if the claimant won their case. As a result, claimants did not need to meet the insurance costs if they lost cases, and their opponents paid those premiums when the claimants won (as they usually did). Clients were similarly unaffected by the level of the insurance premium. Furthermore, the uplift on a lawyer's base costs could be set without the client ever being likely to pay the uplift itself. If claimants lost the case, they did not pay, and if they won the case their opponent paid both the base and success fee. Understandably, defendants were concerned that there was no market pressure exerted by clients to push down on insurance premiums, although research on the way the pre-2000 scheme worked suggested that clients did not understand these costs even when they were imposed upon them – which called into question the extent to which clients *could* exert pressure on such fees.[6] Success fees were similarly set without

[4] The costs savings to the Legal Aid Fund of removing all personal injury cases from the legal aid scheme were originally estimated as being in the region of £37 million. Parliamentary answer, Geoff Hoon MP, Minister of State LCD (2nd February 1999). See, (1999) 1 Litigation Funding 12.

[5] There are possibly apocryphal stories about a senior Minister agreeing the idea in the back of a taxi cab.

[6] S. Yarrow and P. Abrams, 'Nothing to Lose: Clients' Experiences of Using Conditional Fees' (London: University of Westminster, 1999); S. Yarrow, 'Just Rewards: The Outcome of Conditional Fee Cases' (London: University of Westminster, 2000).

the client needing to worry about paying them. As mentioned previously, a statute limited the maximum success fee to 100% of the normal fee. The basis for allowing a 100% uplift was that it would allow lawyers to take on cases approaching a 50:50 chance of success on a basis that reflected their risk. At the time the test was brought in, this mirrored the legal aid test.

Defendants criticised the recoverable fee as riskless to the client. They either side-stepped the important point that the risk was borne by the lawyers[7] or suggested that lawyers bore minimal risk because they only cherry-picked the easier cases. Somewhat counter to that, they encouraged press concerns about a compensation culture that prompted too many claims and, sometimes in the alternative, too many spurious claims. The idea of a compensation culture did not bear academic scrutiny[8] but was twice addressed officially – once under the Labour Government and once under the Conservative-led Coalition[9]; both identified the idea of a compensation culture as imagined rather than real but also felt that the *perception* of a compensation culture made individuals, local authorities and businesses unnecessarily risk-averse. In other words, an imagined phenomenon had real effects. That feeling was fed by the portrayal of lawyers as (suddenly more) motivated by a financial interest because they could now get paid by results. This was coupled with a rise in TV advertising by solicitors and a new breed of claims management companies who did not need to practice as lawyers (and who were only belatedly subject to regulation[10]).

Against the more media-friendly compensation culture debate, a more significant battle was being waged on the minutiae of costs. Under the old systems of legal aid and then non-recoverable CFAs, defendants had, as mentioned, expressed concerns that claimants were under insufficient incentives to restrain the amount of time spent on cases. Claimants in turn blamed this on inappropriate defence tactics (borne out, in part, by what

[7] Claimant lawyers that lose cases invest their time and, not uncommonly, the cost of the disbursements (expenses) on their cases.

[8] A. Morris, 'Spiralling or Stabilising? The "Compensation Culture" and our Propensity to Claim Damages for Personal Injury', Modern Law Review, 70 (3) (2007) 349–378; R. Lewis, A. Morris and K. Oliphant, 'Tort Personal Injury Claims Statistics: Is There a Compensation Culture in the United Kingdom?', Journal of Insurance Research and Practice, 21 (2) (2006) 5–12.

[9] See, Department of Constitutional Affairs (2004) 'Tackling the "Compensation Culture" Government Response to the Better Regulation Task Force Report: "Better Routes to Redress"' (London: DCA); Young (2011) 'Common Sense Common Safety: A report by Lord Young of Graffham to the Prime Minister following a Whitehallwide review of the operation of health and safety laws and the growth of the compensation culture' (London: HM Government) http://www.number10.gov.uk/wp-content/uploads/402906_CommonSense_acc.pdf, last downloaded 24th May 2011.

[10] Established under the Compensation Act of 2006.

little academic research there had been in the area).[11] Control of costs was dealt with by agreement between the parties or through judicial assessment (often by specialist judges known as taxing masters). There were rules designed to shift the burden of proof between the parties in relation to who paid what, but judges struggled to control costs on a case by case basis when presented with schedules of work which were difficult to critique on a line by line basis.

The problem was magnified significantly when costs-shifting applied to insurance premiums and success fees. Getting the level of these fees right was a matter of significant importance. Squeeze the fees too tightly and access to justice would be diminished; fail to squeeze sufficiently hard and claimant lawyers and insurance companies could garner unjustifiably large profits.[12] There was generally an absence of data to gauge which was more likely. Client protection rules (there to protect the claimant) and the indemnity principle[13] were used by defendants as bases of challenge to recoverability. For a time, large numbers of settled cases mounted up and remained unpaid because of open costs challenges.

The Courts did what they could to deal with the costs litigation. Claimant firms regarded the challenges as politically motivated and commercially damaging but also (for some claimant firms at least) the costs litigation was a source of extra profit. Time spent defending unsuccessful cost challenges was itself recoverable (and potentially uplift-able). Defendants nevertheless continued to lobby against the principle that claimants could litigate costlessly and suggested that claimant lawyers were profiteering.

With the costs war in full flow, the Civil Justice Council (a body chaired by the senior civil Court of Appeal judge, the Master of the Rolls, and bringing together the judiciary, practitioners, insurers, academics, and others[14]) hosted various "Big Tent" costs events to bring together the major stakeholders to negotiate industry-wide agreements on elements of the costs problems. Progress was partial but not insignificant. The Council's work led to the kind of approach now embodied in the predictable costs scheme established under Part 45 of the Civil Procedure Rules (CPR).[15] These rules

[11] H. Genn (1988) 'Hard Bargaining: Out of Court Settlement in Personal Injury Actions' (Oxford: Clarendon).

[12] Lord Hoffman recognised the essential problem in *Callery v Gray* [2002] UKHL 28.

[13] The indemnity principle is the rule that a solicitor may not recover from an opponent any costs that he could not recover from the client; this retained some purchase in spite of the fundamental nature of CFAs.

[14] The author is a former member.

[15] The rules can be found at http://www.justice.gov.uk/guidance/courts-and-tribunals/courts/procedure-rules/civil/contents/parts/part45.htm#IDAE5SIC, last downloaded 24th May 2011. For a fuller discussion see, C. McIvor (2011) Jackson and Access to Justice in Oliphant et al (2011) *On A Slippery Slope – A Response To The Jackson Report* (London: Thomsons Solicitors).

provide for the base costs (that is the costs normally established by means of the hourly rate which have been recoverable under all the schemes discussed above) to be fixed in low value road traffic accident (RTA) claims (which make up the bulk of personal injury claims) by reference to a modest percentage of the value of the claim plus a specified amount (£800 in RTA personal injury claims under £10,000 in value). These rules also set the success fees that can generally be recovered for road traffic accidents, employers' liability claims, and employers' liability disease claims (ELD) where claims settle before issue and the success fee if they go to trial. In relation to RTA claims, a fixed solicitor success fee of just 12.5% applies to cases which are settled before trial, for example. The figures were negotiated on the basis that research suggested they were "revenue neutral" (that is, uplifts at this level covered the risk that solicitors took in on cases they lost but did not lead to additional profit).[16] More recently a portal has been introduced to speed up the handling of such claims "by providing a secure medium for the electronic transfer between Claimant Representatives and Defendant Insurer/Compensators of the information necessary to process claims by individuals for personal injury following a road traffic accident."[17] Costs are also fixed in relation to stages within the portal.

The then Master of the Rolls (now Lord Clarke) was frustrated by the Government's slow progress on civil litigation reform and thus appointed Sir Rupert Jackson, a then newly-appointed Court of Appeal judge, to review the costs system. Lord Justice Jackson set about his task with exceptional alacrity producing two encyclopaedic volumes by way of interim reports and then a final report containing a raft of recommendations for reform of the current systems.[18] Whilst his proposals are controversial with claimant lawyers, as are parts of his evidence base –unsurprisingly given the time and resources within which he had to work – the reports are likely to stand as seminal work on the domestic costs regimes for some time. In broad terms, they suggest a return to the position in the late 1990s with some modification. Current indications are that Lord Justice Jackson's 109 recommendations have broadly been accepted by the

---

[16] P. Fenn and N. Rickman (2003), P. Fenn (2003), 'Calculating "Reasonable" Success Fees for RTA Claims', (London: Civil Justice Council) and (2004) 'Calculating "Reasonable" Success Fees for Employers' Liability Claims' (London: Civil Justice Council).

[17] Taken from the portal's website: (http://www.rtapiclaimsprocess.org.uk/how_portal_works.html), 24th May 2011.

[18] R. Jackson LJ, 'Review of Civil Litigation Costs: Final Report' (London: Judiciary of England and Wales, 2010) and R. Jackson LJ, 'Civil Litigation Costs Review – Preliminary Report by Lord Justice Jackson' (London: Judiciary of England and Wales, 2009).

Government,[19] whilst remaining hotly disputed, particularly by claimant lawyers. The recommendations include:

- The recoverability of success fees and ATE insurance premiums would be abolished.
- Those costs would be payable by the claimant, effectively out of their award, and would be capped at 25% of the damages.
- A 10% increase in general damages (damages for pain, suffering and loss of amenity) to compensate for claimants' losses due to success fees that would be payable by them.
- "Part 36" arrangements (offers to settle) would be strengthened which would increase the penalties for failing to accept reasonable offers to settle.
- Qualified one way costs shifting (QOCS) would be introduced to remove, or significantly weaken, the need for ATE insurance. Claimants would be expected to pay costs only where their behaviour in bringing a claim merited it (e.g., very weak claims or claims pursued unreasonably might be subject to attack) or where their own means meant they could afford to meet the costs.
- Of final interest here is the proposal to bring in Ontario-style contingency fees. Under such agreements, the client would agree a percentage fee with his or her lawyer, who (if successful) would seek to recover their normal (hourly or fixed) costs from their opponent; "in so far as the contingency fee exceeds what would be chargeable under a normal fee agreement, that is borne by the successful litigant."[20]

The government has been consulting on these proposals, having broadly indicated support for them. An announcement on the outcome of that consultation is expected at the time of writing. Opponents of the reform have tended to concentrate on the extent to which such reforms undermine the principle of full compensation and also on the risk that limiting success fees to 25% of compensation will significantly inhibit access to justice for cases where the risks and costs cannot be financially supported by a 25% success fee. Such a wide-ranging attempt at one way costs shifting has not been attempted. Insurers might be expected to continue to rely on, and to propagate through the media, folksy arguments about the unfairness of only one side having to pay the costs and to continue to fight cost shifting orders through the courts where they can and where it is in their commercial interests to do so. That the system has shifted back towards the

[19] Ministry of Justice (2011) 'Proposals for Reform of Civil Litigation Funding and Costs in England and Wales Implementation of Lord Justice Jackson's Recommendations' (London: Ministry of Justice).

[20] Jackson, n 18 above, p. 131 of the Final Report.

interests of liability insurers means that the field of battle has narrowed but the war may not have ended. The introduction of Ontario-style contingency fees, which are only marginally different from what will almost certainly be non-recoverable CFAs, would probably lead to lawyers to abandon CFAs in favour of the greater simplicity and slightly greater profitability of contingency fees without their clients noticing. The access to justice and cost impacts of a change from CFAs to Ontario-style contingency fees appears minimal: claimant clients might lose out but probably only marginally.

Other fronts have opened up in the costs battle as well. Liability insurers have begun to use "claims capture" models. They target potential claimants, offer to get their claims settled quickly for them and refer the claimant to a team of lawyers (and paralegals) tied to the insurer in some way who settle the claim without the need to have two sets of lawyers (one for the claimant and one for the defendant). Whether such arrangements operate in the interests of the claimant is questionable, but one can see straight away how they are likely to be cheaper and quicker. Insurers are seeking to de-adversarialise personal injury claims in this way but it would be a brave person that predicted that under such arrangements they would be willing to settle claims at their full value. Similarly, until there is contrary evidence, one would be wise to question whether claimants fully understand the lack of independence involved in such claims-capturing arrangements. The opening up of the England and Wales legal services market encouraged by the Legal Services Act 2007 is also part of the picture here. New models of claims-handling business may yet bypass the courts with one-stop mediation-arbitration services being offered to both claimant and defendant.[21] All these factors plus the growing significance of third party funders means that the direction of travel on litigation costs is both returning to the mid-90s and taking some intrepid steps into an uncertain future.

[21] See, R. Moorhead (2011) 'Paradigm Shifts: Better by Design?' http://lawyerwatch.wordpress.com/2011/04/07/paradigm-shifts-better-by-design/, last downloaded 24th May 2011.

Chapter 9
Cost and Fee Allocation in Finland

Jarkko Männistö

9.1 The Basic Rule

In Finland, the basic rule of cost and fee allocation is that the loser pays all the legal costs incurred by the opposing party. The term "legal costs" refers to (1) costs of preparing and presenting a case (adduction of evidence, witness fees, court costs, etc.), and (2) attorney's fees. Furthermore, compensation is paid for (3) the work done by the party, as well as (4) party's direct losses relating to the litigation. All these types of costs are treated similarly. The "loser", i.e. the party who will be liable for the legal costs of the opposing party, is determined by comparing the plaintiff's claim to what he was awarded. If the plaintiff's claim is partially upheld to the extent that neither plaintiff nor defendant can be considered having lost the action, each party shall bear its own legal costs.[1]

Cost liability is not without restrictions. The losing party shall only be liable for the *reasonable* costs incurred by the *necessary* measures of the winner. That is, before liability is imposed, the winner's costs must pass a two-part test. First, the costs sought to be recovered from the losing party need to be incurred by measures that were necessary for the presentation of the case. Second, the cost of each such measure is recoverable only up to an amount that is deemed reasonable.

For example, it would not be possible to charge an exorbitant amount for a simple written pleading even though such a measure is necessary to file a claim. By contrast, the hourly fee itself can be whatever the client and attorney agree to, as long as the total amount charged is reasonable. Hence, high hourly fees should require high productivity.

In practice, though, the representatives of the parties are understandably reluctant to challenge as unreasonable or unnecessary any costs incurred

[1] Code of Judicial Procedure Section 21 Chapter 3.

J. Männistö (✉)
University of Turku, Turku, Finland
e-mail: jarkko@jarkkomannisto.fi

M. Reimann (ed.), *Cost and Fee Allocation in Civil Procedure*,
Ius Gentium: Comparative Perspectives on Law and Justice 11,
DOI 10.1007/978-94-007-2263-7_9, © Springer Science+Business Media B.V. 2012

or measures taken by the opposing party if they themselves have taken similar measures or incurred similar costs.[2] As the courts cannot adjust the liability of the losing party beyond what a party challenges on motion, the practical significance of these limitations (reasonable and necessary costs) is diminished.

The same basic rules apply to appeals, where the legal costs at stake *cumulate* as the litigation progresses from one instance to another.[3] Hence, in addition to the allocation of appeal costs, the court of appeal decision covers also the *re-allocation* of costs awarded in the previous instance. For example, if the judgment given by the court of first instance is reversed on appeal, the losing party is rendered liable for the appeal costs of the opposing party, and the costs incurred by the opposing party in the court of first instance. In the Supreme Court the costs may once again be re-allocated. Although the re-allocation of costs is the main rule, exceptions may apply. This lessens somewhat the risks associated with the appellate process.

A party pays the witness fees for any witness (expert and other) that he or she calls to testify. A witness is entitled to a reasonable compensation for his or her necessary travel and maintenance expenses as well as for loss of earnings.[4] The witness fees can eventually be charged by the winner against the loser. By a rough estimation, the witness fees account for 10–20% of the legal costs of both parties, although there is of course great variation.

If the parties settle their dispute, they typically bear their own legal costs. Yet, if they are unable to agree on the allocation, the court shall upon request from the parties give a separate order on costs. The costs should be allocated according to the same principles as in disputes litigated to the judgment. Thus, if the court is able to sufficiently and reliably determine who would have lost the dispute had it been litigated, then that party will be treated as the loser. If such a determination cannot be made, the loser will be determined by comparing the original claim to the settlement. In any case, the extent of the actual liability of the "losing party" should be reasonable in the light of the general principles set forth in the Code of Judicial Procedure Chapter 21.[5] There is no exact data on what percentage of cases are settled, as such disputes are often simply cancelled. According to one estimate based on interviews of judges, nearly half of the cases are

[2] In 2008, the median legal costs of plaintiffs and defendants were 6,500 euros and 5,554 euros respectively. The median award on costs was 5,277 euros. Kaijus Ervasti, *Käräjäoikeuksien riita-asiat 2008* (Helsinki: Oikeuspoliittinen tutkimuslaitos, 2009), 21.

[3] *See* Government Bill "Hallituksen esitys Eduskunnalle oikeudenkäyntikulujen korvaamista koskevien säännösten muuttamisesta 191/1993".

[4] Code of Judicial Procedure Chapter 17 Section 40.

[5] *See* Finnish Supreme Court Decisions 1996:131, 1997:77, 2001:68, and 2002:96.

settled.[6] Based on some informal interviews by the author, the proportion of settled cases may even be as high as 75%.

9.2 Exceptions and Modifications

There are a number of important exceptions and modifications to the basic rule related to (1) the nature of the case, (2) actions of the parties, and (3) equity.

First, in cases not amenable to settlement out of court, the parties shall be liable for their own legal costs, unless there is a special reason to render a party liable, in full or in part, for the legal costs of the opposing party.[7] Such special reasons may exist, for example, when the losing party was acting in the capacity of a state authority, or the conduct of the losing party can be deemed abusive.[8]

Second, if the winning party has deliberately or negligently caused a frivolous trial to be held, the winning party shall be liable for the legal costs of the loser, unless there is reason to order that the parties shall bear their own legal costs.[9] A trial is considered frivolous if the result sought in the trial could have been achieved outside court. For example, a defendant may cause a frivolous trial by failing to disclose material facts which would have prevented the plaintiff from bringing the claim, had he been aware of such facts.[10] Furthermore, if a party has deliberately or negligently caused the other party to incur legal costs which could have been avoided, he or she will be liable for such costs regardless of how the allocation of costs is otherwise determined.

Third, if the case involves such complicated or ambiguous legal issues that the losing party had a justifiable reason to pursue the proceedings, the court may order that the parties are liable for their own legal costs in full or in part. It should be noted that the standard for what constitutes a particularly complicated or ambiguous legal issue is rather strict. Such issues arise when the codified law is silent or inconsistent, and there is no complimentary source of law either.[11] A court may also, on its own motion, reduce a party's liability when, taking all aspects of the case into account, if it would be manifestly unreasonable to render one party liable

---

[6] Kaijus Ervasti, "Riita-asiat tuomioistuimissa," in *Katsaus oikeudellisten instituutioiden toimintaan ja oikeuden saatavuuteen*, ed. Marjukka Lasola (Helsinki: Oikeuspoliittinen tutkimuslaitos, 2009), 51.

[7] *Code of Judicial Procedure* Chapter 21 Sections 1 and 2.

[8] Antti Jokela, *Oikeudenkäynti*, vol. III (Helsinki: Talentum, 2004), 298.

[9] Code of Judicial Procedure Section 21 Chapter 4 Paragraph 1.

[10] Hallituksen esitys 191/1993, 13.

[11] Antti Jokela, *Oikeudenkäynti III*, 307.

for the legal costs of the other. In this regard, the court will examine the circumstances giving rise to the proceedings, the situation of the parties, and the significance of the issue.

There are no formal mandatory pre-litigation procedures. Yet, the possibility of a settlement shall be determined at the preparation stage,[12] and the court must endeavor to persuade the parties to settle.[13] Moreover, the pre-trial settlement negotiations may have a significant impact on the eventual cost and fee allocation. In particular, when determining the allocation of legal costs, the court will compare the outcome of the trial to any valid settlement offers preceding the trial. If the outcome of the trial is not better for the winning party than the rejected settlement offer, the winning party may not only have to bear its own costs but may also pay for the loser's.[14]

Party agreements on the allocation of costs and fees in case of litigation are extremely rare. In theory, though, there are no obvious legal barriers to enforce such agreements, as the question of allocating legal costs is amenable to settlement. Since the basic rule employed is that the loser pays the legal costs of the winning party, party agreements would typically entail that the winning party's right to recover its costs would be somehow limited, thus reducing the financial risk of litigation.

The practical barrier to such agreements lies in the insurance terms of litigation insurance contracts, which apply to most consumers and even many companies. The typical insurance terms of litigation insurance require that the insured demand the opposing party to pay for his legal costs in case the insured party prevails. This claim must then be subrogated to the insurance company paying for the insured's legal costs. Any agreement by the insured that results in the reduction in his potentially recoverable legal costs would allow the insurance company to deny coverage. This would significantly increase the expected cost of litigation for the insured. Furthermore, if agreements between companies contain conflict management clauses at all, they typically concern arbitration.[15]

The parties can represent themselves in all civil cases. Self-representation is relatively rare, however. In 2008, only 5% of plaintiffs and 15% of defendants were unrepresented in tried cases. The majority of parties are represented by an attorney (a member of the Finnish Bar Association) or another lawyer. Hence, a person who is not a member of the Finnish Bar Association may represent clients in trials, although members of the bar are in a favored position in some situations, for example when the defendant is appointed a counsel by the court. A person without a law

---

[12] Code of Judicial Procedure Chapter 5 Section 19.

[13] Code of Judicial Procedure Chapter 5 Section 26.

[14] *See* Supreme Court judgment 2008:52.

[15] These views are based on the personal experiences of two experienced attorneys, Mr. Juha Kiiha and Mr. Mats Welin, whom I kindly thank for their assistance on the matter.

degree can represent a party in trials only if the party is a close relative of the representative (parent, offspring, sibling, or spouse).

9.3 Encouragement or Discouragement of Litigation

The rules governing cost and fee allocation are generally intended to affect the *quality*, not the quantity of cases tried. The idea is that legal cost shifting will encourage meritorious claims across a spectrum of different cases, when confident potential plaintiffs expect that they can recover their legal costs. Correspondingly, legal cost shifting is intended to discourage frivolous claims, when less confident plaintiffs will find the expected value of litigation to be negative.[16] Many jurists, including this author, suggest that an unintended consequence of increased financial risk of cost shifting in litigation is that it discourages all, even highly meritorious, claims from middle- and low-income plaintiffs. Similarly, defending against even a frivolous claim brought by a plaintiff with deep pockets may be too risky for such persons.[17]

No up-front payments need to be made into court or to other officials. Attorneys, however, have the right to ask for a retainer. The retainer can cover a portion of attorney's fees and the expected direct expenses arising from the assignment. In practice, up-front payments to attorneys are relatively rare though. Approximately 20% of attorneys never ask for a retainer and only 3% of attorneys ask often.[18] Also, witnesses are entitled to an advance payment, although it is quite rare in practice. At any rate, up-front payments are generally small enough not to deter potential litigants.

9.4 The Determination of Costs and Fees

The court costs are determined solely on the basis of the stages of procedure involved before the case is closed. For example, if the litigation ends after the exchange of pleadings (written preparation) the court cost is 79 euros whereas full trial before three judges will be 179 euros in the court of first instance. Hence, the quality, amount in controversy, or general scale of the case has no effect on the court costs, which are, in most cases, negligible. As court costs are clearly not enough to cover the actual expenses caused by the procedure, courts are clearly providing for a highly accessible public service.

---

16 *See* Hallituksen esitys 191/1993, 21.

17 *See* Jarkko Männistö, "Oikeudenkäyntikulut kannustimena – taloustieteellinen analyysi oikeudenkäyntikulujen korvausvelvollisuuden vaikutuksista," *Lakimies* (2005): 79–97.

18 Suomen Asianajajaliitto, *Asianajajatutkimus 2007,* 26.

Lawyers' fees are determined by the market, except in legal aid cases, where the maximum hourly fee is determined by statute.[19] In 2007, the average hourly fee for attorneys representing a client in trials was 177 euros (all rates excluding a 23% VAT), which makes it slightly less than in cases not involving trial work, where an average hourly fee is 182 euros.[20] Most likely this is due to the inclusion of legal aid cases, where the hourly fee of attorneys is, by statute, only 100 euros. Beyond the case of legal aid, the client's ability to pay for legal services often affects the hourly fee. First, attorneys serving mainly business clients charge an average of 221 euros per hour, whereas attorneys serving mainly private clients charge an average of 150 euros per hour.[21] Second, 70% of attorneys claim that they have given substantial discounts or have sometimes worked pro bono for social reasons.[22]

The judge presiding over the case will determine the final allocation of legal costs. The judge has plenty of discretion in making a costs award because of the exceptions and modifications to the basic rule. At the same time, however, the margin of discretion is narrowed down to what the parties (their attorneys) admit as reasonable fee. To obtain compensation for legal costs, a party must make a claim before the conclusion of the hearing, and the decision on costs is integral to the judgment.[23] The cost decision is separately appealable, although such appeals are rare in practice.

9.5 Special Issues: Success-Oriented Fees, Class Actions, Sale of Claims, and Litigation Insurance

Simple time-based fees independent of the outcome of the case are strongly preferred by attorneys.[24] Although success oriented fees are allowed, the Finnish Bar Association requires that the use of contingency fee arrangements and success premiums be justified by special reasons. Despite this unsympathetic attitude, such fee arrangements are no recent development; instead, they have been explicitly allowed since the ratification of the first Finnish Bar Association fee regulation in 1961.

Success fees are not explicitly regulated by law, but like attorney's fees in general, they must be reasonable.[25] Thus, the loser's liability for the enhanced fee depends on whether the court considers the enhanced fee

---

[19] Legal Aid Act 257/2002.

[20] Suomen Asianajajaliitto, *Asianajajatutkimus 2007,* 23.

[21] Ibid., 25.

[22] Ibid., 26.

[23] Code of Judicial Procedure Chapter 21 Section 14.

[24] Suomen Asianajajaliitto, *Asianajajatutkimus 2007,* 23.

[25] Matti Ylöstalo, and Olli Tarkka, *Asianajajan käsikirja* (Helsinki: WSLT, 1998), 236.

still to be within the limits of reasonability. In the absence of case law on the matter, one can only speculate how courts would approach the problem. A party could probably successfully challenge a fee that would substantially exceed that of his own lawyer.

Selling claims for purposes of litigation is generally allowed. Yet, it is common only with respect to undisputed claims, which companies sell in large scale to debt collection agencies. Individual disputed claims are rarely, if ever, subrogated. Attorneys and law firms are not willing to buy disputed claims, probably for a multitude of reasons. Even if a lawyer or a law firm had the necessary working capital for buying and litigating disputed claims, as well as the necessary experience and talent to recognize winnable cases, such activities would most likely be met with prejudice by colleagues and the judiciary, hence making it a less tempting idea generate business. Class action is available in consumer disputes. The defined group of consumers is represented by the consumer ombudsman. Legal costs in such group litigation are allocated according to the same rules as in normal two-party litigation.[26] But because the costs are borne by the consumer ombudsman in the event of loss, they are not a financially relevant factor for the individual members of the group.

It is possible to insure against the costs of litigation either by buying coverage in general homeowners insurance (consumers), or by buying litigation insurance to protect against specific claims (companies). In fact, litigation insurance is part of homeowners insurance by default, which makes it very common. Unfortunately, the terms of such litigation insurance are generally quite restricted. Many of the most common causes of disputes – employment, investment, divorce, and custody issues – are not covered. The policy will typically cover only the insured's own legal costs, while the policy amount is generally only 8,500 euros, which is on the low side except for the simplest disputes. Companies are not nearly as frequently insured against litigation, although exact data is unavailable. Depending on the terms of the policy, litigation insurance will cover the insured's own legal costs and may include even those of the opposing party, in case the insured is rendered liable for them.

9.6 Legal Aid

There is a publicly funded legal aid system. A legal aid agency grants aid upon application. The applicant is then appointed a public legal aid counsel or an attorney, who shall represent the applicant. Legal aid covers, in part or in full, the applicant's legal costs, including court costs, attorney's fees, and witness fees, along with some other, minor costs. Legal aid is calculated

[26] Group Litigation Act 444/2007, Section 17.

as a percentage of the applicant's total legal costs and is determined on the basis of the applicant's income.

Private legal aid is more limited. The Finnish legal aid system is relatively extensive and accessible, thereby making large scale pro bono work unnecessary. Some local branches of the Finnish Bar Association offer pro bono counsel to assess whether legal representation is required.

Legal aid is awarded selectively and progressively on the basis of financial criteria as a proportion of the applicant's legal costs. It is intended for low- and medium-income people. In particular, if the applicant's monthly available means are less than 1,500 euros, he is entitled to the minimum legal aid of 25% of legal costs, whereas monthly available means below 700 euros entitle him to full legal aid. When the financial conditions for legal aid are met, legal aid is, in practice, always available to the applicant. If public legal aid counsels are not available, the applicant will be appointed an attorney. In a study from 2005, only 4% of attorneys representing legal aid clients felt that there were not enough attorneys and legal aid counsels to satisfy the need, whereas 57% thought that there were too many.[27]

Given the moderate cost of litigation coupled with the rather extensive right to legal aid, the cost of litigation does not, in itself, exclude anyone from access to justice. Yet, the cost-shifting rule coupled with the fact that the loser is rendered liable for the opposing party's legal costs in full significantly increases the financial risk involved in litigation, and thereby creates a barrier to seeking redress in court. The *threat* of having to pay the one's own and the opposing party's legal costs is obviously a strong deterrent to risk averse parties and to parties with limited solvency, such as consumers and small businesses. Legal aid or litigation insurance is of limited help, since they normally do not cover the opposing party's legal costs. Indeed, a little over half of attorneys handling legal aid cases answered in a survey that they often recommended their clients not to pursue their case in court due to the risk of having to pay the opponent's costs.[28] Similarly, in another survey concerning labor law issues, attorneys and legal aid counsels found that the cost shifting rules prevent litigation even if the case should, in their opinion, be tried.[29]

Because of the severe financial risk involved in litigation, disputes between consumers and companies are frequently disposed of by the consumer dispute board, which renders recommendations on how such disputes should be resolved. Although these recommendations are not binding, courts tend to follow them, which is why the parties generally accept

---

[27] Marjukka Litmala, and Kari Alasaari, *Köyhäinavusta kansalaisoikeudeks: Oikeusapu-uudistuksen seurantatutkimuksen I osaraportti* (Helsinki: Oikeuspoliittinen tutkimuslaitos, 2004), 77.

[28] Ibid., 78.

[29] Kairinen Martti et al., *Työsopimuslain toimivuus: Työsopimuslain seurantatutkimus II osaraportti* (Helsinki: Työministeriö, 2004), 100.

them as well. What makes the consumer dispute board such an appealing forum for dispute resolution is the fact that the procedure is simple and cheap. Moreover, both parties bear their own legal costs, which further reduces the risk involved in a dispute.

Given the cost-shifting rule and the way it is typically applied (loser pays all), the amount in controversy alone is not enough to determine whether litigation is economically feasible. The expected value of litigation is a function of the amount in controversy, the litigation costs, and the probability of prevailing. If the probability of prevailing is sufficiently high, practically any claim can be made or defended against with a positive expectation regardless of the litigation costs. Indeed, in approximately half of the cases the combined litigation costs of both sides was more than the actual amount in controversy.[30]

---

[30] Kaijus Ervasti, *Käräjäoikeuksien riita-asiat 2008*, 21.

Chapitre 10
La répartition des frais en procédure civile française

Nicolas Cayrol

1. *Diversité des frais de justice.* Le droit français relatif aux frais de justice distingue plusieurs catégories de frais. Certains, comme les « honoraires » des avocats, sont déterminés librement ; d'autres, au contraire, sont encadrés de manière très précise par la loi : ainsi, par exemple, des « débours » et des « émoluments ». Ces distinctions subtiles se retrouvent à l'issue du procès, au moment de la répartition des frais du procès entre les plaideurs. Les frais réglementés, qui constituent ce que l'on appelle les « dépens », sont en principe mis intégralement à la charge du perdant. Quant à la charge des autres frais, ceux que l'on appelle les « frais irrépétibles », elle fait l'objet d'une décision discrétionnaire du juge. En fait, les plaideurs ignorent le plus souvent le détail de ce qu'ils payent et pourquoi : « dépens », « débours », « émoluments », « honoraires », etc., sont en effet des termes qui appartiennent à un lexique ancien et technique dont seuls les spécialistes maîtrisent vraiment le sens.

2. *Rémunération des juges.* L'explication est à rechercher dans l'histoire : le régime juridique actuel des frais de justice est le résultat d'une longue évolution, dont le sens général est celui d'un allégement des frais pour les plaideurs, par la suppression des « épices » et des « redevances de greffes ». Les « épices » désignaient avant la Révolution française, une gratification que les juges recevaient directement des plaideurs en complément de leurs « gages », c'est-à-dire de la rémunération que leur versait l'Etat royal. On raconte que cette gratification, avant d'être payée en monnaie, fut d'abord payée en nature sous forme de dragées ou de confitures, appelées à l'époque les « épices ».[1] Les épices rémunéraient les actes écrits des juges, alors que les gages correspondaient à

[1] V. R. Perrot, Institutions judiciaires, Montchrestien, 14e éd. 2010, n° 71.

N. Cayrol (✉)
l'Université de Paris II (Panthéon-Assas), Paris, France
e-mail: nicolas.cayrol@univ-tours.fr

M. Reimann (ed.), *Cost and Fee Allocation in Civil Procedure*,
Ius Gentium: Comparative Perspectives on Law and Justice 11,
DOI 10.1007/978-94-007-2263-7_10, © Springer Science+Business Media B.V. 2012

la rémunération de la justice rendue oralement. Les épices furent supprimées lors de la Révolution française par la grande loi des 16 et 24 août 1790.[2] Depuis cette loi, la rémunération des magistrats est à la charge de l'Etat. Cette règle, cependant, ne concerne que le service public de la justice. Elle ne vaut pas pour les arbitres dont la rémunération reste intégralement à la charge des parties, lesquelles en répondent solidairement.[3]

3. *Frais d'actes de justice.* Le coût du service public de la justice ne se limite pas à la rémunération de juges. Pendant longtemps, une partie des frais de fonctionnement des tribunaux, et en particulier des frais d'actes et de secrétariat, pesa sur les plaideurs qui devaient acquitter des taxes diverses : droit de timbre et d'enregistrement des décisions de justice, droit de timbre sur les actes de procédure, et autres « redevances » à verser aux secrétariats-greffes. C'est seulement en 1977, par une loi du 30 décembre, que ces taxes furent supprimées.[4] Seuls furent maintenus et subsistent encore la redevance à acquitter auprès des greffes des tribunaux de commerce[5] et ce que l'on appelle le « droit de plaidoirie », sorte de taxe qui est perçue par les avocats au profit de la caisse nationale de retraite des barreaux français.[6] Depuis 1977, le législateur français a établi deux nouvelles taxes : une taxe sur les actes d'huissier de justice[7] et une taxe temporaire destinée à financer sur la prochaine suppression des avoués de cours d'appel.[8]

4. *Gratuité de la justice, égalité devant la loi, droit d'accès au juge.* La loi des 16–24 août 1790 et celle du 30 septembre 1977 traduisent, chacune à leur manière, l'idée de gratuité de la justice, idée que le législateur français érigea en principe dans la constitution révolutionnaire du 3 septembre 1791 et qui figure aujourd'hui, depuis une ordonnance du 8 juin

---

[2] Tit. II, art. 11. La même loi supprime en même temps la vénalité des charges de magistrat.

[3] V. E. Jolivet et L. Marquis, Les frais de l'arbitrage, Gaz. Pal. 15 déc. 2009, p. 15.

[4] V. C. Freyria, Défunte, la fiscalité des actes judiciaires ?, Mélanges Pierre Hébraud, Toulouse, 1981, p. 329.

[5] La raison est que, lors de la grande réforme des greffes de 1965, les greffiers des tribunaux de commerce, contrairement à leurs collègues des autres juridictions, ne sont pas devenus des fonctionnaires d'Etat : ils sont aujourd'hui encore titulaires d'un office ministériel et ils perçoivent à ce titre des « émoluments » déterminés par les art. R. 743-140 et suivants du Code de commerce.

[6] Code de la sécurité sociale, art. L. 723-3.

[7] Rétablissement de la taxe sur les actes huissiers de justice (L. n° 91-1322 du 30 déc. 1991, art. 22) ; établissement d'une taxe pour financer la suppression des avoués de cour d'appel.

[8] L. 30 déc. 2009, art. 54.

2006, en tête du Code de l'organisation judiciaire.[9] Au fond, le principe de gratuité peut se justifier de deux manières complémentaires. On peut dire d'abord qu'il est le corollaire de l'égalité des justiciables devant la justice, qui est lui-même un prolongement nécessaire de l'égalité des citoyens devant la loi. Ensuite, il est une garantie du droit d'accès au juge, droit fondamental garanti par la Convention européenne de sauvegarde des droits de l'homme et des libertés fondamentales (art. 6, § 1) et par la Charte des droits fondamentaux de l'Union européenne (art. 47).

5. *Autres frais de justice.* Cela dit, les autres frais de justice restent à la charge des plaideurs. Ces frais peuvent être très importants, puisqu'ils comprennent notamment la rémunération des auxiliaires de justice : avocats, avoués, huissiers, notaires, commissaires-priseurs, administrateurs et mandataires judiciaires. Autre poste important de dépense : les frais liés à l'administration de la preuve, et spécialement au paiement des expertises.[10]

6. *Limitation des frais de justice.* Pour limiter ces frais, le législateur français est intervenu de différentes manières. Parfois, de manière radicale, il a purement et simplement « déjudiciarisé » certaines procédures, c'est-à-dire supprimé le recours au juge.[11] Souvent, il a instauré des procédures simplifiées n'imposant pas le recours obligatoire à un avocat. Il en existe aujourd'hui de nombreux exemples. Autre moyen : l'allègement des procédés de notification des actes. Au lieu d'une « signification » par l'intermédiaire d'un huissier de justice, les actes sont portés à la connaissance de leur destinataire simplement par voie postale. La limitation des frais relatifs aux mesures d'administration de la preuve est aussi une préoccupation du législateur. Mais les règles à cet égard expriment surtout des vœux : selon l'article 147 du Code de procédure civile, « le juge doit limiter le choix de la mesure à ce qui est suffisant pour la solution du litige, en s'attachant à ce qui est le plus simple et le moins onéreux ».[12] Pour les plaideurs, une manière de maîtriser les frais consiste à conclure avec leur avocat ce que l'on appelle

[9] C.O.J., art. L. 111-2 : « La gratuité du service de la justice est assurée selon les modalités fixées par la loi et le règlement ».

[10] On ne dira rien ici des incidences financières de la durée du procès, sinon que le droit français impose au débiteur le paiement d'intérêts « moratoires », c'est-à-dire d'intérêts censés compenser le retard dans l'exécution (C. civ., art. 1153). Sur ce point, v. P. Ancel, v° Coûts du procès, in L. Cadiet, Dictionnaire de la justice, PUF, 2004.

[11] V. S. Amrani Mekki, La déjudiciarisation, Gaz. Pal. 5 juin 2008, p. 2. Ainsi, par exemple, depuis la loi du 9 juillet 1991, sauf incident, les procédures de saisies mobilières se déroulent en dehors du juge.

[12] V. aussi, C. proc. civ., art. 264 : « il n'est désigné qu'une seule personne à titre d'expert à moins que le juge n'estime nécessaire d'en nommer plusieurs ».

une « convention d'honoraires », c'est-à-dire une convention encadrant les honoraires de l'avocat.[13]

7. *Plan.* Pour le reste, il faut payer les frais et en répartir la charge.[14] Les plaideurs doivent normalement faire l'avance des fonds (I) avant d'espérer en recouvrer une partie à l'issue du procès, au moment du règlement des comptes (II).

10.1 L'avance des fonds

8. *Abrogation de la cautio judicatum solvi.* Il appartient normalement à chaque partie de faire l'avance de ses frais de procédure. Autrefois, un étranger qui intentait un procès contre un français devait non seulement avancer ses propres frais de procédure, mais il devait en outre consigner une somme d'argent destinée à garantir le remboursement éventuel des frais de procédure exposés par son adversaire français, ce que l'on appelait la *cautio judicatum solvi*. Une loi du 9 juillet 1975 a abrogé cette disposition.

9. *Provision sur les honoraires d'avocat.* L'avocat qui accepte la charge d'un dossier est en droit de demander à son client le paiement immédiat d'une provision fondée sur une « estimation raisonnable des honoraires et des débours probables entraînés par le dossier. A défaut de paiement de la provision demandée, l'avocat peut renoncer à s'occuper de l'affaire ».[15]

10. *Provision sur les frais d'expertise.* Lorsque le juge ordonne une expertise, il désigne en même temps la ou les parties qui doivent consigner au greffe la provision à valoir sur la rémunération de l'expert. A défaut de consignation de la provision dans le délai imparti par le juge, la désignation de l'expert est caduque.[16]

11. *Provisions sur les frais d'une médiation.* Le même dispositif se retrouve en matière de médiation : lorsque le juge donne mission à un tiers médiateur de tenter de concilier les parties, il doit en même temps désigner la ou les parties qui consigneront la provision à valoir sur la

---

[13] « A défaut de convention entre l'avocat et son client, les honoraires sont fixés selon les usages, en fonction de la situation de fortune du client, de la difficulté de l'affaire, des frais exposés par l'avocat, de sa notoriété et des diligences de celui-ci » (L. n° 71-1130 du 31 déc. 1971, art. 10, al. 2).

[14] V. S. Gjidara-Decaix, Les règles de répartition des frais en procédure civile, RIDC 2010, p. 325.

[15] Décret n° 2005-790 du 12 juillet 2005, art. 11.

[16] C. proc. civ., art. 269 s.

rémunération du médiateur. A défaut de consignation, la désignation de celui-ci est caduque.[17]

12. *L'aide juridictionnelle.* La nécessité de faire l'avance des fonds peut constituer en fait un obstacle à l'accès effectif au juge. Une telle conséquence est inadmissible au regard du droit fondamental d'accès à la justice.[18] D'où la mise en place d'un système étatique d'aide à l'accès à la justice. Les premières dispositions datent de la Révolution française.[19] En 1851, est instaurée *l'assistance judiciaire*, remplacée par *l'aide judiciaire* par une loi du 3 janvier 1972 qui consacra formellement le droit à l'accès à la justice. Nous sommes aujourd'hui sous le régime de la loi du 10 juillet 1991, instaurant *l'aide juridictionnelle* et *l'aide à l'accès au droit.*[20]

13. *Régime.* Sauf exception, le bénéfice de l'aide juridictionnelle est réservé aux personnes physiques dont les ressources sont insuffisantes pour faire valoir leurs droits en justice (et qui ne bénéficient pas d'une assurance de protection juridique), et à condition que leurs prétentions ne soient pas manifestement irrecevables ou dénuées de fondement. Il ouvre « droit à l'assistance d'un avocat et à celle de tous officiers publics ou ministériels dont la procédure requiert le concours ». Dans ce cas, l'Etat avance tous les frais nécessaires à la conduite du procès (actes de l'instance, mesures d'instruction, etc.).[21] Cependant, l'aide juridictionnelle ne couvre que les frais engagés par le bénéficiaire, de sorte que si, à l'issue du procès, le bénéficiaire perd et est condamné à payer les frais engagés par son adversaire, en principe, il devra les acquitter.[22] Inversement, s'il gagne, son adversaire sera, en principe et sous réserve du pouvoir modérateur du juge, tenu de rembourser au Trésor public les sommes avancées par l'Etat au bénéficiaire.[23]

14. *Provision ad litem.* Les plaideurs qui ne bénéficient pas de l'aide juridictionnelle peuvent solliciter auprès du tribunal l'allocation d'une

---

[17] L. n° 95-125 du 8 février 1995, art. 21.

[18] V. supra n° 4. Le projet de constitution du 19 avril 1946, qui n'a pas été adopté, le disait très clairement : « La loi assure à tous les hommes le droit de se faire rendre justice ; l'insuffisance des ressources ne saurait y faire obstacle ».

[19] Auparavant, l'accès à la justice des indigents reposait sur la déontologie des avocats qui étaient tenus, dit-on, de leur prêter leur concours gratuitement, conformément à la doctrine du « désintéressement » qui fait d'ailleurs encore partie aujourd'hui de leur déontologie.

[20] Il existe en outre des dispositions propres à l'aide juridictionnelle dans les litiges transfrontaliers au sein de l'Union européenne : v. Règlement du 18 décembre 2008.

[21] L. n° 91-647 du 10 juillet 1991, art. 25 et 40.

[22] V. cep. *infra*, n° 34.

[23] L. n° 91-647 du 10 juillet 1991, art. 43.

« provision pour le procès », ce que l'on appelait autrefois une « provision *ad litem* », c'est-à-dire une provision payée immédiatement par l'adversaire et destinée à couvrir l'avance des frais de procédure.[24] La loi n'en précise pas les conditions. Pour les juges, l'octroi de cette provision ne se justifie qu'à l'égard d'un plaideur n'ayant pas les moyens financiers de faire face aux charges d'un procès alors pourtant qu'une issue au moins partiellement favorable pour lui peut être présumée. Cette possibilité existe depuis 1935. A l'époque, il s'agissait de compenser les insuffisances manifestes du régime de l'assistance judiciaire.[25]

15. *Assurance.* La charge des frais de procédure peut être couverte par une assurance dite de « protection juridique ».[26] Dans ce cas, l'assureur paye les frais de procédure et les honoraires d'avocat. La loi garantit à l'assuré la liberté de choisir son avocat et la stratégie procédurale.[27]

16. *Autres conventions.* Il arrive parfois que les frais de procédure soient pris en charge par un tiers en vertu d'une autre sorte de convention qu'une police d'assurance. Ainsi, par exemple, en matière de crédit-bail, lorsque le crédit-preneur assume la charge et le coût du procès à l'encontre du fournisseur en lieu et place du crédit-bailleur. D'autres hypothèses sont concevables.[28] La position du droit français à l'égard de ces conventions relatives au procès est réservée. Si la validité de certains arrangements a pu être admise, notamment les clauses de transfert d'action en matière de crédit-bail, les conventions par lesquelles une personne ferait le commerce d'une action en justice se heurtent à l'hostilité du législateur et des tribunaux. Traditionnellement, le droit français n'admet pas les agents d'affaires en matière judiciaire.[29] Au milieu du 20e siècle, la jurisprudence condamna les sociétés commerciales dites de « défense en justice » qui s'étaient constituées dans le but d'offrir à leurs clients des consultations juridiques et fiscales en contrepartie d'une somme forfaitaire annuelle,

[24] C. proc. civ., art. 771, 2°.

[25] V. *supra*, n° 12.

[26] v. V. Nicolas, Le procès, risque assurable ?, RGDA 2010, p. 895.

[27] Code des assurances, art. L. 127-1 et s., issus de la loi n° 2007-210 du 19 févr. 2007.

[28] D. Mondoloni, Le procès peut-il être financé par un tiers investisseur?, Mélanges Larroumet, Economica 2010, p. 361.

[29] Par exemple, « sont nulles de plein droit et de nul effet les obligations contractées, pour rémunération de leurs services ou de leurs avances, envers les intermédiaires qui, moyennant émoluments convenus au préalable, se chargent d'assurer aux victimes d'accidents de droit commun ou à leurs ayants droit, le bénéfice d'accords amiables ou de décisions judiciaires » (Loi du 3 avril 1942, art. 1er).

ainsi que la prise en charge, rémunérée par un pacte de *quota litis*, de la conduite et des frais des procès en demande ou en défense.[30]

17. *Honoraires de résultat.* Une évolution doit toutefois être notée à ce sujet, mais celle-ci ne concerne que la profession d'avocat. Depuis 1991, est licite la convention d'honoraires qui prévoit, outre la rémunération des prestations effectuées, un honoraire complémentaire fixé en fonction du résultat obtenu ou du service rendu.[31] On parle dans ce cas d'honoraire « de résultat », par opposition à l'honoraire dit « de diligences », censé rémunérer les prestations de l'avocat. Lorsqu'une telle convention est conclue, le client n'a donc pas à supporter la totalité de la rémunération de son avocat, puisque l'honoraire de résultat sera acquitté sur les sommes payées par l'adversaire. Cette évolution est très remarquable compte tenu de l'hostilité traditionnelle du droit français aux pactes de *quota litis*[32] et, plus généralement, aux spéculations sur l'aléa judiciaire. Il convient néanmoins d'en souligner les limites car, aujourd'hui encore, l'honoraire de résultat ne peut être qu'un complément de la rémunération de l'avocat. La loi est très ferme sur ce point : « toute fixation d'honoraires, qui ne le serait qu'en fonction du résultat judiciaire, est interdite ».

10.2 Le règlement des comptes

18. *Règlement des comptes par le juge.* En rendant son jugement, le juge doit obligatoirement procéder en même temps au règlement des conséquences pécuniaires du procès.

19. *Fondement de la charge des frais au perdant.* En principe, le juge doit condamner le perdant à payer les frais du procès.[33] Cette

[30] V. A. Besson, Les sociétés de défense en justice devant la jurisprudence, RGAT 1951, p. 365. V. N. Cayrol, Les actes ayant pour objet l'action en justice, préf. F. Grua, Economica, 2001.

[31] L. n° 71-1130 du 31 déc. 1971, art. 10, al. 3, dans sa rédaction issue de la loi n° 91-647 du 10 juill. 1991. La loi prévoit d'autre part, dans le cas particulier où le gagnant bénéficie de l'aide juridictionnelle, que son avocat est en droit de demander des honoraires conformes à ceux auxquels il aurait pu prétendre si son client n'avait pas été bénéficié de ce régime (art. 36 et 37, al. 2).

[32] V. C. Jamin, Deux questions préalables à l'instruction du procès de la prohibition des pactes de *quota litis*, Mélanges Geneviève Viney, LGDJ, 2008.

[33] C. proc. civ., art. 696 : « La partie perdante est condamnée aux dépens [...] » et 700 : « [...] le juge condamne la partie tenue aux dépens, ou à défaut la partie perdante à payer à l'autre partie la somme qu'il détermine au titre des frais exposés et non compris dans les dépens. [...] ».

solution est traditionnelle[34] mais son fondement est discuté.[35] Plusieurs explications ont été proposées mais aucune ne fait l'unanimité. La jurisprudence ancienne considérait que la condamnation du perdant à payer les frais du procès était justifiée par sa faute : qui perd son procès a commis une faute dont il doit répondre à l'égard de son adversaire. Cette explication n'a jamais vraiment convaincu, car il y a des cas où le perdant n'a manifestement commis aucune faute en agissant en justice ou en n'acquiesçant pas aux prétentions de son adversaire. Pourtant l'absence de faute n'a jamais été, en soi, une cause d'exonération. En outre, si le perdant devait répondre de sa faute, il devrait alors, selon les principes du droit de la responsabilité civile, être condamné à rembourser au gagnant *l'intégralité* des frais exposés par celui-ci pour le procès, ce qui n'est pas non plus le cas.

20. *Pouvoir modérateur du juge.* Le régime de la répartition des frais en procédure civile française n'est donc pas un régime de responsabilité civile. En réalité, en la matière, le droit français se caractérise par l'importance du *pouvoir modérateur du juge* davantage que par des principes généraux que le juge n'aurait qu'à mettre en application. En effet, le juge, s'il décide de mettre les frais à la charge du perdant, dispose du pouvoir d'aménager cette condamnation au cas par cas, en fonction de considérations particulières à l'espèce (A). Mais le juge peut aussi, par exception, décider de ne pas condamner le perdant aux frais et d'en reporter la charge sur quelqu'un d'autre (B).

10.2.1 La condamnation du perdant

21. *Notion de partie perdante.* Le principe est que le juge doit condamner la partie perdante à payer les frais du procès. Or il arrive que chaque partie au litige soit à la fois gagnante et perdante. Ainsi en cas de pluralité de prétentions, lorsque le tribunal en adjuge certaines et en rejette d'autres. Ainsi encore en cas de litige portant sur le montant d'une créance, lorsque le tribunal l'estime à 1000, alors que le créancier réclamait 1200 et que le débiteur ne reconnaissait que 800. Il appartient alors au tribunal de répartir la charge des frais entre les parties. Il dispose à cet égard d'un pouvoir « discrétionnaire », c'est-à-dire qu'il n'a pas à motiver spécialement sa décision.

---

[34] Elle existait en droit romain et, de là, elle est passée en droit canonique et en droit français dans les pays de droit écrit (les provinces du sud de la France). Dans les pays de droit coutumier (les provinces du nord), en revanche, la règle fut initialement que le perdant devait être condamné à de fortes amendes au profit du Trésor. Ce n'est que vers le 13e siècle que, dans les pays de coutumes, le perdant s'est vu imposer la charge des dépens. Depuis cette époque, la solution est constante.

[35] R. Japiot, Le fondement de la dette des dépens, RTD civ. 1914, p. 523.

22. *Pluralité de parties perdantes.* En cas de pluralité de parties perdantes, il incombe au tribunal de répartir les frais entre elles. Les frais sont personnels et divisibles, c'est-à-dire que les perdants n'en garantissent pas solidairement le paiement, sauf s'ils ont été condamnés solidairement sur le fond ou si le juge le décide spécialement. Lorsqu'un plaideur assigné en paiement appelle un tiers en garantie et obtient la condamnation de celui-ci à titre principal, dans ce cas, la charge des frais pèse au premier chef sur ce dernier. Ce n'est qu'en cas d'insolvabilité du plaideur appelé en garantie que les dépens seront supportés par le défendeur originaire.[36]

23. *Notion de partie.* Seules les parties au procès peuvent être condamnées à payer les frais. Les personnes qui ne font qu'assister ou représenter une partie *stricto sensu* n'ont, en principe et sauf exceptions,[37] rien à payer.

24. *Notion d'instance.* A l'égard du règlement des frais, la jurisprudence retient une interprétation large de la notion de procès. Ainsi, en cas d'appel, le plaideur qui succombe en appel après avoir triomphé en première instance, doit supporter la charge des frais des deux instances.[38]

25. *Distinction des dépens et des autres frais.* Cela dit, en droit français positif, il convient de distinguer deux sortes de frais de justice : les « dépens » et les autres. En effet, la condamnation du perdant aux dépens est de droit.[39] Au contraire, la condamnation aux autres frais que les dépens *stricto sensu* est laissée à l'appréciation souveraine du juge qui doit alors tenir « compte de l'équité ou de la situation économique de la partie condamnée. Il peut, même d'office, pour des raisons tirées des mêmes considérations, dire qu'il n'y a pas lieu à cette condamnation ».[40]

26. *Notion de dépens.* Que recouvrent les dépens ? *Grosso modo,* il s'agit des frais réglementés. Inversement, les frais qui ne sont pas obligatoires ou dont le montant n'est pas tarifé ne sont pas compris dans les dépens. La liste exhaustive des frais compris dans les dépens figure à l'article 695 du Code de procédure civile. Sans entrer dans le

---

[36] C. proc. civ., art. 338.

[37] Sur lesquelles, v. infra, n° 35.

[38] Sous réserve de l'article 88 du Code de procédure civile qui dispose que les frais afférents au « contredit », c'est-à-dire à la contestation devant la cour d'appel d'une décision rendu par le premier juge sur sa compétence, reste à la charge de la partie qui succombe sur la question de compétence. Peu importe que celle-ci gagne ensuite le procès au fond.

[39] C. proc. civ., art. 696.

[40] C. proc. civ., art. 700.

détail de ce texte, relevons que sont compris dans les dépens, 1° les taxes et redevances des greffes lorsque, par exception, celles-ci sont dues[41]; 2° les frais liés aux mesures d'administration de la preuve.[42] Parmi les frais d'administration de la preuve, citons la rémunération des « techniciens » (c'est-à-dire principalement des experts), les indemnités des témoins et les frais liés à une enquête sociale ; 3° les frais d'interprétariat, de traduction et de notification des actes de procédure à l'étranger ; 4° les « débours » et les « émoluments » des auxiliaires de justice.

27. *Les débours.* Les débours correspondent aux frais avancés par les auxiliaires de justice (avocats ou autres) pour les besoins de leur activité. Entrent dans les débours, par exemple, les frais de déplacement et de correspondance. Les débours, qui font l'objet d'un tarif réglementé, sont compris dans les dépens dans la mesure prévue par la règlementation.

28. *Les émoluments.* Les émoluments désignent la rémunération des officiers publics ou ministériels et une partie de la rémunération des avocats. La rémunération des officiers publics ou ministériels (huissiers, notaires, commissaires-priseurs, administrateurs et mandataires judiciaires, greffiers des tribunaux de commerce) fait l'objet d'une tarification réglementaire. Elle est toujours comprise dans les dépens dans son intégralité. Au contraire, la rémunération des avocats n'est pas toujours comprise dans les dépens, et lorsqu'elle l'est, ce n'est que partiellement. La rémunération d'un avocat n'est considérée comme émolument, et par conséquent n'est comprise dans les dépens, que si son ministère est obligatoire et dans la mesure seulement où elle correspond à l'accomplissement d'actes de procédure réglementés.[43]

29. *Les honoraires.* Tout le reste de la rémunération des avocats, tout ce qui ne correspond pas aux débours ou aux émoluments, est considéré comme « honoraires ».[44] Cette partie de la rémunération des avocats, qui correspond à son activité de conseil et de plaidoirie ainsi

---

[41] V. supra, n° 3.

[42] A condition toutefois que ces mesures aient été ordonnées par le juge ou, lorsqu'elles sont antérieures à l'instance, à condition qu'elles soient dans un rapport étroit et nécessaire avec celle-ci.

[43] On parle alors de frais dits « de postulation ».

[44] Cette qualification emporte une conséquence très remarquable que les limites de ce rapport ne permettent que de signaler brièvement : en droit français, suivant une règle directement issue du droit romain, les honoraires – contrairement au salaire ou au prix – sont réductibles. Le juge est en droit de réduire le montant des honoraires réclamés lorsque celui-ci parait exagérée au regard du service rendu. La portée de cette règle est générale : peu importe que les honoraires aient fait l'objet d'une convention préalable ; peu importe qu'il s'agisse d'honoraires de diligences ou d'honoraires de résultat (sur cette distinction, v. supra, n° 17).

qu'aux actes de procédure qu'il accomplit lorsque son ministère n'est pas obligatoire, n'est pas réglementée : les honoraires sont libres, et pour cette raison, ils n'entrent pas dans la catégorie des dépens. C'est ainsi que lorsqu'il demande le règlement définitif de ce qui lui est dû, l'avocat doit présenter à son client un compte détaillé faisant « ressortir distinctement les frais et débours, les émoluments tarifés et les honoraires ».[45]

30. *Frais irrépétibles.* Les frais non compris dans les dépens ne se limitent pas aux honoraires des avocats. Les consultations rédigées par un professeur de droit ne sont pas non plus compris dans les dépens. *Idem* des recherches ou des enquêtes menées par des organismes privés en dehors des mesures d'instruction ordonnées par le juge. On appelle traditionnellement tous ces frais, honoraires ou autres, les frais « irrépétibles », parce qu'ils ne peuvent faire l'objet de « répétition », c'est-à-dire d'une demande de remboursement. En réalité, cette qualification traditionnelle est trompeuse, car le juge est bien en droit de décider discrétionnairement de condamner le perdant à payer ces frais non compris dans les dépens.[46]

31. *Calcul des frais.* Le calcul des dépens *stricto sensu* ne soulève pas de difficultés majeures dans la mesure où ils correspondent à des frais dont le montant est réglementé ou est contrôlé par le juge.[47] En cas de difficultés, c'est le greffier du tribunal qui opère, sous le contrôle du juge, les vérifications qui s'imposent.[48] En revanche, le montant de la condamnation éventuelle du perdant aux frais non compris dans les dépens relève d'une « arithmétique » beaucoup plus arbitraire. En fait, le juge ignore le montant exact des sommes payées par le gagnant. Son seul repère est la somme demandée par le plaideur au titre des frais non compris dans les dépens. Mais cette demande ne fait l'objet d'aucune justification, l'avocat n'ayant pas à présenter au juge le décompte de ses honoraires. Pour fixer le montant de la condamnation aux frais non compris dans les dépens, le texte du Code de procédure civile recommande au juge de « tenir compte de l'équité ou de la situation économique de la partie condamnée ». Mais là encore, sauf si l'instruction du litige lui a révélé quelques aspects de la situation économique réelle des parties, il est laissé dans l'ignorance. Il en résulte qu'au moment de fixer le montant de la condamnation au titre des frais non compris dans les dépens, le juge en est souvent réduit à modérer la demande formulée par le gagnant en fonction de la plus ou moins bonne foi de son adversaire...

[45] D. n° 2005-790 du 12 juillet 2005, art. 12.

[46] V. supra, n° 24.

[47] Ainsi notamment de la rémunération de l'expert.

[48] C. proc. civ., art. 704 s.

10.2.2 Exceptions

32. *Dépens à la charge du gagnant.* Par exception à la règle de principe, le tribunal peut décider de mettre tout ou partie des dépens à la charge du gagnant.[49] Toutefois, il s'agit là d'une faculté exceptionnelle qui doit être dûment motivée par le tribunal. Le législateur contemporain ne précise pas les motifs susceptibles de justifier un tel renversement de la charge des dépens laissant au juge le soin de les énoncer.[50]

33. *Frais non compris dans les dépens à la charge du gagnant.* Le tribunal peut également décider de laisser à la charge du gagnant les frais engagées par celui-ci non compris dans les dépens. Mais dans ce cas, il n'a pas à motiver sa décision.

34. *Ministère public.* Par exception, le ministère public, représentant l'Etat et agissant dans l'intérêt général de la société, lorsqu'il perd le procès auquel il est partie en matière civile, ne peut pas être condamné aux dépens. Le gagnant supportera donc toujours la charge des frais qu'il a exposés. Cette solution, constante en jurisprudence, ne repose pourtant sur aucun fondement juridique vraiment convaincant.[51]

35. *Dépens à la charge de l'Etat.* Lorsque le perdant bénéficie de l'aide juridictionnelle, il doit normalement payer les dépens exposés par son adversaire. Toutefois, par exception, le juge peut, même d'office, en mettre une partie à la charge de l'Etat.[52] Dans ce cas, l'aide juridictionnelle couvre alors non seulement les frais engagés par le bénéficiaire, mais également une partie de ceux de son adversaire.

36. *Frais frustratoires à la charge des auxiliaires de justice.* Par exception, le tribunal peut décider de mettre certains dépens, non pas à la charge du perdant, mais à la charge de l'auxiliaire de justice qui les a engagés, avocat ou autre. Il en est ainsi des frais engagés par les auxiliaires de justice en dehors de leur mandat, des frais relatifs aux actes

---

[49] C. proc. civ., art. 696, in fine.

[50] Autrefois, dans l'espoir d'apaiser les rancunes familiales, la loi avait expressément prévu la répartition des dépens lorsque le procès avait opposé des plaideurs d'une même famille...

[51] Pour le Conseil constitutionnel français, si la règle selon laquelle le gagnant peut obtenir du perdant le remboursement des frais qu'il a exposés n'a pas valeur constitutionnelle, la possibilité d'un tel remboursement affecte néanmoins l'exercice du droit d'agir en justice. Il estime en conséquence, vu l'égalité des justiciable devant la loi et la justice, ainsi que le principe d'une procédure juste et équitable garantissant l'équilibre des droits des parties, qu'est contraire à la Constitution, le texte qui prive arbitrairement une catégorie de plaideur de la possibilité de demander le remboursement de ses frais (Cons. const., déc. n° 2011-112 QPC, 1er avr. 2011, cons. n° 4). Ce raisonnement devrait conduire à l'abandon de la solution traditionnelle exposée au texte.

[52] L. n° 91-647 du 10 juillet 1991, art. 42, al. 2.

déclarés nuls par l'effet de leur faute et, de manière plus générale, des frais considérés comme injustifiés.[53] On les appelle les « frais frustratoires ». A noter que le juge peut décider de mettre ces frais à la charge des auxiliaires de justice d'office, c'est-à-dire même en l'absence de toute demande des parties en ce sens.

37. *Règles particulières.* Il existe, pour certains types de procès, des règles particulières de répartition de frais de procédure. Ainsi, par exemple, pour certains types de divorce. En matière de divorce par consentement mutuel, la règle est que les dépens de l'instance sont partagés par moitié entre les époux, à moins que leur convention n'en dispose autrement.[54] En matière de divorce pour altération définitive du lien conjugal, les dépens de l'instance sont à la charge de l'époux qui l'en a pris l'initiative, à moins que le juge n'en dispose autrement.[55]

38. *Perspectives.* Ce rapide survol du droit français des frais de justice fait apparaître quelques zones d'ombre, spécialement autour du report de la charge des honoraires d'avocat sur le perdant. La manière dont elle est décidée, au titre des frais non compris dans les dépens, n'est en effet guère satisfaisante. Pour améliorer ce point, il faudrait que le juge puisse se déterminer en connaissance de cause et donc sur la base d'une demande motivée. Certains auteurs le suggèrent. Mais exiger de l'avocat qu'il déclare au juge les honoraires réclamés à son client n'est-ce pas nécessairement introduire une forme d'appréciation de leur montant au regard du service rendu, en contradiction avec le principe de la liberté de la fixation des honoraires?[56] Plus généralement, ira-t-on vers une forme de normalisation des honoraires avec, comme en Italie, des minimums et des maximums?[57] Au demeurant, une telle tarification existe déjà d'une certaine manière lorsque le client bénéficie de l'aide juridictionnelle. La rétribution à laquelle a droit l'avocat à ce titre est déterminée en fonction d'une unité de valeur de référence fixée annuellement et affectée d'un coefficient pour chaque type de procédure.[58] L'équilibre économique du système d'aide juridictionnelle en dépend évidemment, et avec lui l'accès effectif au droit pour

[53] C. proc. civ., art. 697 et 698.

[54] C. proc. civ., art. 1105.

[55] C. proc. civ., art. 1137.

[56] Le barreau français garde en mémoire qu'en 1976, fait exceptionnel, les avocats français firent grève pendant une semaine parce que le législateur avait mentionné les honoraires au titre des frais non compris dans les dépens, considérant que cette simple référence portait en elle le risque d'une immixtion du juge dans la fixation des honoraires ! Le législateur retira aussitôt cette mention.

[57] La Cour de justice de l'Union européenne a jugé que l'instauration de barèmes indicatifs d'honoraires, fixant des minimums et des maximums, n'était pas contraire au droit de l'Union européenne (v. CJCE, 19 févr. 2002, aff. C-35/99).

[58] V. L. n° 91-647 du 10 juill. 1991, art. 27 et Décr. n° 91-1266 du 19 déc. 1991, art. 90.

tout un chacun. Cette observation en appelle une autre, sur l'avenir des honoraires de résultat. Les deux questions sont en effet objectivement liées. Si ce n'est pas l'Etat qui fait l'avance des frais aux plaideurs, il faut que les avocats eux-mêmes acceptent de le faire, mais on conçoit qu'ils n'accepteront de le faire qu'en contrepartie d'un intéressement substantiel sur les gains éventuels du procès. Dans une telle perspective, les honoraires de résultat peuvent-ils rester un simple complément de rémunération ? A cet égard, la perspective sans cesse repoussée de l'introduction en droit français d'une action de groupe, cette action en justice à l'économie si particulière puisqu'elle suppose pour être engagée à une certaine échelle une avance de fonds considérable que seuls peuvent assumer les plus gros cabinets d'avocats, n'ouvrira-t-elle pas une brèche dans la prohibition traditionnelle du pacte de *quota litis* ? On peut d'ailleurs se demander si les deux questions ne sont pas liées, si les hésitations du législateur français à l'égard des actions de groupe ne reposent pas, au fond, sur la crainte d'une « marchandisation » de la justice.

Chapter 11
Cost and Fee Allocation in German Civil Procedure

Burkhard Hess and Rudolf Huebner

11.1 Basic Rules

11.1.1 Cost and Fee Allocation – The Loser Pays

In Germany, the losing party must bear all statutory costs of the litigation in civil and commercial matters, including the costs incurred by the opponent and the costs for the taking of evidence, sec. 91 (1) ZPO ("loser pays" rule[1] and indemnity principle). If each party is successful in part and fails in part, costs are mutually cancelled or proportionally divided, sec. 92 (1) ZPO.

Appellate proceedings entail additional and higher costs. These costs are allocated according to the general principles with minor exceptions, as set out in sec. 97 ZPO. According to sec. 97 (1) ZPO, the losing party must pay the complete costs of the litigation and reimburse the costs of the winning party – even if the losing party won in the first instance.

The winning party can only recover the necessary costs of the litigation, sec. 91 (1) ZPO. The term *necessary* refers to the statutory costs. Consequently, a winning party that agreed to pay higher fees to its attorney than provided for by the Attorneys Remuneration Act (RVG) will only receive a reimbursement of the legally fixed fees, and not of the additional agreed costs. This limited recoverability reduces the financial risk of civil litigation and thus protects the losing party.

The reimbursable costs for the taking of evidence include not only court appointed expert witnesses,[2] but also expert witnesses hired by the prevailing party as long as the hiring of the expert was *necessary* as provided by

[1] *Murray/Stürner*, German Civil Justice (2004), p. 341.

[2] As a rule, the court selects and appoints the expert, see sec. 404 ZPO.

B. Hess (✉)
University of Heidelberg, Heidelberg, Germany
e-mail: hess@ipr.uni-heidelberg.de

M. Reimann (ed.), *Cost and Fee Allocation in Civil Procedure*,
Ius Gentium: Comparative Perspectives on Law and Justice 11,
DOI 10.1007/978-94-007-2263-7_11, © Springer Science+Business Media B.V. 2012

sec. 91 (1) ZPO.[3] If the court appoints an expert, parties have to advance the costs according to the burden of proof.[4] These advance payments are later recoverable according to the general principles (sec. 91 ZPO). The remuneration of court appointed experts (and interpreters) is governed by law (JVEG) and based on hourly rates.

The German system is designed to provide equal access to justice of a high standard at reasonable costs. As an additional objective, the "loser pays" rule shall encourage potential claimants to pursue valid claims, but at the same time discourage the pursuit of unmeritorious claims. Thus, it also promotes the efficient use of the judiciary. Taken as a whole, the basic rule corresponds to the general procedural objective[5] of protecting and implementing substantive private rights. However, the basic rule also has constitutional underpinnings as it is closely related to the constitutional guarantee[6] of free access to justice, derived from articles 2 (1), 20, 3 GG.[7] Accordingly, the constitutional guarantee prohibits any unnecessary and disproportional costs in civil litigation, although it still leaves large discretion to the legislature when elaborating a cost system.

11.1.2 Exceptions and Modifications

11.1.2.1 Statutory Exceptions

For some family proceedings and non-contentious proceedings, there are wide ranging exceptions from the loser pays rule, sec. 81 FamFG. The most important family proceedings (marital matters and contentious family matters) are, however, governed by the general rules of the ZPO as described above, sec. 112, 113 FamFG. Non-contentious proceedings predominantly comprise matters concerning the supervision of natural persons and the confinement of supervised persons and the mentally ill, (*Betreuungs- und Unterbringungssachen*), decedents estates and issues of their distribution (*Nachlass und Teilungssachen*), matters concerning public registers

[3] *Bork* in: Stein/Jonas, ZPO (2004), sec. 91, 42 (p. 425) and 79 et seq. (p. 440 et seq.); note 22, *infra*.

[4] For acts of the court requested by a party cf. sec. 17 GKG, 379, 402 ZPO. For ex officio acts of the court cf. *Zimmermann* in: Binz/Dörndorfer/Petzold/Zimmermann, GKG, JVEG, sec. 17 GKG 16, 17.

[5] Cf. *Hartmann* in: Baumbach/Lauterbach/Albers/Hartmann, ZPO[66] (2008), Einl III, 9 (p. 9).

[6] Cf. BVerfG, December 12, 2006 – 1 BvR 2576/04, BVerfGE 117, p. 163 (186 et seq.); also cf. *Brehm* in: Stein/Jonas, ZPO[22] (2003), vor sec. 1, 287–288 (p. 103 et seq.).

[7] Cf. *Hartmann* in: Baumbach/Lauterbach/Albers/Hartmann, ZPO[66] (2008), Grdz § 128, 14 (p. 619).

and specific company law matters (*Registersachen und unternehmensrechtliche Sachen*). Where applicable, sec. 81 FamFG gives the court wide discretion when allocating the costs among the parties.[8] The court may also decide that no one shall be charged for the proceedings. However, limiting the court's discretion, sec. 81 (2) enumerates several situations where the court shall allocate the costs to a specific party.

According to a general objective, the German cost system tends to discourage the parties from persevering in litigation – even after the case has been filed – and to settle the case. Accordingly, several provisions permit a reduction or even a shifting of the costs if one or both parties terminate the litigation. Specific provisions address the discontinuation of the proceedings (*Erledigung der Hauptsache*, sec. 91a ZPO[9]) and the immediate acknowledgment of the claim by a defendant who gave no motivation for the litigation (sec. 93 ZPO[10]).

An additional guiding principle of the German cost system tends to discourage procedural misbehavior by (rather limited) sanctions. If a party fails to observe a time limit and the hearing is adjourned, the negligent party must bear the additional costs – irrespective of the outcome of the litigation (sec. 95 ZPO). If a party prevails on appeal by presenting new facts – which by negligence were not presented at the first instance – the court may (at its discretion) order the prevailing party to partly or fully reimburse the costs of the appeal (sec. 97 ZPO[11]). Additional costs for unsuccessful or unnecessary motions (sec. 96 ZPO) can also be allocated to the responsible party. As far as the allocation of (additional or unnecessary) costs is concerned, German law provides for limited judicial discretion. However, the court is not permitted to deviate from the general rule in sec. 91 ZPO. In this context, the principle guiding the discretion provides that the party who caused additional costs (cf. sec. 96 ZPO) must compensate the other side for these costs.

11.1.2.2 Party Agreements and Settlements

Party agreements allocating costs and fees are very uncommon unless parties reach a settlement. For settlements, sec. 98 ZPO explicitly provides for

---

[8] Also see the materials of the German Federal Parliament (*Bundestags Drucksache*) BT Drs. 16/6308, p. 215 et seq.

[9] In this case there will be no judgment on the merits. Moreover, as the parties no longer seek such judgment, the court will only decide on the costs, based on the information brought forward until that moment.

[10] This provision is intended to prevent claimants from pursuing undisputed claims in court.

[11] Additionally, unsuccessful appeals have to be paid for by the party that appealed (sec 97 (1) ZPO).

agreements on fees and costs.[12] Such cost agreements are enforceable if they are a part of a settlement in court. If the parties of a settlement do not agree on the allocation of costs, each party bears its own costs and court costs are equally divided, sec. 98 ZPO.

11.1.3 Encouragement or Discouragement of Litigation

In general, cost rules shall encourage parties to bring valid lawsuits and to discourage parties from pursuing unmeritorious claims. In addition, German law provides for two major incentives to encourage settlements. Firstly, the renouncing of litigation – including settlements –involves considerably lower court charges, cf. appendix 1 to sec. 3 (2) GKG, KV 1211, 1222, 1232. Secondly, lawyers receive an additional settlement fee, cf. appendix 1 to sec. 2 (2) RVG, VV 1000, 1003, 1004, providing for an incentive to encourage their clients to agree on the settlements.

11.1.4 Advance Payments

For most of the litigation costs, advance payments are either necessary (court charges and expenses,[13] cf. sec. 12, 17 GKG) or at least permitted (attorney remuneration, cf. sec. 9 RVG[14]), in some cases such payments are made upon request of the court for witnesses of fact and court appointed experts (cf. sec. 379, 402 ZPO). The actual amount usually depends on the amount in controversy (for court charges and attorney fees). The advancement of fees may hinder the parties' access to justice although a party entitled to legal aid does not have to advance any fees.[15]

11.1.5 The Determination of Costs and Fees

11.1.5.1 Court Costs

Court charges are generally calculated on the basis of the amount in controversy, sec. 3 GKG and sec. 3 FamGKG. The amount in controversy is defined by sec. 39–65 GKG, sec. 2–9 ZPO and sec. 33–56 FamGKG. In

---

[12] For further information see *Bork* in: Stein/Jonas, ZPO[22] (2004), sec. 98, 11 et seq. (p. 559 et seq.).

[13] Court charges include the remuneration of court appointed translators and experts, cf. KV 9005 of appendix 1 to the GKG.

[14] Lawyers regularly request an advancement of the remuneration from the client.

[15] Jauernig/Hess, Zivilprozessrecht (30rd ed. 2011), §§ 93–95.

some cases concerning the violation of intellectual property rights[16] or competition laws, amounts in controversy are assessed generously on a rather abstract calculation of possible damages. As a result, high court and attorney fees are used by claimants as a threat against the alleged violators. For example, most recently, a producer of plastic toys with a turnover of approximately 100 million EUR sued the single (woman) producer of hand-made teddy bears over the use of her last name as a trademark she had registered. The business of the woman generates an annual profit of 500–700 EUR but the amount sought by the plastic toy producer is 250,000 EUR.[17]

As the court fees are solely based on the amount in controversy, they do not depend on the efforts actually undertaken by the Court. Neither the length nor the difficulty of the proceedings is taken into account. Court fees rise with the amount in controversy on a digressive scale. This is based on the consideration that the workload of the court does not usually increase proportionally to the amount in controversy. Therefore, in comparison to the workload, court charges are comparatively low for small claims and increase enough to constitute a system of cross subsidization in which large claims financially subsidize smaller cases.[18] Since 2002, the amount in controversy is capped at a maximum of EUR 30 million, sec. 39 (2) GKG, 33 (2) FamGKG.[19] There are also lower caps to the amount in controversy for some special types of proceedings.

11.1.5.2 Lawyers' Fees

Lawyers' fees are also regulated by statute. According to the Attorney Remuneration Act (RVG) the fees of lawyers are usually fixed according to the amount in controversy. Yet, lawyers are permitted to negotiate higher fees, sec. 2, 3a RVG. By contrast, a negotiated decrease is not permitted for court related attorney work, sec. 49b (1) BRAO, 4 (1) RVG. Sec. 4a RVG, a provision enacted in 2008, permits success fees under specific and very

---

[16] E.g. illegal downloads of music, cf. Tyra, ZUM 2009, 934 (940 et seq.).

[17] Cf. http://www.spiegel.de/wirtschaft/unternehmen/0,1518,671570,00.html (2011-03-31).

[18] While usually small claims are less complex to pursue and thus also require less work, the work required for the pursuit of larger claims on average does not increase proportionally to the value in dispute. Rather, the workload usually increases slower than the value in dispute. This finding is also the reason for the declining design of the amount in controversy based cost structure, cf. sec. 34 GKG, 13 RVG. Hence the subsidies result from a – on average – lower than adequate decline of the costs in comparison to the (typical) actual workload of a rising value in dispute. Cf. *Hommerich/Kilian/Jackmuth/Wolf*, Anwaltsblatt 2006, p. 406 (406).

[19] This legislative change immediately increased the volume of high value litigation in Germany.

restricted circumstances. However, as a rule, German law does not permit contingency fees, cf. sec. 49b (2) BRAO (but see C.I. infra).

The calculation of the amount in controversy for lawyer fees is defined by sec. 22–33 RVG, which largely refer to the GKG and ZPO (see supra B.V.1.). There is a cap of EUR 30 million to the amount in controversy here as well.

11.1.5.3 Cost Allocation and Determination Decisions

In contentious proceedings, courts determine the allocation of costs among the parties as part of the judgment, cf. sec. 308 (2) ZPO (*Kostengrundentscheidung*[20]). The amount in controversy will also be calculated and fixed by the court. This decision will – at the latest – be made together with the decision on the material claim but in a separate court order, cf. sec. 63 (2) GKG. The actual taxation of potential reimbursement claims, i.e., the determination of the exact sum, however, is determined in completely separate proceedings, sec. 103–107 ZPO, 85 FamFG (*Kostenfestsetzungsverfahren*).

11.2 Litigation Financing

11.2.1 Success-Oriented Fees

Traditionally, success-oriented fees were not permitted by the German lawyers' remuneration laws, cf. sec. 49b (2) BRAO. In 2006, the Federal Constitutional Court (*BVerfG*) ruled that the ban on success-oriented fees was, in part, not in accordance with the German Constitution (*GG*).[21] The constitutional guarantee of access to justice requires the ban to allow for exceptions in cases in which parties could be deterred from pursuing their rights unless they had the possibility to negotiate a contingency fee. With very reluctant changes to the RVG, effective since July 1st 2008, the legislature tried to implement the standards demanded by the *BVerfG*. Still, the regulation on success-oriented fees is criticized for both

---

[20] Usually the last part of the decision. An exemplary decision dividing the costs could be: *Von den Kosten des Rechtsstreits trägt der Beklagte 4/5 und die Klägerin 1/5* (Of the litigation costs, the respondent bears 4/5 and the claimant 1/5.).

[21] BVerfG, 12.12.2006 – 1 BvR 2576/04, BVerfGE 117, p. 163 et seq.

its consequences[22] and its reach.[23] Some critics fear that even the limited permission of contingency fees will be a substantial step towards an unwelcome Americanization[24] of German procedural law.[25]

The German legislature endorsed these criticisms and permitted success fees in a very restricted fashion. According to sec. 4a RVG, success-oriented fees are only permitted in case the client would otherwise be deterred from pursuing his or her right because of his or her economic situation. Consequently, success-oriented fees can only be agreed to on a case by case basis. If these conditions are met, different types of remuneration can be negotiated. Accordingly, the parties can agree on contingency fees (a percentage of the sum won), no win-no fee arrangements, success premiums (higher fees in case of a victory) and other arrangements.[26] Importantly, success-oriented fees that are higher than the statutory remuneration cannot be recovered from the losing party under sec. 91 ZPO. These costs are – in general – not considered necessary to pursue a claim in light of this provision.[27]

11.2.2 Sale of Claims

Claims can be *sold and transferred* for purposes of litigation within the limits of substantive law. Sec. 398 BGB determines that all claims can be subrogated unless a special provision prohibits the cession of the claim. The two most important of these limiting provisions follow immediately. Sec. 399 BGB excludes claims from transfer if the parties have agreed to a prohibition of any transfer or if the claim cannot be ceded without a change of its content. Sec. 400 BGB defines that a claim cannot be transferred to the extent it is not subject to pledge.

However, if claims are to be (collectively) enforced by a third party, such business is restricted by sec. 2 (2) and 3 RDG. Under these provisions, only

---

[22] Cf. e.g. *Mayer*, Anwaltsblatt 2008, p. 473 (477) criticizing the changes for the consequential lack of form in remuneration agreements.

[23] Cf. e.g. *Hartung*, Anwaltsblatt 2008, p. 396 et seq.

[24] Cf. *Hartung*, Anwaltsblatt 2008, p. 396 (398) on what is understood as Americanisation in Germany.

[25] Cf. e.g. *Stüer*, Anwaltsblatt 2007, p. 431 et seq.

[26] Cf. *Mayer*, Anwaltsblatt 2008, p. 473 (474, 475); materials of the German Federal Parliament (*Bundestags Drucksache*) BT Drs. 16/8384, p. 10 et seq.

[27] *Herget* in: Zöller, ZPO[27] (2009), sec. 91, 13 (p. 376); *Giebel* in MünchKomm-ZPO[3] (2008), sec. 91, 49 and 105.

persons with a license to offer legal services and some exempt organizations, such as consumer protection agencies (sec. 8 (1) No. 4 RDG),[28] may engage in such business. At the litigation stage, sec. 79 (1), (2) ZPO reflect these restrictions. In other cases, the transfer of the claim is considered void (sec. 134 BGB).

Recently, the BGH permitted an action brought by a Belgian stock company (CDC) against several German corporate defendants for the collection of damages caused by a cartel.[29] The plaintiff had bought the claims from several German companies which had been victims of the cartel. The defendant relied on sec. 8 (1) No. 4 RDG and argued that the assignment of the claim to the plaintiff was null and void. The BGH did not directly decide the issue but held that the lawsuit was admissible. This judgment demonstrates a growing willingness to permit innovative forms of litigation financing.

11.2.3 Litigation Insurance

In Germany, 90% of funds for civil procedure costs emanate from three sources:

(1) Self-financing of the client (47%),
(2) Legal Expenses Insurance (LEI) (35%) – approximately 43% of the German population hold a LEI policy,[30]
(3) Legal aid (8%).[31]

This data demonstrates that Germany can be considered a stronghold of Legal Expenses Insurance. During the last two decades, it has become widespread in Germany.[32] This insurance usually covers specific risks such as legal costs arising out of motor accidents. The main advantage of this kind of insurance, compared with legal aid, is that the insurance covers the risk of losing the lawsuit. The typical legal cost insurance reimburses the whole litigation costs which include the representation by a lawyer and

---

[28] Also cf. *Hess* in: *Mansel/Dauner-Lieb/Henssler*, Zugang zum Recht, 2008, p. 61 (67 et seq.). Please note that at the time, the RDG was not yet in force. The RDG replaced the RBG that covered the same topic.

[29] BGH, April 7, 2009 – KZR 42/08 and press release 80/2009, both available on http://www.bundesgerichtshof.de/ (in German).

[30] Cf. *Hommerich/Kilian/Jackmuth/Wolf*, Anwaltsblatt 2006, p. 200 (200); *Köbl*, Prozesskostenhilfe vor Erfolgshonorar?, FS Leipold (2009), p. 63 et seq.

[31] Cf. *Hommerich/Kilian/Dreske*, Statistical Yearbook of the Laywers Profession 2007/2008, p. 139.

[32] In 2002, German insurance companies earned approximately €2.8 billion in LEI premiums from issuing about 25 million policies (the total amount of the German population is about 80 million people).

the obligation to pay the opponent's cost in case of defeat. This growth of legal cost insurances has been criticised by judges: they complain about a "litigation explosion" in Germany and the bringing of lawsuits without serious chances of success.[33] Insurers are not legally bound to offer only specific types of LEI. The freedom of contract leaves them many options for designing their policies. However, insurers offering LEI usually use a standardized policy under the Uniform Conditions on Legal Expenses Insurance (*Allgemeine Bedingungen für die Rechtsschutzversicherung – ARB 2010*).[34]

Legal expenses insurance can also be included in various types of liability insurance. However, liability insurance usually offers only passive protection. This means that the insurer will only pay for the costs of a defense against claims the insurer believes to be non-meritorious.

11.2.4 Legal Aid

Sec. 114–127a ZPO and sec. 76–78 FamFG provide for general and publicly funded legal aid. Legal aid is available to all individuals who are unable to pay for parts or any of the procedural costs, either immediately or at all, sec. 114 ZPO, sec. 76 FamFG. As a second condition, the applicant's claim or defense has to have an adequate chance of success. If these conditions are met, legal aid is granted either as an interest-free loan[35] (sec. 114, 115 and 120 (1) ZPO) or as a full grant without any repayment obligation (sec. 127 (III) 1 ZPO[36]), depending on the ability of the applicant to financially contribute to the litigation. Interest-free loan legal aid has to be repaid in monthly installments (sec. 120 (1) and 115 ZPO).

Applications for legal aid have to be filed with the same court deciding the merits of the case, sec. 117 (1) ZPO. Legal aid is granted or denied without an oral hearing although the opposite party is heard, sec. 127 (1) ZPO. The decision can be appealed, sec. 127 (2), (3) ZPO. Grants are awarded independently in every instance of the proceedings, sec. 119 (1) ZPO.

Representation based on legal aid is less attractive for lawyers as their statutory compensation is significantly reduced, cf. sec. 49 RVG. Legal aid also carries significant risks for its recipients. If the recipient of legal aid loses the litigation, he or she must still reimburse the necessary costs of the prevailing party, cf. sec. 91 (1), 123 ZPO, sec. 76 (1) FamFG.

---

[33] Statistics did not confirm these critics, *Murray* and *Stürner*, German Civil Justice, p. 124.

[34] Available online (2011-03-31): http://www.gdv.de/Downloads/Bedingungen/Musterbedingung_Rechtsschutz_ARB2010_September2010.pdf.

[35] Note: The applicant never receives any payment; rather, the state pays the costs on behalf of the applicant.

[36] Cf. *Philippi* in: Zöller, ZPO[27] (2009), sec. 120, 7 (p. 565), sec. 127, 14 (p. 605).

11.3 Class Actions and Group Litigation

American-style class actions are unknown to the German civil procedure system. Yet, since 2005, investors can collectively sue companies under the KapMuG (Capital Markets Model Case Act) for certain violations of capital market rules.[37] Under the KapMuG, individual proceedings are temporarily merged into one model case to resolve the issues common to all the individual claims.[38] The KapMuG contains two provisions on litigation costs for model cases, sec. 17, 19 KapMuG. Pursuant to sec. 17 KapMuG, the costs of the model case are part of the costs of the subsequent continuation of individual proceedings (dealing with the particularities of each individual case). The costs are allocated to the individual proceedings according to the proportion of the net worth of each individual claim to the overall net worth of all claims merged. Sec. 19 KapMuG, in contrast to sec. 17 KapMuG, is a separate rule on the allocation of costs in case of an appeal against the decision in the model case. Whereas the costs of the original model case become part of the costs of the individual proceedings (sec. 17 KapMuG), costs of an appeal against the model case are allocated among the parties of the appeal (sec. 19 KapMuG). Although it is a special provision in relation to sec. 91 et seq. ZPO, sec. 19 KapMuG roughly follows the same principle of allocating the costs to the loser of the appeal.[39]

Despite the traditional concept of two parties litigating against each other, either side can consist of more than one party (*Streitgenossenschaft* – group litigation), sec. 59–63 ZPO. In that case, sec. 100 ZPO provides a special rule on the allocation of litigation costs among the group. According to sec. 100 (1), as a general rule, costs are shared equally among the members of the group. Only if the extent of the involvement in the litigation is considerably uneven, the court can allocate the costs among the members of the group according to its discretion, sec. 100 (2).

11.4 Conclusion

Due to its high level of regulation, civil litigation costs in Germany are comparatively predictable. This predictability of the costs is perceived as a strong advantage of the German litigation system.[40] Yet, there are two factors that may lower the predictability in specific cases. Firstly, the costs

---

[37] For details consult *Hess*, in *Hess/Reuschle/Rimmelspacher*, KapMuG (2008), Einl. (p. 3 et seq.).

[38] Cf. *Kruis* in: *Hess/Reuschle/Rimmelspacher*, KapMuG (2008), sec. 17, 1–2 (p. 547).

[39] Cf. *Kruis* in: *Hess/Reuschle/Rimmelspacher*, KapMuG (2008), sec. 19, 1–3 (p. 561).

[40] Cf. "Law – Made in Germany", p. 29, the booklet is available on the website (2011-03-31) http://www.lawmadeingermany.de/.

incurred by the taking of evidence cannot be calculated easily in complex cases even though they are also highly regulated. This applies especially when court appointed experts are involved. These experts are paid on a – relatively low – hourly basis. Secondly, statutory costs are sometimes insufficient for rewarding sophisticated legal advice. In such cases parties have to negotiate a higher remuneration. However, as mentioned, under the compensation regime of sec. 91 et seq. ZPO, a negotiated higher remuneration cannot be recovered.

The basic concept of the "loser pays" rule, which does not leave any discretion for the court, entails an effective deterrent for unmeritorious lawsuits. It also promotes the access to justice for valid claims.

The German lawyers' remuneration system is based on the idea of a cross subsidization (among lower and higher claims). However, this basic assumption has considerably lost momentum due to growing specialization within the German bar. It is noticeable that the pressure to change the whole system is growing as the overall trend is likely to make the pursuit of small claims more difficult in the future. Therefore, the elaboration of adequate remuneration structures for small claims will be a major challenge.

During the last few years, the legal framework of attorney remuneration has been somewhat deregulated. The relatively low costs level and the high transparency of costs are major economic advantages of the regulated system compared with the situation in less regulated or even unregulated markets.[41] Deregulation may cause adverse effects, e.g., a lack of transparency or an insufficient protection of inexperienced parties.[42]

The present cost system in Germany seems to be appropriate and competitive, at least at a European level. Its basic structures guarantee a comparatively efficient and highly qualified judicial system. The predominant legal literature suggests preserving the present system and its two fundamental principles: the "loser pays" rule and the lack of judicial discretion with regard to the allocation of costs.

---

[41] *Von Seltmann*, BRAK-Mitteilungen 2008, p. 118 (119).

[42] *Von Seltmann*, BRAK-Mitteilungen 2008, p. 118 (119).

Abbreviations

	Full Term (German)	Translation
BGB	Bürgerliches Gesetzbuch	Civil Code
BGH	Bundesgerichtshof	Federal Court of Justice
BRAO	Bundesrechtsanwaltsordnung	Federal Attorneys Code
BVerfG	Bundesverfassungsgericht	Federal Constitutional Court
FamFG	Gesetz über das Verfahren in Familien-sachen und den Angelegenheiten der freiwilligen Gerichtsbarkeit	Code of Family Proceedings and Non-Contentious Proceedings
FamGKG	Gesetz über Gerichtskosten in Familien-sachen	Family Matters Court Charges Act
GC	Grundgesetz	Federal Constitution (Basic Law)
GKG	Gerichtskostengesetz	Court Charges Act
GVG	Gerichtsverfassungsgesetz	Court Organization Code
JVEG	Justizvergütungs- und Entschädigungs-gesetz	Judicial Remuneration and Compensation Act
KapMuG	Kapitalanleger-Musterverfahrensgesetz	Act on the Initiation of Model Case Proceedings in Respect of Investors in the Capital Markets (Capital Markets Model Case Act)
RDG	Rechtsdienstleistungsgesetz	Legal Services Act
RVG	Rechtsanwaltsvergütungsgesetz	Attorney Remuneration Act
ZPO	Zivilprozessordnung	Civil Procedure Code

Chapter 12
Lawyers' Fees in Greece at a Turning Point: Recent Legislative Changes in Litigation Costs

Kalliopi Makridou

12.1 The Civil Trial in Greece: The Financial and Time Framework

Over the past two months in Greece, there has been an "over-production" in legislation relating to procedure. Among others, laws 3900/2010 (21-12-2010) and 3904/2010 (27-12-2010) have modified respectively the legal framework of administrative and criminal procedure to expedite proceedings. In the meantime, the amendment of the Code of Civil Procedure will soon become law to accelerate civil proceedings.

Furthermore, recently legislators passed the law 3919/25-2-2011 on "The principle of professional freedom, abolition of unjustified restrictions on access to and pursuit of professions", which in Article 5 amends the way lawyers' fees are determined and, in particular, liberalizes legal fees. The legislature aims to bring down attorneys' fees through free market competition.

Delays plague the Greek judicial system. As a result, the courts are currently extremely overburdened. For example, in the case of a civil trial it usually takes at least six months for a temporary arrangement of the dispute by means of provisional remedies. In an ordinary proceeding it usually takes two to three years for a judgment in the first instance and at least another two for a final judgment. The reasons for this delay are numerous. Principal among them are the lack of an adequate infrastructure and the insufficient number of judges.

To make matters worse, Greece is one of the most litigious nations on earth. It has become commonplace for Greeks to resort without a second thought to the courts to conduct even less significant disputes. There are several reasons for this situation. First of all, there is the excessive number of lawyers. In a country like Greece, with an estimated population of

K. Makridou (✉)
Aristotle University of Thessaloniki, Thessaloniki, Greece
e-mail: lioka2004@yahoo.gr

M. Reimann (ed.), *Cost and Fee Allocation in Civil Procedure*, 163
Ius Gentium: Comparative Perspectives on Law and Justice 11,
DOI 10.1007/978-94-007-2263-7_12, © Springer Science+Business Media B.V. 2012

11,000,000 inhabitants, there are approximately 42,000 lawyers, of whom 22,000 (representing ca. 50% of the total) are enrolled in the Athens Bar Association. Thus there is currently approximately one lawyer for every 250 Greek citizens.

Second, the percentage of disputes that are resolved before the civil courts through settlement is extremely low in Greece today; in fact, it is almost disappointingly low. Less than 5% of all disputes end with a settlement. The situation has not improved even after the introduction of a mandatory extrajudicial settlement procedure (Article 214A of the Hellenic Code of Civil Procedure).

At the beginning of the settlement procedure, all parties are obliged to pay their lawyers the minimum fee reserved for the lawyers' appearance in court. The minimum fee is to be determined on the basis of the amount involved and the issues covered, using specific evaluation methods.[1] Where a trial ends in a court settlement, the lawyer is only entitled to the settlement fee and not to the cumulative fee for all his pre-court and out-of-court acts.[2] If no settlement is achieved, no fee is payable to the lawyer for the settlement; instead, he or she must be paid for the specific remunerable activities he was engaged in.[3] The fees play an important role in the failure of the settlement system because the fee that a lawyer receives in a settlement falls far short of the fee he would receive if he pursued the case to final judgment. Lawyers thus have no significant financial incentive to contribute to the settlement of a conflict.

Last but not least, the excessive burden on the courts is due to the fact that scheduled and thus reimbursable fees are extremely low. As the General Report points out,[4] Greece is among the countries with the lowest shifting of litigation costs to the loser. Court costs especially are so low that citizens do not consider them to be a barrier to lodging any form of action, even if the odds of winning the case are weak. In Greece there is a strong policy that litigation costs should not constitute a barrier for access to justice and that all Greeks be able to bear the financial burden of a trial.

In practice, the costs awarded for minimum lawyers' fees rarely reflect the actual amount paid by the client to the lawyer so that the winning party is rarely awarded the entire fee paid. Recent law 3919/25-2-2011 radically changed the framework for attorneys' fees, and hence litigation costs, shifting towards free market prices for lawyers. Under the new system there is a risk of follow-up litigation, as in England and similar systems.

---

[1] Greek Supreme Court Judg. No. 42/2006, Nomos Legal Databank.

[2] Greek Supreme Court Judg. No. 212/2004, Nomos Legal Databank. Amounts paid as a fee for work done up until the time of the settlement are deducted from the lawyer's fee. Greek Supreme Court Judg. No. 736/1998, Legal Tribune Law Review 1999. 1557.

[3] Greek Supreme Court Judg. No. 1028/1995, Review of Labor Law 1995. 619.

[4] General Report II.2.b.

Extremely low official fees are counterbalanced, however, by the common use of contingency fee arrangements. Yet, there are strict conditions on the validity of such arrangements (e.g., a requirement that agreements expressly provide for the case of failure, a cap of 20% of the amount in controversy, certification by the tax authority, etc.). Finally, in Greece, public legal aid is the only available kind of legal aid.

12.2 The "Loser Pays" Principle

12.2.1 The Basic Rule

One of the fundamental rules of Greek law is that each litigant must pay court costs up-front (Article 173 (1) to (3) of the Hellenic Code of Civil Procedure).[5] For clearly social purposes there is an exception to the rule of advance payment in maintenance cases (Article 173 (4) of the Hellenic Code of Civil Procedure). In such a case, the party that owes maintenance, i.e., the respondent, pays the plaintiff's costs and charges which are set by the judge and capped at €150 (Article 174 of the Hellenic Code of Civil Procedure). If the respondent fails to pay up-front costs, he or she is deemed in default (Article 175 of the Hellenic Code of Civil Procedure).

When it comes to ex post allocation of court costs, it is not important who paid the ex ante costs. Here, the 'loser pays' principle applies (Article 176 of the Hellenic Code of Civil Procedure). The losing party is ordered to pay the litigation costs, which include both the court costs and lawyers' fees. In practice, however, the official lawyers' fees are extremely low, because they are the minimum scheduled and do not cover, even in the slightest, the fee that the winning party must actually pay to her lawyer.

Court costs are also allocated on the basis of the 'loser pays' principle even in a case where a party is only partially successful. Article 178 (1) of the Hellenic Code of Civil Procedure states that 'the court shall allocate costs depending on the extent to which each party wins or loses'.

The Greek legislature links the 'loser pays' principle to the principle of fault.[6] The losing party is deemed to be responsible for the court proceedings and for that reason must pay all litigation costs. Article 177 of the Hellenic Code of Civil Procedure, which actually deviates from the basic rule, further reinforces the connection between the loser pays principle and the principle of fault: litigation court costs can be imposed on

[5] Kerameus, Civil Procedural Law (1986), p. 342. Nikas, Civil Procedure II (2005), par. 101 § 1–3.

[6] Kerameus, Civil Procedural Law, p. 343.

the winning party if the respondent did not, due to his attitude, cause the action to be opened and, immediately after the action was lodged, admitted or accepted the grounds of the action.[7] The winning party is ordered to pay only those costs that are necessary for conducting the trial both in and out of court[8] but not costs arising from a party's contempt, negligence[9] or excessive delay[10] (Article 189 of the Hellenic Code of Civil Procedure).

It should also be noted that Greek law contains a significant deviation from the principle of equality of the parties because the State enjoys a certain favorable treatment (Article 22 of Law 3693/1957). In particular, when the State loses an action, costs it has to pay are limited to half of the scheduled lawyers' fees and cannot, in any event, exceed €300 at any court level.

Article 189 (1) of the Hellenic Code of Civil Procedure contains a list of the individual types of recoverable costs. These expressly include amounts paid to witnesses to cover their costs or as remuneration, and to expert witnesses for their costs and fees[11] in line with the applicable fee schedules. They also include costs to preserve evidence,[12] and the cost of private expert opinions.[13] However, recoverable costs do not include the fee agreed with the expert witnesses.[14]

Moreover, court costs do not include technical consultant fees[15]– in other words, the fee of any specialist whom a party appoints on his own behalf when the court orders that an expert opinion to be prepared. The litigant is entitled (but not obliged) to submit a detailed table of the expenses incurred. The court will include a ruling on court costs in its final order.

---

[7] Athens One-Member District Court Judg. No. 203/1986, Hellenic Justice Law Review 1987. 360.

[8] E.g. translation/legalisation expenses for documents, property title deed searches for the respondent's assets, etc.

[9] E.g. service of the action to the wrong address and repeat service, Keramefs, Civil Procedural Law, p. 346.

[10] Greek Supreme Court Judg. No. 1101/1993, Hellenic Justice Law Review 1995. 145.

[11] Greek Supreme Court in plenary session, Judgement No. 9/1996, Hellenic Justice Law Review 1996. 1054.

[12] Article 348 of the Hellenic Code of Civil Procedure. Preservative evidence shall be ordered even before the start of the trial where there is a risk of certain evidence being lost or its use being hampered, or in order to determine the provisional state of a thing or project. It is also allowed following the proceedings for provisional measures.

[13] Kerameus/Kondylis/Nikas (-Orfanidis), Interpretation of the Hellenic Code of Civil Procedure, (2000), Article 189 § 2.

[14] Athens Court of Appeal Judg. No. 896/1988, Hellenic Justice Law Review 1990. 588. Piraeus Court of Appeal Judg. No. 1101/1995, Hellenic Justice Law Review 1996. 1160.

[15] Kerameus/Kondylis/Nikas (-Orfanidis), Interpretation of the Hellenic Code of Civil Procedure, (2000), Article 189 § 3.

Article 191 of the Hellenic Code of Civil Procedure states that if the judgment fails to include a ruling on litigation costs, a party may petition the court to issue a separate ruling on costs.[16] A judgment for costs in the first instance may not be enforced until the judgment is final (Article 909 (2) of the Hellenic Code of Civil Procedure). Only a final judgment (in other words the judgment of an appellate court or a judgment for which the deadline for lodging an appeal against the first instance judgment has lapsed) is enforceable for court costs. Moreover, it is expressly prohibited to detain a losing party for failure to pay a costs order (Article 1047 of the Hellenic Code of Civil Procedure).[17]

12.2.2 Exceptions and Modifications

The "loser pays" principle is abandoned in certain specific cases, primarily on grounds of clemency.[18] More specifically, the court is entitled[19] to off-set all litigation costs or a part thereof (Article 179 of the Hellenic Code of Civil Procedure) in two cases: firstly, in the case of disputes of a personal or proprietary nature between spouses or between relatives by blood or marriage; and secondly, in any trial where interpretation of the law is extremely complicated.

In civil courts, the parties are represented by authorized attorneys at law (Article 94 (1) of the Hellenic Code of Civil Procedure). An exception to this rule enables parties to represent themselves in cases before Justices of the Peace, or when seeking an injunction. Parties may also represent themselves in small claims litigations (amount requested below €1,500) and in all special proceedings where the Justice of the Peace procedure applies (i.e., labor disputes[20] or disputes arising from work provided by freelance professionals).

---

[16] Greek Supreme Court in plenary session, Judg. No. 918/1972, Legal Tribune Law Review 1973. 355.

[17] Kerameus/Kondylis/Nikas (-Nikopoulos), Interpretation of Civil Procedure Code (2000), Article 1047 § 16.

[18] Kerameus/Kondylis/Nikas (-Orfanidis), Interpretation of the Hellenic Code of Civil Procedure, (2000), Introduction to articles 173-193 § 2.

[19] Not mandatory, Greek Supreme Court Judg. No. 859/2002, Hellenic Justice Law Review 2003. 1290.

[20] Moreover, in labour disputes it is even possible (under Article 665 of the Hellenic Code of Civil Procedure) for one employee to be represented by another employee engaged in the same profession, and for the employer to be represented by one of his employees at first instance. However, in practice this provision is not frequently utilised since the parties feel safe only when they are represented by lawyers.

12.3 The New Legislative Framework for Lawyers' Fees

Until recently, the fees shifted to the losing party were calculated according to a schedule, which is payable on the basis of the Lawyers' Code and set from time to time by ministerial decisions. In addition to scheduled attorneys' fees, court costs also included a certain percentage of this amount to cover the operating costs for Bar services, the lawyers' insurance fund, and to support a special account for new lawyers. Again, however, attorney costs imposed on the loser were still far from reality. Despite serious objections raised by the Greek Bar Associations, the recent law number 3919/2011 has radically changed the framework for attorneys' fees and hence overall litigation costs: under the new system, shiftable attorney's fees are no longer limited to the scheduled amount but can now reflect the actual fees paid by the winning party to his attorney.

The official attorney fee schedule has become less important with the shift towards free market pricing for legal services. The promotion of the freedom of the profession and of competition facilitates a free market for lawyer fees. Under the new legislative framework, the lawyer and his client are free to contract for payment through a written agreement, and "the official fee" is maintained as a minimum. Importantly, a costs award is then based on the actual fee on if there is written agreement between the lawyer and the client; the officially scheduled fee is used only if there is no such agreement (article 5 section 6). The deductions mentioned above (in favor of the Bar Association, the lawyers' insurance fund, and young lawyers' fund) are calculated over a "reference amount", which is determined by a ministerial decision (arthr. 5 par. 8).

The new legislative framework in Greece clearly follows the trend found in most countries – particularly in Europe – in the direction of free market prices for lawyers' fees. It entails all the disadvantages of such a system, as identified in the General Report,[21] and will certainly lead to constant legal disputes by the losing party over the proper amount of attorneys' fees. Losing parties may contest an adverse judgement on grounds related to the merits of the case as well as the court costs awarded (Article 193 Hellenic Code of Civil Procedure). On appeal, the court determines on a case-by-case basis whether the victorious party's attorney fees are "reasonable".

Moreover, there is a widespread fear in lawyers' circles that the free market system will impoverish thousands of lawyers by completely eliminating the "middle class lawyers", who will be unable to survive professionally. This fear seems justified, considering the large number of Greek lawyers currently in the market, as well as the fact that attorney's fees are no longer strictly linked to the schedule.

---

[21] General Report II.2.b.

12.4 Special Issues

12.4.1 Success-Oriented Fees

Contingency fee arrangements are particularly common in Greece. They have advantages not only for lawyers, but especially for their clients, who pay their lawyers only if the case is won.

Article 92 (3) of the Lawyers' Code states that "An agreement making the fee or type of fee dependent on the outcome of the trial or on the result of work or subject to any other condition, and a fee agreement by assignment or transfer of part of the amount in controversy or work amount is permitted. Such agreement may not account for more than 20% of the amount in controversy." Article 92 (5) of the Lawyers' Code also provides that "An agreement making the fee dependent on the outcome of the trial shall only be valid if the lawyer undertook the obligation to conduct the trial until the judgment is rendered final, without him or any joint attorney or replacement at any level receiving any fee in a no-win case."

The law obviously lays down strict conditions on the validity of contingency fees arrangements. A client only owes a contingency fee if she achieves a successful outcome at trial. Additionally, agreements must expressly provide that the lawyer gets nothing if the case is lost.[22] If that term is missing, the arrangement is deemed invalid.[23] Moreover, an agreement for more than 20% of the amount in controversy, which is the maximum limit set by law, is also invalid.[24]

There are further formal conditions which need to be met. The agreement has to be certified by the competent tax authority within ten days from the date on which it was signed; otherwise it is null and void. Also, in certain categories of disputes, the competent Bar Association has to be notified of the arrangement within twenty days from the date on which it is signed, or else the agreement is invalid. This condition applies to disputes of which the Bar Association withholds a percentage of the lawyers' fee.[25]

---

[22] Greek Supreme Court Judg. No. 396/2008, Nomos Legal Databank.

[23] Greek Supreme Court Judg. No. 451/2000. Greek Supreme Court Judg. No. 1308/2004, Nomos Legal Databank.

[24] Greek Supreme Court Judg. No. 564/1983, Legal Tribune Law Review 1984. 61.

[25] Recently, the Greek Supreme Court in plenary session held a conditional fee agreement in a compulsory purchase order trial to be invalid because it was not sent within twenty days to the Piraeus Bar Association, Greek Supreme Court in plenary session, Judg. No. 27/2008, DIKE Law Review 2008. 998.

This agreed fee is payable to the lawyer even if the dispute was resolved by settlement.[26]

12.4.2 Legal Aid

As the General Report points out,[27] in Greece, as in other countries, "public legal aid is the only kind of legal aid systematically available". However, the mechanism of legal aid is uncommon in practice. Various factors such as tight restrictions and the cautious response of the courts have led to its deterioration in recent years.

Law 3226/2004 transposed Council Directive 2002/8/EC of 27 January 2003 into Greek law and better organized the system of legal aid for low-income citizens. The new law replaced Articles 194 to 204 of the Hellenic Code of Civil Procedure in all civil and commercial law cases. Beneficiaries of legal aid include all Greek and foreign[28] citizens (individuals only) and stateless persons provided they reside in or have their normal place of residence in the European Union (Article 1).

Moreover, legal aid does not affect the allocation of court costs in the judgement.[29] If the indigent party loses the trial, he or she must nevertheless pay the litigation costs. Moreover, if the opponent party loses the case, he will be ordered to pay the court costs even though they were not paid by his opponent.[30] In that case, the costs are not awarded to the indigent party but to his attorney, the State, and the jurists' welfare funds.

[26] Greek Supreme Court Judg. No. 59/2007, Nomos Legal Databank. However, the contingency fee agreement does not automatically entail the lawyer acquiring a percentage of the amount in controversy after the successful final outcome of the trial. The latter has a contractual claim against his client for transfer of or payment of the percentage, Greek Supreme Court Judg. No. 423/2000, Hellenic Justice Law Review 2000. 1318. Greek Supreme Court Judg. No. 48/2006, Hellenic Justice Law Review 2006. 1382. Athens Court of Appeal Judg. No. 5638/2001, Archive of Jurisprudence 2002. 182.

[27] General Report III.1.a.

[28] Legal aid was payable to foreigners under mutuality conditions (Article 195 of the Hellenic Code of Civil Procedure). That provision was found to be unconstitutional and non-enforceable.

[29] Kerameus, Civil Procedural Law, p. 349

[30] Greek Supreme Court Judg. No. 1359/1986, Review of Greek Jurists 1987. 522.

Chapter 13
Shifting Sands and Pyrrhic Victories – The Case of India

Neela Badami

13.1 Introduction

Court fees have always been a controversial subject in India. Prior to the advent of British rule, the concept of court fees was unknown. Court fees were first levied in the eighteenth century by regulations applicable in the then provinces of Madras, Bengal and Bombay, since which time they have become an important feature of the administration of civil justice in India. The Bengal regulation, in particular, recorded in its preamble that the justification for the imposition of court fees was that it would discourage frivolous litigation. It is interesting to note that Lord Macaulay (the first Law Member in the British Governor-General's Council) considered this statement indefensible and described it as the "most eminently absurd preamble that was ever drawn."[1] Subject to his caveat, court fees were conceived, in the eighteenth century as restraints on frivolous litigation, but have been increasingly regarded by the States, in whose power it lies to legislate on them, as sources of revenue. Court fees are levied on the value of the subject matter in dispute, and are thus called "ad valorem" fees.

India has since had a long line of legislative and judicial thought behind the principle that access to justice should not be hindered by an excessive levy of court fees, keeping in mind constitutional dictates as well as

---

Neela Badami received her first law degree (B.A., B.L (Hons.)) from the National Academy of Legal Studies and Research, University of Law, India, and her LL.M from the University of Michigan Law School, Ann Arbor, where she was a Hugo Grotius Fellow. She is currently a Senior Associate at *Narasappa, Doraswamy and Raja*, a Bangalore-based law firm (neela@narasappa.com).

[1] Quoted in the 128th Report of the Law Commission of India on the Costs of Litigation in India (1988) available at http://lawcommissionofindia.nic.in/101-169/Report128.pdf.

N. Badami (✉)
Senior Associate at Narasappa, Doraswamy and Raja, Bangalore, India

University of Michigan Law School, Ann Arbor, MI, USA
e-mail: neela@narasappa.com

M. Reimann (ed.), *Cost and Fee Allocation in Civil Procedure*,
Ius Gentium: Comparative Perspectives on Law and Justice 11,
DOI 10.1007/978-94-007-2263-7_13, © Springer Science+Business Media B.V. 2012

the principle that it is the duty of the state to provide a system of justice administration[2] whose costs should be met out of general appropriations (taxpayer funding) and not through the levy of court fees alone. In fact, when the question was referred to the Law Commission of India as to whether court fees should be enhanced to discourage frivolous and vexatious litigation, that Commission vehemently argued against such a move, listing legislative and judicial reasons as to why such a measure "cannot, and has never been accepted as a reason in the last 150 years."[3]

13.2 The Framework of Court Fee Rules – Both Central and State

The Indian Constitution of 1950 divides all legislative competences into three lists: first, subjects that the Central Government, through the Union Parliament can legislate upon for the whole country; second, subjects that each state of the Union can legislate upon; and third, subjects upon which both the Union and the States enjoy concurrent competences. Court fees (except at the Supreme Court level) are a subject that the Constitution exclusively empowers the various states to regulate. Therefore, any discussion of cost and fee allocation needs to keep in mind that there are a plethora of different rules operating in India – the pre-Independence and pre-Constitution central "Suits Valuation Act, 1870" remains in force but several states have opted out of its application, exercising their constitutional competence to enact their own rules for valuation of suits. Court fees may therefore be governed by either the Suits Valuation Act of 1870, or specific enactments in force in particular states, or a combination thereof (if a State has chosen to apply the Suits Valuation Act after making desired amendments.)

The fact that states have discretion in fixing court fees has led the Supreme Court of India to observe that there are vast differences in the scales of court fees charged in the different states of the country (in some cases it can be as high as 10% of the value of the suit) and has called for standardizing them.[4] The Law Commission submitted its 220th Report in

[2] Since any analysis of cost and fee allocation is intrinsically tied in with the structure of the Indian judiciary, it is worth taking a quick moment to understand the hierarchy of the Indian courts. India has a quasi-federal structure with 29 States further sub-divided into about 601 administrative Districts. The Judicial system however has a unified structure, with the Supreme Court, the High Courts and the lower Courts comprising a single Judiciary. Each District has a District Court, and each State, a High Court. Each State has its own laws constituting Courts subordinate to the District Courts.

[3] *Supra*, note 2.

[4] See *Secretary to Government of Madras v.P. R. Sriramulu* (1996) 1 SCC 345.

2009, recommending that the Government fix the maximum fees that may be charged in subordinate courts.[5] The Government has not yet taken steps to do so.

13.3 Shifting Sands

In response to the General Reporter's question "to shift or not to shift", this section will look at the legislative provisions dealing with the award of costs and fees, and the implementation of such provisions by India's courts.

We begin with another pre-Independence and pre-Constitution statute, the Code of Civil Procedure, 1908.[6] Under this Code, and subject to such conditions and limitations as may be prescribed, "*the costs of and incident to all suits shall be in the discretion of the Court, and the Court shall have full power to determine by whom or out of what property and to what extent such costs are to be paid, and to give all necessary directions for the purposes aforesaid.*"[7] The fact that the Court has no jurisdiction to try the suit shall be no bar to the exercise of such powers. It is expected that the wide discretion granted in the Code to courts to award costs should be exercised on legal principles, including those of reason and justice, and not capriciously.

Importantly, the Code also mandates that "*Where the Court directs that any costs shall not follow the event, the Court shall state its reasons in writing.*"[8] The expression "costs [to] follow the event" indicates that the Code presumes cost-shifting from the winner to the loser, and expects that this rule be followed except where the court feels that there are reasons not to so shift. This means that the successful party is entitled to costs unless he is guilty of misconduct or there is some other good reason for not awarding costs to him.

In theory then, India appears to fall in the first category of the General Reporter's tripartite categorization of countries (major shifters). However, the practice of Indian courts, as discussed below, would suggest that India does not appear to "be serious about it" (to borrow another phrase of the General Reporter's), denying her a seat in the first category.

The provisions of the Code set out above are honoured more in the breach than in the observance. Courts do not cost-shift routinely, leading the Supreme Court to observe in one case that

[5] Available at http://lawcommissionofindia.nic.in/reports/report220.pdf.

[6] The Code consolidates the law relating to the procedures to be followed by the civil judicature, and it is a central statute. Available at http://www.legalhelpindia.com/bareacts/THE%20CODE%20OF%20CIVIL%20PROCEDURE,%201908.doc.

[7] Section 35, Code of Civil Procedure.

[8] Section 35(2), Code of Civil Procedure.

> *many unscrupulous parties take advantage of the fact that either the costs are not awarded or nominal costs are awarded on the unsuccessful party.* ***Unfortunately, it has become a practice to direct parties to bear their own costs, despite the language of S. 35(2) of the Code.*** *Such a practice also encourages the filing of frivolous suits or taking up of frivolous defences.* ***Further wherever costs are awarded, ordinarily the same are not realistic and are nominal.*** *Section 35(2) provides for costs to follow the event. It is implicit that the costs have to be those which are reasonably incurred by a successful party except in those cases where the court in its discretion may direct otherwise by recording reasons thereof.* ***The costs have to be actual reasonable costs, including the cost of the time spent by the successful party, the transportation and lodging if any, or any other incidental cost beside the payment of the court fee, lawyer's fee, typing and other costs in relation to the litigation. It is for the high courts to examine these aspects*** *and wherever necessary, make requisite rules, regulations or practice direction so as to provide appropriate guidelines for the subordinate courts to follow.*[9]

As empowered by the Code of Civil Procedure,[10] (and exhorted by the Supreme Court) the High Courts of various States have made rules regulating their own procedure and the procedure of civil courts subject to their superintendence. These rules also deal with the various fees involved in litigation (apart from the court fee itself) including schedules of attorney's fees. Two important state jurisdictions that this article looks at show no deviation from the Code's general prescription that costs should follow the event, as shown below.

Looking first at the example of Karnataka,[11] the High Court of that state has framed the Karnataka Civil Rules of Practice, 1967 (the "Karnataka Rules"), which provide that "*unless the Court otherwise ordered, the costs of a party in any proceeding, shall mandatorily include*" [...] a list of 14 different types of costs, ranging from the fees paid by the party on his pleadings and other relevant documents to his witness fees, expenses incurred in giving required notices, as well as on typing up his pleadings, among others.[12] Also included are advocates' fees, as computed according to the prescribed rules, and subject to the caps specified, in original suits, in regular appeals, in small cause suits, in execution cases, in execution appeals, and in other proceedings such as land acquisition, motor accident claims, insolvency, rent control, and other proceedings[13]: a minimum of Rs. 100 – 200 (USD 2.5 to USD 5) to a maximum of Rs. 1000 – 5000 (USD 22.5 to USD 112) (assuming a conversion of 1 USD = 45 INR); obviously, there are

[9] Salem Advocate Bar Association v. Union of India AIR 2005 SC 3353, quoted in Mulla, The Code of Civil Procedure, 17th Edition (2007), (hereinafter, "Mulla") at p. 614 (emphasis added).

[10] Section 122, the Code of Civil Procedure.

[11] A prosperous state in the Southern peninsula, and one of the most developed in India. Home to its capital city, Bangalore, which has achieved fame as India's Silicon Valley.

[12] Chapter XIII, Rule 99 of the Karnataka Rules.

[13] Rule 100 of the Karnataka Rules.

really small amounts. It is worth noting that in the state of Maharashtra,[14] the fees payable to advocates at the Bombay High Court (Original Side) are higher than those provided for in Karnataka.[15]

The Rules of the Delhi High Court[16] also state the general rule that "*costs follow the event of the action; that is the costs of the successful party are to be paid by the party who is unsuccessful*". They proceed to set out detailed scenarios when costs may, and when they shall, be disallowed by the court, always, for reasons to be recorded.[17]

Despite such clear statutory language, both Karnataka's and Delhi's courts follow the example of courts in the rest of the country in that they do not shift costs, although exhorted by their governing rules to do so.

Another statutory provision requiring mention is one designed to discourage frivolous litigation, i.e., S. 35A of the Code of Civil Procedure, a provision that deals with compensatory costs in respect of false or vexatious claims or defenses.[18] While the intention of this section is no doubt laudable, its deterrent value is almost completely nullified by the limit placed on such compensatory costs – effectively, three thousand Indian rupees (roughly $67). This is not a sum that will deter much frivolous or vexatious litigation.[19]

Apart from this provision, in India, costs cannot be imposed as a penalty beyond the costs of the suit.[20] Punitive costs, therefore, in the sense in which it is understood in other jurisdictions, is not permitted. Certain other kinds of fees, such as success or contingency fees are also not allowed in India, as the Bar Council of India's Standards of Professional Conduct and

[14] Situated on India's western seaboard, and home to India's financial and business capital, Mumbai.

[15] See Rule 606 of Chapter XXXI (Taxation and Advocates' Fee) of the Bombay High Court (Original Side) Rules, Available at http://bombayhighcourt.nic.in/libweb/BHCRULESGUIDELINES.htm.

[16] Available at http://delhihighcourt.nic.in/rules/Vol.1/Part1Chapter11.html.

[17] See Rules 1 – 4 of Part C (Award of Costs in Civil Suits) of Chapter 11, ibid.

[18] It provides that "*If any suit or other proceedings including an execution proceedings but excluding an appeal or a revision any party objects to the claim of defence on the ground that the claim or defence or any part of it is, as against the objector, false or vexatious to the knowledge of the party by whom it has been put forward, and if thereafter, as against the objector, such claim or defence is disallowed, abandoned or withdrawn in whole or in part, the Court if it so thinks fit, may, after recording its reasons for holding such claim or defence to be false or vexatious, make an order for the payment to the object or by the party by whom such claim or defence has been put forward, of cost by way of compensation.*"

[19] Section 35(2) provides that "*No Court shall make any such order for the payment of an amount exceeding three thousand rupees or exceeding the limits of it pecuniary jurisdiction, whichever amount is less.*"

[20] Mulla, at p. 600.

Etiquette which prescribes an advocate's duty to his or her clients, prohibits the stipulation of fees contingent on the results of litigation; or any agreement to share the proceeds of litigation. Advocates cannot buy, traffic in, stipulate for or agree to receive any share or interest in any actionable claim.

13.4 Special Issues – Legal Aid

The Indian Constitution mandates that the State "secure that the operation of the legal system promotes justice on a basis of equal opportunity, and shall in particular provide free legal aid, by suitable legislation or schemes or in any other way, to ensure that opportunities for securing justice are not denied to any citizen by reason of economic or other disability." Accordingly, India has enacted the Legal Services Authorities Act, 1987 (brought into force 1995) and constituted the National Legal Services Authority as well as State Legal Services Authorities.

The mode of providing legal aid varies from state to state, as well as from one practice area to the next. In Karnataka, legal aid is delivered, inter alia, to the following categories of persons: members of a scheduled caste or tribe, women, children, trafficked persons, victims of natural or industrial disasters, ethnic violence, caste atrocities, and any person whose income is below Rupees 50,000 per annum (a little over USD 1,000). The legal aid system is funded by the government, and administered by the relevant high court of each state. There is however a general dearth of good, competent lawyers in the legal aid system, since it is not as lucrative as private practice.

13.5 Conclusion

India presents a paradoxical picture: the legislative intent seems clear that costs, including reasonable attorney fees, should be awarded to the winning party as a matter of course, but practice in the Indian courts is otherwise. In addition, there seems to be a tug-of-war between the executive and the legislature on the one hand and the judiciary and Law Commission of India on the other regarding the lens through which costs are to be viewed – as a source of revenue for the state or a token fee which does not seek to cover the state's outlay on justice administration. There is, though, a definite commitment to give meaning to the "access to justice" principle, in terms of inter alia, the provisions for legal aid that have been discussed as well as through exceptions from court fees for indigent persons.

Chapter 14
It's for the Judges to Decide: Allocation of Trial Costs in Israel Report on Israel

Talia Fisher and Issi Rosen-Zvi

14.1 Introduction

The law governing court and attorney fees (hereinafter "trial costs") is of utmost importance for the scope, shape and outcome of civil litigation, as well as for access to justice. The rules governing litigation costs affect all stages of litigation. First, they substantially influence whether a dispute will result in a trial or not. If, due to high costs, the case is not worth pursuing (trial costs equal or exceed the expected recovery in a monetary case), no litigation will ensue even if the claim is meritorious. And people who cannot afford the costs of litigation are unable even to bring a suit. For them, costs can completely block access to justice. Second, litigation costs influence the parties' litigation strategy – what steps they take, how much money they invest, what risks they bear – which affects the overall efficiency of litigation. Third, costs play an important role in determining the outcome of the litigation – whether the case is abandoned, settled, or pursued to its conclusion, as well as the accuracy of the trial's result.

14.2 The Basic Rules Governing Trial Costs: Who Pays?

The rules regulating trial costs and fees are specified in the Rules of Civil Procedure of 1984.[1] The fundamental rule (Rule 511) grants the court very wide discretion with regard to both the allocation and the amount of trial

Fisher is a senior lecturer at the Tel Aviv University Buchmann Faculty of Law; Rosen-Zvi is a senior lecturer at the Tel Aviv University Buchmann Faculty of Law. We would like to thank Mathias Reimann for his invaluable comments and suggestions. Shay Fischer provided the research assistance, for which we are also most thankful.

[1] Sections 511–519 to the Rules of Civil Procedure, 1984 (the "Rules").

T. Fisher (✉)
Buchmann Faculty of Law, Tel Aviv University, Tel Aviv, Israel

Harvard Law School, Cambridge, MA, UK
e-mail: tafisher@post.tau.ac.il

M. Reimann (ed.), *Cost and Fee Allocation in Civil Procedure*,
Ius Gentium: Comparative Perspectives on Law and Justice 11,
DOI 10.1007/978-94-007-2263-7_14, © Springer Science+Business Media B.V. 2012

costs, subjecting it to only a limited set of rules (prescribed in Rule 512). These rules instruct the court to base its cost decision on, among other things, the amount or value of the relief asked for by the plaintiff and the remedy granted by the court. It also authorizes the court to take into consideration the behavior of the parties during the trial. Courts are not required to distinguish between the two components of trial costs (namely, court costs and attorney fees),[2] but may treat them jointly.

The Supreme Court has issued several important rulings dealing with trial costs. In 2005, the Supreme Court's registrar delivered a decision according to which judges should award the winning party its actual costs, unless such an award would unreasonably impair access to justice and equality or cause over-deterrence.[3] In a subsequent decision, the Supreme Court explained that awarding the winning party its actual costs is intended to prevent financial loss by the winning party, to deter potential plaintiffs from filing frivolous claims, and to discourage potential defendants from defending against a rightful suit. However, the Court continued, the award of actual costs is subject to their being "reasonable, proportional and necessary for the litigation." This limitation is intended to avoid over-deterrence, prevent inequality between rich and poor parties, inhibit inappropriate increases in the cost of litigation, and foster access to justice.[4] Another decision specified some of the factors judges should consider when awarding litigation costs: the character of the suit and its complexity, the relief sought, and the proportionality between it and the relief granted, the amount of work invested by the party on the litigation, the actual amount paid or payable as attorney fees, and the behavior of the party during the litigation.[5] Notwithstanding these decisions, it is clear to those acquainted with Israeli civil litigation that, in the majority of the cases, the awarded litigation costs do not reflect the actual costs expended on the litigation and a great deal of variation exists in the scope of trial costs that are awarded by different judges. This is so in part because courts do not know what the actual litigation costs were, since parties are not required, and rarely do, introduce into evidence of the actual costs and fees expended on the litigation.

In 2002 the Supreme Court's President, Justice Aharon Barak, issued administrative guidance regarding the award of attorney fees. According to the guidance, judges are *allowed* to take into account when calculating attorney fees, the written retainer agreement between the party and her

---

[2] Rule 512(a) of the Rules of Civil Procedure.

[3] H.C. 891/05 *Tnuva v. The Authority for the Licensing of Imports* (delivered on 31.3.2005). It should be noted that due to the status of the registrar as a magistrates' court judge his rulings are not binding on trial court judges.

[4] R.C.A 6793/08 *Luar v. Meshulam Levinshtein Handasa Vekablanut* (delivered on 28.6.2009).

[5] C.A. 9535/04 Siat "Biyalik 10" v. Siat "Yesh Atid Biyalik", P.D. 60(1) 391 (2005).

attorney, introduced into evidence by the attorney in the course of the trial or as an annex to the written summations. The second part of the guidance qualifies this instruction by saying that attorneys are by no means obligated to introduce retainer agreements into evidence and courts are not obligated to take them into account when calculating the fees.[6] Later on, the succeeding President, Justice Dorit Beynish, issued an amendment to the administrative guidance stating that "as a general rule, the attorney fees to be awarded should approximate the actual costs expended on the litigation, subject to their being reasonable, proportional and necessary under the circumstances. In this regard, each party is allowed to introduce, alongside the summation, the written retainer agreement between that party and her attorney, as well as proof of any money paid as attorney fees". The second part of the administrative guidance remained as it was.[7] These administrative guidelines on the books have not changed the practice on the ground and retainer agreements are rarely introduced into evidence. This is so probably due to lack on incentives on the part of the lawyers to reveal information about their fees with no benefit to them (since attorney fees are awarded to the clients).

Historically, courts have tended to disregard the actual amounts expended by winning parties when awarding costs. This led to substantial under-compensation. In recent years, however, following the "constitutional revolution"[8] that began with the enactment of the Basic Law: Human Dignity and Liberty and the constitutionalization of civil procedure, the awards of trial costs tend to be higher, thus probably *more* in line with actual costs,[9] although in most cases they still do not reflect the full costs expended on the litigation. Awards of trial costs in appeal proceedings are treated in the same manner.

Trial costs are subject to fierce criticism. In 2008, the Israel Bar's standing committee on civil procedure and evidence issued a proposed amendment to the Rules of Civil Procedure that deal with litigation costs. The opening statement of the proposal states as follows: "the problem with regard to the ruling on court costs and attorney fees is very well known. Although the decided ruling is that the amounts awarded as litigation costs should reimburse the winning party for its actual expense on the litigation, subject to it being "reasonable, proportional and necessary" to the litigation, in fact courts do not follow this ruling. There is a great divergence

---

[6] *See* Administrative Guidance of the President of the Supreme Court 1/98, Calculating Attorney Fees (17/11/2002).

[7] See Chief Justice Instructions: Carrying Guidelines, State of Israel Judicial Authority website, available at http://elyon1.court.gov.il/heb/dover/html/hanchayot_new.htm.

[8] Aharon Barak, Interpretation in Law (Vol. III – Constitutional Interpretation) (1994).

[9] Shlomo Levin, The Theory of Civil Procedure: Introduction and Basic Principles (Second edition, 2008) 48.

in ruling on court costs and attorney fees between different courts that prevents predictability. Usually the amounts awarded are not realistic, even when the expenditure on the litigation was reasonable. In such cases, the winning party comes out with a financial loss. Sometimes courts even refrain from awarding litigation costs to the winning party without providing any explanation."

In addition to court costs and attorney fees, the costs of taking evidence can also be quite high and a burden on the parties in certain types of cases, such as tort litigation involving bodily injury as well as other cases in which expert testimony is essential.[10] Each party bears its own costs of collecting evidence, including expert testimony. One important exception is court-appointed experts, the costs of which are allocated by the court. Under Section 513(1) of the Rules of Civil Procedure, the parties' outlays on experts are a component of trial costs and, as such, are treated in the manner described above.

A high percentage of civil cases are settled out of court, whether through direct negotiation or via court-affiliated ADR mechanisms.[11] In such cases, the parties typically reach an agreement regarding the manner in which trial costs will be allocated among them. When agreement on this issue cannot be reached, the parties may turn to the court for a ruling specifically on this matter.

14.3 Exceptions and Modifications

There are a number of regulatory exceptions to the requirement to pay court fees, which are based either on the party's financial need or on the nature of the proceedings. Courts will exempt plaintiffs in full or in part on a showing of economic inability to pay.[12] This provision is applied narrowly, and the applicant must demonstrate not only inadequate personal financial resources but also the unavailability of access to financial assistance from other sources (such as family members). Exemptions based on the nature of the proceedings include such cases as prisoner petitions,[13] claims for damages for bodily harm, and governmental takings,[14] as well as many others listed in Section 20 of the Court Rules (Court Fees). In all such cases, the exemption from payment of court fees may be partial.

---

[10] Special rules govern proof of medical matters in which expert testimony is required. See Rule 127. In order to contest such testimony, counter expert testimony must be submitted. See Rule 128.

[11] For statistics on mediations conducted in the year 2008 see http://www.israelbar.org.il/article_inner.asp?pgId=79649&catId=178.

[12] Section 14 of the Court Rules (Court Fees), 2007.

[13] Section 9 of the Court Rules (Court Fees), 2007.

[14] Section 3(8) of the Court Rules (Court Fees), 2007.

In 2008 the Rules of Civil Procedure were amended to incorporate mandatory introductory mediation meetings in most types of civil cases (above a certain monetary threshold). Mandatory pre-litigation procedures impact trial costs both formally and informally. Formally, plaintiffs may be reimbursed for court fees if such mediation is successful.[15] Informally, courts take into account the parties' willingness to engage in mediation when ruling on trial costs. Since mandatory pre-litigation mediation is a recent development, it has not yet been fully implemented so that the full scope of its impact remains unclear.

Parties are permitted to represent themselves in civil cases,[16] and in small claims proceedings, self-representation is mandated while attorney representation is greatly restricted.[17] In cases of self-representation, trial costs are calculated as if the party were a witness on his or her own behalf.[18] Statistical data on the prevalence of self-representation are not available, but one may assume a negative correlation between the value of the claim and the incidence of self-representation.

14.4 Encouragement or Discouragement of Litigation

Rules governing trial costs are interpreted by judges as intended to affect a party's decision to litigate. Court fees are designed, among other things, to decrease the incidence of frivolous claims. Court fees are set as a percentage of the value of the relief sought, and thus serve as a disincentive to overstating a plaintiff's claim.[19] This is counterbalanced by restricting reimbursement of trial costs to amounts that are "reasonable, proportional and necessary," the intent of which is to prevent over-deterrence in filing suits, as well as to facilitate more equal access to justice.[20]

Court fees are paid in two installments: the first half upon filing the claim, and the second half 20 days prior to the date set for the opening of trial.[21] The court is authorized to order the plaintiff to deposit a security to insure the future reimbursement of the defendant's costs of trial in case she loses. The security is usually deposited at the initial stages of trial.[22] This mechanism is rarely used by the courts, and is usually restricted to

---

[15] Section 6(b) of the Court Rules (Court Fees), 2007.

[16] Rule 472 of the Rules of Civil Procedure.

[17] Section 63 of the Courts' Act, 1984.

[18] Rule 516 of the Rules of Civil Procedure.

[19] R.C.A. 2623/02 **Sys v. Bezek**, P.D. 57(1) 717, 720 (2002); C.A. 10537/03 **State of Israel v. Yesh Gad Industries**, P.D. 59(1) 642, 648 (2004).

[20] R.C.A. 6793/08 **Luar Ltd. V. Meshulam Levinstein Engineering** (decided 6.28.2009).

[21] Rule 6(a) of the Court Rules (Court Fees), 2007.

[22] Rule 519 of the Rules of Civil Procedure.

foreign plaintiffs. Attorney fees are paid pursuant to the agreement that is reached between the lawyer and the client which can take a variety of forms (including, but not limited to, retainer agreements). No data exists as to the prevalence of upfront fee payments, which constitute a de facto barrier to access to the courts.

14.5 The Determination of Costs and Fees

As a rule, court fees in the general civil courts amount to 2.5% of the value of the relief sought, with a minimum threshold updated periodically.[23] For any claim exceeding a certain upper limit, the court fees drop to 1% of the amount in controversy.[24] There are particular rules governing court fees in specific types of cases such as declaratory relief, contempt of court, derivative claims, among others. In addition, specialized courts and tribunals (such as family courts, labor courts, small claims courts, etc.) are governed by special rules with respect to court fees.

In principle, attorney fees are established by agreement between the lawyer and the client. There is also some regulation, although much of it comes in the form of soft law. The Israel Bar Act authorizes the Bar to issue recommendations for minimal attorney fees,[25] and the Bar has issued such non-binding recommendations for various categories of legal services.[26] In addition, the Minister of Justice is authorized to declare that with respect to particular types of legal services, a cap on attorney's fees is required, in which case the Bar's national council will set the maximum fees permitted.[27] Such fee caps currently apply pursuant to the context of the Compensation for Victims of Car Accidents Act.[28]

According to Rule 511 of the Rules of Civil Procedure, the court has broad discretion in deciding both the size and allocation of trial costs. Rule 512(a) restricts the court's discretion by mandating that the attorney's fee component should be no less than the minimal fee recommended by the Bar unless special circumstances exist, in which case such circumstances must be specified in the ruling on costs.

[23] As of May 2011, the minimum amount is set at 711 NIS. *See*: Second Supplement (item 1) of the Court Rules (Court Fees), 2007.

[24] As of May 2011, the amount is set at 22,749,919 NIS. *See*: Second Supplement (item 8) of the Court Rules (Court Fees), 2007.

[25] Section 81 of the Israel Bar Act, 1961.

[26] Israel Bar Rules (Recommended Minimal Fees), 2000.

[27] Section 82 of the Israel Bar Act, 1961.

[28] Section 16(b) of the Compensation for Victims of Car Accidents Act, 1975.

14.6 Special Issues: Success-Oriented Fees, Class Actions, Sale of Claims, and Litigation Insurance

The basic rule governing attorney fees permits monetary compensation only.[29] Success-oriented fees are allowed in civil cases,[30] conditioned on an explicit written agreement to that effect between the attorney and the client.[31] Contingency fee arrangements are quite common, especially in tort cases.

The law provides for regulation of success-oriented fees. The Bar is authorized to intervene in an agreement between an attorney and the client, and to lower the agreed-upon fee if it finds the amount asked by the lawyer to be excessive.[32] In addition, specific regulatory restrictions can be found in the Compensation for Victims of Car Accidents Act, under which the amount a lawyer can charge for a successful outcome is capped, based on the manner in which the case was concluded (out-of-court settlement prior to filing a suit, 8%; out-of-court settlement after the suit was filed, 11%; trial verdict, 13%).[33]

The sale of tort claims is prohibited by statute.[34] As regards other types of suits, the situation is more ambiguous. The champerty doctrine applies in Israel and prohibits the sale of claims to third parties. However, over the years this principle has been eroded by the courts, which now draw a distinction between the selling of the right to sue (which is prohibited), and the selling of the right to collect damages (which is allowed). Courts are also more likely to permit such a transfer when the purchaser of the right to sue has some property interest in the claim.[35]

In class action suits, special rules apply both with respect to courts fees and to attorney fees. The Class Action Act of 2006 requires the regulation of court fees by the Minister of Justice.[36] These regulations are still pending. In the meantime, courts usually require class action plaintiffs to pay court fees only with respect to their personal claim (which is typically very small). Attorney fees are regulated by the Act, which requires the court's approval of the amount charged, even when the suit is settled out of court.[37] The general rules governing the imposition of trial costs on the losing party also apply to class action suits. Courts use their discretion

---

[29] Rule 9(a) of the Israel Bar Rules (Professional Ethics), 1986.

[30] Rule 9(b) of the Israel Bar Rules (Professional Ethics), 1986.

[31] R.C.A. 4723/05 **Levi, Adv. v. Brosh** (decided 12.09.2005).

[32] Section 84(b) of the Israel Bar Act, 1961.

[33] Section 16(a) of the Compensation for Victims of Car Accidents Act, 1975.

[34] Section 22 of the Tort Ordinance [New Version], 1968.

[35] R.C.A. 2077/92 **Sheldon Adelson v. Reif**, P.D. 47(3) 485 (1993).

[36] Sections 44 of the Class Action Act, 2006.

[37] Sections 18 and 23 of the Class Action Act, 2006.

cautiously (perhaps too cautiously) in order to achieve the goals underlying the class action mechanism and they impose high costs on the plaintiffs only when the action is considered frivolous.[38]

There is no legal prohibition on legal expenses insurance. However, such insurance is not common.

14.7 Legal Aid

Israel provides publicly funded legal aid for the indigent. Since 1975, the Legal Aid Department of the Ministry of Justice has provided legal assistance in civil matters for low-income individuals with meritorious claims. Legal aid includes both counseling and representation in court by attorneys appointed by the Legal Aid Department.[39] Numerous NGOs, law school clinics, and private law firms provide legal aid pro bono. The Israel Bar Association established a pro bono program ("Schar Mitzva") in 2002. According to sources of the Bar, over 3000 lawyers are currently volunteering in this program.[40] All law schools have established clinics offering legal aid in a variety of matters. Nonetheless, demand greatly exceeds supply, and many people in need are unable to receive legal aid. Litigation costs thus remain a serious barrier to access to the courts not only for the indigent but also for individuals of average income.

14.8 Conclusion

Litigation costs in Israel are a barrier to access to justice, especially for low and middle class individuals, as well as for small businesses. Judicial discretion in cost allocation is broad, resulting in unpredictability. Moreover, in most cases fees awarded do not reflect actual costs expended on the litigation. This fact, supplemented by the tendency of appellate courts not to intervene in costs awarded by the trial courts, means that there are no "cost wars" of the type existing in the England and Wales.

There is some hope that litigation expenses in Israel will decline, or at least not rise, in the future because lawyer fees are likely to become cheaper. Over the last 15 years, the number of lawyers per capita in Israel has increased dramatically, and is expected to reach 1 in 160 within three years. The downside is the concern that the quality of legal services will suffer accordingly.

---

[38] B.S.C. (Tel-Aviv) 14471/01 **Azualus v. The American-Israel Gas Corp.** (decided 12.19.2006).

[39] http://www.justice.gov.il/MOJHeb/SiuaMishpati/.

[40] Nurit Rot, *Schar Mitzva: Over Three Thousand Lawyers in Fifty Three Centers,* THE MARKER (5.26.2011) (http://www.themarker.com/law/1.647185).

Chapter 15
Italy: A Tale of Successful Resistance?

Alessandra De Luca

15.1 The Basic Rule About Cost Shifting and Its Exceptions

Like most continental European systems, Italy falls into the first category defined in the General Report, that of "major shifting" systems. Actually, the basic rule concerning cost and fee allocation set by the code of civil procedure is that the losing party has to reimburse *all* his or her opponent's expenses: court costs, lawyer fees, and other expenses such as those incurred by taking evidence.[1]

As to lawyer fees, they are determined according to an official tariff. But it should be noted that this does not mean absolute predictability of the costs that the loser will have to pay. In fact, the tariff has some flexibility because it establishes a minimum and a maximum fee for each procedural step that can be remunerated. Therefore, the actual amount of lawyer fees in a given case will depend on two variables that cannot be predicted at the outset: the number of procedural acts performed, and the amount chosen within the permitted range.

The exact sum to be awarded to the victorious party is determined by the court, on the basis of an itemized bill submitted by each party at the end of the proceeding. The court has the power to check the fees and exercises discretion regarding their determination, albeit within the limits set by the fee scale. As a result, the court may not award all the fees claimed, so that the successful party may have to pay *some* fees to his/her lawyer in excess of the amount awarded by the court.

But what happens more frequently is that the court decides that each party bears his or her own costs in whole or in part. This may happen in case of a split outcome or if there is another "good cause".[2] While the first

[1] Art. 91, paragraph 1 of the Code of Civil Procedure.

[2] Art. 92, paragraph 2 of the Code of Civil Procedure.

A. De Luca (✉)
Comparative Law, Faculty of Law, University of Florence, Florence, Italy
e-mail: adeluca@unifi.it

M. Reimann (ed.), *Cost and Fee Allocation in Civil Procedure*,
Ius Gentium: Comparative Perspectives on Law and Justice 11,
DOI 10.1007/978-94-007-2263-7_15, © Springer Science+Business Media B.V. 2012

hypothesis is common to most countries, as the General Report points out, the exception based on the existence of a so-called "good cause" is more peculiar and gave rise to some problems.

The origin of these problems does not lie in the fact that the provision confers discretion on courts, but in the position of our Court of Cassation. The Court has recognized such wide discretionary power that the lower courts do not even have to state explicitly what the good cause was.[3] As a result, the decision to let each side bear its own expenses did not require a justification and could not be reviewed by the appellate courts. Over time, the recourse to this exception has become more and more frequent, so that, notwithstanding the will of the legislator and the general opinion of the public, it has turned into the actual rule.

In order to limit judicial discretion and restore the loser pays all rule, the relevant provision was changed twice in the last five years. In 2005, an amendment to the relevant code provision introduced the requirement to state explicitly the "good cause" in the decision.[4] But this amendment only provided for a formal requirement that, at worst, could be satisfied by the use of a standard phrase, thereby leaving the question of the disproportionate use of the exception to the loser pays all rule almost untouched. This may be part of the reason for a new legislative intervention on the same provision just a few years later, in 2009,[5] when the "good cause" condition was replaced with the more stringent "serious and exceptional reasons" requirement. Both amendments were well received because they tackled what was largely perceived as a problem by scholars and practitioners, and the general public as well. Still, any attempt to predict their effectiveness would be premature.

15.2 The Emergence of Instrumentalist Considerations: Access to Justice v. Abuse of Process

As in the majority of the systems covered by the General Report, in Italy the justification for the cost-shifting rule is based on considerations of fairness to the winner: as a result of litigation, the successful party should be put in

[3] See, e.g. Cassazione civile, sezione I, decision no. 8540 of April 22, 2005, *Giurisprudenza italiana* (2006) Part 2 336. Some examples of the reasons why Italian courts declined to award all or part of the costs are given in Andrew Colvin and Vincenzo Vigoriti, *Transnational Civil Procedure in Italy*, *Civil Justice Quarterly* 23 (2004) 38 at 51.

[4] Law No. 263 of December 28, 2005, art. 2, paragraph 1, letter a). See Giampiero Balena and Mauro Bove, *Le riforme più recenti del processo civile* (Bari 2006) 110–111. For the judicial interpretation of the new text, see Cassazione, sezioni unite civili, 30 luglio 2008, n. 20598, *Giustizia civile* (2009) Part 1 115.

[5] Law No. 69 of June 18, 2009, art. 45, paragraph 11.

the same situation as he or she would have been if the other party had not brought or defended the claim. However, there are signs of a growing awareness of the possibility to use the rules governing cost and fee allocation to influence party behaviour, in order to strike a balance between the right of access to justice and the prevention of frivolous litigation and abuses of process.

In the Italian civil procedural culture, "access to justice" is generally understood to mean "access to a court". This is an individual right protected both by Article 6 of the European Convention on Human Rights[6] and Article 24 of the Italian Constitution.[7] The meaning of this constitutional guarantee can be understood in the light of the basic philosophy prevailing in the nineteenth century and still widespread today among many scholars and most practitioners. This philosophy has been rightly described as a "strictly adversarial approach providing parties' lawyers with virtually absolute powers over the development of procedural options and strategies".[8] As a consequence, civil justice was and still is conceived by many as a means intended only to protect individual rights: the proceedings entirely belong to the parties who are completely free to exercise their rights of action and of defence and to use all possible procedural devices to pursue their interests.

The emergence of the notion of abuse of process is one of the major trends currently affecting Italian civil justice. In fact, while the notion of abuse of a substantive right is well known in Italy, the idea that parties could abuse process is of recent vintage. It is the result mainly of the 1999 constitutional amendment that for the first time explicitly introduced the principle of reasonable length as one of the elements of a fair trial.[9] Obviously, this principle was not unknown in our system, but its explicit provision in the Constitution, followed by the enactment of a statute introducing the possibility of lodging a complaint with the Italian courts in respect of excessively long proceedings and obtaining compensation for the resulting loss,[10] brought the notion of a fair trial more to the fore. According to this notion, while civil justice is still conceived as a means to protect

---

[6] *Case of Golder v. The United Kingdom* of 21 February 1975 (Series A no. 18).

[7] Article 24: "Everyone is entitled to go to court for the protection of his rights and legitimate interests. Defence is an inviolable right at every stage and instance of the proceedings." See N. Trocker, *Civil Procedure as a Part of the Constitutional Project: The Fundamental Guarantees of the Parties*, in M. De Cristofaro, N. Trocker (eds.), *Civil Justice in Italy* (Tokio 2010), p. 55 ff., 56.

[8] A. Dondi, *Abuse of Procedural Rights: Regional Report for Italy and France*, in M. Taruffo (ed.), *Abuse of Procedural Rights: Comparative Standards of Procedural Fairness* (The Hague/London/Boston, 1999), p. 109 ff., 115.

[9] Art. 111 of the Italian Constitution as amended by Constitutional Law No. 2 of November 22, 1999.

[10] Law No. 89 of March 24, 2001, known as the "Pinto Act".

individual rights, it is also true that each party is not completely free to determine the progress of the proceedings, but must base his or her conduct on principles of fairness and good faith.

As far as cost and fee allocation is concerned, this trend is reflected, for example, in an alternative justification of the cost-shifting rule that has recently been suggested: the obligation to reimburse the opponent's expenses is precisely a sanction for an abuse of process.[11]

The emergence of the notion of abuse of process has also led to a re-evaluation of article 96 of the Code of Civil Procedure. According to this provision, on application by the victorious party, the opponent may be ordered to pay for damages caused by bringing or defending a claim "in bad faith or with gross negligence, in addition to reimbursing costs and fees. In some cases (e.g. if the claim on which the party obtained and enforced a provisional remedy was unfounded) the provision only requires that the unsuccessful party acted "without normal prudence". Until recently, this rule, obviously aiming at punishing but also preventing unlawful behaviours, has been strictly construed and scarcely used. Currently, however, judicial recourse to this provision as a means of preventing abuses of process is reportedly increasing, and such a trend meets with civil procedure scholars' approval.[12]

Moreover, the legislature also showed its intent to enhance cost sanctions against abuse of process. In fact, the Law No. 69 of June 18, 2009 added a new paragraph to article 96 that confers on courts the power to order the losing party to pay to the other side a further amount besides the costs, even on their own motion and without proof of actual damage.[13]

This new provision was widely criticised by legal scholars for several reasons. The first problem rests with the possible infringement of the right to be heard, considering that the judge can act on his or her own motion. Furthermore, there is some ambiguity because it is not clear whether the measure has a compensatory or a punitive nature. Then – and this is probably the main problem – there is the vagueness of the provision since it says nothing about the conditions that should be satisfied in order for the court to use this power, nor does it set any limits to the amount that the sanctioned party may be ordered to pay.[14] This flaw seems even more serious if one compares the provision with a similar one that was introduced in 2006

---

[11] Francesco Cordopatri, *L'abuso del processo e la condanna alle spese*, *Rivista trimestrale di diritto e procedura civile* (2005) 249.

[12] See, also for further references, Luigi P. Comoglio, *Abuso del processo e garanzie costituzionali*, *Rivista di diritto processuale* (2008) 319 esp. at 322–327 and 347–353; Rosaria Giordano, *Responsabilità delle parti per le spese ed i danni e abuso del processo*, *Giurisprudenza di merito* (2007) 43 at 43–49.

[13] Law No. 69 of June 18, 2009, art. 45, paragraph 12.

[14] See e.g. Andrea Proto Pisani, *La riforma del processo civile: ancora una legge a costo zero (note a prima lettura)*, *Foro italiano* (2009) Part V 221, column 222.

by the Legislative Decree that reformed the procedure before the Court of Cassation. In fact, the 2006 amendment vested the Supreme Court with a similar power, but established that the amount of the sanction could not be more than twice the maximum court costs and required at least gross negligence.[15] As the legislature clearly intended the 2009 provision to replace and generalize the 2006 provision (which was therefore abrogated), it could be expected that requirements of this sort were retained.

The risk is that, given these flaws, the new provision will not be used much. The courts, however, are showing a certain willingness to use this tool in order to sanction (and possibly prevent) abuses of process.[16] Actually, in the first reported decisions applying the rule the courts seem to make wise use of this power, adequately explaining the reasons why they ordered the losing party to pay the further sum besides costs (usually the party's bad faith or gross negligence), and the factors taken into consideration in deciding its amount.[17]

The 2009 law has also amended article 91 of the Code of Civil Procedure in order to introduce a further exception to the loser pays all rule. If the victorious party fails to obtain a judgment more advantageous than a conciliation proposal which she refused without good reason, the party will bear all the fees and costs incurred after the proposal was made.[18] Similarly, though less stringent, provisions already exist for specific types of disputes – namely labour[19] and corporate[20] cases. Furthermore, this same mechanism has been provided also by the Legislative Decree No. 28 of March 3, 2010, that for the first time contains a comprehensive and detailed regulation of mediation in civil and commercial disputes.[21]

---

[15] Code of Civil Procedure, art. 385, paragraph 4 added by Legislative Decree No. 40 of February 2, 2006.

[16] See the opening speech delivered at the beginning of this year by the First President of the Court of Cassation, Ernesto Lupo at 33–34 http://www.cortedicassazione.it.

[17] See the decisions annotated by Giuliano Scarselli *Il nuovo articolo 96, 3° comma, c.p.c.: consigli per l'uso* and Paolo Porreca *L'art. 96, 3° comma c.p.c., tra ristoro e sanzione*, *Foro italiano* (2010) Part I 2229; the three decisions by the Tribunale di Verona annotated by Giuseppe Finocchiaro, *Accessi infondati alla giustizia e abusi del rito: nel mirino della nuova responsabilità aggravata*, *Guida al diritto* (2010) issue 49–50, December 18, 18; the decision by the Tribunale di Piacenza annotated by Giuseppe Buffone *Estesa al processo sommario di cognizione la condanna per aver agito in mala fede*, *Guida al diritto* (2011) issue 3, January 15, 46.

[18] Law No. 69 of June 18, 2009, art. 45, paragraph 10.

[19] Article 412 of the Code of civil procedure as amended by the Law No. 80 of March 31, 1998. After the very recent reform of labour law made by the Law No. 183 of November 4, 2010 this provision moved to article 411 of the Code of Civil Procedure.

[20] Legislative Decree No. 5 of January 17, 2003, arts. 16 and 40, respectively abrogated by the Law No. 69 of 2009 and the Legislative Decree No. 28 of March 3, 2010.

[21] Arts. 10 and 13.

These provisions are a clear sign that the legislature intends to use the allocation of costs as a tool to encourage the parties to accept reasonable conciliation proposals. This should reduce the workload of ordinary courts and deter dilatory behaviour amounting to an abuse of process. Although the effectiveness of these measures is far from certain, the trend is likely to continue.

15.3 Lawyer Fees Between Liberalization and Resistance

As in most continental European systems, in Italy lawyer fees are set by an official schedule tied to the amount in controversy and to the level of the court in which the case proceeds. The schedule provides for two kinds of fees: *diritti*, for single procedural acts (e.g. service, attending a hearing), and *onorari*, for the services performed (e.g. study of the controversy, preparation of the claim or the defence). *Diritti* are predetermined by the decree and are binding, but they represent the lesser element of lawyer fees. As for *onorari*, which are by far the most important heading, only a minimum and a maximum amount are set, together with the criteria to be followed in the determination of the sum due in the single case. If the particular characteristics of the case require it, it is possible to go beyond the maximum, although this requires a special leave by the Local Bar Council.[22] Instead, until recently, the minimum was binding.

The binding minimum fee was traditionally founded on the need to protect the "dignity" and "decorum" of the profession together with its financial independence. Recently, however, it has come under attack as a barrier to free competition and to the free circulation of lawyers within the EU. According to its opponents, binding minimum fees prevented or at least impeded young lawyers' entry to the market, because they could not charge lower fees despite being less experienced. Furthermore, the existence of this limit was seen as a barrier for foreign lawyers willing to practice in Italy, because they could not charge a fee below the minimum although in their country of origin such a limit did not exist.[23]

[22] Ministerial Decree No. 127 of April 8, 2004, Chapter 1, art. 4 and Chapter 3, art. 9.

[23] See Commission of the European Communities, *Report on Competition in Professional Services*, COM(2004) 83 final, February 9, 2004, paragraphs 31–36; id., *Commission Staff Working Document. Progress by Member States in reviewing and eliminating restrictions to Competition in the area of Professional Services*, COM(2005) 405 final, September 5, 2005, paragraphs 65–73 and Opinion of Advocate General M. Poiares Maduro in Cases C-202/04 *Macrino*, *Capodarte* and C-94/04 *Cipolla* at http://eur-lex.europa.eu.

Deciding the joined cases C-94/04 *Cipolla* and C-202/04 *Macrino*, *Capodarte*, on December 2006[24] the European Court of Justice established that

> legislation containing an absolute prohibition of derogation, by agreement, from the minimum fees set by a scale of lawyer's fees such as that at issue in the main proceedings for services which are (a) court services and (b) reserved to lawyers constitutes a restriction on freedom to provide services laid down in Article 49. EC. It is for the national court to determine whether such legislation, in the light of the detailed rules for its application, actually serves the objectives of protection of consumers and the proper administration of justice which might justify it and whether the restrictions it imposes do not appear disproportionate in the light of those objectives.[25]

In order to implement these very EU principles and to promote greater competition in the market for professional services, the Decree Law No. 233 of July 4, 2006,[26] abolished minimum (but not maximum) fees and established that within January 1, 2007 all codes of ethics were to be amended in order to comply with the new regulation. This occurred even before the ECJ decided the two cases just mentioned.

The same Decree Law No. 233 of 2006 also repealed the traditional prohibition on contingency fees provided by article 2233 paragraph 3 of the Civil Code. That provision was replaced with the requirement that all agreements concerning fees be in writing. Apart from this formal requirement, no other regulation is provided by the law, such as a percentage cap, limits on the type of cases where contingency fees are allowed, or informational duties for lawyers. The code of ethics, by contrast, only provides that in any case lawyer fees should be "proportional to the work done"[27] (which, by the way, is illogical, since the contingency fee is agreed *before* the litigation begins, and conflicts with the very nature of a contingency fee that by definition is proportional to the *result* achieved for the client[28]). The lack

[24] [2006] ECR I-11421. See Martin Illmer, *Lawyers' Fees and Access to Justice – The* Cipolla *and* Macrino *Judgment of the ECJ (Joined Cases C-94/04 and C-202/04)*, *Civil Justice Quarterly* 26 (2007) 301. This decision was confirmed by the Order of the Court (Seventh Chamber) of 5 May 2008 in the case C-386/07 *Hospital Consulting Srl and Others v Esaote SpA and Others* [2008] ECR I-67.

[25] Paragraph 70.

[26] Converted into law and amended by the Law No. 248 of August, 4, 2006. It is usually referred to as the "Bersani Decree Law", after the name of its proponent.

[27] Codice deontologico forense, art. 45, as amended on June 12, 2008. The Code of Ethics is available on the site of the Consiglio Nazionale Forense www.consiglionazionaleforense.it.

[28] Lotario Dittrich, *Profili applicativi del patto di quota lite*, *Rivista di diritto processuale* (2007) 1141 at 1150–1152.

of regulation of contingency fees is rightly criticized by many scholars.[29] Perhaps more importantly, the legal profession seems determined to resist this liberalization and to fight for a return to the traditional regime. Actually, the most probable reason for the current lack of ethical regulation of contingency fees is the Bar's opposition to them *tout court* – and the hope to have them abolished.

This opposition to the liberalization of lawyer fees is typically explained by the need to protect clients against unscrupulous behaviour and to preserve the quality of the services provided by lawyers.

One can get the impression that this is mainly rhetoric. As the General Report points out, the trend towards liberalization of lawyer fees is general, and contingency fees already exist in practice in some areas (e.g. for labour disputes)[30]; they are apparently not causing particular problems. Furthermore, if consumer protection were the real aim, an explicit regulation providing some limits and safeguards – especially a maximum percentage that lawyers may charge by way of a contingency fee, or detailed informational duties – would be a much better solution.

In a recent decision regarding a case regulated by the pre-2006 provisions, our Court of Cassation seemed to endorse the bar's argument, at least as far as binding minimum fees are concerned. Actually, this decision takes into consideration the *Cipolla* and *Macrino* judgment of the European Court of Justice and explicitly maintains that binding minimum fees do not infringe free competition and the free circulation of lawyers. The Court opined that since the Italian market is characterised by an extremely large number of lawyers, a tariff imposing minimum fees avoids excessive competition and prevents lawyers from offering services at a discounted rate, which may lead to deterioration in the quality of the services provided.[31]

To be sure, the large number of lawyers in Italy is undisputable,[32] but the Court of Cassation does not offer any proof of a causal link between

[29] See e.g. Ugo Carnevali, *Compenso professionale e autonomia privata: il patto di quota lite: problemi civilistici*, in Remo Danovi, a cura di, *Compenso professionale e patto di quota lite* (Milano 2009) at 2–3, 5–7; Matteo Lupano, *Compensi "speculativi" e patto di quota lite*, *Rivista trimestrale di diritto e procedura civile* (2009) 323 at 343–346; Lotario Dittrich, *Profili applicativi del patto di quota lite*, cit., at 1148–1150; Piero Schlesinger, *Liberalizzazione e avvocati*, *Corriere giuridico* (2006) 1337.

[30] See Alexander Layton and Hugh Mercer, eds., *European Civil Practice Vol. 2*, 2nd ed. (London 2004) at 331.

[31] Cassazione civile, sezione lavoro, decision no. 20269 of September 27, 2010, *Foro italiano* (2010) Part I 3301 at 3306.

[32] Actually, according to the 2010 Report of the European Commission for the Efficiency of Justice (CEPEJ) Italy is among the Council of Europe member states with the highest number of lawyers per 100,000 inhabitants. European Commission for the Efficiency of Justice, *Edition 2010 (data 2008): Efficiency and Quality of Justice*, Strasbourg, 2010, at 237–239. Available at www.coe.int/cepej. And the data of the National Bar Association show that this number is increasing at a significant rate, now being well over 200,000.

the setting of minimum levels of fees and the attainment of adequate quality standards of legal services, nor does it determine whether other professional rules suffice to protect consumers and to ensure the proper administration of justice. As these very points were questioned in the *Cipolla* and *Macrino* case by the Commission,[33] it seems that the issues raised by the judgment of the European Court of Justice remain still unanswered.

There is another argument against the abolition of binding minimum fees that is based on the reported experience under the regime established by the 2006 measure. As the tariff sets the minimum fees at a rather low level, in practice lawyers have seldom agreed to fees below the minimum. More importantly, they have done so only with "big clients", such as banks or insurance companies, who have always been in a stronger bargaining position because they can guarantee large amounts of work. In other words, only repeat players – who already enjoyed a preferential treatment – have benefitted from the abolition of this lower limit, not ordinary consumers.[34]

While we thus have some idea of how mandatory minimum fees work, we do not have any information regarding the experience with contingency fees after their liberalization. This may be an indication that the bar's resistance against them is so strong that they are seldom used.

Actually, the legal profession's resistance seems so strong that the legislative trend towards liberalization of fees is likely to be reversed. The occasion for such a reversal is the ongoing attempt to reform the whole regulatory framework of the legal profession, which is presently still contained in the Royal Decree Law No. 1578 of November 27, 1933. The bill for the reform of the statute regulating the legal profession was passed by the Senate on November 23, 2010 and is presently pending before the Chamber of Deputies. It explicitly re-establishes binding minimum fees and the prohibition on contingency fees.[35]

As was to be expected, the restoration of binding minimum fees is one of the bill's aspects that have been criticized by the Italian Competition Authority,[36] which in general is in line with the European Commission. It is noteworthy, however, that the support for this leap backwards is bipartisan. Both the government and the opposition introduced two bills on this subject, which shared the same restrictive attitude towards lawyer fees,

---

[33] See Cases C-202/04 *Macrino*, *Capodarte* and C-94/04 *Cipolla* [2006] ECR I-11421 paragraph 63.

[34] See, e.g., Guido Alpa, *Accorpamento e semplificazione degli onorari per assicurare al cliente una scelta consapevole*, in *Guida al diritto* (2010) issue 46, November 20, 11.

[35] Camera dei Deputati, XVI Legislatura, Progetto di legge (Bill) No. C3900, art. 12, available at www.camera.it.

[36] The report of the Autorità Garante della Concorrenza e del Mercato on the Bill for the reform of the statute regulating the legal profession of September 16, 2009 can be read at http://www.agcm.it.

although to different degrees. This may seem odd, considering that the proponent of the measure providing for the liberalization of lawyer fees is the present leader of the parliamentary minority. The common attitude of both majority and opposition is undoubtedly prompted by the powerful lobby of the National Bar Association, which actually draw up the bill introduced by the government. Therefore, there is reason to believe that, short of early elections, the present bill is likely to pass and thus reverse the trend towards liberalization of lawyer fees in Italy.

Chapter 16
Recent Issues of Cost and Fee Allocation in Japanese Civil Procedure

Manabu Wagatsuma

16.1 Litigation Costs and Attorney Fees

In Japan, the cost of litigation consists of court fees (*saiban hiyo*) and party costs (*tojisya hiyo*). The court fee comprises a filing fee and the costs of taking evidence. The party costs consist of expenses, such as for traveling, and the cost of hiring a lawyer. The amount of court costs is basically determined by the amount in controversy. If the dispute is difficult to estimate or not regarded as a financial dispute, the amount of the dispute is regarded as 1,600,000 JPY (ca. $16,000 USD).

The concrete amount of the court costs is determined by the court clerk in the court of the first instance upon motion after the decision to impose costs has become executable (Art. 71 of Code of Civil Procedure). The court clerk does not have discretion. The cost decision takes a separate court order (ketei). Yet, the application of the cost order is not generally used. That is why the winner does not reimburse the costs and fees in practice. The lawyer usually explains to his client that each party bears its own cost in advance.

The basic rule is that the losing party shall bear the cost of litigation (Art. 61 of Code of Civil Procedure). This, however, only applies to court fees. Attorney fees are not included in the reimbursable cost of litigation so that as a general matter, each party bears its own.

The exclusion of attorney fees is justified in various ways. To begin with, it is to predict the outcome of litigation.[1] When making a judgment, the court must decide, according to its free determination, whether the factual allegations presented by the parties are true and whether their legal arguments are convincing, in light of the entire presentation of the case at

[1] T. Tanase, The Cost of administration of justice, *Koza Minji soshoho,* Vol. 1, p. 216 (*Japanese*).

M. Wagatsuma (✉)
Tokyo Metropolitan Law School, Tokyo, Japan
e-mail: wagatsum@tmu.ac.jp

M. Reimann (ed.), *Cost and Fee Allocation in Civil Procedure*,
Ius Gentium: Comparative Perspectives on Law and Justice 11,
DOI 10.1007/978-94-007-2263-7_16, © Springer Science+Business Media B.V. 2012

oral argument and as the result of the examination of evidence (Art. 247 of Civil Procedure). This suggests that it may not be fair to shift the entire cost, including attorney fees, to the loser simply based on the outcome of the litigation.[2] Furthermore, the resolution of a dispute benefits not only the parties but also helps to maintain peace in society; thus, the cost of litigation, including attorney fees, can be regarded as an administrative cost that each party must bear for itself. Finally, representation by the attorney is not compulsory in Japan; it is the choice of a party whether to hire an attorney. As a result, attorney fees are not strictly speaking necessary costs.

There are several exceptions to the general rule. First, if the suit is frivolous, i.e., essentially an abuse of the court system, the attorney fees necessary to defend oneself are regarded as necessary cost.[3] Second, in tort cases for personal injury (e.g., traffic accidents), representation by an attorney is regarded as necessary expense in order to protect tort victims;[4,5] about 10% of the amount of damages is usually regarded as appropriate and thus reimbursable. In addition, tort plaintiffs do not have to pay the defendant's attorney's fee even if they lose; such a rule of one-way fee shifting is supported, inter alia, by Professor Kojima,[6] although others have argued that it is not rational to distinguish between, e.g., tort and contract cases in this fashion.[7] Third, attorney fees are regarded as necessary if incurred by local residents against local government (Art. 242-2 of Local Administrative Law) and by shareholders against a corporation (Art. 852 of Commercial Law). Again, if the plaintiff loses, she does not have to pay the defendant's attorney fees. These exceptions are justified mainly by the public interest inherent in such litigation. Fourth, if the court prohibited the making of a statement, it may order an attorney to assist the opposing party upon determining that such assistance is necessary (Art. 155 of Code of Civil Procedure); if the party then hires the attorney according to the court order, the proper amount of attorney fee is regarded as a necessary cost (Art. 2 of Civil Cost Law).

---

[2] M. Ito, The burden of litigation cost and compensation of attorney fee, Hanrei Minsjisoshyo no hori, Vol. 2, p. 93 (1995) (*Japanese*).

[3] In 1984, the Tokyo High Court made a decision to recognize the litigation itself as abuse and admit the defendant's attorney's fee as a necessary cost. In1988, the Supreme Court reversed the decision and declared that it is necessary for the plaintiff to file a case knowing that there is no legal basis to recognize the litigation as an abuse. (Decision of the Supreme Court, January 26, 1988, *Minshu* Vol. 42, No. 1, p. 1.).

[4] Decision of the Supreme Court, February 27, 1969, *Minshu* Vol. 23, No. 2, p. 441.

[5] T. Sono, Damage claim of attorney's fee, *Shin Jitsumu Minji Soshoho*, Vol. 4, p. 104 (1982) (*Japanese*); M. Tamura, Attorney's fee, *Jitsumu Minnji Soshoho* Vol. 2, p. 158 (1969) (*Japanese*).

[6] T. Kojima, Review of Decision of the Supreme Court, February 27, 1969, Hanrei Hyakusen, 2nd (1982) (*Japanese*).

[7] Ito, supra note 2 at 101; Y. Hirai, *Saiken Soron*, 2nd, p. 95 (1994) (*Japanese*).

16.2 Representation by an Attorney and Self-Representation

Whether or not to shift attorney fees is one of the most controversial issues in Japanese reform debates about civil litigation. This is because civil litigation is becoming more complex and technical and thus increasingly difficult to handle without an attorney. If a plaintiff's fees are not shiftable to the loser, a plaintiff's ability to pursue his rights will be diminished.[8]

The discussion about including attorney fees in the shiftable costs is related to the issues of mandatory use of an attorney and of fixed attorney fees. These matters were discussed already by the Judicial Reform Committee (*shihoseido chosakai*) from 1967 to 1969, but attorney fees were not included in the necessary costs.

Parties who have attained the age of majority (20 years) are allowed to represent themselves in all cases. This rule reflects in part the fact that the number of attorneys in Japan has been very small. In addition, most attorneys are concentrated in the big cities, especially in Tokyo (48.5%) and Osaka[9] (13.5%).[10] The number of new registered attorneys also focuses on Tokyo and Osaka so that in rural area self-representation is often simply inevitable. This situation is slowly changing, however. In 2004, the new law school system was established to improve legal education and to increase the number of practicing lawyers. There are currently 74 such law schools,[11] and the number of graduates passing the bar exam has increased.[12] As a result, the number of attorneys in Japan has been increasing: from 21,185 in 2005 to 28,789 in 2010 – in increase of 36%.

Nonetheless, self-representation remains fairly common, especially in bad loan and debt collection cases, or where consumers sue lending companies to return the payment of interests above the permissible rate.[13] Here, the issues are often mainly prescription and scope of lending contract. More

[8] T. Nakano, The cost shifting rule, *Kashitsu No Suinin*, p. 256 (1978) (*Japanese*).

[9] Before 1975, the number of attorneys was less than 10,000 (White Paper on Attorneys by Japan Federation of Bar Associations in 2010, p. 60 (2010)).

[10] Id. at 98.

[11] Law schools in Japan provide a two-year curriculum mainly for pre-law graduates and a three-year curriculum mainly for other undergraduates.

[12] The number of successful takers of the bar exam more than doubled from 1,009 in 2006 to 2,079 in 2010. The success rate, however, dropped quite dramatically from 48% in 2006 to 25.4% in 2010. The main reason for that is that the number of people trying to pass it increased dramatically from 2,091 in 2006 to 8,163 in 2010. One can try to pass the bar exam three times.

[13] The largest lending company applied for Chapter 11 (Corporate Reorganization) in September of 2010. The number of creditors will be 1 million and the total amount of claims will reach around 1trillion JPY (ca. US $10 billion). The number of bad loan cases will be decreased.

generally, in 2009, in about a quarter of all cases (25.3%) before the district courts (*chihosaibannsyo*) both parties represented themselves;[14] in summary court (*kanisaibannsyo*) that was even true in almost two thirds (63.8%) of all cases.[15] Most companies are represented by an employee with permission of a summary court (Art. 54 of Code of Civil Procedure). In 2009, in another 16.1% of all cases, only one side was represented by an attorney (plaintiff: 13.4%, defendant: 2.7%) in summary court.

Critics have argued that attorney fee shifting may be unfair vis-à-vis parties representing themselves (especially in rural areas)[16] because a self-represented party will not be able to shift any of the costs of representation that a represented party would be able to. In response, Dr. Nakano has proposed partial attorney fee shifting, and only in large cities.[17] If the self-represented party wins, a specific amount of her cost would be regarded as necessary and thus would be shifted, which would help to treat self-represented parties more fairly.[18]

The amount of attorney fees is determined by the agreement with the client. Attorney fees should be just and appropriate, and depend on the economic profit at stake, the difficulty of the issues, and the attorney's efforts (Art. 2 of the schedule of attorney fees). Some attorneys still use the formerly official schedule to determine their fees.

Attorney fees generally consist of a handling charge (*chakushkuin*) and a contingency fee of usually 10% of recovery (*hoshu*). The amount of success premiums (uplift) is thus very low compared with other countries, especially the US.[19] The contingency fee also depends on the difficulty of the case as well as on the amount in controversy. It is not regulated by law.

If the parties settle, each side generally bears its own costs, including attorney fees, unless a different arrangement has been made (Art. 68 of Civil Procedure). In 2010, 28.6% of cases in the district courts, and 14.0% of cases in the summary courts, were settled.

---

14 District courts have jurisdiction over claims where the value of the subject matter exceeds 1,400,000 JPY (ca. US $14,000).

15 Summary courts have jurisdiction over claims where the value of the subject matter does not exceed 1,400,000 JPY (Art. 33 of Court Act).

16 Tabe, Attorney fees, Jitsumu Minji Soshoho, Vol. 2, p. 175 (*Japanese*).

17 For example, only the retainer fee (T. Nakano, The Cost shifting rule of attorney fees, Jurist No. 388, p. 83 (1968) (*Japanese*).

18 The special provision for litigation in person is implemented in England and Wales (Rule 48.6 of Civil Procedure Rule 1998).

19 M. Reimann, Cost and Fee Allocation in Civil Procedure, General Report III.4.c (2010).

16.3 The Reform of Litigation Cost Shifting

In 1995, the Study Group on the Cost System of Civil Procedure (*minso-hiyoseidotou kenkyukai*) was established to consider the current amount of court fees and the implementation of some part of attorney fees shifting.[20] Its report was published in 1997. The majority of the Study Group supported the inclusion of attorney fees in the amount of shiftable costs in the near future. Yet, the Study Group also concluded that it is first necessary to increase the number of attorneys and to extend legal aid to all people lacking the resources for civil litigation.

It is difficult to decide the proper amount of shiftable attorney fees. The bar is also in part opposed because determining that amount will lead to regulation of attorney fees by the courts and thus infringe the autonomy of attorneys.

It is difficult to reach an agreement to support the necessary legislation. In 2001, the Final Report of the Legal Reform Committee (*shihoseidokaikaku shingikai*) recommended the implementation of the loser pays rule for part of the attorney fees in order to increase access to litigation. The Committee also mentioned, however, that it is necessary to avoid a chilling effect on litigation. In addition, the Access to Justice Committee (*akusesu kentoukai*) was established to discuss court fees and the attorney fees. The opinion of the Committee is divided. One view is that part of the attorney fee must be regarded as a necessary cost because it is often necessary for ordinary people to hire an attorney; thus, the loser should bear some part of attorney fees. The other view is that shifting even part of the attorney fee to the losing party will have a chilling effect on litigation because it may deter people from bringing a lawsuit. It is difficult to decide how broad an exception from a loser-pays rule should be in order to avoid a chilling effect. Should it, for example, apply to small claims or to administrative litigation?

The Final Report of the Legal Reform Committee recommended that the basic rule remain that each party bears its own attorney fees but that some part of the attorney fee must be borne by the loser if the both sides appoint an attorney and if they agree that the loser must bear also the winner's attorney fees. The amount of attorney fees shifted to the loser depends on the amount in controversy. For example:

- For 1,000,000 JPY (ca. US $100,000) it would be 100,000 JPY (ca. US $1,000).
- For 5,000,000 JPY (ca. US $50,000) it would be 200,000 JPY (ca. US $2,000).

---

[20] The chairman is Professor Aoyama.

- For 10,000,000 JPY (ca. US $100,000) it would be 300,000 JPY (ca. US $3,000).
- For 1,000,000,000 JPY (ca. US $1,000,000) it would be 3,270,000 JPY (ca. US $32,700).

Note that these amounts are considerably lower than the real attorney fees a party must usually pay. Still, the Japan Federation of Bar Associations and consumer groups strongly criticize the proposal because it may have the impact of denying access to justice to certain parties for financial reasons. As a result, the current proposal of shifting attorney fees was abandoned.

If the shifting cost rule were to be implemented, it would also influence an attorney's decision whether to settle or continue litigation (for average settlement rates, see supra. (II.)). It will also be necessary to discuss the issue of litigation insurance.

The current discussion of cost and fee determination and shifting in many countries around the world may provide important information for the reform efforts in Japan as well.

Chapter 17
Attorney Fee Arrangements Really Matter in Terms of Access to Justice in Korea

Gyooho Lee

17.1 Introduction

Korea is one of the most litigious societies on earth. In other words, the Korean legal community has witnessed an "epidemic of hair-trigger suing"[1] like the United States in the closing decades of the twentieth century.[2] As of 2002, the number of court filings per 100,000 persons in civil cases in Korea is more than those of the states of California, Illinois, and Texas, although it is lower than in the state of New York. The statistical data is shown in Fig. 17.1.

Also, the number of civil cases exceeding 100,000,000 Korean won [roughly US $88,650] is steadily increasing in Korea, which is among the main reasons why the Korean courts are choked by a heavy caseload.[3] The increase of court filings in terms of civil cases that exceed 100,000,000 Korean won can be attributed to the rapid growth of the Korean economy.[4] None of this, however, means that the Korean legal community offers easy access to justice. For example, Korea has a much higher incidence of pro

This article was previously published at the Journal of Korea Law, Vol. X, No. 1 (2010), pp. 65–97. Reprinted and modified with the permission of the Journal of Korean Law.
Associate Professor, Chung-Ang University School of Law in Seoul, Republic of Korea; J.S.D., Washington University School of Law, St. Louis, MO, USA; LL.M, Yonsei University College of Law, Seoul, Republic of Korea and University of Washington, Seattle, Washington, USA; LL.B, Yonsei University College of Law.

[1] Warren E. Burger, *Isn't There a Better Way?*, 68 A.B.A.J. 274, 275 (1982).

[2] Gyooho Lee, *A Model as to Whether to Bring or Settle a Lawsuit and an Economic Analysis of Litigation Explosion in Civil Cases*, Civil Procedure, Vol. 8, No. 2, at 12–16 (2004) (hereinafter referred to "Lee, *Litigation Explosion*.").

[3] The National Court Administration (NCA) of the Supreme Court of Korea ed., *Future of Civil Procedure*, Journal of Korean Judicature, Vol. I, at 732–33 (2008).

[4] Id. at 733.

G. Lee (✉)
Chung-Ang University School of Law, Seoul, Republic of Korea
e-mail: ghlee@cau.ac.kr

M. Reimann (ed.), *Cost and Fee Allocation in Civil Procedure*, 201
Ius Gentium: Comparative Perspectives on Law and Justice 11,
DOI 10.1007/978-94-007-2263-7_17, © Springer Science+Business Media B.V. 2012

Country's or state's name	Total no. of court filings	No. of court filings per 100,000 persons
California	1,569,672	4,470
Illinois	712,727	5,656
New York	2,326,378	12,143
Texas	1,022,919	4,697
Republic of Korea	3,210,247	6,981[a]

Fig. 17.1 Number of court filings per 100,000 persons in civil cases in California, Illinois, New York, Texas, and Republic of Korea in 2002
[a]Statistics Korea has surveyed the population of Korea for every 5 years. Hence, the number of court filings per 100,000 persons in 2002 in Korea was calculated at the total number of court filings in 2002 divided by the population of Korea in 2000.
Source: http://ncsconline.org/D_Research/csp/2003_Files/2003_SCCS_Tables9.pdf (last visit on June 8, 2010).
Court of Court Administration, Annual Judicial Report for Year 2002, available at http://www.scourt.go.kr/justicesta/JusticestaListAction.work?gubun=10 (last visit on June 8, 2010).

se participation than do either the United States or Germany. Even in substantial cases it is common that one or both parties are without a lawyer. In 2005, lawyers represented both parties in fewer than 20% of cases initiated in the District Court or Branch Court.[5] This suggests that attorney fees can be one of the most important obstacles to access to justice in Korea.

The overall increase of court filings in civil cases in Korea is the result of factors external to the courts, as well as of the costs parties incur as they directly use the courts.[6] The external factors may include the increase in the number of disputes resulting from the Korean economy's rapid growth and the increasing weakness of traditional dispute resolution mechanisms such as families, churches, and neighborhoods. The internal costs may include litigation costs.

In order to improve access to justice in Korea, the Article mainly focuses on how attorney fee arrangements affect a litigant's incentive to bring a lawsuit.

The Article explains the basic rules as to who pays fees and costs in a lawsuit. In this regard, it discusses in particular whether the one party can be ordered to pay the opposing party's attorney fees. It then delves into the basic mechanism of attorney fee arrangements in Korea. Afterwards, it deals with special issues including success-oriented fees, litigation insurance, and legal aid in terms of attorney fee allocation rules. In the Conclusion, I propose that in the context of civil litigation, both the Filing Fees Act and the Rules Regarding Attorney Fees as part of the litigation costs be

[5] *See* Hyun Seok Kim, *Why do We Pursue "Oral Proceedings" in Our Legal System?*, 7 J. KOREAN L. 51, 71–73 (2007).

[6] Lee, *Litigation Explosion*, *supra* note 2, at 12.

incorporated in to Rules of Costs for Civil Procedure. Afterwards, I make some comments on contingency fee arrangements and pro se litigation.

17.2 The Basic Rules: Who Pays?

Litigation costs are one of many significant factors to determine whether a potential litigant brings a suit or settles a case.[7] Litigation costs refer to costs prescribed by laws and regulations as part of the expenses incurred by parties to an action and by the court.[8] In Korea, litigation costs are mainly governed by the Civil Procedure Act (hereinafter referred to "KCPA"), the Act on Costs for Civil Procedure, the Rules of Costs for Civil Procedure, the Act on the Stamps Attached for Civil Procedure, etc. (hereinafter referred to Filing Fees Act), the Rules on the Stamps Attached for Civil Procedure, etc. (hereinafter referred to Filing Fees Rules), the Rules regarding Attorney Fees Included in Litigation Costs, the Securities Class Action Act, and the Securities Class Action Rules.

The KCPA prescribes the basic rule and its exceptions and modifications as to who pays litigation costs. The Act on Costs for Civil Procedure and the Rules of Costs for Civil Procedure stipulate the general rule as to how to compute all types of litigation costs. The Filing Fees Act and Filing Fees Rules govern the calculation of court filing fees as part of the litigation costs in civil cases, administrative cases, non-litigation cases, and others. The Securities Class Action Act and Securities Class Action Rules determine court filing fees with respect to a securities class action. A part of fees paid to lawyers are included in litigation costs as determined by the Rules Regarding Attorney Fees Included in Litigation Costs.[9]

The Korean legal system compels the losing party to pay for all litigation costs incurred by both sides in accordance with Article 98 of the KCPA. The basic rule in Korea is that the losing parties must bear the winning parties' legal expenses. This rule is not intended to employ fault liability but to follow the principle under which the losing party shall bear the litigation costs incurred by both parties.[10] This is regardless of the cause of the defeat, and regardless of whether he or she intentionally or negligently lost

---

[7] James Fleming, Jr., et al., CIVIL PROCEDURE § 1.21 (4th ed. 1992).

[8] Si Yoon Lee, NEW CIVIL PROCEDURE 600 (Pak Young Sa, 2009); Ki Taek Lee, *Burden of Litigation Costs*, at A COMMENTARY TO NEW CIVIL PROCEDURAL LAW(II) 61 (Sang Won Kim et al. eds. 2004); Dong Yoon Chung and Byung-Hyun Yoo, CIVIL PROCEDURE 1015 (Beop Mun Sa, 2005).

[9] Supreme Court Rules No. 2116, amended on November 28, 2007, effective on January 1, 2008.

[10] Judgment rendered by the Korean Supreme Court on June 30, 1995, Case No. 95Da12927; Gyooho Lee, In Search of the Optimal Tort Litigation System: Reflections

the case. The rationales for the basic rule cannot be found in Korean legal literature.[11] In my view, this basic rule is judicially fair.

However, the basic rule does not necessarily mean that the KCPA follows the English Rule under which the losing party pays for all costs and fees incurred by both parties.[12] Article 109 (1) of the KCPA provides as follows:

A fee paid or to be paid by a party to his or her attorney, who institutes a lawsuit on behalf of the party, shall be the cost of lawsuits up to the limit of the amount as determined by the Supreme Court Rules.[13]

Therefore, only a part of the fee of a winning party's attorney must be directly reimbursed by the losing party. In other words, only a part of the fees paid to lawyers are included in litigation costs as determined by Rules Regarding Attorney Fees Included in Litigation Costs.[14] As shown in Fig. 17.2, the attorney fees included in litigation costs are determined in proportion to the amount in controversy.

17.3 Attorney Fee Arrangements

To curtail excessive retainer fees and contingency fees, the Korean Bar Association originally established the Rules of Standards on Attorney Fees as the Korean Bar Association Rules No. 19 on May 21, 1983. Yet, the Rules were abolished as of January 1, 2000 because they violated the unfair competition law in Korea. Even though the Rules were effective from 1983 to 2000, attorneys were not strictly bound by the Rules; these rules were merely standards that the attorneys could take into account if they chose.

---

on Korea's Civil Procedure Through Inquiry into American Jurisprudence 179 [J.S.D. dissertation (Washington University School of Law)(1998)].

[11] See, e.g., Si Yoon Lee, *supra* note 8, at 602; Dong Yoon Chung and Byung-Hyun Yoo, CIVIL PROCEDURE 1026 (Beop Mun Sa, 2009); Moon Hyuk Ho, CIVIL PROCEDURE 574 (Beop Mun Sa, 2009).

[12] In England, the practice is that the loser often pays only part of the winner's costs.

[13] The official English version of Civil Procedure Act in Korea, available at http://elaw.klri.re.kr/ which has been run by the Korea Legislation Research Institute, prescribes as follows:

> A fee paid or to be paid by a party to a lawyer who performs a lawsuit on behalf of the party shall be admitted as the costs of lawsuit within the limit of the amounts as prescribed by the Supreme Court Regulations.

However, the term, "Supreme Court Rules," is preferable as compared to the word, "Supreme Court Regulations," because the rules have been enacted and amended by the Supreme Court rather than the Executive branch. Hence, my translation of Article 109(1) of Korean Civil Procedure Act is a little different from that of its official English version.

[14] Supreme Court Rules No. 2116, amended on November 28, 2007, effective on January 1, 2008.

Amount in controversy (Unit: Korean won(hereinafter referred to "KW"))	Percentage of attorney fees included in litigation costs (%)
Up to 10 million KW	8
Amount exceeding 10 million KW up to 20 million KW [800,000 KW + (amount in controversy – 10 million KW) × 7/100]	7
Amount exceeding 20 million KW up to 30 million KW [1,5 million KW + (amount in controversy – 20 million KW) × 6/100]	6
Amount exceeding 30 million KW up to 50 million KW [2.1 million KW + (amount in controversy – 30 million) × 5/100]	5
Amount exceeding 50 million KW up to 70 million KW [3.1 million + (amount in controversy – 50 million KW) × 4/100	4
Amount exceeding 70 million KW up to 100 million KW [3.9 million KW + (amount in controversy – 70 million KW) × 3/100]	3
Amount exceeding 100 million KW up to 200 million KW [4.8 million KW + (amount in controversy – 100 million) × 2/100]	2
Amount exceeding 200 million KW up to 500 million [6.8 million + (amount in controversy – 200 million KW) × 1/100]	1
Amount exceeding 500 million KW [9.8 million + (amount in controversy – 500 million KW) × 0.5/100]	0.5

Fig. 17.2 Annexed Chart 3 in accordance with Article 3 of the rules regarding attorney fees included in litigation costs

Today, attorney fees are determined by an agency contract between a client and an attorney under the principle of freedom of contract. The attorney fee arrangement usually consists of initiation fees (retainer) and contingency fees.

Initiation fees normally range from 2 million to 5 million Korean Won (roughly US $1,770–4,424). Initiation fees are non-refundable unless an attorney fails to perform his/her duty based on the agency contract with the client.

A court finally determines the concrete amount to be awarded to the parties to an action according to the table above. A court shall, in the final judgment on a case, render ex officio a decision on the entire litigation costs in each specific instance.

17.4 Success-Oriented Fees and Litigation Insurance

Contingent fee arrangements are common in Korea.[15] They are allowed in civil cases, including family disputes, and even criminal cases. There are no ceilings for contingency fee arrangements since the Rules of Standards on Attorney Fees were abolished in 2000. Hence, such arrangements are

[15] Jae Won Kim, *The Ideal and the Reality of the Korean Legal Profession*, 2 Asian-Pacific L. & Pol'y J. 45 (2001).

permitted even in criminal cases unless the arrangements are unfair legal acts. In 2007, the Korean National Assembly introduced a bill to revise the Attorney Act by restricting contingency fee arrangements in criminal cases. However, several members of the Judiciary Subcommittee reviewing the bill, including a number of former judges and public prosecutors, opposed its adoption. Thus, the use of contingency fee arrangements in criminal cases survived, mainly because many of the former judges and public prosecutors wanted to take advantage of their former status even though that is not permitted by law. In contrast to contingency fees, however, no win-no fee arrangements are not available because, as mentioned, attorneys in Korea are usually paid retainer fees in advance, i.e., before commencing a lawsuit.

Contingency fees are determined on the basis of all circumstances of the case, including the importance and difficulty of the case in question, the amount in controversy, the location of evidence, and the parties' residence. Normally, contingency fees are set between 5 and 10% of the amount awarded to the winner in litigation or in settlement.[16] The attorney will not receive contingency fees, however, in "unimportant cases", such as litigation about provisional disposition or provisional seizure.[17]

A client may reduce attorney fees by shopping online for favorable fee arrangements. For example, a client may sign up on the website http://www.lawmarket.co.kr and propose the amount of attorney fees that he or she wishes to pay, and then an attorney can accept the offer via an Internet auction for attorney fees.[18] As of June 1, 2009, approximately 2,300 cases were posted by clients on the website and auctioned for attorney fees. Normally, contracts created through this website are 20–50% cheaper than ordinary offline contracts between an attorney and a client.[19]

A plaintiff is not permitted to subrogate his claim to an attorney, a law firm, or an entrepreneur who finances the litigation, and thus assumes the litigation risk, in Korea.

The public had long called for legal costs insurance, but it was only introduced in October of 2009. Legal costs insurance was first offered by D.A.S., a subsidiary of Munich Re Group in Germany. It covers legal costs, such as lawyer fees, stamp fees, fees for service of process, all up to 50 million Korean won (approximately US $44,235)[20] Also, LIG Insurance Co., Ltd, one of Korea's domestic insurance companies, has been selling legal costs

---

[16] http://www.oseo.com/people/qna/view3.asp?bd_cd=CM120&sp=1&cp=1&no=5293&s_chk=N (last visit on March 15, 2011).

[17] Id.

[18] http://www.lawmarket.co.kr/auction/auction_guide.asp (last visit on March 10, 2011).

[19] Id.

[20] See http://www.das.co.kr/MainServ?cmd=homepage (last visit on March 4, 2011).

insurance since October 19, 2009. Its policy covers attorney fees, filing fees, and the fees for service of process in civil cases except domestic relations disputes, especially divorce cases.[21]

17.5 Legal Aid

The KCPA allows, but does not require, courts to provide civil litigation aid. Aid is usually provided in the form of deferment of payment rather than as a free service.[22] Under certain conditions, the court provides financial assistance to a person who cannot afford to pay the attorney fees. In other words, a court may grant litigation aid, either ex officio or upon request of a person who falls short of the solvency threshold, unless he or she will obviously lose the case.[23] A motion for litigation aid shall be in writing in accordance with Article 24(1) of the Civil Procedure Rules. The motion shall also include a statement that states the financial abilities of the movant and his or her cohabitants.[24]

The movant must demonstrate need for litigation aid.[25] The court that keeps the record of litigation shall render judgment on the motion.[26] Litigation aid is awarded only for deferral of litigation costs, deferral of fees payable to a lawyer and an enforcement officer, exemption from security for the litigation costs, and deferral or exemption from other expenses as prescribed by the Supreme Court Rules.[27] The court can also limit litigation aid to a part of these costs for appropriate reasons.[28] When a person who has been granted litigation aid is found to have the solvency to pay the litigation costs or when he or she becomes solvent, the court keeping the record of litigation may cancel the aid at any time, either ex officio or upon request of an interested person, and order the aided party to pay all deferred litigation costs. Those deferred costs may be collected directly from the aided party, who is obligated to pay them pursuant to the court's ruling.[29]

---

[21] http://www.lig.co.kr/product/p_03/p_0303/p_0303_01.shtml (last visit on March 1, 2011).

[22] Articles 128 and 129 of KCPA.

[23] Article 128(1) of KCPA.

[24] Article 24(2) of KCPA.

[25] Article 128(2) of KCPA.

[26] Article 128(3) of KCPA.

[27] Article 129(1) of KCPA.

[28] Article 129(1) of KCPA.

[29] Article 132(1) of KCPA.

Only 5,155 of the 1,314,833 civil cases filed in 2008 were financed by litigation aid.[30] It is fair to say that litigation aid is not generally available to the public in need, but only in cases where a party to an action meets certain requirements mentioned above.

In Korea, the legal aid currently available is largely provided by the Korea Legal Aid Corporation, which was established pursuant to Legal Aid Act of 1987. As a public interest organization, the Korea Legal Aid Corporation is under the supervision of the Ministry of Justice. Some scholars criticize that governmental support for legal aid by private organizations such as the Korean Legal Aid Center for Family Relations is trivial. The private sectors' legal aid is independent from the legal aid provided by courts and the public interest organizations.

17.6 Conclusion

As mentioned above, litigation costs are mainly governed by a variety of statutes and rules: the KCPA, the Act on Costs for Civil Procedure, the Rules of Costs for Civil Procedure, the Filing Fees Act, the Filing Fees Rules, the Rules Regarding Attorney Fees Included in Litigation Costs, the Securities Class Action Act, and the Securities Class Action Rules. The complexity and multiplicity of the laws and rules hardly permits lay persons to understand the system. Hence, I propose first that the Filing Fees Act be incorporated within the Act on Costs for Civil Procedure. I next propose that both the Filing Fees Rules for Civil Procedure and the Rules Regarding Attorney Fees Included in Litigation Costs be incorporated within the Rules of Costs for Civil Procedure.[31] According to my proposal, the Act on Costs for Civil Procedure and the Rules of Costs for Civil Procedure can cover litigation costs including filing fees and some portion of attorney fees. This would provide some of the much needed clarity.

In my view, contingent fee arrangements should not be permitted in criminal cases in Korea because those cases are related to the public interest. Also, contingency fee arrangements for domestic relation cases should not be allowed because it can encourage the dissolution of families.

---

[30] Office of the National Court Administration of the Supreme Court of Korea, Annual Judicial Report for Year 2008. http://www.scourt.go.kr/justicesta/JusticestaListAction.work?gubun=10 (last visit on March 8, 2011).

[31] Cf. HANKUK MINSASOSONGBEOP HAKHOI [KOREA ASSOCIATION OF THE LAW OF CIVIL PROCEDURE], MINSASOSONGJEDO UI JEONGBIBANAN YEONGU [A STUDY ON THE REFORM OF THE LAWS ON CIVIL LITIGATION COSTS] 286–288 (2009); Byungseo Chon, *Sosongbiyong Jedo ui Gaeseon e ganhan Yeongu* [*A Suggestion on the Improvement of Civil Litigation Costs*], 14-1 MINSASOSONG [CIVIL PROCEDURE] 313–325 (2010).

Pro se actions in small claims cases have resulted from the fact that the parties are reluctant to pay attorney fees. Pro se actions can encourage a court to look primarily for justice in the concrete case rather than worry about legal consistency and certainty In other words, individual justice[32] sometimes prevails over legal certainty in Korea because in pro se litigation, courts may function as quasi-arbitrators *ex aequo et bono*. One should hope, nonetheless, that even litigants in small claims cases can be represented by a lawyer. The problem is partially solved by the legal aid system and will be somewhat alleviated by the ongoing increase of the number of attorneys as well as by the increasing availability and popularity of legal service insurance.

[32] Chaewoong Lim, *A Study on the Target of Avoidance in Korean Bankruptcy Law: When There is No Debtor's Action*, Journal of Korean Law, Vol. 7, No. 2, at 344 and n. 24 (2008) (Saying that "*The appropriate in the concrete* is an important word in legal practice in Korea, especially for the judges. Put it simply, it is the question who must win the case. New comers are taught to consider it when they make a decision. They are told to think of who must win apart from the superficial logic. If *the appropriateness in the concrete* is not agreed to the superficial logic, for example in the case that the plaintiff would win by the latter, but the defendant should win by the former, they are asked to give it a second thought and to seek a new logic. To understand the Korean judges' behavior on the work, it is necessary to understand the role of *the appropriateness in the concrete*.")

Chapter 18
The Particularities of the Macau Special Administrative Region of the People's Republic of China: Legislation on Costs and Fees in Civil Procedure

Cândida da Silva Antunes Pires

18.1 Introduction

Macau, including the Macau Peninsula, Taipa Island and Coloane Island, since the 20th December 1999 has been a Special Administrative Region of the People's Republic of China,[1] authorized by the National People's Congress to exercise a high degree of autonomy and enjoy executive, legislative and independent judicial power, including that of final adjudication,[2] under the principle "one country, two systems".

Portuguese, living in Macau since 1985, a permanent resident of Macau SAR. Master of Law, Classic University of Lisbon. Bachelor of Law, Classic University of Lisbon. Former Lawyer. Former Legal Advisor on Registry and Notary. Co-drafter of the Civil Registration Code of Macau. Co-drafter of the Code of Civil Procedure of Macau. Former member of the "Conselho Superior da Advocacia" of Macao. Member of the Editorial Council of the academic journal "Boletim da Faculdade de Direito", of the University of Macau. Member of the Editorial Council of the magazine "Direito e Cidadania", City of Praia, Cape Verde. Responsible for the chairing of the following classes in the Law Bachelor Degree Programme of the University of Macau: Comparative Law and Legal Systems; Civil Procedural Law I and Civil Procedural Law II, since 1989/1990 to date. Given the chair of Civil Procedural Law in the Master of Law Degree Programme of the Faculty of Law of the University of Macau, as well as of Labour Law in the Higher School of Security Forces of Macau (Training Course for Public Security Police Officers). Given the chair of Arbitration Courses in the Macau Legal and Judiciary Training Centre. A large participation in Congresses and Seminars in Portugal, Spain, Brazil, Mozambique, Cape Verde, Mainland China and Macau. A number of publications in those Countries, including papers presented in Congresses and Seminars, as well as books (textbooks for students, and others) on Civil Procedural Law, Labour Law, Family Law and Environmental Law. Co-author of the "Código de Processo Civil de Macau – Anotado e Comentado" (two volumes already published). Writing a Commentary on the new Code of Civil Procedure of Cape Verde.

[1] In short **MSAR** or **Macau SAR**.

[2] See Art. 2 of the Macau SAR Basic Law.

C.S.A. Pires (✉)
Faculty of Law, University of Macau, Taipei, China
e-mail: csap@umac.mo

M. Reimann (ed.), *Cost and Fee Allocation in Civil Procedure*, 211
Ius Gentium: Comparative Perspectives on Law and Justice 11,
DOI 10.1007/978-94-007-2263-7_18, © Springer Science+Business Media B.V. 2012

Considering some of the questions raised in the questionnaire sent out by the General Reporter, it is important to emphasize that the Macau Special Administrative Region legal system is a civil law system with Portuguese roots. This system has, in turn, influenced the Chinese and Taiwanese legal systems in Macau. Considering the establishment of the Macau SAR as very recent (10 years), some data on the reporting subject will therefore be somewhat scarce, concerning either bibliography or legal opinions. Yet, there is a panoply of specific domestic legislation on the subject. It comprises, in particular:

i. On costs and fees in Civil Procedure, the Decree-Law no. 63/99/M, dated 25 of October (Arts. 1–50)[3] and, of course, some regulations in the Macau Civil Procedure Code[4] (Decree-Law no. 55/99/M, dated 8 of October), *maxime* Arts. 376–384, 565, 2 and 232, 2 *in fine*;[5]
ii. The Law no. 21/88/M, of 15th August, and the Decree-Law no. 41/94/M, dated 1 of August (general regulations on legal aid); as well as
iii. The special rules on attorney's fees, mainly the Decree-Law no. 31/91/M, of 6th May (Lawyers' Statute), the Rules on Legal Opinions of the Macau Lawyers' Association.[6]

18.2 The Macau Sar Legislation on Costs and Fees

18.2.1 The Basic Rules of Cost and Fee Allocation and Their Justification

At the outset, one must understand that court costs and attorney's fees are treated distinctly because they refer to different types of civil litigation expenses. Still, there are some cost allocation rules that are common to both court costs and attorney fees (in Portuguese "procuradoria") and that regulate what the loser must pay to the winner.[7] One must also consider that the term "court costs" has a broad meaning in the domestic legal regime of the Macau SAR, since it includes various amounts of money, i.e., reimbursements, transportation expenses and other forms of compensation.[8]

The basic allocation rule is that the loser pays the total costs of the winner as determined by the special rules of the CCR (see infra. IV.). Some

[3] Here referred as **CCR** (Court Costs Regime).
[4] In short **CPC**.
[5] Website: http://www.imprensa.macau.gov.mo or http://www.io.gov.mo/ or http://www.court.gov.mo.
[6] Website: http://www.informac.gov.mo/aam/portuguese/legisla.html.
[7] See Art. 26 of the CCR.
[8] See Art. 21 of the CCR.

major exceptions are certain private and labor law disputes which are free of charge[9] and whose parties are the state authorities, as well as the official organizations and the government departments or similar entities (e.g., municipalities), or the victims of a labor accident. There are other procedures which are free of charge, such as in adoption cases. In addition, various situations are treated under special rules. For example, the plaintiff may have to pay all litigation expenses even in case of victory if the case ends because the suit has become moot (unless that situation is the defendant's fault,[10] e.g., if the obligation is not yet enforceable because of a future maturity date).[11] Also, if the case ends because the parties ultimately agree on arbitration, each party will pay half of the costs amount.[12]

In general, whenever the law does not expressly stipulate who pays, cost allocation depends on the judge's decision under various fundamental concepts, such as "dar causa à acção" (meaning to cause a needless litigation), or "ficar vencido na acção" (to be the unsuccessful party), or "tirar proveito da acção"[13] (the party who achieves certain advantages through the judgment).[14] Ultimately, therefore, much depends on the concrete situation, such as the particular proceedings, the situation and conduct of the parties, etc. The court decides on a case-by-case basis, and sometimes, not all of the winner's costs and fees are reimbursed.

There are special rules for appeals, but no additional costs and fees. On the contrary, there are some reductions of the general amounts, depending on the kind of the appeal (in the domestic legal system of the Macau SAR there are two main species of appeals) or on the subject of the litigation.[15]

In general, the expenses of taking evidence, especially the costs of (expert and other) witnesses are paid by the loser. Again, however, there are exceptions, e.g., in cases where evidence introduced by the winner are not considered useful by the court.[16] In such a case, the winner bears its own expenses. Whether such expenses are a significant factor in the overall costs of litigation depends on the circumstances of the case, especially on the kind of evidence taken or on its location.

---

[9] See Arts. 2 and 3 of the CCR.

[10] See CPC, Art. 377,1.

[11] See CPC, Art. 565, 2 in fine.

[12] See Art. 232, 2 of the CPC.

[13] Please note that Macau SAR legislation is written both in Chinese and Portuguese, the two official languages of the Region. Any available English version is an unofficial translation, for reference only.

[14] See, e.g., Arts. 376, 1, 2 and 3–382 of the CPC.

[15] See CCR, Arts. 17 and 18.

[16] See Art. 378, 1 of the CPC.

In case of settlement, each party typically pays half of the costs and fees, unless they agree otherwise.[17] Unfortunately, data on the percentage of law suits settled are not available in the Macau SAR.

18.2.2 Exceptions and Modifications of the Basic Rules

In the Macau SAR civil procedure, there are no general rules mandating pre-litigation procedures, such as mediation. In certain kinds of cases, or certain phases of procedure, however, the Macau CPC requires the parties to attempt conciliation before the judge.[18] If the conciliation attempt is successful, each party typically pays half of the costs and expenses, again, unless they agree on a different arrangement.

There are no data pertaining to party agreements on cost and fee allocation (e.g., in a contract). In consumer disputes, however, such agreements would be subject to review by the Arbitration Centre of the Consumers Council according to its own regulations.

According to the general rules in the Macau CPC, whether the parties are allowed to represent themselves depends on the kind of proceedings and on the amount in controversy. Representation by an attorney is *mandatory* if the value of the case exceeds $50,000.00 patacas (ca. US $6,000) – the legal jurisdiction, or "*alçada*", of the courts of first instance,[19] in appellate proceedings, and in the context of judgment enforcement.[20] In practice, however, self-representation is not common.

18.2.3 Encouragement or Discouragement of Litigation

Generally speaking, the existing rules governing cost and fee allocation are not intended either to encourage or to discourage civil litigation. From a significant part of the Macau SAR residents' perspective, it also seems improbable that a party would forego litigation just because of the rules of cost and fee allocation. There is, moreover, hardly a general answer to the question whether such rules will encourage or discourage litigation. The issue is broad and complex and requires consideration of differences between kinds of proceedings. It is also tied to the heterogeneous composition and specific characteristics of society in Macau SAR.

Requiring up-front payments may, of course, discourage litigation. As far as court costs and the expenses of taking evidence are concerned,

[17] See Art. 380, 2 of the CPC.

[18] See Arts. 428 and 555, 2 of the CPC.

[19] See Art. 18 of the Law no. 9/1999, of 20th December.

[20] See Art. 74 of the CPC.

such payments may be required, and their amount depends on the kinds of litigation and the amount in controversy.[21] Attorneys are allowed to charge an up-front retained fee; the matter is regulated in certain Rules on Legal Opinion of the Macau Lawyers' Association. The concrete amounts are determined on the basis of the *usus fori* and various other factors, prominently among them the amount in controversy. The practice does not appear to be common so that its potential deterrent effect is limited.

18.2.4 The Determination of Costs and Fees

As mentioned, the amount of court costs is determined by a variety of factors, especially the type of the dispute (e.g., family, commercial, labor cases); the respective amount in controversy; the court level (first instance or appellate level); and other considerations, such as the type and number of the procedural acts requested by the parties during the litigation process.[22]

Whereas there are schedules determining lawyer fees, their rates are not strictly binding between the client and his or her attorney. It is thus common practice to determine lawyers' fees by the market.

The amount of attorney fees awarded by the court to the winning party is a different matter, however. The court determines this amount depending on the value and on the complexity of the case. Often, the court will set it at around half of the legal judiciary rate[23] (*taxa de justice*).

According to article 12 of the Decree-Law no. 63/99/M, dated 25 of October (CCR), the judiciary rate in civil litigation is determined by a statutory schedule, an Annex of that DL, on the basis of the lawsuit value.

Courts have considerable discretion in setting the concrete amount awarded to the party/parties. In exercising this discretion, the court should take into consideration the concrete circumstances of the case, including the conduct of the parties during the lawsuit. The decision on this matter is an integral part of the judgment.

18.2.5 Special Issues: Success-Oriented Fees, Class Actions, Sale of Claims, and Litigation Insurance

In the Macau SAR system, success-oriented fees are not allowed, either in arrangements between clients and their attorneys or with regard to court-shifted fees. Both the Rules on Legal Opinions of the Macau Lawyers'

[21] See CCR, Arts. 28–35.

[22] See Arts. 5 and 6 of the CCR.

[23] See Art. 27 of the CCR.

Association (Arts. 3 and 4) and the Lawyers' Deontological Rules (Art. 18) forbid those kinds of agreements. In particular, *quota litis* agreements are expressly declared illegal.

There are no specific rules directly governing the sale of claims for litigation purposes. Yet, any agreements with lawyers are forbidden if such agreements are done for the lawyer's advantage in matter he or she is entrusted with (see Art. 17 of the Lawyers' Deontological Rules).

Under the CCR, class actions and other lawsuits brought by the official departments and organs listed in Articles 2 and 3 of the CCR are cost free. This also comprises civil and labor disputes[24] to which public authorities are parties, as well as the official organizations and the government departments or similar entities (e.g., the municipalities). The same is true for victims of a labor accident as well as a few other special kinds of procedures (e.g., on adoption).[25]

The Macau Insurance Companies Ordinance (Decree-Law no. 27/97/M, of 30 June[26]) foresees one class of non-life insurance concerning legal expenses. This type of legal insurance permits the possibility of effecting and carrying out contracts to insure against the covered party's risks of loss associated with his legal expenses, including the cost of litigation. There are no reliable statistics on how many of such contracts exist although it seems that they are not very common in practice.

18.2.6 Legal Aid and Access to Justice

In the Macau SAR, there is a publicly funded legal aid system. There are various general rules governing public legal aid (see Art. 36 of the Basic Law of Macau SAR and Art. 1, 1 of the Civil Procedure Code – access to justice, including legal advice), and there is also more specific legislation (the Law no. 21/88/M, of 15th August, and the Decree-Law no. 41/94/M, dated 1 of August). The granting of legal aid is decided case by case and consists of total or partial exemption from costs and fees, including free attorney's representation. The Macau Lawyers' Association provides free service as well.

By and large, the legal aid system applies for any kind of litigation. The requesting party must file an application before beginning, or during, the litigation. The court's decision depends mainly on whether the petitioner lacks the economic resources for litigation.

24 See Arts. 2 and 3 of the CCR.

25 See Arts. 2 and 3 of the CCR.

26 Available on http://www.asianlii.org/mo/legis/laws/micodl2797368.

There is also privately organized help for indigent or other clients. Some local non-governmental organizations, namely Foundations and Associations, provide relief for low income and very poor people. Legal aid is generally available to all parties in need, if they are Macau SAR residents.[27]

In the Macau SAR legal system, no Macau resident is excluded from access to justice. Still, access to justice may sometimes be difficult for a variety of reasons, and litigation costs in particular can be a serious access barrier. This is usually not true, however, because even where the amount in controversy would be too low to be worth litigating, there is a special court for small claims with procedures in which litigation costs are kept at a minimum.

18.2.7 Some Examples

It is very difficult to provide reliable examples of litigation costs in Macau SAR courts (which are, of course, all in the local currency, i.e., *patacas*) because many variables are involved: the level of court (first instance or appeal), the type of litigation, and, more generally, the overall circumstances of the case. Statistical information about litigation costs is not available.

It is noteworthy, however, that disputes about litigation costs are rather frequent; appeals in this matter are not lacking, and some controversies reach the Macau Court of Last Instance.[28] As a result, there is a fairly rich jurisprudence about cost and fee allocation issues which illustrates the complexity of the rules and the variability of outcomes.

---

[27] See Art. 36 of the Macau SAR Basic Law and Art. 4 of the CCR.

[28] The Macau SAR Judiciary Organization is comprised of three levels of courts: The Judicial Basis Court, the Second Instance Court and the Court of Final Appeals, named Last Instance Court (see Law no. 9/1999, dated 20 of December – www.court.gov.mo).

Chapter 19
Cost and Fee Allocation in the Netherlands

Marco B.M. Loos

19.1 The Basic Rules

19.1.1 Cost and Fee Allocation – Loser Pays All

In principle, all costs incurred by the winning party are compensated provided that they are reasonable. However, with regard to attorneys' fees, the scheme for liquidated costs indicates that a costs award is for specific services and acts of the attorney only. Thus, additional costs – for example, those based on extra time the attorney was required to spend on a case without performing additional procedural acts – are not compensated by the losing party. The same rules apply for appeals.

Both the costs of expert opinions and of witnesses are ultimately to be borne by the losing party. The costs involved will depend on how complicated the case is, particularly with regard to the taking of evidence, but they usually constitute only a fragment of the overall costs of litigation. These overall costs are dominated by the attorney fees.

Witnesses are entitled to compensation for the costs of travelling and, if need be, for accommodation, as well as for loss of income. These costs are to be advanced by the party that has summoned them.[1]

Expert opinions are solicited by the court (usually upon a request by one of the parties), and the court determines whether one or both parties are required to pay an advance of the costs of the expert opinion (art. 195 Code of Civil Procedure). As a general rule, these costs are to be advanced by the

[1] Art. 182 Code of Civil Procedure.

M.B.M. Loos (✉)
University of Amsterdam, Amsterdam, The Netherlands
e-mail: M.B.M.Loos@uva.nl

M. Reimann (ed.), *Cost and Fee Allocation in Civil Procedure*,
Ius Gentium: Comparative Perspectives on Law and Justice 11,
DOI 10.1007/978-94-007-2263-7_19, © Marco B.M. Loos 2012

claimant, but the court may derogate from this, particularly when facts are to be established for which the defendant bears the burden of proof.[2]

Where parties settle a case, the division of costs is normally kept secret. In practice, the parties will often make an estimate on the chances of winning and losing and apportion the costs accordingly, or they may simply agree that each party bears its own costs.

19.1.2 Exceptions and Modifications

There are some exceptions to the general principle that the loser pays all, particularly in the context of family proceedings. Art. 237 of the Code of Civil Procedure provides that the court may "compensate" the costs in full or in part if the parties are married to each other, are registered partners, or otherwise live together; if they are family in direct vertical relation; or if they are siblings or the partner thereof.[3] In this case, each party bears its own costs.[4] Similarly, the court may order that each party bears its own costs in full or in part if the parties have both won and lost aspects of the case.[5]

Party agreements allocating costs and fees in case of litigation are not common. Where such agreements would be included in standard contract terms that are invoked against a consumer, the terms may be considered unfair under standard contract terms legislation. In this regard, a court may find such a term to have the effect of deterring consumers from litigating, invoking their contractual rights, or opposing a claim by the other party. The term would thus fall within the wording of point q of the Annex to the Unfair Contract Terms Directive,[6] which indicates that terms which have the object or effect of excluding or hindering the consumer's right to take legal action or exercise any other legal remedy may be considered as unfair within the meaning of Article 3(1) of that Directive. If the court indeed considers the term to be unfair, it is not binding on the consumer,[7] implying that the court would disregard the term.

Parties are free to represent themselves if the claim is within the competence of the *kantonrechter* (subdistrict court, justice of the peace). This is

---

[2] D.J. Beenders, note 2 at art. 196 Code of Civil Procedure, in: A.I.M. van Mierlo, C.J.J.C. van Nispen, M.V. Polak (eds.), *Tekst & Commentaar Burgerlijke Rechtsvordering*, 3rd. edition (Deventer: Kluwer, 2008).

[3] Art. 237, para. (1), second and third sentence, Code of Civil Procedure.

[4] P.A. Stein and A.S. Rueb, *Compendium van het burgerlijk procesrecht*, 16th edition, p. 213 (Deventer: Kluwer, 2007).

[5] Stein/Rueb 2007, p. 213.

[6] Council Directive 93/13/EEC of 5 April 1993 on unfair terms in consumer contracts, OJ 1993/L 95/29.

[7] Cf. Art. 6(1) Unfair Terms Directive.

the case if the claim is for no more than €5,000 (including the interest accumulated until the date of the summons), or cases of undetermined value if there are clear indications that the value is below that threshold. Moreover, all cases pertaining to labour law, collective labour agreements, commercial agency, rental contracts and hire-purchase contracts are within the competence of the *kantonrechter*. According to a bill about to be formally approved by Parliament, all cases with a value up to €25,000, all cases based on a consumer sales contract, and all cases on the basis of the Consumer Credit Act will also be within the *kantonrechter*'s competence.

19.1.3 Encouragement or Discouragement of Litigation

The system of cost shifting is, among other things, designed to discourage excessive litigation. Moreover, according to article 237 of the Code of Civil Procedure, the court may leave outside of the normal allocation of costs any amounts that were spent or caused needlessly. This means that such costs will always have to be borne by the party who has incurred them, even if that party has won the case. For example, where a claim is submitted to the court without prior communication between the parties (*rauwelijkse dagvaarding*), the court may determine that the summons was premature (as the defendant may have been willing to perform his or her obligations voluntarily and/or to settle the claim). In such a case, the court may determine that the costs of the procedure have been incurred needlessly and refuse to award compensation of these costs by the defendant.[8]

As of 1 January 2009, the cost of bringing a summons was €72.25.[9] The amount of court fees will depend on the value of the claim and which court is competent to hear the case. Where the *kantonrechter* is competent, the court fees vary. As of 1 January 2009, court fees may be as low as €36 (as in a claim for payment in a labour case); €63 (for other kinds of monetary claims with a value of no more than €90); or up to €297.[10] Where the *sector civiel* (the "normal" court for civil cases) is competent (i.e. when the *kantonrechter* is not), the fees vary from €110 (in the extraordinary case where the normal court is competent to hear a labour case) to €4,941 in a case of expropriation, where the party is not a consumer.[11] These amounts are adjusted annually. In the case of appeal, higher court fees apply.[12] Where

[8] Stein/Rueb 2007, pp. 202–203.

[9] Cf. *Besluit tarieven ambtshandelingen gerechtsdeurwaarders* of 4 July 2001, *Stbl.* 2001, 325, as amended by the *Regeling wijziging tarieven ambtshandelingen gerechtsdeurwaarders 2009* of 25 November 2008, *Stcrt.* 2008, 246.

[10] Cf. art. 2 para. (2) sub 1° *Wet tarieven in burgerlijke zaken.*

[11] Cf. art. 2 para. (2) sub 2° *Wet tarieven in burgerlijke zaken.*

[12] Cf. art. 2 para. (3) *Wet tarieven in burgerlijke zaken.*

the *kantonrechter* is the competent court, the defendant need not pay any court fees. In other cases, however, the defendant is required to pay the same amount if he opposes the claim.[13]

Attorney fees are advanced by the party that has incurred them, according to the contractual arrangement between that party and the attorney. As these costs are generally considerable, they may operate as a deterrent for submitting a case to court or opposing such a claim, in particular where the value of the claim is relatively low. In this respect, it should be noted that *Carla J.M. Klaassen*, in her national report to the European research project of *Hodges*, *Vogenauer* and *Tulibacka* indicated that the hourly fees in the Netherlands vary from €75–700.[14] As even the simplest procedure will take several hours (including the time spent at the acceptance of the case and the preparation of the trial), the hourly fee would have to be multiplied by at least 3 or 4 to give an accurate impression of the costs of legal assistance. *Ab van der Torre*'s research into the costs of legal assistance, dating back to 2005, supports this picture. He estimated the costs for legal assistance to range between €979–1,400 for a commercial lawyer in an ordinary case, where the total amount of time invested in the case does not exceed 6.6 h.[15] This comes to an hourly fee of (on average) €180.

19.1.4 The Determination of Costs and Fees

Court fees are primarily determined on the basis of the value of the claim, but specific (and comparatively lower) court fees are charged in the case of labour cases and in family law cases. It should be noted, however, that in response to the economic crisis and the budget cuts which are now being made, the Dutch government has recently announced its plans to fundamentally change the system of court fees. According to the government's plans, the court fees should equal the costs the government incurs for the adjudication of the claim, although individual claimants and defendants from low and middle income groups would be required to pay lower court fees.[16] The announcement is strongly contested by the *Raad voor de rechtspraak*, an organisation representing the courts, as it is at odds with

[13] Cf. art. 2 para. (1) *Wet tarieven in burgerlijke zaken*.

[14] See Annex III, p. 55, in the report by C. Hodges, S. Vogenauer, M. Tulibacka, *Costs and Funding of Civil Litigation: A Comparative Study,* Oxford Legal Research Paper Series 55 (2009), available for download at http://papers.ssrn.com/sol3/papers.cfm?abstract_id=1511714 (last checked on 4 April 2011).

[15] A. van der Torre, *Advocaat met korting. Een analyse van de prijsgevoeligheid van de rechtsbijstand*, Den Haag: Sociaal Cultureel Planbureau, 2005, p. 55, available at http://www.scp.nl/dsresource?objectid=20764&type=org (in Dutch; last viewed on 4 April 2011).

[16] Cf. E. Bauw, F. van Dijk, F. van Tulder, "Een stille revolutie? De gevolgen van de invoering van kostendekkende griffierechten", *Nederlands Juristenblad* 2010/39, p. 2528 (in Dutch).

the fundamental right of every citizen to have a case adjudicated by a court. The *Raad voor de Rechtspraak* indicates that persons of lower and middle incomes as well as small companies will have difficulty in enforcing their claims through the judiciary and, in particular, to appeal from the decision in first instance.[17] In a letter to Parliament, the government announced that the system will be cost-neutral for the government at system level (for all civil and administrative claims for which court fees are due), not at the level of individual cases. The government also indicated budget cuts for legal aid by raising the amount that citizens are required to pay themselves and by lowering the amounts attorneys will receive in such cases.[18]

Attorneys' fees are determined on the basis of the contractual agreement between the parties. Where the parties have not determined the amount of the fee, the client is required to pay the ordinary fee charged by the attorney, or – if no such fee is established – a reasonable fee.[19]

In practice, several ways of calculating the fee are used. Most common is a fee based on an hourly tariff. The parties may agree that the hourly fee depends on whether the case is won or lost, i.e., provide for a higher fee in case of success. "No win, no fee" arrangements, however, are not permitted. The parties may also agree to a fixed price for the services of the attorney.

The court ultimately decides the amount of costs that the losing party is to compensate the winning party. As indicated above, the court has some discretion, and this decision is an integral part of the judgment.

19.2 Litigation Financing

19.2.1 Success-Oriented Fees

Contingency fees and no win-no fee arrangements are not allowed in the Netherlands. Article 25, paragraph (1) of the *Gedragsregels 1992* provides that the attorney is required to demand payment of a reasonable fee, taking into account all circumstances. Paragraph (2) adds that the attorney may not agree that the client is only required to pay if a certain result is achieved (no win-no fee). Moreover, the attorney may also not agree to a fee determined as a percentage of the result achieved in court (para. (3)).

The *Orde van Advocaten*, the organisation of attorneys, which has regulatory powers in this matter, contemplated an experiment with "no win-no fee" in personal injury cases, but the Dutch Council of Ministers (cabinet)

---

[17] Cf. Raad voor de Rechtspraak, *Standpunt Raad voor de Rechtspraak over kostendekkende griffierechten*, available at http://www.rechtspraak.nl/NR/rdonlyres/E49495FB-36A9-49F6-BD29-4A1836E29190/0/StandpuntRaadvoorderechtspraakoverkostendekkendegriffierechten.pdf (last checked on 4 April 2011).

[18] Bijlage Handelingen Tweede Kamer 2010–2011, 31 753, no. 27.

[19] Cf. art. 7:405 para. (2) Civil Code.

declared that it would forbid the experiment as contrary to the principle of good professional practice, which requires the attorney to avoid any risk of a conflict of interest. According to the responsible Minister of Justice, in the case of "no win-no fee" arrangements, the attorney has an important financial interest in the outcome of the case, resulting in a clash between his financial interest and his obligation to properly represent the client. Moreover, it may lead attorneys to litigate only cases with a high chance of success or cases with a high financial value, and to disregard cases with a lower chance of success or with a lower financial value, as the chance of a (sufficient) financial reward would become too low.[20] The experiment never took place.

19.2.2 Sale of Claims, Collective Settlement, and Litigation Insurance

Sale of claims (in Dutch: *cessie*) is permitted in some circumstances. A client may sell a claim, as the claim represents monetary value. In practice, companies often sell their claims to attorneys or to bailiffs, who then claim the amount themselves in their own name. Equally customary is the situation where the claim is not sold to the attorney or bailiff, but transferred to a debt collecting company who then collects the claim in the name of the client. In both cases, the costs for the services of the collecting party are added to the original claim. In practice, these costs amount to approximately 15% of the original value of the claim. The client's contractual counterpart has normally agreed to such levies by accepting the standard terms of the client. If no such agreement is made (e.g. because the standard terms of the other party were applicable), such costs may be recovered as reasonable costs for attempts to settle the claim out of court.[21] These costs are not included in the liquidated costs mentioned above, as those only encompass the costs incurred with a view to the court procedure itself.

The Law of Collective Settlement of Mass Damage (*Wet collectieve afwikkeling massaschade*) provides for the possibility of a binding collective settlement for all victims of a party or parties liable for damages, although an individual may opt out of the settlement.[22] The individual consumers, who are represented by a consumer organization, bear no costs

[20] Ministry of Justice, *Kabinet geen voorstander van no cure no pay*, press release 4 March 2005. This press release is no longer available; its essence is reported (in Dutch) at http://www.emea.nl/?p=2800 (last checked on 4 April 2011).

[21] Art. 6:96 paragraph (2)(b) of the Dutch Civil Code.

[22] See extensively M.B.M. Loos, *Evaluation of the effectiveness and efficiency of collective redress mechanisms in the European Union – country report The Netherlands*, 2008, available at http://ec.europa.eu/consumers/redress_cons/nl-country-report-final.pdf (last checked on 4 April 2011).

for the procedure to declare the settlement binding. However, in practice the consumers finance the ad hoc creation of the consumer organization through a (relatively modest) membership fee. These membership fees facilitate the process of negotiating the settlement (and likewise pay for the organization's attorneys costs). Settlements in this context thus often arrange for the compensation of these costs.

Legal aid insurance is widely available in the Netherlands and is becoming increasingly popular. A 2003 survey enquiring into the manner of how disputes are settled found that 53.6% of those in the highest income classes have legal aid insurance, compared with only 22.6% in the lowest income class.[23]

19.2.3 Legal Aid

Under Dutch law, the starting point is that each party bears its own costs during the court procedure.[24] Of course, for financially disadvantaged consumers (citizens), these costs weigh more heavily than for parties with sufficient finances. As a result, there is a risk that such consumers will abstain from defending their rights in court for purely financial reasons. This obviously puts these consumers' access to the court system in jeopardy.[25] Moreover, even for consumers with sufficient income, the value of claims in many consumer cases will in practice prevent consumers from going to court.[26]

The Legal Aid Act (*Wet op de rechtsbijstand*) aims to secure access to the court system for consumers with a low income. On the basis of this act, a consumer is eligible for legal aid if his or her annual income in 2007 was no more than €23,800 before income tax but after deducting the costs of interest for a home mortgage, and assuming the consumer is single and does not have assets exceeding €20,661. (For consumers who are married

[23] B.C.J. van Velthoven, M.J. ter Voert, *Geschilbeslechtingsdelta 2003. Over verloop en afloop van (potentieel) juridische problemen van burgers*, Den Haag: Boom Juridische uitgevers/WODC, available at http://www.wodc.nl/onderzoeksdatabase/geschilbeslechtingsdelta.aspx (last checked on 4 April 2011). A new report, available online at http://www.wodc.nl/onderzoeksdatabase/geschilbeslechtingsdelta-2008-burgers.aspx (last checked on 4 April 2011) was published in 2009 and contains similar figures.

[24] W. Hugenholtz and W.H. Heemskerk, *Hoofdlijnen Nederlands burgerlijk procesrecht*, 21st edition, no. 128 (Den Haag: Elsevier juridisch, 2006).

[25] Hugenholtz/Heemskerk 2006, no. 128.

[26] Cf. M.B.M. Loos, "Individuele handhaving van het consumentenrecht", in: M.B.M. Loos, W.H. van Boom, *Handhaving van het consumentenrecht*, preadviezen Nederlandse Vereniging voor Burgerlijk Recht 2009, p. 37 (Deventer: Kluwer, 2010).

or live together, other amounts apply.) The monetary ceiling for people eligible for legal aid is only slightly above the minimum wage, which amounts to €18,000 on the basis of full-time employment (as of 1 January 2009). Moreover, every consumer who wishes to invoke legal aid is required to pay a contribution to the costs of legal aid. The amount of the contribution depends on the income and resources of the consumer and varies (as of 1 January 2009) from €98 for the poorest of consumers to a maximum of €732 for the party with the highest income and bracket of assets who is still eligible for legal aid. Drastic financial cutbacks on the money invested in the legal aid system have already been announced, restricting the access to legal aid even further.[27]

When a consumer who is awarded legal aid loses the case, he is nevertheless required to pay for the (liquidated) costs of the other party.[28] Given the risk of having to pay a high amount of costs, such a consumer may hesitate to submit a claim to the court or to defend his position against it.

An application for legal aid is evaluated by the *Raad voor de Rechtsbijstand* (Council for Legal Aid). The Council determines whether the consumer is eligible for legal aid and whether the claim of the consumer justifies the involvement of an attorney or mediator.

There are also some forms of private legal aid in the Netherlands. In particular, law students offer legal assistance free of charge through *rechtswinkels* and *wetwinkels* (legal aid clinics). Law firms may offer pro bono services though only relatively few lawyers do so on a regular basis. Often, "pro bono" really means that they offer their services on the basis of the Legal Aid Act, which means that they will receive a (rather modest) remuneration from the state.

19.3 Conclusion

All in all, it seems that the Dutch system of cost and fee allocation works reasonably well for the majority of cases. The key to this success is the fact that although the starting point of the Dutch system is the "loser pays" rule, the effects of this rule are mitigated because with regard to attorney fees, the winning party does not receive full compensation but only a portion thereof on the basis of the liquidated tariff. As a consequence, the winning party always bears a part of the costs sustained itself. It is not likely that this system is to change fundamentally in the next years. However, problems arise when a claim is made by or on behalf of a consumer or a small company, as for them the risk of the "loser pays" principle is much more serious than for big(ger) companies. Such parties will think twice before

[27] See also above, Section 19.1.4.

[28] Hugenholtz/Heemskerk 2006, no. 129; Stein/Rueb 2007, p. 204.

submitting their (relatively low value) claims to the judiciary, as they know they will incur part of these costs themselves in any event, but also may have to pay the liquidated costs of the procedure in case they lose. This is the case even when the consumer or the small company itself did not have legal representation, but the other party did. From the perspective of consumer law enforcement, this is problematic: as attorney fees in consumer cases may easily be higher than the original value of the claim, there is a substantial risk that consumer claims are not submitted for fear of having to pay for the other party's attorney fees. This leads to underenforcement of consumer law.

The new governmental plans to amend the court fee system in such a manner that (at the system-level) all costs of operating the court system are covered by the parties will only further hinder enforcement of small claims. In practice, such claims will most likely be handled only by ADR institutions – in particular by the so-called *geschillencommissies*, as is already the trend. The use of such ADR institutions has been promoted by the government for many years now, as these ADR institutions tend to be much cheaper and faster than the civil courts. These *geschillencommissies* do not operate on the basis of the "loser pays" principle. Quite to the contrary: the idea is that parties bear their own costs and that legal assistance by an attorney is not necessary as formalities are significantly reduced and costly procedures regarding the gathering of evidence are simply abolished. The non-application of the loser-pays principle before the *geschillencommissie* means that the principle's practical importance is considerably reduced. Since submitting a claim in a consumer case to the ordinary courts will become increasingly problematic due to the announced budget cuts,[29] civil procedure will increasingly become a business-to-business-affair, because claims by and against consumers will largely be dealt with outside the ordinary court system.

[29] See also Loos 2010, pp. 109–110.

Chapter 20
Court Costs and Fee Allocation in the Russian Federation: A Civil Law System with a Free Market

Alena Zaytseva

20.1 Introduction

The Russian Federation has always belonged to the civil law tradition. It remains a member of this tradition, notwithstanding the changing notions of judicial precedent introduced into the Russian legal system in 2010.[1] Thus in Russia, it is statutory law that primarily regulates allocation of costs and fees. In addition, the higher courts can adopt mandatory explanations with respect to statutory interpretation, and thus provide more particular rules on certain legal matters. In the commercial context, such explanations may also come from judgments of the Supreme Commercial Court of the Russian Federation (SCCRF, or RF for short).[2]

With regard to civil practice, one of the most interesting features of the Russian legal system is the coexistence of two independent branches of the judiciary: there are general courts (i.e. courts of general jurisdiction) and commercial courts (initially designed to resolve business-related disputes). Both systems are distinctly organized with regard to their court structure and the respective powers of their courts. They are headed by the Russian Supreme Court and the Russian Supreme Commercial Court, respectively. Both systems hear civil cases (including private and commercial disputes), and both systems apply civil procedure rules. The difference is that such rules are incorporated in two codified statutes – the Commercial Procedure Code RF (ComPCRF) and the Civil Procedure Code RF (CivPCRF). This often means that the same procedural institutions are being regulated

---

[1] Judgement of the Constitutional Court RF № 1-P from 21.01.2010: http://ksrf.ru/DECISION/Pages/default.aspx.

[2] The above mentioned perception of judicial precedent affected only commercial courts – judgments of the SCCRF were declared mandatory for the commercial courts of lower instances.

A. Zaytseva (✉)
Deputy Chief of the Private Law Department, Supreme Commercial Court of the Russian Federation, Moscow, Russia
e-mail: 7746817@mail.ru

M. Reimann (ed.), *Cost and Fee Allocation in Civil Procedure*, Ius Gentium: Comparative Perspectives on Law and Justice 11,
DOI 10.1007/978-94-007-2263-7_20, © Springer Science+Business Media B.V. 2012

differently in the two Codes. Moreover, the general and commercial courts often pursue diverse approaches when applying similar rules.

Given the idiosyncrasies in key attitudes of both systems, having two distinct procedural codes seems appropriate. Commercial courts resolve disputes arising in connection with economic activity and business. Parties to such disputes bear normal business risks, as well as the financial risks of civil litigation. Consequently, the commercial courts are far more demanding and stricter with the litigants and thus ready to apply procedural sanctions in case of abusive conduct, etc. Beyond their role as decision-makers, general courts primarily provide aid and counsel to citizens. Due to the lack of free legal aid in private litigation (see infra.), the general courts have had to explain to individuals the meaning of legal rules, help them to formulate claims, etc. General courts thus tend to be very protective and will rarely sanction individual litigants or postpone trials even if a party appears to have no valid reason not to appear in court. Obviously, general courts have never been fit to resolve commercial disputes. Subsequent to the development of the market economy after the USSR ceased to exist, commercial courts were created to hear all business-related cases.

Given these circumstances, it seems logical that commercial courts and general courts should hear different cases. However, both systems retain concurrent jurisdiction over civil cases with respect to individuals engaged in commercial activity. Provided that such individuals have the special status of individual entrepreneur – meaning that they were registered for economic activity – they clearly fall within the jurisdiction of the commercial courts.[3] But if an individual acts as a private person and nevertheless is involved in economic activity that does not require a special status (e.g., he or she rents property to companies), the general courts will have jurisdiction over a dispute arising from this activity. Since similar disputes between legal entities or individual entrepreneurs will be heard either by a commercial court or a general civil court, these two branches may adopt different attitudes when deciding the same legal issues. In practice, however, the two court systems interpret rules allocating litigation costs quite similarly.

20.2 Basic Principles

The basic approach of the Russian legal system is to encourage litigation in principle, i.e. not only lawsuits the plaintiff is confident to win but also lawsuits the plaintiff thinks he or she may lose. This approach has never been declared officially,[4] but follows from some generally accepted premises.

[3] Such individuals – entrepreneurs – are actually treated like legal entities.

[4] On the contrary, the CivPCRF contains a rule discouraging unmeritorious claims.

The Russian Constitution guarantees the right of access to justice (right to court). Thus the system is designed to facilitate access to court through certain coordinated means. What is guaranteed is not only access to court but very fast and rather cheap court proceedings.

This rather unrestrained conception of access to justice encourages even unmeritorious claims. A person who initiates a lawsuit believes she is right and thus apparently has a reason to sue. Whether her claim is meritorious or not is known only at judgment. Although there are certain situations when suing proves to be unnecessary – as may be illustrated by the withdrawal of a lawsuit – there is always room for doubt, and Russian courts will err on the side of caution to permit greater access to courts.

Encouragement of litigation became an actual barrier for the proper development of alternative dispute resolution. At the same time, absence of mediation[5] and other settlement procedures forces the state to do even more to ensure an access to court.[6] A vicious cycle is born.

Whether a policy of encouraging litigation is actually of any benefit to the legal system is a very complex question beyond the scope of this analysis. It definitely has led to a huge burden on courts.[7] Consequently, whether it is possible to provide proper administration of justice or judgments of good quality within such an approach is open to substantial doubt.

20.3 Basic Rules of Costs Allocation

According to the basic rule, the loser is to compensate the winner for all litigation costs that the winning party has incurred (art. 110 CPCRF, art. 98 CivPCRF). Court costs consist of the filing fee (a fee collected upon initiating a case in court) and costs incurred in the course of proceedings (costs of evidence taking, attorney's fees, postal costs etc.). Thus the Russian legal system, using the terms of the General Report, is "major shifting", i.e. court costs, lawyer fees, and evidence expenses are all shifted to the losing party.

This basic approach is based on the fundamental principle of fairness. A decision in favor of one party confirms that this particular party – the winner – has substantive rights which were proven in court. At the same time, it implies that the losing party breached such (lawful) rights and thus breached the law. Hence, the winning party may recover all expenses incurred in connection with protecting his rights and interests in court.

[5] The institution of mediation was introduced in the 2011 Statute on Mediation.

[6] Only 4,7% of all commercial cases, and around 2,5% of all private cases in general courts were settled in 2010.

[7] In 2010 ca. 1, 3 million cases in commercial courts, 20 million civil cases in general courts.

Therefore, a decision on court costs allocation is a necessary component of the right of access to justice.

The General Report distinguishes two versions of the fairness approach (para. 3. Policies: Fairness and Instrumentalism). For the Russian system both policies are true: the winner is compensated because she won, and she won because she was proven right. Thus while it is not completely correct to define the Russian system as an exclusively procedural liability system, such a characterization comes very close.

Notwithstanding the basic rule, procedural rules do not guarantee the winner full compensation for all litigation expenses. Court costs and the costs of evidence taking (witnesses, expertise, etc.) are usually reimbursed in full. Other costs, however, are reimbursable only up to a reasonable amount (e.g., economical travel and accommodation costs). Russian procedural laws explicitly establish that compensation of attorney's fees is also limited by a reasonableness requirement.

A commercial court may reduce the amount shifted upon request of the party liable for litigation costs. This party will have to prove that the winner's expenses are excessive and unreasonable.

There are not many exceptions from the basic rule. The most interesting ones are sanctions for causing unnecessary costs and cases of split outcomes. For example, each party may be liable to the other for all or part of the total litigation costs in the event of abusive conduct, failure to fulfill procedural duties or to comply with a court order. This is true regardless of the overall outcome, meaning that a winning party may win yet be forced to pay. Such liability, however, arises only if there are negative consequences – disruption of a trial, delays in proceedings, obstruction of justice, etc.

According to the General Report, situations with split outcomes are usually regulated in detail in most systems. This is not the case in Russia. In fact, such situations seem very under-regulated.[8] Pursuant to the commercial procedure rules, in case of a split outcome costs and fees are allocated between parties proportionally to the amount won. The CivPCRF contains a clearer formula: if a plaintiff wins just a part of his claim, he recovers the incurred expenses in proportion to the amount he won; at the same time a losing party is compensated by the winner in proportion to her amount lost. However, this rule is not ideal. Simple mathematics proves that it can easily become unfair if the losing party's overall costs are bigger than those of the winner.

[8] Given a large number of split outcomes, they do need a detailed regulation.

20.4 Court Costs – The First Step

Court costs – i.e. a state filing fee – are a tax and are determined by the Tax Code RF. They depend on the type of court and the amount in controversy.

In the court of first instance, court costs are determined under a schedule in a degressive manner. For example, the percentage charged upon recourse to a commercial court of first instance varies from 4 to 0,5% of the lawsuit's value. Still, the higher the amount in controversy, the higher the filing fee: in commercial proceedings court costs range from the equivalent of around $70–6,896, and in general courts from $14–2,100. The General Report indicates that appeals usually cost more than first instance proceedings. This is not the case in Russia. A very small flat fee is charged upon filing an appeal – around $138 as a maximum for any kind of appeal. The result is very predictable – parties are encouraged to seek review, and normally up to 20% judgments of first instance are appealed.[9] There are four instances in the commercial courts system, and multiple instances in the general courts system; litigants tend to try all of them.

The fact that the highest filing fee is charged in the court of first instance is often considered a factor discouraging potential plaintiffs, especially in the event of a large claim. This is not completely true if one takes into account the fact that these costs may be deferred. Both commercial and general courts have a great deal of discretion in granting a postponement of the filing fee payment or allowing a payment in installments. The decision takes a form of a special court order. In 2010 there were 71,226 lawsuits (6% of all lawsuits) brought in commercial courts with requests for a postponement or an installment of the filing fee payment. 97% of such requests were granted. The numbers in the general courts are even higher because they deal mostly with individuals.

However, courts cannot grant immunity from court costs. Special provisions for exemptions from the filing fee payment are set in the Russian Tax Code. The list of persons exempt from court costs is fairly extensive. It can be divided into two categories – with regard to the type of a case (labour disputes, cases involving alimony and support) and type of a litigant (indigent, military invalids); sometimes both criteria are used together. State authorities are exempt from court costs when they in the public interest.

20.5 The Costs of Evidence Taking

As the General Report points out, in civil law countries evidence costs are usually secondary in importance to both court costs and lawyer fees. This is mostly true for Russia as well: evidence costs can have an impact on

[9] This is the case in the commercial courts.

overall costs, although this depends on the category of case. Witnesses are rare in commercial courts, where written evidence – documents and expert reports – are common given the nature of disputes under their jurisdiction.

Expert witnesses are appointed by the court, usually upon a party's request. There are certain situations, explicitly established in the Codes, when a court may call for evidence on its own initiative, e.g. order an investigation by an expert or call a witness. In such a case, the expense of taking evidence is borne by the state (usually the federal budget).

Expert witnesses are paid according to an official schedule which is slightly below market rate for wages and services. A party to a dispute may hire her own expert instead of relying on the one appointed by the court. However, she will probably not be able to obtain reimbursement for such expenses even if she wins, as this can be considered an excessive and unreasonable cost.

Advance expenses for evidence taking are usually borne by the party requesting an appointment of expert or other witnesses. An interesting exception applies where a party lacks the necessary funds: in such a case, a court may order that such expenses be covered by the federal budget. These costs will subsequently be recovered from the losing party for the benefit of the state.[10]

The costs of evidence taking are always shifted to the losing party.

20.6 Representative's Fees

At the outset one must note that paying for legal representation can be avoided in Russia. Self-representation is allowed in both civil and commercial proceedings, and in any court at any level. Possible restrictions on self-representation have been discussed recently, but only academically.

A more relevant question for the Russian society is whether a representative must be an attorney – a professional lawyer from the bar association, or any professional lawyer. Current laws provide that a party may be represented by any person whatsoever. Of course, this approach does not guarantee proper representation, and it forces judges to play a more active role in litigation. Most experts agree, however, that introducing any restrictions with respect to both self-representation and legal representation in courts now will restrict access to justice. In this regard, there are significant differences between two branches of the Russian judiciary and their impact on the development of civil procedure. While the commercial court system has long been ready to restrict representation to legal professionals, general courts cannot afford to do so. Postponing reforms in this respect seems just, given the absence of a developed legal aid system which is a

[10] Section 15 of Plenary Resolution No. 66, 20/12/2006, of the Supreme Commercial Court RF.

more immediate issue for Russia at the moment. Of course, such reform delays slow down the progress of the commercial courts' procedure.

Representation by attorneys – or at least professional lawyers – has gradually become common in civil litigation, particularly in commercial courts, which hear very complex cases. Thus the question of shifting attorney fees and of their magnitude becomes more relevant for Russia.

In the Russian Federation, there is no official attorney fee schedule with respect to civil litigation. Such fees are to be set in an agreement between the lawyer and his or her client. This agreement has priority even where basic fee rates have been established by the relevant bar association.

However, in spite of any agreements made, a court will resort to the market when reimbursing the winner for his lawyer's fees. In this way, courts try to comply with the legal requirement of compensating merely a reasonable amount of such fees. The amount of reasonable lawyer fees is determined by analyzing the legal services market in the given region, the duration of proceedings, and the complexity of each case. Such criteria are used in the aggregate.

20.7 Success-Oriented Fees

In the Russian legal system there is no distinction between several types of success-oriented fees – they all treated equally and allowed with very few restrictions.

The Supreme Commercial Court has ruled that the only relevant condition with respect to the reimbursement of legal costs incurred by the winning party is whether such costs have been actually incurred. Neither the method of determination (e.g., hourly rates, fixed fees, subscription fees, fees as a percentage of a lawsuit value) nor the conditions of payment (e.g., only if the court decides in favor of the client)[11] are relevant. It is important, though, whether such fees are reasonable. These factors – whether the fees were actually paid and whether they were reasonable – are thus the only limits for reimbursing attorney fees, even under a contingency fee or a "no win-no fee" agreement.

20.8 Legal Aid

The Russian Bar is a professional association of attorneys and, as a civil institution, is not a part of the system of governmental entities or local authorities. A major purpose of the Bar is to provide professional legal aid.

[11] Section 6 of Information Letter of the Supreme Commercial Court of the Russian Federation No. 121, dated December 5, 2007 "Review of caselaw on issues relating to representative fees allocation between parties to the case", available at http://www.arbitr.ru:80/as/pract/vas_info_letter/18473.html.

In Russia, public legal aid is available only in criminal cases (it is guaranteed by the Russian Constitution and the Russian Criminal Procedure Code). There is no generally available public legal aid for private litigation although there are very limited categories of cases – e.g. recovery of alimony – in which the Bar must provide legal representation for indigents.[12] Presumably, individuals of low income must apply directly to a certain bar association with a request for pro bono legal aid, and must support their application by relevant documents.

In Russia, there are some other institutions which provide legal help for parties in need. In fact, Member States of the Russian Federation try to solve the problem of legal aid on their own. Some of them are in the process of organizing state bureaus (Moscow Region, Chechnya, and many others). In several regions parties can receive legal help from clinics operated by law faculties. Despite all these efforts, there is no unified or organized legal aid system yet.

Recently, however, there has been considerable progress towards an organized system of legal aid. The non-profit organization «Association of Lawyers of Russia» had created more than 300 legal aid centers in 42 regions of Russia (half of all Russian Federation Members) by the end of 2009. Usually help is provided for the most unprotected people (World War II veterans, pensioners, handicapped persons, public sector workers, students, foreign citizens, and persons without any citizenship). The circle of potential beneficiaries is thus rather large and wider than the group of litigants entitled to legal aid by law.

20.9 Conclusion

As we have seen, the Russian Federation embraces the loser-pays principle. Moreover, the losing party compensates the winning party for all litigation costs. The implementation of this statutory rule differs dramatically, however, depending on the court system hearing the case. While the commercial courts tend to be serious about making the winner by and large whole, the general courts' approach often results in only partial cost shifting. Again, this latter approach can easily turn into a major-shifting attitude depending on the concrete circumstances of a case. Ultimately, wide judicial discretion means that the general courts often shift costs and fees at levels close to those of the partial-shifting jurisdictions.

Furthermore, with regard to attorney's fees, Russia is a market oriented system, with a very open market approach. Attorneys and their clients can agree to nearly any variation on the method of payment. Success-oriented fees are common and are limited by only a reasonableness requirement.

---

[12] Article 25 of the Federal Statute *On Advocacy in the Russian Federation*.

All of the features mentioned above are designed to implement the Russian Federation's policy of facilitating access to justice. In fact, the only factor that seems to contradict this approach is a rather high filing fee (e.g., compared to the US). However, a wide range of exemptions from court costs and broad discretion by the judge to grant installment payments or to postpone the filing fee payment reduces the deterrent effect of this factor dramatically.

The main disadvantage of the Russian approach is that individuals resort to courts from the outset rather than to attempt to settle disputes. Insufficient development of an alternative dispute resolution system and an increasing burden on the courts are the direct consequences.

However, a rapid development of the commercial courts' procedure may, and probably will, trigger a new cycle of reforms concerning mandatory mediation in certain categories of cases, reassessment of the current computation method for court costs, and professional legal representation, in the near future.

Chapter 21
Rigidity, Discretion and Potential Reform: Cost and Fee Allocation in Scotland

Greg Gordon

21.1 Introduction

There have been few revolutions in Scots civil procedure over the years. Instead, the courts and (especially) the legislature have tended to tinker around the edges of the machinery of justice. This has resulted in a system which, at its best, displays the robust common sense born of long experience and which, at its worst, appears cumbersome and old fashioned.

A revolution, or something close to one, may be on the horizon. The Report of the Scottish Civil Courts Review (generally referred to as The Gill Report after its lead author, Lord Gill, a senior Scottish judge) was published in September 2009. The Gill Report makes many far-reaching proposals and if implemented will change the face of the Scottish civil justice system. Where the Gill Report proposes changes which are germane to the subject matter of this report, these are noted and discussed below. However as it is not known if, when, or to what extent the recommendations in the Gill Report will be implemented, this Chapter generally proceeds on the basis of current procedure and practice.

Some of the terminology used and structures described may be a little alien to those unfamiliar with Scots procedure and a few introductory words of explanation are offered here. Firstly, a few words should be said about the hierarchy of courts in Scotland. In civil proceedings, the Court of Session is the senior court before which the most high-value and significant business is generally conducted. However, as we shall see, it is possible to raise relatively low-value actions in the Court of Session, and this has led to the court becoming overwhelmed with business. It has also unnecessarily raised the cost of litigation, as Court of Session proceedings are in general significantly more expensive than those in other courts. Within

G. Gordon (✉)
University of Aberdeen, Aberdeen, UK
e-mail: law339@abdn.ac.uk

M. Reimann (ed.), *Cost and Fee Allocation in Civil Procedure*, 239
Ius Gentium: Comparative Perspectives on Law and Justice 11,
DOI 10.1007/978-94-007-2263-7_21, © Springer Science+Business Media B.V. 2012

that court, a variety of different forms of procedure are utilised for different actions. For our purposes the most significant are the court's Ordinary Procedure and its Commercial Procedure. Lower in the court hierarchy is the Sheriff Court, which is essentially a local court used for low and low-to-mid value claims. Again, there exists a multiplicity of different forms of procedure within the Sheriff Court; Small Claim procedure (for low value claims), Summary Cause Procedure (for slightly higher value claims, but the difference is so slight that it hardly justifies the existence of two low-value claims procedures), Ordinary Cause procedure (for claims which exceed the ceiling value of Summary Cause procedure) and Commercial Procedure. The people litigating within these courts are known as pursuers (claimants/plaintiffs) and defenders (defendants). What is generally known as "costs" in other jurisdictions is described as "expenses" in Scotland (but for the ease of comparison, other than in direct quotations, the term "costs" will be used in this Chapter). Finally, by way of introduction, we should say a few words about the Scottish legal profession. Like the profession in England and Wales, Scotland has a split bar, where the more senior branch of the profession (advocates) enjoy rights of audience in all Scottish courts, while the more junior branch (solicitors) have rights of audience in the Sheriff Court, and also most specialist tribunals, but do not generally[1] have rights of audience in the Court of Session or the new Supreme Court, which has taken over the judicial function of the House of Lords and, although based in London, is Scotland's highest court of civil appeal.

21.2 The Basic Rules: Who Pays?

The basic rule of cost and fee allocation in Scots civil litigation is often said to be that the loser pays the winner's expenses (henceforth "costs"). This, however, is something of an over-simplification. It is more accurate to say that the judge has a discretion as to which party should bear the costs of a particular litigation, but that in exercising that discretion the judge will be guided primarily by the principle that the party whose conduct made the litigation (or the particular procedural step in an overall litigation) necessary bears the expense of the litigation (or step). Because Scots law accepts the notion that "the rights of the parties are to be taken all along such as the ultimate decree declares them to be,"[2] the application of this

[1] Especially experienced solicitors may apply to become solicitor-advocates, who enjoy rights of audience in the most senior courts. In general, however, it continues to be the case that when litigation is conducted in the Court of Session or the Supreme Court the function of the advocate is to present the clients case while the function of the solicitor is to do the majority of the pre-hearing preparation.

[2] *Shepherd v Elliot* (1896) 23 Rettie's Reports 695 per the Lord President (Robertson) at 696.

principle generally results in the loser paying. However, where success is divided, the judge's discretion results in a wide range of potential outcomes: for instance, partial awards may travel in each direction, or the judge may simply find in the circumstances the parties have fought each other to a draw, and no costs are due to or by either party. Similarly, as the rule lays emphasis upon the way in which the litigation has been conducted, the judge will also bear in mind whether the litigation was conducted properly and efficiently.[3] So a litigant who ultimately wins, but who, along the way to that victory, led evidence from a witness whose testimony is found by the court to be wholly irrelevant, is likely to find that the court will make an award of costs in favour of the loser in relation to the costs associated with that witness's testimony.

The usual position in Scots law is that the loser will have to pay the winner's legal fees "as taxed" (i.e., as assessed by an expert and approved by the judge[4]) on what is called a party and party basis. Here, the winner receives the amount that the Auditor of Court considers was reasonably necessary for the proper conduct of the case. This basis of calculation has been found to significantly under-estimate the amount of work which is typically done by a lawyer both before litigation commences and in preparation for proof (which is to say, the trial of fact).[5] An award calculated on this basis will almost invariably be at least somewhat lower than the fees actually charged by the winner's lawyers, and the restrictive nature of the items which are allowable on a party and party basis can, most notably in complex commercial cases, lead to a very wide divergence between the cost of the service as billed by the lawyer to the client and the amount which the rules and practice of the court permit. Recent research suggests that recovery rates of 50–60% of actual lawyers' fees are normal for commercial actions in the Court of Session, and that in complex cases the recoverable element can fall below 50%.[6] It is generally considered that the recovery rate in non-commercial actions is higher and lies at around 60%.[7]

It is competent for awards to be made on what is called an indemnity (also known as agent and client) basis. Here the norms used in calculating

---

[3] See e.g. *Fowler v Gruber* [2009] Court of Session (Outer House) 156.

[4] For a further discussion on the process of taxation, see Section 21.5, below.

[5] Law Society of Scotland Professional Remuneration Committee, *Shortfall in Judicial Costs: Response of the Committee to the Scottish Civil Courts Review*, ("Law Society Remuneration Committee, *Evidence to Gill*") available at http://www.scotcourts.gov.uk/civilcourtsreview/Responses_to_the_Consultation_Paper/L/Law_Society_of_Scotland_Remuneration_Committee.pdf (visited 7 June 2011).

[6] Lord Gill et al., *Report of the Scottish Civil Courts Review*, Edinburgh, 2009, ("The Gill Report") Volume II at p. 76.

[7] Law Society of Scotland Remuneration Committee, *Evidence to Gill*, p. 1.

an award on a party and party basis are rejected in favour of the overarching principle that the successful party should be reimbursed in full.[8] Such awards are rarely made in the Scottish courts, and when they are, the court is almost always expressing its considerable displeasure at some aspect of the way in which the case has been conducted.[9] For instance, if a litigant completely changes the basis on which its claim or defence is formulated, and the other party can demonstrate that it has been inconvenienced by investigating a case which is no longer being proceeded with, then the court may well order that all of the costs incurred up to the time of the rewriting must be met by the amending party on an indemnity basis.

There are no especial rules for appeals. This position is generally justified on the basis that, as noted above, the rights of the parties are to be taken all along such as the ultimate decree declares them to be.

The costs associated with preparing for proof, and in particular the costs of expert and other witnesses, are borne in first instance by the litigant who wishes that witness to give evidence on his behalf, and, (so long as the judge and the Auditor of Court are satisfied that this particular witness's evidence was reasonably necessary for the conduct of the case), these costs will generally be included at taxation as an allowable cost recoverable from the losing party. These costs are likely to form a significant part of the overall costs of litigation, and the fact that the instructing party (usually the pursuer) may have to settle these outlays months or even years before being reimbursed is perceived to be a weakness in the existing system. The Gill Report recommends taking at least some account of the hardship which may be associated with having to fund such outlays by allowing interest to be recovered.[10]

The great majority of civil suits settle without the need for a formal determination by the court. As is the case in England and Wales, reliable statistical information is not available, but it is widely estimated that some 90–95% of cases are concluded without the need for a final judicial determination If parties settle their dispute by the acceptance of a judicial tender (i.e., a formal offer to settle the case lodged in court by the defender), then the defender will be bound to pay the pursuer's costs incurred only up to the point when the tender was lodged. If an extra-judicial settlement is reached outside the tendering framework, costs are a matter for agreement between the parties, but it would ordinarily be the case that at least some agreed contribution towards costs would be made by the defender. A relatively common way of addressing this issue is for the parties to agree that

[8] *Baker Hughes Ltd v CCG Contracting International Limited* 2005 Session Cases 65 at 69.

[9] See e.g. *APPA (UK) Limited & Anor v The Scottish Daily Record and Sunday Mail Ltd* [2007] Court of Session (Outer House) 196 per Lord MacPhail at paras 7–17.

[10] The Gill Report Vol. 2 at p. 87.

the defender will pay the pursuer's costs on a party to party basis, which costs will be determined after the event by the Auditor of Court in the event that they cannot be agreed upon by the parties themselves.

21.3 Exceptions and Modifications to the Basic Rule

There are a number of situations where the basic rule is deviated from. A special category of Small Claims is recognized (consisting of defended claims worth less than £200) where an award of costs will only be granted if a party has behaved unreasonably or has not defended the action in good faith. Similarly, awards of costs are granted only very rarely, and for similar reasons, in proceedings before Employment Tribunals.

Where the losing party to a litigation enjoyed the benefit of Legal Aid,[11] awards of costs may be applied for against either the losing party itself or the legal aid fund. However, such applications are not determined in accordance which the usual rules; statutory guidelines require the court to limit any award of costs. In determining an application for costs against a legally aided party, the court must limit any award to the amount "that is reasonable [for the party] to pay, having regard to all the circumstances including the means of all the parties and their conduct in connection with the dispute".[12] In practice this means that, in the absence of wholly unreasonable conduct by the losing litigant, the court will generally find that no or at most very limited costs are payable by a legally aided party.[13] In the case of an award of costs against the legal aid fund, the test for making an award is that it is "just and equitable in all the circumstances".[14] Such awards are made only rarely, and usually only when the party seeking the award can demonstrate that he or she will suffer serious hardship if an award is not made, and if the conduct of the party having legal aid can fairly be subjected to criticism.[15]

---

[11] Legal Aid is discussed more fully in Section 21.7, below.

[12] Legal Aid (Scotland) Act 1986 s. 18 (as amended).

[13] For an illustration of what will constitute unreasonable conduct leading the court to decline to vary an award of expenses, see *Bell v Inkersall Investments Ltd* (*No. 2*) 2007 Session Cases 823.

[14] Legal Aid (Scotland) Act 1986 s. 19 (as amended). If the application for an the award of costs relates to first instance proceedings, there are additional criteria to satisfy, namely that the proceedings must have been commenced by the legally aided person, and the court must be satisfied that the unassisted party will suffer financial hardship unless an order is made.

[15] *Clegg v Clegg* 1999 Scottish Civil Law Reports (Sheriff Court, Notes) 773.

I am not aware of any other special or protected categories of litigants.[16] For instance, no rule exists stating that awards of costs cannot be made against consumers, or that an award of costs are incompetent against the state.

Contractual agreements about who will bear certain legal costs are relatively common in Scotland in some commercial contexts: commercial leases, for instance, will often contain clauses to the effect that in case of a lawsuit, some of the landlord's legal costs will be borne by the tenant. However, party agreements on who will bear the cost of litigation are unknown in this reporter's experience and must be, at most, very rarely used. It is unlikely that the courts would consider themselves bound by such agreements, particularly if they produced a manifestly unjust result, and any clause in a standard form contract which provided that a consumer was required to bear the costs of a commercial organization would in any event be potentially unenforceable as a result of consumer protection legislation.[17]

Parties are permitted to represent themselves in all civil cases. Self-representation is commonplace in Small Claims and Summary Cause procedure, and in some Sheriff Courts advisors are on hand to guide party litigants on court presentation and procedure. Self-representation is also commonplace before some specialist tribunals (the most relevant of which, for present purposes, is the Employment Tribunal; most of the rest of these would be considered to be administrative in nature). Self-representation is relatively uncommon in mainstream civil litigation (i.e. under Sheriff Court Ordinary Cause procedure and in the Court of Session) but has still been identified as a significant waste of court time, particularly at the appellate stage. The Gill Report is at best agnostic about party litigants, and perceives a need both for strong case management powers to control the unruly,[18] and the enhanced use of in-court advise services to encourage and assist the responsible.[19]

21.4 Encouragement or Discouragement of Litigation

The most commonly given justification for the special rules which exist for very Small Claims and in the Employment Tribunal (discussed in Section 21.3, above) is that they encourage claimants to bring cases which

---

[16] It may be worth noting in passing that there is limited scope for an award of costs against the state in criminal or administrative proceedings, but a discussion of these areas lies outside the scope of this paper.

[17] Unfair Terms in Consumer Contracts Regulations 1999 (SI 1999/2083). See in particular Schedule 2(1)(e) and 2(1)(q).

[18] The Gill Report Vol. 1 pp. 234–238.

[19] The Gill Report Vol. II 17–19.

would otherwise be uneconomic. To that rather limited extent only, the rules governing cost and fee allocation encourage litigation.

The "loser pays" rule is not really designed to discourage litigation. The purpose of the rule is to ensure that the winner suffers as little loss as possible as a result of a litigation which he or she has won. The rule nevertheless has the effect of discouraging litigation. In particular, it can act as a barrier to the bringing of cases which break new legal ground. In such cases, the idea, discussed in Section 21.2, above, that "the rights of the parties are to be taken all along such as the ultimate decree declares them to be" is particularly artificial – and the consequences flowing from it especially harsh. However, the courts still continue to apply the general rule and order the loser to pay in such situations.

The chilling effect of an approach to expense which, whatever its apparent subtleties, generally reduces down to a loser pays rule is problematic, not only from the perspective of the individual litigant, but also from the perspective of the systemic interest. The point was recently made by Lord Rodger, a Justice in the UK's Supreme Court, that Scotland, a small jurisdiction with a low throughput of cases, can ill afford to deter litigation if its law is to develop.[20] The Gill Report recommended the institution of a procedure, modeled on the Protective Costs Orders of the law of England and Wales, whereby, where litigation involves a serious matter of public interest, an order clarifying the issue of costs (generally by stating that no costs are to be awarded to or by either party) can be obtained ab initio, thus providing the pursuer with a degree of certainty on costs.[21] The Court of Session has recently accepted that it has a common law power to make such an order. However, among the qualifying criteria for the making of such an order is "that the applicant has no private interest in the outcome of the case".[22] This criterion would seem to mean that such orders will be possible only in the context of an application of an essentially public character. It is suggested that this limitation is to be regretted.

The up-front court costs associated with initiating an action are relatively small in Scotland. The fee for initiating a Small Claims action is either £15 or £65 (depending on the value of the claim), a Summary Cause costs £65 to initiate, an Ordinary Case £100 and a Court of Session action £175. It is in addition common for solicitors to demand a certain amount of money "up front" to cover the initial stages; the amount taken will vary depending on the size and degree of complexity of the action. A solicitor might request as little as £2,000 to allow him to take steps to initiate an Ordinary Cause

---

[20] Lord Rodger of Earlsferry, *Where Have We Come From, Where To Next?*, (2008) 53.8 Journal of the Law Society of Scotland, p. 14.

[21] The Gill Report Vol. II pp. 37–44.

[22] *McGinty Petitioner* [2010] Court of Session (Outer House) 5.per Lady Dorrian at paras 1 and 2.

action worth around £100,000. He or she would be likely to seek a retainer measured in tens of thousands of pounds to initiate a more complex commercial action. Most solicitors will now also issue interim bills as the case progresses.

There is little evidence that up front payments (in the sense of payments required to commence a litigation) of themselves have a significant deterrent effect upon potential litigants. However, the fact that the overall cost of litigation is so large, and the risk that the litigant may not be able to recover all of his or her costs or, in the worst case scenario, may have to make a significant contribution towards the costs of the other side, have a notable deterrent effect upon potential litigants.

21.5 The Determination of Costs and Fees

Court fees (which are not charged to litigants who have the benefit of Legal Aid, or who are in receipt of certain welfare benefits) are fixed by delegated legislation.[23] Different fees apply for different courts and for different forms of procedure within individual courts. Small Claim and Summary Cause fees are cheaper then Ordinary Cause or Commercial proceedings in the Sheriff Court, and fees in the Court of Session are somewhat higher again. However even in the Court of Session court fees are not especially high, and rarely will court fees comprise the main or even an especially significant part of the overall cost of litigation.

Scots law operates a hybrid system where, for most forms of civil litigation block fees are set out in delegated legislation stating what will be payable in respect of the various constituent phases of the litigation if the party entitled to costs wishes to proceed on a block fee basis. However, and except for the cases of Small Claims and Summary Cause procedure, where the block fees are ordinarily mandatory, the successful party has a choice: he or she may accept payment on the block fee basis, or may opt to submit a "time and line" account, which seeks to weigh up with greater precision the amount of work done by the parties' lawyer(s) in the case. It is usually the case that parties will opt for block fees where a case was reasonably straightforward and will opt for a time and line account where the case was more complex. Either way, the account will have to be "taxed" before being approved by a judge (see below).

The final determination of the amount to be paid to the entitled party/parties is a multi-stage (not to say cumbersome) process. A judge will

[23] The current fees chargeable in the Sheriff Court are to be found in The Sheriff Court Fees Amendment Order 2008 (SI2008/236). Court of Session fees may be found in The Court of Session Fees Amendment Order 2008 (SI2008/239).

make a determination, usually at the same time as determining on the merits of the case, but possibly at a subsequent hearing convened specifically to address the issue, deciding who, in principle, is to bear the costs. Any party who has received an award of costs will then prepare accounts setting out what it believes itself to be entitled to. If agreement is not reached between the parties, these accounts are remitted to the Auditor of Court (or the Sheriff Clerk in the case of Small Claim or Summary Cause procedure) who "taxes" (i.e. tests, or assesses) the account. The Auditor reports the outcome of the taxation back to the court. Ordinarily, the court will pronounce a decree approving the Auditor's report, but the court can depart from the Auditor's recommendations if satisfied that he or she has erred in law. The Gill Report notes the rather cumbersome nature of this procedure and proposes some relatively minor amendments (principally the enhanced use of IT and telephone taxations), but it appears that the current system will otherwise remain substantially in place.[24]

21.6 Special Issues: Success-Oriented Fees, Class Actions, Sale of Claims, and Litigation Insurance

Contingency fees cannot be charged by qualified members of the legal profession (i.e. by solicitors, advocates or solicitor-advocates). This is known as the rule against *pactum de quota litis*. This rule, which is civilian in origin, has been recognized in Scotland since at least the seventeenth century and exists as it is thought to be undesirable for lawyers to have a direct financial interest in the outcome of a litigation.[25] A contingency fee, if levied, would be void and legally unenforceable, and attempting to levy such a fee would be unethical and likely to render a qualified legal professional liable to be proceeded against for professional misconduct by their professional body.[26] However, it has been held that contingency fees are not invalid when levied by an unqualified or quasi-legal advisor, such as a claims handling agency.[27] In Scotland, a considerable amount of personal injury claims are handled by such agencies on a contingency fee basis. If the agency is unable to settle a case before advancing to litigation, it will employ professionally qualified lawyer(s) to commence litigation. The qualified lawyer(s) cannot directly

[24] The Gill Report Vol. II pp. 89–92.

[25] James Dalrymple the Viscount Stair, *The Institutions of the Law of Scotland*, Edinburgh, 1693, paragraph I.10.8.

[26] Alan Paterson and Bruce Ritchie, *Law Practice and Conduct for Solicitors*, Edinburgh, 2006 at pp. 234f.

[27] *Quantum Claims Compensation Specialists Ltd v Powell* 1998 Scots Law Times 228. Note, however, that the work done by the claims handling agency prior to the transfer of the case to a qualified lawyer cannot be adopted by that lawyer and recovered from the other party in the litigation: *Smith v Highland Council* 2010 Scots Law Times 2.

share in the contingency fee, but will usually be employed on a no-win, no-fee basis.

No-win no-fee arrangements (usually coupled with success premiums, discussed further below) are permissible and increasingly commonplace. They are seen most commonly in actions for personal injury but are competent across the board.

While success premiums are permitted,[28] they cannot be recovered from the other side. This has allowed Scots law to avoid some of the difficulties caused to defenders (and arguably the systemic interest in justice) in systems where success fees are recoverable from the losing party, but of course gives rise to the converse problem of markedly increasing the successful pursuer's unrecoverable element of costs.

Claims may be sold for the purposes of litigation, but the only context in which this occurs commonly is the sale of commercial debts for a certain proportion of their value; this is commonly done by companies in order to enhance liquidity.

The sale of claims by a client to his or her attorney is by and large unknown. Such action could very well give rise to professional misconduct proceedings against the lawyer on the basis of a conflict of interest between the lawyer and the client, and would probably be prohibited by the rule against *pactum de quota litis*, discussed above.

There are no special rules of court for class actions, group litigation or actions brought by consumer organizations. The Gill Report considers Scots law to be underdeveloped in this area and recommends the introduction of a new dedicated multi-party procedure. The Gill Report does not propose to deviate from the default position on costs for such actions.[29]

It is possible to obtain insurance against the cost of litigation. This may take the form either of specific litigation insurance (used primarily in the context of personal injury actions) or coverage under other policies such as automobile or homeowners insurance. Although specific litigation insurance is available, it is used somewhat less commonly in Scotland than in other jurisdictions (for instance, England and Wales) because of the continued availability of civil legal aid (discussed in further detail, below). Where used, specific litigation insurance is generally organized for the client by his or her solicitor, who will require to certify that probable cause exists. The cost of the premium for buying the insurance is responsibility of the claimant and is not a recoverable expense in the event that the pursuer wins an award of costs. Where legal costs insurance is obtained as part of another policy, this usually involves the payment of an additional premium, the total amount payable in any one claim will usually be capped (often at £100,000 or £250,000) and the pursuer will usually be obliged to make use

[28] Solicitors Scotland Act 1980 s. 61A(3) and (4).

[29] The Gill Report Vol. 2 at 66f.

of the services of a lawyer recommended by the insurance company. Certain types of litigation (for instance family disputes and claims relating to inheritances) will usually be excluded from the scope of cover.

21.7 Legal Aid

A publicly funded legal aid system has existed in Scotland since the 1950s. The system is currently administered by the Scottish Legal Aid Board (generally abbreviated to SLAB). Only registered legal aid practitioners can act in cases supported by Legal Aid. The system operates by providing means-tested financial support on a sliding scale, with those on the lowest incomes receiving the greatest amount of support and the amount of assistance provided "tapering off" for those with more means. In consequence, someone who only just satisfies the means test will still require to make a significant contribution towards the cost of his or her litigation. Claw-back provisions also exist whereby the cost of legal aid will often be deducted from any damages awarded in the litigation.

Pro bono work is undertaken by some lawyers, sometimes because of sympathy for a particular cause (some lawyers, for instance, have a reputation for offering pro bono work for charities or other causes for which they feel a particular empathy or association) or on occasions where they consider the law to be unjust or in need of reform. The relevant professional bodies support the undertaking of pro bono work. There is however no enforceable professional obligation to undertake pro bono work and this remains a matter for the conscience of the individual lawyer. Litigation costs and fees are considered by many to be excessive and as such a serious barrier to justice,[30] especially for small businesses and for private individuals who earn too much money to get any significant benefit out of the legal aid system, but who could not be described as wealthy. The differential between actual charges and the recoverable element has been identified as especially problematic. Following recommendations in the Gill Report, the Scottish Government has recently commissioned a review of the costs and funding of litigation (the Taylor Review)[31] which is charged with, among other things, considering the affordability of litigation. The Report is expected in late 2012.

[30] See e.g. Law Society Remuneration Committee, *Evidence to Gill* at 10.

[31] Scottish Government Press Release, "Costs of Litigation Review", available at http://www.scotland.gov.uk/News/Releases/2011/03/04133056 (visited 7 June 2011).

21.8 Conclusion

Scots civil procedure has over time evolved a system of rules which can, rather paradoxically, be characterized as both rather rigid and somewhat capricious. The rigidity is brought about by the system's all but total adherence to the notion that the rights of the parties are to be taken all along such as the ultimate decree declares them to be. This leads, almost invariably, to a finding that the loser pays. But what, exactly, does the loser have to pay? This is where the variability comes into play. The answer will depend upon the complex interaction of many factors, including the conduct of the parties (and their lawyers), the particular court that the pursuer has chosen to play the dispute out in, the question of whether one or more of the parties has the good fortune to be legally aided, the scale that the winning party chooses to be paid upon, or whether preparatory work has been carried out by a qualified legal professional or by a claims handling company. While some of these factors (the conduct of the parties in particular) are clearly appropriate factors for the court to bear in mind when making a costs order, others reduce the amount of costs which must be borne to a matter of happenstance. Discretionary decisions made by the pursuer and/or the winning party have too much influence on the overall cost of the litigation.

Scots civil procedure is likely to be entering a period of considerable upheaval and change over the next few years. The proposals of The Gill Report, if implemented, will effect the most radical structural alteration to the machinery of civil justice since at least the 1850s. Yet the recent establishment of the Taylor Review and the Gill Report's support for the institution of a Civil Justice Council suggests that we may be about to enter an even more thoroughgoing period of reform. The Scottish system is by no means entirely bad, but a thorough review is long overdue. It is to be hoped that the Scottish authorities will take this opportunity to reduce costs, make the system less capricious, and improve access to justice.

Chapter 22
Cost and Fee Allocation in Slovenia – From Major to Partial Shifting?

Nina Betetto

22.1 General Legal Background

Basic rules on cost and fee allocation in civil procedure are found in the Civil Procedure Act (CPA).[1] Besides the CPA there are other important formal sources of civil procedural law affecting cost and fee allocation.

Obviously, regulations on court and attorneys' fees and on legal aid are important from a financial point of view. The Slovenian Constitutional Court dealt with the problem of the relationship between the financial burden of litigation and the right of access to court. According to the Constitutional Court, the right of access to court can be violated if the financial burden of litigation forms an insurmountable obstacle for a poor party's access to court.

The court fees are determined and calculated according to the Court Fees Act.[2] In ordinary proceedings, court fees must be paid for each instance of proceedings (i.e., including access to the Supreme Court, up to three court fees; Article 18/1, Court Fees Act). Parties must advance the payment for certain procedural acts and a failure to do so has direct procedural effects. For example, the court fee for the claim and the appeal must be prepaid at the time of filing; if the party fails to pay the court fee even after the court has ordered him or her to do so, the claim or appeal is deemed withdrawn (Article 105a, CPA). Also, the party proposing a motion for taking evidence must pay in advance the amount necessary to cover the anticipated costs of producing this evidence. If the party fails to do so, the motion for taking such evidence is also deemed withdrawn (Article 153, CPA).

[1] Official Gazette RS, No. 26/99 – 45/08.

[2] Official Gazette RS, No. 37/08.

N. Betetto (✉)
Supreme Court of the Republic of Slovenia, Ljubljana, Slovenia
e-mail: nina.betetto@sodisce.si

M. Reimann (ed.), *Cost and Fee Allocation in Civil Procedure*, 251
Ius Gentium: Comparative Perspectives on Law and Justice 11,
DOI 10.1007/978-94-007-2263-7_22, © Springer Science+Business Media B.V. 2012

Under Slovenian law, parties may represent themselves (it is common, for example, in small claims proceedings and family cases) or perform procedural acts through an attorney. If a party chooses to be represented by another person, he or she can only authorize an attorney at law or another lawyer who has passed the state bar exam. Only in the lowest courts (county courts) are there no limitations on whom the power of attorney can be conferred (Article 87/1, CPA). The only exception to this rule concerns proceedings with "extra-ordinary legal remedies" (for example, revision and action for annulment of a court settlement). In such a case, a party is obliged to be represented by an attorney at law (except if a party him- or herself passed the state bar exam).

Formerly, one of the unfortunate features of Slovenian law often resulting in dilatory tactics of attorneys and thus encouraging protracted litigation was that an attorney at law was entitled to reimbursement for every single procedural act performed (for example, for filing the claim, for every written preparatory submission, for attendance at every hearing) rather than a certain phase of the proceedings as a whole. This rule was recently changed by the Attorneys' Fees Act (which came into force on 1 January 2009)[3] and a system (following the German model) was introduced under which an attorney at law is entitled to reimbursement for an entire phase of the proceedings. Currently, attorneys' fees are calculated in accordance with the Attorneys' Tariff contained in the Attorneys' Fees Act. Yet, under strong pressure from the side of the Attorneys' Chamber (bar association), an amendment to the Attorneys' Act in 2009[4] transferred competence to determine attorneys' fees to the Attorneys' Chamber. The new Attorneys' Tariff, which is subject to approval of the Minister of Justice, has not been adopted yet and the Attorneys' Tariff contained in the Attorneys' Fees Act is currently still in force.

Assistance to indigent parties is regulated by the Free Legal Aid Act.[5] Some provisions concerning free legal aid were previously contained in the CPA, but after the adoption of a comprehensive system of the Free Legal Aid Act, there is no further need to retain a parallel system in the CPA. Legal aid is provided by attorneys at law and (except for representation in court) by private bodies and NGOs licensed by the state. A party granted legal aid can choose an attorney from a list submitted by the Attorneys' Chamber. Attorneys are remunerated for services accomplished exclusively according to the Attorneys' Tariff. Yet there is a lower fee for attorneys representing a client on a free legal aid basis than in the case of providing services for "ordinary" clients. If the applicant succeeds in litigation, the state has the right to claim costs incurred through free legal aid from the opponent.

[3] Official Gazette RS, No. 67/08 – 35/09.

[4] Official Gazette RS, No. 35/09.

[5] Official Gazette RS, No. 48/01 – 23/08.

A grant of free legal aid does not affect the relation between the applicant and the other party in civil proceedings. Thus, if the opponent wins, he is entitled to claim costs from the losing party – the free legal aid beneficiary – and legal aid does not cover that risk.

An application for free legal aid is decided upon by the president of the district court after the draft is prepared by the Legal Aid Services Department of the court. The rules of the Administrative Procedure Act apply. An unsuccessful applicant may bring an administrative complaint before the Administrative Court of the Republic of Slovenia. If the Legal Aid Services Department grants aid, it may condition it on a request that the aided party attempt to settle the case by using one of the ADR mechanisms before pursuing the case in court (Article 28, Free Legal Aid Act).

An applicant is entitled to free legal aid if he or she is unable to cover the costs of legal proceedings without jeopardizing his or her financial position or that of the family. The detailed criteria regarding the financial eligibility are determined by the Free Legal Aid Act. Legal aid includes legal advice, representation in court through an attorney at law, and partial or full exemption from payment of the costs of proceedings (for example, court fees, costs of experts, witnesses). Free legal aid may be restricted to certain phases of procedure (for example for the procedure at the first instance court). Only a natural person and certain categories of non-profit NGOs that operate in the public interest can qualify for free legal aid. If circumstances regarding the financial status of the applicant change during the procedure, the decision granting the legal aid may be revoked. Pursuant to the amendment of the Free Legal Aid Act in 2004,[6] residents of other EU Member States are guaranteed the same level of access to free legal aid as Slovenian residents.

Case law in Slovenia is not formally recognized as a source of law. In practice, however, established case law is an important authority and lower courts tend to follow positions of the appellate courts and of the Supreme Court. Courts are not authorized to determine procedural rules by themselves.

Because of the compulsory character of the norms contained in the CPA, party agreements (in a contract) allocating costs and fees in case of litigation are not allowed and could not be enforced. The conclusion of a settlement (Article 159, CPA) is the exception to the rule that it is the court – not the parties- that decides on claims relating to costs in litigation. In such a situation, the parties who have resolved their substantive dispute can agree on cost and fee allocation by themselves.

[6] Official Gazette RS, No. 50/04.

22.2 The Basic Rule: The Loser Pays

The basic rule of cost and fee allocation is that the losing party must reimburse costs to the winning party. If a party succeeds only in part, such a party is entitled to a proportionate amount of costs. In that case, the court may also order that each party bear his or her own costs (Article 154, CPA). The principal justification for the rule that the losing party must reimburse costs to the winning party is that the winner deserves to recover the costs of successfully claiming a right or defending against such a claim. In addition, it is believed that this principle is designed to encourage litigants to bring meritorious claims to court.

When allocating costs and fees, courts will only take into account whether a party is successful upon final judgment; the success of individual procedural acts is disregarded. Appellate and revision (extra-ordinary legal remedy) proceedings necessarily result in additional costs. If the appellate court annuls the judgment of the first instance and remands the case for retrial, this results in almost doubling the costs. With regard to appeals, the same basic rule of cost and fee allocation used in first instance courts applies: the losing party must reimburse the costs of the winning party. As only the final success is taken into account (not the success of individual procedural acts), the party who successfully appealed against a judgment is not automatically entitled to reimbursement of his or her costs: if the appellate court could make no final determination of the issue, but instead annuls the judgment and remands the case to the court of first instance, then it is the final judgment of the court of first instance that will decide any claims relating to costs, including the costs for appeals. If the challenged judgment is altered in favor of the appellant, however, then the appellate court will decide any claims relating to costs in litigation, including costs incurred in the first instance court.

Concerning the calculation of the proportion of success, usually the ratio between the amount sought and the sum granted is taken into account. For example, if the plaintiff demanded $10,000 in damages and the court orders the defendant to pay $5,000, the plaintiff will be entitled to reimbursement for half of his expenses. In turn, the defendant will be entitled to reimbursement from the plaintiff for half of her expenses.

The costs of proceedings include the expenses incurred during or due to the litigation (Article 151 CPA). The major costs incurred in litigation are attorneys' fees, court fees and costs for the taking of evidence, including the costs of experts and witnesses. With regard to reimbursement, all of them are treated in the same way.

The winning party is not automatically entitled to reimbursement of *all* costs. When deciding which costs are to be refunded, the court takes into account only the expenses that were necessary for the litigation (Article 155, CPA). The court may, for example, find that the attorney's fee for filing a certain written preparatory submission cannot be considered a necessary expense because it contained nothing new or relevant to the case. By using its power to deny reimbursement of costs that were not necessary for the litigation, the court can expedite the proceedings. Yet it must be emphasized that in practice the court should use this power more often.

22.2.1 Exceptions to the Basic Rule

There are several exceptions to the basic rule. Thus, irrespective of the outcome of the litigation, a party shall refund to her opponent any costs arising due to her default or by accident (Article 156, CPA). Take, for example, the case where a plaintiff files an extensive written preparatory submission at a hearing instead of properly sending it to the court in advance to permit her opponent to review it. As it is now necessary to adjourn the hearing to permit her opponent to comment on the submission, the plaintiff is the party responsible for the adjournment and shall thus be required to bear the costs caused by adjourning the hearing. The same rule applies in the case of a hearing that is adjourned not through a party's lack of due care, but still as a result of circumstances within this party's sphere (for example, the defendant was involved in a car accident while going to the court hearing, which therefore had to be adjourned).

Special rules which are aimed at stimulating parties to participate diligently in the proceedings also apply for certain specific procedural situations. If a plaintiff withdraws the claim, he must reimburse the defendant's costs unless he withdrew the claim immediately after the defendant had satisfied it (Article 158, CPA). In the case of an acknowledgement of the claim, the costs must be paid by the defendant. Yet, if the defendant did not provide any cause for bringing the action in the first place and has acknowledged the claim in the defense plea or at the main hearing before becoming engaged in trying the main subject of dispute, then the plaintiff must reimburse the costs of the proceedings (Article 157, CPA).

22.3 The Determination of Costs and Fees

The amount of court fees and attorneys' fees depends on the amount in controversy and is calculated according to the court fees and attorneys' fees tariffs. As noted above, court fees are determined according to the Court Fees Act. They must be paid for each instance of proceedings.

In their contractual relationship, an attorney and a client can agree on criteria for payment other than the application of the Attorneys' Tariff.

The major principle regulated by the Attorneys' Act[7] is that in patrimonial matters, an attorney and a client can agree on a contingency fee, which, however, must not exceed 15% of the value of the claim. They can also agree to an hourly rate on the basis of the time actually spent working on the case, or a payment pursuant to rates higher or lower than those in the Attorneys' Tariff (Article 17, Attorneys' Act). The agreement determining details of the contractual relationship between an attorney and a client must be in writing. Only if no special agreement is made between the party and the attorney does the Attorneys' Tariff apply. Therefore, the Tariff does not restrict the autonomous position of attorneys as private entrepreneurs. The advance payment of attorneys' fees is allowed (Article 10, Attorneys' Fees Act); in fact, such agreements are quite common.

The court finally determines the concrete amount to be awarded to a party (or parties). The decision on costs forms an integral part of the judgment or decree, and it can be appealed in the same manner as the decision on the principal claim. The real importance of the Attorneys' Tariff in this context is that it provides the basis for the court's determination of costs and fees, irrespective of the actual agreement between the winning party and the attorney. Thus, for the court it will be irrelevant if the winner agreed to pay, for example, a double fee to his or her attorney; the losing party will be ordered to reimburse only the amount that corresponds to the fee as prescribed by the Attorneys' Tariff.

22.4 Contingency Fees – From Major Shifting Toward Partial Shifting?

In looking at cost and fee allocation in civil procedure, the first question is: which of the parties has to bear litigation expenses? Groupings of legal systems with regard to who pays various categories of expenses (court costs, lawyer fees and evidence expenses) tend to oversimplify reality. Slovenia as a civil country embraces the loser-pays principle. Yet, as mentioned, cost and fee allocation rules do not guarantee the winner full compensation for all litigation expenses. Thus while success oriented fees are allowed to limited extent, a court will shift costs on the basis of the applicable statutory tariff.

Thus, in evaluating what cost shifting really means, one must include information on the amount of attorneys' fees that the winner can recover from the loser. It must be emphasized that although in most cases the tariff fees currently cover the winner's attorney fees either completely or at least to a very large extent, there is a strong pressure from the side of the

[7] Official Gazette RS, No. 18/93 – 35/09.

Attorneys' Chamber to move from the schedule-based approach towards a market-oriented model. Such deregulation of attorneys' fees could dramatically complicate the loser-pays rule in the future. Where the determination of lawyer fees is left to the market, fee shifting becomes more problematic as far as the protection of the loser is concerned, and can result in a situation where full reimbursement of the winner is becoming the exception rather than the rule.

Chapter 23
The System of Costs in Spanish Civil Procedure

Francisco López Símo and José Ángel Torres Lana

23.1 The Basic Rule on Cost Under the Spanish Law of Civil Procedure

The basic and general rule is that the loser pays all costs (art. 394.1 of Law of Civil Procedure (CPL), *Ley de enjuiciamiento civil*). Yet, according to recent decisions of the Spanish Supreme Court, this rule is fully applied only if all the petitions of the respective party have been defeated, or at least substantially defeated, in court. In other cases, i.e., in case of merely partial defeat, another rules applies, which is described below (Section 23.2.1, Step 1).

What does it mean that the loser has to pay *all* costs? Under article 241 CPL, the following items are included: fees of the attorneys and solicitors (though not in all cases, as we will explain in the next paragraph); compulsory advertisements which have to be published during the litigation; compulsory advance payments required for filing appeals; fees of experts and compensation for the first three witnesses; the price of copies, certificates and other documents (except those requested from Public Registrations Offices which are free) and finally fees of public notaries. Obviously these items are not all the expenses generated by litigation, but they are the only ones that may be counted as "costs".

As mentioned, the fees of attorneys and solicitors are considered costs when the participation of these professionals in a litigation is mandatory.

The present essay is a summary of Spanish Report written by the authors and sent to the General Reporter (Mathias Reimann) for the XVIIIth World Congress of the International Academy of Comparative Law, held in Washington D.C. on July, 25–31, 2010. López Simó has written the paragraphs n. 1–4 and Torres Lana n. 5–8. The conclusions (paragraph n. 8) have been prepared and written by both authors. Both authors take responsibility for the entire work.

F.L. Símo (✉)
University of the Balearic Islands, Balearic Islands, Spain
e-mail: francisco.lopezsimo@uib.es

M. Reimann (ed.), *Cost and Fee Allocation in Civil Procedure*, 259
Ius Gentium: Comparative Perspectives on Law and Justice 11,
DOI 10.1007/978-94-007-2263-7_23, © Springer Science+Business Media B.V. 2012

This is true if the amount in controversy exceeds €2,000 (arts 23.2, 1st and 31.2, 1st *a contrario sensu* CPL, as amended March 2011). Since this amount is very low it means attorneys and solicitors participate in a very high percentage of controversies – practically in all cases. Their fees are usually the most important part of the costs.

The role of these professionals requires some explanation. We have just used the English term "solicitor" to designate the Spanish *procurador* A *procurador* is a legal professional (i.e., a holder of a law degree) who must be distinguished from an attorney (*abocado*). The *procurador* represents a party (never both) but he does not appear in court. Instead, he takes care of notifications, scheduling of trials, the procurement of evidence, etc. He has also to receive the documents from the other party and to forward them to the attorney who defends to his client in court. For all these activities, the solicitor receives his own fees. These fees are included in the item of costs when his participation is mandatory (i.e., when the amount in controversy exceeds €2,000). All in all, it is fair to say that *procuradores* work much like English solicitors whereas Spanish *abocados* are similar to English barristers. We can thus call the *procurador* a "solicitor".

The basic rule that the loser pays all is justified by the principle that the winner should not to suffer any kind of damage or economic loss which would decrease the total amount he wins under to the judgment.

There is, however, a limit to which fees of attorneys and experts can be shifted. The loser has to pay such fees only up to one third (33.3%) of the amount in controversy (art. 394.3 CPL). This cap is rarely reached in practice. There is also an exception: the cap does not apply if the court concludes that the loser has behaved recklessly or acted in bad faith; in that case, the loser has to pay the total amount of the fees, i.e., even if they exceed one third of the amount in controversy.

A somewhat different rule applies for appeals. If the appellant loses all his petitions, he has to pay all the cost of the appeal. In any other case, the costs are equally shared between the parties, and each party pays the fees of its own legal experts (art. 398 CPL).

The expenses incurred by taking evidence are considered part of the cost as well (art. 241, 4th, CPL) and their allocation follows the rules established by the CPL in articles 394 et seq. But these expenses – mainly the fees of experts – are usually not a significant item on the overall bill.

The CPL does not provide a particular rule for cost allocation in case of settlement. The basic rule is that the agreement between the parties governs which usually involves the allocations of the cost. Typically, the agreement provides that each party pays the fees of its own attorneys, solicitors and experts, and that the court fees are shared equally. Note, however, that in Spain, the percentage of cases ending in settlement is very low – even where settlement is legally permitted. There are certain kinds of litigation in which settlements are not allowed because the case is closely linked to personal status, e.g., personal competence of incompetence, filiation and protection of minors, marriage, and state of minority. These cases involve a public interest (arts. 19.1 and 751.1 CPL) and cannot be settled by the parties. On the whole, probably less than 10% of all civil cases are settled in Spain.

23.2 Exceptions and Modifications of the Basic Rule

23.2.1 Exceptions

There are several specific provisions which involve exceptions to the basic rule. The most important ones are the following:

1. When the matter of the litigation is obscure, highly complicated or involves serious doubts of fact or law, the cost are split between the parties, i.e., each side has to pay its own court costs and fees of its attorneys, solicitors and experts (art. 394.1, *in fine,* CPL).
2. The same rule applies, if the petitions of the plaintiff or of the defendant result only in partial victory (art. 394.2 CPL).
3. There are also exceptions for specific procedural situations. If the defendant admits the claim before filing an answer (art. 395 CPL), each side has to pay its own cost. And if the plaintiff withdraws the claim, he or she has to pay all the costs, unless the withdrawal has been accepted by the defendant (art. 396 CPL).
4. There are also exceptions pertaining to specific parties. Public attorneys, representing the state, never have to pay costs, even if they lose the case (art. 394.4 CPL). Indigent litigants who are entitled to "free justice" are not obliged to pay the costs, unless and until their economic situation improves (394.3, last paragraph CPL).

23.2.2 Contractual Agreements About Cost Allocation

Ex ante (e.g., contractual) agreements between the parties on cost allocation are unusual. Judges would not be bound by such an agreement because the rules about costs are mandatory. They must be applied ex officio by the judge, i.e., even without petition by the parties. Agreements in derogation of mandatory rules are void (art. 1255 Spanish Civil Code).

23.3 Encouragement or Discouragement of Litigation

Generally speaking, the current Spanish system (which dates back to 1984 when the "the loser pays all" was established) tries to discourage litigants who doubt the validity of their claim and thus have reason to be unsure about the outcome of the litigation. Yet, it also encourages parties who are confident to win because if they do, they do not incur costs diminishing the amount their gain.

Another factor of discouragement are the upfront payment requirements by attorneys or solicitors. They can especially deter people who do not have the financial means to make such payments. To be sure, in case of victory, their expenses will be reimbursed, but that can take more than one year in the first instance an another year in case of appeal.

23.4 Amounts and Time of Payment

As a general rule, the costs of the litigation (fees, expenses for evidence, etc.), including the court costs (a special kind of taxes), have to be paid by each party at the time these costs are generated (art. 241.1 of CPL), i.e., without waiting until the end of the litigation (art. 241.2). That means that the winner, under the "loser pays" rule, obtains a reimbursement claim for the amounts he has paid up front at the end of the litigation.

There are special rules concerning a kind of court fee which is considered a type of tax (*tasa*). This kind of tax is like a price one has to pay for using a public service or when one attends or benefits from the activity of a public office. This tax, however, is so low that it is almost symbolic. Also, certain parties to a controversy, such as individuals, non-profit organizations and small business entities are exempt from these taxes according to the Law of the Taxes for Companies. In any event, since they are so low, these taxes represent a very small percentage of the total litigation costs. They are determined by combining by a fixed amount of about €150 (depending of the kind of the proceedings) and a variable amount depending on the amount in controversy (at a very low percentage, i.e., 0.5% per €100 up to €1,000,000 and 0.25% above €1,000,000). For appeals these amounts are doubled. These taxes are not provided in the CPL but rather in arts. 5 and 6 of Spanish Law 53/2002, of Dec. 30.

Regarding the amount of attorney and solicitor fees, there are neither mandatory rules nor fixed criteria. Attorneys and solicitors may ask for upfront retainers of up to 100% of their fees although usually, only about 50% are requested. We will turn to the determination of the amount of fees below (Section 23.5).

The costs of taking evidence also have to be paid when they are being incurred (art. 241 of CPL). The particular amount depends of the kind of the evidence. As a general rule, an expert (e.g., an engineer, an architect or a doctor) has the right to receive his or her own fees which are determined freely by each expert according to the respective professional rules. Without doubt, expert testimony is often the most expensive item on the litigation bill, together with the fees of attorneys and solicitors. Witnesses receive compensation only for the losses they suffer (e.g., through absence from work or by having to travel) which have to be paid by the party calling the witness. The total amount of these compensations is fixed by the court according to the circumstances alleged and proved by each witness (art. 375 of CPL).

23.5 The Determination of Costs and Fees

As mentioned, the amount of court costs is basically determined according to the amount in controversy. If such an amount cannot actually be established due to the nature of the case, it is set at €18,000. The determination of the amount in controversy also depends on the kind of the process involved and on the type of court.

Attorney fees are set by a free agreement with the client. If there is no express agreement, the attorney can apply the statutory rules of his own Bar. Still, these rules are not mandatory, i.e., they do not bind to the attorney but only serve as a reference point for fee determination (art. 44.1 of General Statute of Spanish Advocacy, approved by Real Decreto – Royal Decree – 658/2001, of June, 22). Note that formerly, these rules used to set binding minimum fees so that an attorney could not charge less (that would have been considered unfair competition).Today, however, attorney and client can agree to increase or decrease these officially set fees as they wish.

As a result, attorney fees are now left to the market. Still, the freedom to determine attorney fees is not unlimited but rather follows by several important criteria. These criteria may consist of an hourly rate, or, more frequently in the case of litigation, the amount in controversy and the level of complexity of the case. It also very common to use a mixed approach, i.e., a combination of two factors: a fixed amount and a percentage of the final result of the litigation if the client wins (arts. 44.2 and 44.3 of the current Statute of Advocacy). There is also a specific protection for the loser against excessively high amounts of costs, which has been previously described: according to art. 394.3 CPL, the loser only has to pay, as a general rule, the fees of the winner's attorney and experts up to a third of the amount in controversy (although if there are several winners, each is entitled to that percentage). Again, if the amount in controversy cannot actually be determined (*cuantía inestimable*), it is fixed by law at €18,000 so that the maximum payable by the loser for the winner's attorney and expert fees is €6,000. If there is no a clear winner because each party has prevailed in part, it is not necessary to determine the amount of the costs because each side has already paid in advance all the costs caused by it, and there will be reimbursements. An exception is, as mentioned, the situation in which one of the parties has acted recklessly or in bad faith (*mala fides*); in that case, the party can be condemned to pay all costs even it has not lost.

If the party liable for costs does not pay them voluntarily, the secretary of the court will assesses them. This assessment can be challenged in which case the judge makes the final decision. The assessment of costs is enforceable (arts. 242–246 f CPL).

23.6 Success Oriented Fees and Similar Arrangements

The CPL says nothing about success oriented fees and thus leaves the matter to the private and contractual relationship between clients and attorneys. Such fees could also be regulated by the statutes of each Spanish bar association (there is, at least, one bar association in each province) but, again, these statutes do not provide special rules concerning success oriented fees either, again, leaving attorneys and clients by and large to agree as they wish.

There is a major exception, however, for pure contingency fees, which are termed *quota litis* agreements in Spain (and other Latin countries, such as France, Italy, and Portugal because the attorney takes part of the sum won). Pure *quota litis* agreements – i.e., on a no-win-no–fee basis – between the attorney and his client are strictly forbidden by all the particular rules of the statutes of the different Spanish bar associations as well as by the General Statute of Advocacy (art. 44.3). The services of the attorney cannot be left entirely unpaid even he loses the case because an attorney's obligation is one of effort, not of result (see arts. 1583 of Spanish civil Code, which contain the regulation of the contract of services).

Success premiums, however, have long been common. They are considered *quota litis* agreements only in wider sense which is allowed by General Statute of Advocacy (art. 44.3). They involve a previously fixed amount which must be paid in any event (i.e., win or lose) plus an additional amount which becomes due only if the case is won. Usually, this second amount consists of a percentage – which has to be reasonable – of the benefit or advantage received by the winner. As the success premium is purely based on the private agreements between the attorney and the clients, it is not considered part of the "costs" which can be charged against the loser.

The reality, however, is somewhat more complicated. Ultimately, the loser has to pay the costs which have been fixed by the court secretary, and that, of course, encompasses the bill of the winner's attorney. Yet, this bill often includes part of the supplementary (success oriented) amount agreed with the client. The result is that part of the success premium *can* actually be recovered by the winner, albeit not directly and expressly. Remember though that the loser has to pay the bill only up to one third of the amount in controversy (art. 394.3 CPL). As a result, the winner's attorney cannot exceed this amount; if he or she did, it could be reduced by the court or by the bar after a short proceeding.

23.7 Legal Aid

There is a constitutional rule (art. 119 of Spanish Constitution) which states that justice will be free in cases settled by Law (i.e., according to ordinary legislation approved by Parliament). This rule is repeated in the Judicial Power Law and developed by the Free Legal Aid Law, 1/1996, January, 10 (FLAL). That Law states that free legal aid is a "public service". This means that it is paid by the state, in fact by the Ministry of Justice. The system also involves the bar associations: they receive funds from the Ministry of Justice and then pay the fees of the attorneys included in the system. It is important to note that these attorneys do not work for free or pro bono. They have the right to receive their fees, which are fixed in an official schedule and are usually lower than those for regular clients.

A person seeking legal aid has to send an application form to the bar association of the province where litigation will take place. He or she has to show that the requirements legally established are met, in particular, in the case of individuals, associations or foundations, that they lack the funds to present a claim and pursue the litigation. The Bar designates an attorney – called attorney ex officio – for the petitioner on a provisional basis. A specific commission has the last word to confirm or revoke this provisional designation, after examining the evidence presented within 30 days (arts. 12–18 FLAL). There is no private system to help indigent people.

The following parties are eligible for legal aid (according to art. 2 FLAL and various further rules):

1. Spanish citizens, citizens of European Union countries, and foreigners who live in Spain when they show that they have no money to pursue the case;
2. Entities who manage the social security system (subject to no other requirements);
3. Associations, foundations and consumer organizations if they have no funds to initiate and pursue the litigation;
4. The Spanish Red Cross (subject to no other requirements);
5. Public aid associations created to protect disabled people.

In art. 3, the FLAL determines that for individuals, "lack of economic funds" means an income below twice the minimum salary fixed annually by the Spanish Government in the Law of Budgets (currently, between €600 and 700 per month for Spain). This minimum is includes the whole family of the applicant. For entities included in number 3 above, a lack of funds is established when their annual earnings do not exceed three times the minimum salary.

Legal aid is supplied widely in Spain. A judgment of Spanish Constitutional Court (95/2003) abolished the requirement that foreigners had to have "legal residence" in Spain so that currently, even an illegal residence is sufficient.

Further decisions of the Constitutional Court interpreted the FLAL to mean that the purpose of legal aid is to ensure that no one remains unable of defending him- or herself because of a lack of funds to litigate (Auto Constitutional Court 188/1998, followed by Sentence of the Constitutional Court 10/2008).

23.8 Conclusions

The most important features of the Spanish system can be summarized in a few sentences. The basic rule is that the loser pays all. It applies only, however, in case of a clear victory; otherwise costs are normally split. In addition, the loser's liability for the winner's attorney and expert fees is capped at one third of the amount in controversy (under art. 394.3 CPL), thus protecting the losing party from excessive cost liability. This protection does not apply when the losing party behaved recklessly or in bad faith.

The fees of attorneys and solicitors, which are the main part of the costs, are included in calculating recoverable costs if the participation of these professionals is mandatory (i.e., where the amount in controversy exceeds €2,000). The determination of lawyer fees is largely left to the market; there are official tariffs set by the bar associations but they are no longer binding. Success oriented fees are allowed with the exception of pure contingency fees (*quota litis*); success fees are not officially recoverable from the loser although in practice, they are often included in the attorney's bill and then included in the assessment by the secretary of the court.

Legal aid is a constitutional right, financed by the state and managed through the bar associations. It is widely available in Spain to individuals, organizations, and enterprises who lack the funds to pay for litigation.

Chapter 24
Loser Pays – But Only a Reasonable Amount

Cost and Fee Allocation in Sweden

Martin Sunnqvist

24.1 Principles for the Assessment of Costs

In small claim cases, where the dispute concerns values below 21.400 SEK (2011),[1] the winning party only has a right to reimbursement for the cost of legal advice given for a maximum of 1 h (according to the fees of legal aid[2]), the court fee, the cost of the journey of the party or an attorney, witness costs and translation costs.[3] In these cases, this means that a party choosing to hire an attorney will have to pay most of the cost herself, even in case of victory.

In all other civil cases, the winner has a right to full reimbursement of the costs for preparation and performance of the trial including the attorney's fee. However, the reimbursement is restricted to an amount that is "reasonably required for the protection of the party's rights".[4] Unless the losing party has accepted the reasonableness of the required amount, the court has to try this issue.

In the case NJA[5] 1997 p. 854, the Supreme Court made some general statements clarifying how this rule is to be applied: If the losing party shall pay all of it, the cost must be *reasonable*; it is *not* enough that the cost is *not unreasonable.* The amount of the attorney's fee – when legal aid is not involved – shall not be decided according to the time the attorney has used but according to the character and extent of the case and the care and skill of the attorney. The value of the dispute and its importance to the

[1] Approx. €2,300 or $3,200.

[2] 1.166 SEK (2011), approx. €130 or $180.

[3] CJP Ch. 18, § 8 A, section 1–5.

[4] CJP Ch. 18 § 8.

[5] "Nytt juridiskt arkiv", the series of Supreme Court cases.

M. Sunnqvist (✉)
Faculty of Law, University of Lund, Lund, Sweden
e-mail: martin.sunnqvist@jur.lu.se

M. Reimann (ed.), *Cost and Fee Allocation in Civil Procedure*, Ius Gentium: Comparative Perspectives on Law and Justice 11,
DOI 10.1007/978-94-007-2263-7_24, © Springer Science+Business Media B.V. 2012

party may also be considered. A party is not required to specify in detail the work done by himself or the attorney, neither as regards the amount of time used nor the specific measures taken.

In the particular case, the winning party had actually specified the measures taken, approximated the time used and provided the cost per hour, all with regard to the work done both by the party itself and the attorney. The Supreme Court accepted the correctness of the specified time and the reasonability of the cost per hour. Also, the case had been pending for eight years, involved a considerable amount of money, contained several alternative sets of facts, and also presented complex issues as to what law should govern different parts of the case. The winning party thus received full reimbursement.[6]

If a party has hired an attorney, it is easy to establish what the cost actually was and whether it was reasonable or not. If a party was represented by an in-house lawyer, however, it is more difficult to determine the costs. In the case NJA 2009 p. 441, the Supreme Court held that a calculation of the actual cost for such a lawyer's work is not required. Instead, a reasonable cost for hiring an attorney to do the work should be estimated, and that amount should be presumed to be equivalent to the real cost. In the next step, it then needs to be assessed whether such an amount is reasonable with regard to the criteria mentioned in the 1997 case.

The 1997 case provides a good illustration of the factors used by the courts in Sweden to assess the reasonableness of costs. What is striking, however, is that the Supreme Court actually used criteria which it just had said should not be used. It is not easy to reconcile what the Court said with what it actually did. Perhaps the most plausible reading is that the character and extent of the case as well as the care and skill of the attorney may be determined *partly* through a consideration of the reasonable amount of time used and a reasonable fee per hour,[7] albeit without determining appropriate hourly rates by case law and thus losing the discretion of reasonableness in a wider sense.

---

[6] See for an analysis of this case Lars Heuman, "Skäligt ombudsarvode i tvistemål där klienten inte beviljats rättshjälp" in *Juridisk Tidskrift* 1997/1998 pp. 796–808.

[7] In the 1997 case, the attorney's fee per hour was 1.431 SEK and in the 2009 case 1.800 SEK, both numbers exclusive of VAT. Probably one could say that a reasonable fee per hour for a member of the bar association in 2011 would be between 1.500 and 2.500 SEK (approx. €160–280 or $230–380) exclusive of VAT; for work done outside civil proceedings before a court, the fee could be substantially higher, presumably 3.000–5.000 SEK (approx. €330–550 or $460–760). Cf. note 11 as regards work done according to the legal aid tariff.

24.2 Efficiency Measures to Control Litigation Costs

Why are then Swedish litigation costs, seen as a whole, ultimately fairly reasonable? I can think of a few explanations.

24.2.1 Efficient Procedure?

The procedural reform of 1948 not only changed the distribution of costs from a damage-oriented to a rights-oriented approach, it also took some steps from an inquisitorial to an adversarial civil procedure. However, some elements of judicial control over the procedure were kept.

Civil procedure in the first instance is divided into two stages. In the preparatory stage, normally a session is held before a judge with the goal that the parties should clarify all issues and make all the factual allegations they want to make.[8] The judge can ex officio, or on demand of the other party, dismiss evidence, e.g., if it is irrelevant, unnecessary or meaningless or if it can be replaced by other evidence more conveniently.[9] At the trial state, it is then the duty of the court (normally consisting of three judges) to make sure that nothing irrelevant is drawn into the case.[10] This enables the court to ensure that the attorneys do not waste times on irrelevant issues, which in turn has the effect that if such work is done anyway, it cannot be reimbursed.

As long as the evidence is relevant, the parties may rely on it and the court has to assess it.[11] Given that the assessment of the relevance of the evidence will normally take place at the preparatory session or after a written procedure, this means that there will be no costly preliminary proceedings about which evidence is to be allowed. The evidence is put forward by the parties and the witnesses are interrogated by the attorneys, but there is practically neither a Swedish counterpart to the United States discovery procedure, nor are there any "fishing expeditions" which generate high lawyer costs.[12]

Additional proceedings, which might be costly – such as sessions on, or judgments in, preliminary issues – are kept to a minimum. For example, a declaratory or an interlocutory judgment is allowed only after an assessment of whether it would promote a fast and simple decision and in a way that keeps costs down.[13]

---

[8] CJP Ch. 42 § 8.

[9] CJP Ch. 35 § 7.

[10] CJP Ch. 43 § 4.

[11] CJP Ch. 35 § 1.

[12] *See* General Report I.1.c note 49 and II.3.

[13] Cf. NJA 2005 p. 517 and 2007 p. 108.

A civil case cannot be tried by an appellate court unless it has given leave to appeal.[14] On the appellate level, a party cannot put forward new facts or evidence, unless he was unable to do so in the first instance or had a reasonable excuse for not presenting such evidence.[15] The admissibility of new factual allegations or of new evidence is tried by the court ex officio.

These procedural rules together illustrate that the legislature and the courts value procedural economy. The judges are supposed to be, and they actually are, careful that cases do not cause the parties unnecessary costs. The discretion of judges in deciding the reasonableness of costs means that they seldom have to use the specific rules about negligent parties and attorneys who cause unnecessary costs in a culpable fashion.[16] If such a party wins the case, the amount to be paid by the other party is usually mitigated through the general rule of reasonableness.

Most civil claims involving criminal conduct are brought within the criminal proceedings. The prosecutor has a duty to act as a counsel for the injured party as regards civil claims unless such are claims are particularly complicated. Thus, prosecutors generally claim, as counsels for the injured party, damages for infringement of the injured party's integrity, pain and suffering, or the right to stolen property. If the claim is too complicated to be handled by the prosecutor, a special counsel for the injured party – who is an attorney or other lawyer – is appointed by the court. Only if the civil claim is disproportionally complicated – e.g. because it is legally doubtful or requires additional evidence – it will be transferred to a civil trial.[17] This means that most civil claims connected to criminal cases will cause no separate costs.

24.2.2 Strict Assessment of Costs?

When it comes to cost shifting, the lion's share consists of the fees for legal advice and representation in court. Witnesses get paid for their loss of income and their cost of attending court, e.g. travelling and hotel costs.[18] The courts themselves charge near to nothing – only the cost for filing a case which is SEK 450.[19] Paying the costs for keeping a judiciary and an organization of courts has been seen as a self-evident task for the state, safeguarding access to justice.[20]

[14] CJP Ch. 49 § 12.

[15] CJP Ch. 50 § 25.

[16] CJP Ch. 18 § 3, 3 A and 6.

[17] CJP Ch. 22 § 1–2, Lag (SFS 1998:609) om målsägandebiträde.

[18] CJP Ch. 36 § 24, cf. as regards expert witnesses Ch. 40 § 17.

[19] Approx. €50 or $70.

[20] See e.g. Jacobsson 1964 p. 11.

In ensuring that the winner's costs are reasonable, the courts follow what the Supreme Court said in the 1997 case, and in doing so, they have developed a few rules of thumb. One of them is, as indicated in the 1997 case, to compare the cost with the amount in dispute. If the cost is close to, or exceeds, the value of the dispute, which occurs in small to medium cases,[21] such a cost is reasonable only if the dispute has an importance to the party beyond the actual amount.

Often, the specifications of the cost provide little more information other than the total of the fee the attorney has charged the client. One method for the judge is, of course, in relation to the 1997 case, to try to figure out what a reasonable amount of time and a reasonable hourly rate would be and assess whether the resulting total sum is reasonable. In legal aid civil cases and in penal cases, where the state pays attorneys according to a fee per hour, a reasonable amount of time is often considered to be three times the total time actually spent in court. This may also sometimes apply in ordinary civil cases on the district court level. Still, all the other factors indicated in the 1997 case must be taken into account, so that this rule of thumb does not provide all that much help. Especially if the case has been problematic, e.g., if the plaintiff initially has made arguments that later have become unnecessary because of concessions from the defendant, a higher amount of time is reasonable. If the appellate court gives leave to appeal, as a result of a recent reform, the oral evidence will generally be introduced via audio and video recordings of the lower court hearings.[22] This means that the time necessary for the attorney to prepare the case will be reduced and that the reasonable amount of time there would not even be three times the total time of the appellate court session.

There are good reasons for a party to give a fairly detailed account of how much work was done by the attorney. If the party wins the case but the court does not find the cost for the attorney reasonable, the party needs a leave to appeal to get the issue of the costs tried by the appellate court. A leave to appeal is to be granted, e.g., if there is reason to doubt the correctness of the district court's conclusion or if the correctness of the conclusion cannot be determined without a full trial of this issue in the appellate court.[23] Since the amount of costs should be reasonable, there is – according to the Supreme Court in case NJA 2009 p. 738 – room for different conclusions. The appellate court should grant leave to appeal only if there is reason to doubt that the conclusion of the lower court is within the frame of reasonableness. This means that the appealing party needs to show why the amount claimed is reasonable in order to get a leave to

[21] Cf. General report II.4.b.

[22] CJP Ch. 35 § 13.

[23] CJP Ch. 49 § 14.

appeal, something which is likely to make parties more inclined to specify their costs better in the first instance.

24.2.3 Judges Separate from Advocates?

The Swedish judiciary in civil and criminal cases was professionalized through reforms in the seventeenth century. The first appellate courts (*hovrätt*) were established then and the district courts were reformed. Young lawyers gathered around the courts and served as clerks to the district and appellate court judges. By contrast, the bar was professionalized only in the nineteenth and twentieth centuries, with the organization of the bar association (*Sveriges advokatsamfund*) and when parties were represented by attorneys in court more frequently.

Since the seventeenth century, ordinary judges been recruited mainly from among the clerks to the appellate courts. In recent years, this has changed to a certain extent. It is not unusual anymore that attorneys and prosecutors are appointed to the bench. Still, the primary way of becoming a judge is to start as a clerk in the district court and then continue in the court of appeals.

The traditional career of judges and the late professionalization of the bar means that Sweden is more judge-oriented than attorney-oriented, despite the fact that procedure has been largely adversarial for the last 60 years. For better or worse, a Swedish judge does not have the experience as an attorney which his or her English or United States colleagues have. This may make it easier for Swedish judges to cut costs: many of us have no experience in dealing with clients, preparing cases, and arguing them before courts. In addition, judges do not have a common interest with attorneys in keeping costs high. Surely, as far as I have seen, judges that have been attorneys apply the same standards in cost issues their colleagues who did not come from the bar. There is nonetheless reason to believe that the strictness of judges in these matters is deeply rooted in the judicial culture and in the separation of judges and attorneys.

24.3 Remaining Problems

The discussion above is based on the assumption that the costs in Swedish civil procedure are kept lower than one would expect in the light of the fact that attorney's fees are determined by the market.

Still, in Sweden, the question has occasionally been raised whether parties actually bear costs in an equitable way. This question may arise, inter alia, because the "loser pays"-principle applies also to cases where the law is unclear and where the Supreme Court lays down what rules are to be applied in the future. For example, the Supreme Court has decided that a strict liability rule applies in a case where not even the winning party seems to have expected it.[24] The Supreme Court has also, in plenary, shifted the burden of proof in a certain type of fairly common disputes from one party to the other, overruling earlier precedents.[25] In such cases, and in cases where legislation is considered unconstitutional and thus not applied, the "loser pays"-rule can be regarded as too strict. The loser might have started the process in good faith, relying upon published statutes and cases, which are then considered unconstitutional or out-of-date. In such cases the decision by the Supreme Court is to the benefit of the legal order at large and of future cases but the costs caused by the development of law is paid by a party who had good reasons for thinking he or she was right. Of course, the loser still paying both sides' costs fits with the fiction that the Supreme Court only interprets the law as it is, but it does not fit the reality that the Supreme Court occasionally changes established truths. It has been argued convincingly that in such cases, it would be reasonable if the state paid for the costs, or at least that the court could order each party to bear his own.[26]

---

[24] NJA 1991 p. 720.

[25] NJA 2001 p. 177, 2005 p. 205.

[26] Cf. e.g. Jacobsson 1964 pp. 35–46, 119–121, Sven Larsson, "De stigande rättegångskostnaderna" in *Svensk rätt i omvandling. Studier tillägnade Hilding Eek, Seve Ljungman, Folke Schmidt,* Stockholm 1976, pp. 251–262, and Lars Welamson, "Några synpunkter på HD:s verksamhet efter 1971 års fullföljdsreform" in *Svensk rätt i omvandling. Studier tillägnade Hilding Eek, Seve Ljungman, Folke Schmidt,* Stockholm 1976, pp. 626–627. – There is a rule to this effect in Norway, Norwegian Code of Civil Procedure Ch. 20 § 2.

Chapter 25
Pricey But Predictable: Civil Litigation Costs and Their Allocation in Switzerland

Caspar Zellweger

25.1 Introduction

As a result of Swiss federalism, the regime of costs and fees in civil litigation is not entirely uniform throughout the country, although it has recently become more so. Switzerland is a federation of 26 cantons with a history of strong cantonal and relatively weak federal powers. Thus, under the Constitutions of 1848 and 1874, civil procedure was governed by cantonal law (with the exception of proceedings in the Swiss Federal Supreme Court). Finally, with the new Constitution of 1999/2000, the federal legislature acquired the power generally to regulate civil procedure. After several years of drafting, a new (federal) Code of Civil Procedure (CCP) was adopted. It built largely on the various cantonal codes and entered into force on January 1, 2011.[1]

[1] Practice under the new CCP is virtually non-existent to date but literature on the new law is being published literally by the pound. A choice of first publications are: JACQUES Hardy, Jean-Marc Reymond, Laura Jacquemoud-Rossari, Denis Tappy, JEAN-FRANÇOIS POUDRET, FRANÇOIS BOHNET, NICOLAS JEANDIN, Le Projet de Code de Procédure Civile Fédérale, Traveaux de la journée d'étude organisée à L'Université de Lausanne le 8 mars 2007, édités par Suzana Lukic, Publication CEDIDAC 74, Lausanne 2008; BERNHARD BERGER, Zivilprozessrecht – Unter Berücksichtigung des Entwurfs für eine schweizerische Zivilprozessordnung, der bernischen Zivilprozessordnung und des Bundesgerichtsgesetzes, Stämpfli Verlag Bern 2008; ADRIAN STAEHELIN, DANIEL STAEHELIN, PASCAL GROLIMUND, Zivilprozessrecht nach dem Entwurf für eine Schweizerische Zivilprozessordnung und weiteren Erlassen – unter Einbezug des internationalen Rechts, Schulthess Verlag, Zürich 2008; DOMINIK GASSER, BRIGITTE RICKLI, Schweizerische Zivilprozessordnung (ZPO) – Kurzkommentar, Dike Verlag, Zürich/St. Gallen 2010; MYRIAM A. GEHRI, MICHAEL KRAMER (Editors), ZPO Kommentar, orell füssli Verlag AG, Zürich 2010; THOMAS SUTTER-SOMM,

C. Zellweger (✉)
Attorney-at-Law, Basel, Switzerland
e-mail: zellweger@ballmer.ch

M. Reimann (ed.), *Cost and Fee Allocation in Civil Procedure*,
Ius Gentium: Comparative Perspectives on Law and Justice 11,
DOI 10.1007/978-94-007-2263-7_25, © Springer Science+Business Media B.V. 2012

This unification of civil procedure law still leaves some room, however, for diversity with regard to litigation costs. While the *allocation* of costs and fees is governed by the CCP (and thus uniform), their *rate and calculation* continues to be a matter of cantonal law (and thus somewhat varying).

This essay will concentrate on the principles and rules under the new federal Code and point to cantonal regulations only where needed.

25.2 Costs in Swiss Civil Procedure: An Overview

The new Federal Code of Civil Procedure contains an entire chapter on "Costs of the Proceedings and Legal Aid".[2] The respective Title 8 of the CCP comprises 28 articles (Arts. 95–123). The Title is subdivided into four chapters dealing with "Costs of the Proceedings", "Determination and Collection of Costs", "Special Rules", and "Legal Aid".

The chapter on "Costs of the Proceedings" (Arts. 95–103) contains a definition of court costs and party costs and deals with questions relating to the claimant's obligation of having to advance prospective court costs and providing security for the defendant's costs.

According to the statutory definition set forth in Article 95 CCP, court costs comprise a flat fee for the (mandatory) conciliation proceedings, the judgment fee, the costs of the evidentiary proceedings, translation costs, and the costs for the representation of a child in family law proceedings. Party costs consist of the fees for professional counsel, necessary expenses and, if justified in a particular case, appropriate compensation for the inconvenience caused to parties not represented by an attorney.

Prospective court costs have to be advanced if so ordered by the court (Art. 98).[3] In that case, the timely payment of the advance is, among other things, a condition precedent for the rendering of a judgment on the merits (Art. 59). A respondent can, pursuant to Article 99 CCP, request from the claimant security for his prospective party costs (*cautio iudicatum solvi)* if (i) the claimant is domiciled or has its seat in a country with which

---

Franz Hasenböhler, Christoph Leuenberger (Editors), Kommentar zur Schweizerischen Zivilprozessordnung (ZPO), Schulthess Verlag, Zürich/Basel/Genf 2010; Baker & McKenzie (Editors), Schweizerische Zivilprozessordnung (ZPO), Stämpfli Verlag, Bern 2010; Karl Spühler, Luca Tenchio, Donimik Infanger (Editors), Basler Kommentar zur Schweizerischen Zivilprozessordnung, Helbing Lichtenhahn Verlag, Basel 2010; Christoph Leuenberger, Beatrice Uffer-Tobler, Schweizerisches Zivilprozessrecht, Stämpfli Verlag, Bern 2010. For an exhaustive overview on pertinent literature *see* http://:www.zpo.ch (Literatur).

[2] The application of Title 8 of the CCP in arbitration is subject to the parties' choice: parties may choose that the costs are equally shared by the parties or applied according to the tribunal's discretion.

[3] Arbitral tribunals enjoy equal powers pursuant to Article 378 CCP. If a party fails to advance the costs requested, the other party can advance all of the costs or withdraw from the arbitration proceedings. In the latter event the withdrawing party may introduce new arbitration proceedings or bring action in a state court.

Switzerland does not maintain a treaty on court and party costs, (ii) the claimant appears to be insolvent, or (iii) the claimant owes costs from previous proceedings or where there are other grounds for assuming that the claim for party costs may be at risk.[4] Article 100 and Article 101 CCP define the type and manner in which advances have to be paid and securities have to be provided. Article 102 CCP deals with the costs and their application in connection with taking evidence.

The chapter on "Determination and Collection of Costs" (Arts. 104–112) sets forth the principle that all of the costs of the proceedings are to be determined and allocated by the court ex officio (Arts. 104 and 105). The principles to be applied by the courts are defined in Articles 106 through 108 CCP which will be discussed in more detail below. Article 109 CCP deals with costs in the event of a settlement, Article 111 CCP defines the manner in which court costs shall be collected, and Article 112 CCP deals with deferment and waiver of court costs in case of hardship. Court costs are subject to a uniform 10-year statute of limitations and subject to a statutory interest rate of 5% which is payable on arrears.

The chapter on "Special Rules" (Arts. 113–116) relate to proceedings in which the levy as well as the application of court costs and/or party costs follows special rules. Details shall be discussed below under "Exceptions and Modifications".

The chapter on "Legal Aid" (Arts. 117–123) will also be discussed in detail below. Legal aid is only available for proceedings before state courts. Article 380 CCP states explicitly that it is not available for arbitration proceedings.

Any court order and ruling regarding costs and their application can be subject of a separate appeal, albeit only the subsidiary form of appeal in accordance with Article 319 et seq. CCP. The same applies to court orders denying legal aid in whole and in part.

The principles set forth in Title 8 of the CCP apply equally to courts of first instance and cantonal appellate courts. Where a court of appeals renders a new judgment on the merits of a case, it is required to also rule on the costs of the proceedings before the court of first instance (Art. 318 al. 3).

25.3 The Basic Rule: Who Pays?

The principal rule in all of Switzerland is under the unified Federal Code of Civil Procedure that cost and fees are allocated in accordance with the outcome of the case (Art. 106). If the plaintiff is fully successful, then the

[4] Article 379 CCP grants the same power to arbitral tribunals if the claimant appears insolvent with equal consequences as set forth in Article 378 CCP in the event of default. This provision is a novelty without a respective counterpart in the Federal Code of Private International Law.

defendant has to pay all of the costs and compensate the plaintiff in accordance with the applicable schedule. If the action is dismissed, then the plaintiff has to bear all of the costs and owes compensation to the defendant in accordance with the applicable schedule. In between these two extremes, the costs and the fees are distributed between the parties in accordance with the plaintiff's degree of success. The CCP provides for two important exceptions to this general rule which shall be discussed in the next chapters.

While only the claimant has to advance court costs (Art. 98) and possibly provide security for the prospective costs of the respondent (Art. 99), the obligation of advancing costs for the taking of evidence falls on both parties. Article 102 CCP provides that each party is obliged to advance to the court the costs caused by the taking of evidence which it has offered. Where both parties have offered the same evidence, they shall each advance half the costs. If one party fails to make the advance, the other can do so, failing which the evidence will not be taken, save for cases in which the facts have to be established ex officio.[5] The rule of Article 102 is in line with the general rule contained in Article 160 which states that the litigants as well as third parties have a duty to cooperate and participate in the taking of evidence, subject to a party's right of refusal as defined in detail in Article 163 CCP.

Costs associated with the taking of evidence (witnesses, expert opinion etc.) are to be allocated in accordance with the basic principle. Yet, with regard expert witnesses, one must distinguish between those which are appointed unilaterally by one party (so called party experts) and those which are court appointed (so called court experts). The payment of party experts is primarily the responsibility of the appointing party; it is possible to ask that those costs are compensated together with the attorney fees as necessary expenses (Article 95 al. 3a CCP) but courts are reluctant to award costs for party experts and rarely award full costs, if any. By contrast, the costs associated with court appointed experts are usually distributed like all other court fees.

In the event of a settlement, the parties are free in principle to agree on any distribution of the costs (Art. 109), save in the event that one party has been granted legal aid. In practice, the costs (court, experts, etc.) are usually shared equally and each party bears its own lawyer fees. If the settlement agreement contains no provision regarding costs, costs shall be allocated by the court in accordance with the general rule and its exceptions discussed in the next chapter.

---

[5] *See* Article 55 al. 2 CCP which applies currently only to cases involving children in family law matters (Art. 296).

25.4 Exceptions and Modifications

There are number of exceptions where the court is obligated or permitted to deviate from the basic rule that loser pays all.

The perhaps most important set of exceptions is contained in Article 107 CCP: the court can depart from the general rule set forth in Article 106 CCP *at its discretion* if it upheld the action, albeit not to the extent of the sum claimed; if the court had to determine the amount of the claim at its discretion; if the claim was difficult to quantify; if the action was brought in good faith, in matters of family law and registered partnerships; if the proceedings were terminated because the issue become moot (save where the applicable substantive law provides otherwise); or if there are other circumstances which for reasons of fairness justify a different allocation of costs.[6] In the alternative, the court can also charge court costs which have been caused neither by the litigants nor by an (identifiable) third party to the canton in which the court has its seat.

Equally important is the exception mentioned in Article 108 CCP which states, without much ado, that unnecessary costs shall be charged to whoever caused them. This rule applies in particular in cases where one party causes undue delay because a deadline was missed, because the party filed submissions which are unnecessary in substance or in length, or because of a change in argument which could have been made much earlier. Another example for the application of this rule is the widespread practice that each party shall, as mentioned, usually bear the costs of self-appointed experts.

Articles 113 and 114 CCP list a number of proceedings which are either free of charge or require only a minimal court fee, and in which each party has to bear its own costs. Article 113 CCP deals with costs of conciliatory proceedings which are mandatory under the CCP.[7] As a general rule, in conciliatory proceedings court costs are shared by both parties in accordance with their agreement if the case is settled (Art. 109) or by the claimant if the case is referred to the court for further adjudication (Art. 207) whereas party costs are borne by each party, definitely if the case is settled, and temporarily if the case is referred to the court for further adjudication.[8] In certain areas, the conciliatory proceedings are free of court costs,[9] and

---

[6] There is a heated and hitherto unsettled discussion whether (and if so, to what extent) Article 107 CCP shall be applied in case the claimant is not awarded more by the Court then what she/he has been offered by the defendant during conciliation.

[7] *See* Article 197 et seq. CCP. For more details *see* the next chapter on "Encouragement or Discouragement of Litigation".

[8] *See* DOMINIK GASSER, BRIGITTE RICKLI, *supra* note 1, p. 101.

[9] Article 113 al. 2 CCP lists the following types of disputes: those arising under the Equality Act dated 24 March 1995, under the Equality of Handicapped Persons Act dated 13

Article 114 CCP contains a further list of special proceedings not subject to court costs.

Article 115 CCP provides, in the spirit of the somewhat crafty Article 108, that parties who proceed in bad faith or wantonly can be held liable for costs even in proceedings for which, as a rule, no costs are charged.

Article 116 CCP gives the cantons the power to exempt further types of proceedings from court costs. Some cantons have made use of this delegation of powers and provide free court services involving lease contracts relating to private or commercial housing or agricultural leases.

25.5 Encouragement or Discouragement of Litigation

Just as with regard to the calculation of costs, every canton has a different system regarding the up-front payments required from the plaintiffs. The general rule, however, is that plaintiffs, save for those who benefit from legal aid, have to make some sort of a down payment (Art. 98). Some cantons follow a practice of asking the full amount of the presumed court costs in advance, whereby others require that a fraction is paid subject to further requests during the proceedings.

Counsel are allowed, but no longer obligated, to ask for an advance for their fees up to the presumed maximum,[10] unless the client is destitute and would qualify for legal aid.[11]

Under the former system there was no uniform policy with regard to either encouraging or discouraging litigation, apart from the traditional deterrent effect of costs in general. The new Federal Code of Civil Procedure, however, attaches great importance to settling disputes at the earliest possible stage. It requires that parties first make an attempt at conciliation or go through a mediation procedure before they can take the case to the court proper[12] (save for a defined set of exceptions listed in Articles 198 and 199[13]). Instead of the mandatory formal conciliation proceedings, the

---

December 2002, arising from a lease contract relating to private or commercial housing or agricultural leases, arising from employment relationships or under the Personal Employment Leasing Act dated 6 October 1989 with an amount in controversy of less than CHF 30.000, under the Employee Participation Act dated 17 December 1993 or relating to supplemental medicare under the Illness Insurance Act dated 18 March 1994.

[10] The request of excessive advance payments is deemed to constitute a violation of Article 12 lit. (a) of the Federal Attorneys-at-law Act, SR 935.61, dated 23 June 2000.

[11] Article 12 lit. (g) of the Federal Attorneys-at-law Act provides for a statutory obligation for all attorneys-at-law to accept legal aid cases going to court in the canton in which they are registered.

[12] *See* Article 194 et seq. CCP.

[13] Of particular interest is Article 199 subparagraph 2 CCP, which exempts all litigation against defendants living outside of Switzerland from mandatory conciliation.

parties may also jointly opt for out-of-court mediation in accordance with Article 213 et seq. CCP.

In sum, when it comes to encouragement or discouragement of litigation, the new system pursues a middle course: it seeks to guarantee everyone access to court while at the same time requiring the parties to first go through the motions of conciliatory proceedings, the aim of which is a rapid and cheap settlement. A strong incentive to settle cases in the context of a conciliatory proceeding is provided by the costs which formal court proceedings may entail. Settlement of the case at a very early stage is thus quite common in Switzerland, especially in regard to "small" and "medium" claims, i.e., claims of up to about CHF 100.000 (ca. US $100,000).

25.6 The Determination of Costs and Fees

The calculation of court costs and party costs is, as previously mentioned, subject to schedules which form part of cantonal law. These schedules follow by and large the same method of calculation but are very diverse in result. In most cases the costs are calculated as a percentage of the amount in dispute. The advantage of this system is that the costs and fees become largely predictable.

Court fees are regarded as duties. Thus, they have to be set at a level sufficient to cover the expenses incurred by the judicial system while at the same time remaining proportionate to the amount in controversy.[14] This seems like a conundrum without a satisfactory solution.[15] Despite a constant increase of their fees, cantons do not cease to complain about the financial burden of the judicial system which they are required to maintain. For the time being, the outcome of these complaints is not clear. It is undeniable, however, that litigation in Switzerland is generally considered expensive and that costs pose a potential threat to the principle of free access to court.[16]

---

[14] *See* MATIN STERCHI, Gerichts- und Parteikosten im Zivilprozess, in: CHRISTIAN SCHÖBI (editor), Gerichtskosten, Parteikosten, Prozesskaution, unentgeltliche Prozessführung (und Modelle zur Beschränkungen ihrer Kosten), Stämpfli Verlag AG Bern 2001, p. 13.

[15] For an interesting discussion of the necessary planning process required from a canton *see* URS HODEL, Die Planung und Bereitstellung der Ressourcen für die Justizbehörden im Kanton Aargau, in: CHRISTIAN SCHÖBI (editor), Gerichtskosten, Parteikosten, Prozesskaution, unentgeltliche Prozessführung (und Modelle zur Beschränkungen ihrer Kosten), Stämpfli Verlag AG Bern 2001, p. 71 et seq.

[16] *See* MAX PLATTNER, JEAN-PIERRE SCHMID, Gerichtskosten und Rechtsschutzversicherung, in: CHRISTIAN SCHÖBI (editor), Gerichtskosten, Parteikosten, Prozesskaution, unentgeltliche Prozessführung (und Modelle zur Beschränkungen ihrer Kosten), Stämpfli Verlag AG Bern 2001, p. 65.

Most schedules for court costs and attorney fees provide a so-called basic fee determined in proportion to the amount in controversy. The basic fee usually consists of a range between a minimum and maximum figure. This system is then supplemented by a catalogue of a great variety of reasons which allow for an up- or downgrade of the basic fee. The most common factors for an upgrade are the complexity of the controversy, the requirement of special knowledge, the urgency of the matter, the application of foreign law, and the involvement of foreign languages, whereas the most important ground for a downgrade is the termination of proceedings before final judgment.

Attorney fee schedules are in general binding for court related services. An increasing number of cantons haves introduced new legislation, however, pursuant to which attorneys and clients are free to agree on the type and manner of remuneration, albeit only within the fairly narrow limits defined in the Attorney-at-law Act.[17] Yet, these agreements are binding only for the parties. They do not bind the court when determining the party costs which the loser has to pay the winner. Thus, by entering into such agreement, the client accepts the risk that the fee owed to his or her attorney may exceed what he receives from the other side even in case of full success.

From a practical point of view it should be noted, though, that an attorney faced with the risk of a disproportionate amount of work in relation to the expected fee under the applicable schedule will ask for an agreement which allows him or her to bill services on a different and more agreeable basis.

25.7 Special Issues: Success-Oriented Fees, Class Actions, Sale of Claims, and Litigation Insurance

Article 12 lit. e of the Attorney-at-Law Act[18] explicitly prohibits any attorney-client agreements before the conclusion of the proceedings which would give the attorney a percentage of the sum won instead of a fee, or which provide for a no win-no fee arrangement. This provision prohibits solely the undiluted *pactum de quota litis* and applies strictly only to court related work.[19] The Swiss Federal Supreme Court has recently ruled that an arrangement pursuant to which the client pays a reduced fee and in turn, the attorney gets a share in the sum won (*pactum de palmario*)

[17] *See* above note 10. Regarding the permissibility of success oriented fees see the next chapter below.

[18] *See supra* note 10.

[19] *See* WALTER FELLMANN, GAUDENZ ZINDEL, Kommentar zum Anwaltsgesetz, Schulthess Verlag, Zürich 2005, p. 174 *et seq*.

compatible with Federal law in principle, if permitted under the respective cantonal law.[20] This decision may well be the dawn of contingency fees in Switzerland.

Class Actions are not known in Switzerland. The closest equivalents are the simple joinder of actions in accordance with Article 71 CCP and actions brought by an association under Article 89 CCP.[21] Under the latter provision, associations and other organisations of Swiss national or regional importance that are authorized by their by-laws to safeguard the interests of particular groups can bring an action in their own name against *violations of the personality rights* of members of such groups. Similar provisions are contained in other statutes.[22]

Claims can, as a matter of principle, be sold under Swiss law, but there is no widespread practice in that regard, much less an industry. A possible exception is large insolvency cases like the one involving the former national airline Swissair. Before the Attorney-at-law Act came into force in 2000, practicing counsel were subject to the law of the canton in which they had their practice; several of those cantonal laws did explicitly prohibit the sale of claims to counsel.[23] Under the Attorney-at-law Act, however, a sale of a claim by a client to the law firm is deemed permissible, provided the deal is done at arms' length, i.e., not to the sole advantage of the law firm, and the law firm in question does not advise the client in regard to such sale.[24] The most common form, however, is the retention of the services of a professional debt collector who, in most cases, acts in the name and on the account of the creditor for a fee or percentage of the sum collected.

---

[20] ATF 135 (2009) III 259 (in French).

[21] *See* ISABELLE ROMY, Litiges de masse – Des class actions aux solutions suisses dans les cas de pollutions et de toxiques, Editions Universitaires Fribourg Suisse, AISUF 161, 1997; ADRIAN STAEHELIN, DANIEL STAEHELIN, PASCAL GROLIMUND, *supra* note 1, p. 160.

[22] Examples are: actions by unions in connection with collective bargaining of employment contracts under Article 357b of the Swiss Code of Obligations, SR 220, dated 3O March 1911 as revised, actions by Professional and Economic Associations or Consumer Protection Organisations under Article 56 of the Trademark Act, SR 232.11, dated 28 August 1992 as revised and under 10 al. 2 of the Unfair Trading Act, SR 241, dated 19 December 1986 as revised.

[23] *See* WALTER FELLMANN, GAUDENZ ZINDEL, above note 19, p. 179.

[24] *See* KASPAR SCHILLER, Schweizerisches Anwaltsrecht, Schulhess Verlag, Zürich 2009, p. 241 who argues for a wide application of this rule whereas WALTER FELLMANN, GAUDENZ ZINDEL, *supra* note 19, p. 179 defend a more reserved view by pointing out that the sale of a claim is only permissible if the client participates in all of the profit.

Outside litigation investment is now permissible pursuant to a judgment rendered in 2004 by the Swiss Federal Supreme Court,[25] and it is available in Switzerland. Yet, such outside investment does not play a significant role in everyday litigation, because the acceptance thresholds set by agents offering such services are relatively high. Disputes for sums below CHF 300.000 are usually not eligible. In addition, agents very often require that the party who seeks such investment first submit a fully reasoned complaint at his or her own costs. As a result, outside litigation investment is essentially limited to what one may call high end litigation.

Legal insurance has been known in Switzerland since about 1925.[26] Today, it is regulated in the Insurance Contract Act[27] and in more detail in Article 161 *et seq*. of the Federal Ordinance on the Supervision of Private Sector Insurance Companies.[28] It is a widespread industry providing a variety of legal coverage. Traditionally, three types of legal insurance have been available: for car owners, for the private sector and for the professional and business sector. Many insurance companies provide only partial protection by excluding certain types of cases such as family or estate matters and/or construction and neighbour disputes. Usually, legal insurance covers all costs related to bringing or defending a claim, though not the claim itself. Most of the insurance companies provide a maximum coverage of CHF 250.000,00 (ca. US $250,000). If an insurance company denies coverage because it deems the case hopeless, the company must provide the insured with a written opinion together with a notice that the insured can appeal the company's denial of coverage before a quasi-arbitration tribunal to be maintained by the insurance company.[29]

---

[25] ATF 131 (2004) I 223 (in German); for a discussion of the duties of the lawyer suggesting outside litigation investment to his or her client, *see* WALTER FEHLMANN, Anwaltsrecht, Stämpfli Verlag AG Bern 2010, p. 136.

[26] For a detailled discussion of legal insurance in Switzerland *see* MAX PLATTNER, JEAN-PIERRE SCHMID, Gerichtskosten und Rechtsschutzversicherung, in: CHRISTIAN SCHÖBI (editor), Gerichtskosten, Parteikosten, Prozesskaution, unentgeltliche Prozessführung (und Modelle zur Beschränkungen ihrer Kosten), Stämpfli Verlag AG Bern 2001, p. 59 and seq.

[27] SR 221.229.1, dated 2 April 1908 as revised.

[28] SR 961.011, dated 9 November 2005, as revised.

[29] *See* Article 119 of the Federal Ordinance on the Supervision of Private Sector Insurance Companies.

25.8 Legal Aid

Public legal aid is a constitutional right in Switzerland. Article 29 al. 3 of the Constitution[30] provides that anyone who does not have sufficient funds has the right to free legal advice, assistance and representation unless their case appears hopeless. Legal aid is provided by the canton in which the respective court has its seat. The constitutional right is limited to state courts, however, and legal aid is not available for arbitration (Art. 380 CCP).

The new Federal Code of Civil Procedure contains a detailed set of rules dealing with all aspects of legal aid (Arts. 117–123). Legal aid is available to anyone, regardless of residency or citizenship, except for legal entities. To the latter, legal aid is available only under extremely narrow circumstances.[31]

Legal aid comprises a dispensation from the obligation to advance costs and to furnish security, a dispensation from having to bear court costs and, if necessary for the safeguarding of rights, e.g., when the opposing party is represented by counsel, the appointment of an attorney. Counsel can already be appointed to prepare proceedings. Legal aid can be granted completely or partially. Under no circumstances, though, does legal aid dispense a party from the obligation to reimburse the opponent's party's costs awarded by the court in accordance with the general rules. Courts are permitted to revoke legal aid when the conditions for entitlement have ended or are found never to have existed.

Legal aid has to be applied for separately before each instance. Applications for legal aid can be made before or after proceedings have been brought. The applicant is required to disclose income and assets, present his or her case and show the evidence; the applicant is allowed to propose a counsel of choice to the court. The court rules on the application in summary proceedings. The opposing party may be heard. Proceedings about legal aid applications or about the grant of legal aid are free of charge, unless the application is made in bad faith or wantonly. Decisions on legal aid can be appealed by means of a subsidiary appeal in accordance with Article 319 CCP.

A party that has been granted legal aid must repay the benefits received if, and as soon as, he is in a position to do so.

---

[30] SR 101, dated 18 April 1999, in force since 1 January 2000; for an (unofficial) English translation provided by the Federal Department of Justice see http://:www.admin.ch/org/polit/00083/index.html?.

[31] For a discussion *see* DOMINIK GASSER, BRIGITTE RICKLI, *supra* note 1, p. 103/104; FRANÇOIS PAYCHÈRE, Principes de l'assistance judiciaire gratuite en droit international et constitutionnel et application devant les tribunaux : un état de la question, in: CHRISTIAN SCHÖBI (editor), Gerichtskosten, Parteikosten, Prozesskaution, unentgeltliche Prozessführung (und Modelle zur Beschränkungen ihrer Kosten), Stämpfli Verlag AG Bern 2001, p. 125.

25.9 Conclusion

The new Federal Code of Civil Procedure is certainly a further landmark in the creation of a single legal market in Switzerland. At the same time, the fact that the Code is not an entirely new piece of legislation but rather a restatement of common cantonal procedural principles is a sure sign that the diversity among the former cantonal Codes of Civil Procedure had decreased over time. The main reasons for this convergence of cantonal law are the practice of the Swiss Supreme Court regarding fundamental constitutional principles, and the application of federal private law, and the ever growing number of international treaties dealing with aspects of civil procedure of which Switzerland is a member.

The ease, or difficulty, of access to court must be measured not only in light of applicable procedure rules. Equally important are the costs and financial risks involved. As shown, the cost risks are manifold.

A major problem is that the costs can easily be disproportionate to the amount in dispute. This is normally true in Switzerland for claims below ca. CHF 100.000–150.000 (ca. US $100,000–150,000). In this realm, full-fledged litigation requires either legal aid or legal insurance or nerves of steel with total disregard of costs. If none of these are available, then the prosecution of such claims in court is feasible only by way of an early settlement, i.e., in the context of the mandatory conciliation proceedings. The success of the conciliation proceeding depends largely on the ability of the presiding judge to mediate rather than to adjudicate.

The other big cost risk in Swiss litigation stems from the newly introduced Articles 107 and 108 CCP which allow courts to deviate from the general loser-pays rule if the court deems that fair under the particular circumstances. These rules apply to all litigation falling within the purview of the Federal Code of Civil Procedure. Since experience with these rules is still lacking, one cannot yet tell whether deviations from the basic principle will remain the exception or will become the general rule over time. The latter would mean that sooner or later both parties must bear their own costs and share in the court costs without regard to the outcome of the case.

Chapter 26
The American "Rule": Assuring the Lion His Share

James R. Maxeiner

The (D. D.) Field of Gold, or The Lion's Legal (?) Share
Thomas Nast, HARPER'S WEEKLY MAGAZINE, January 15, 1876[1]

© 2011, James R. Maxeiner, J.D., Cornell; LL.M., Georgetown; Ph.D. in Law, Ludwig Maximilian University (Munich, Germany). Associate Professor of Law and Associate Director, Center for International and Comparative Law, University of Baltimore School of Law.

[1] The lawyer is the great reformer, David Dudley Field, Jr. The cave in the background is marked "The Lawyers' Den." All three of the illustrations in this article are of Field.

J.R. Maxeiner (✉)
Center for International and Comparative Law, University of Baltimore School of Law, Baltimore, MD, USA
e-mail: jmaxeiner@ubalt.edu

M. Reimann (ed.), *Cost and Fee Allocation in Civil Procedure*, Ius Gentium: Comparative Perspectives on Law and Justice 11, DOI 10.1007/978-94-007-2263-7_26, © Springer Science+Business Media B.V. 2012

26.1 Rules, Practices and Reasons

26.1.1 Main Features

The system of attorneys' fees in the United States has two characteristic features: (1) no fee-shifting (the "American rule"); and (2) fees set by agreement between lawyers and clients unrestricted by law ("unregulated fee agreements").

American practice of no indemnity. The practice in America is that each party pays his own lawyer her fee. Consequently losers do not make winners whole through paying their attorneys' fees. Winners recover less than their full claims after they pay their lawyers. Although called the "American Rule," it is better named the American practice, since rarely is it compelled by statute or precedent. It does not apply to court costs, which even in America, by rule are shifted to losers.

Unregulated fee agreements. Attorneys' fees are set by agreement of lawyers and their clients. They are usually unregulated by fee schedules or judicial determinations. Most common in the United States are hourly fees, contingent fees in litigation, and flat charges for specific services. Lawyers and their clients are free, however, to structure their fees using a combination of these three elements in just about any way they wish.

26.1.2 American Exceptionalism

According to the General Report, the American practice of "open rejection of the loser pays principle and the actual refusal to shift the lion's share of litigation expenses in the vast majority of cases sets the United States apart from the rest of the systems covered here." [1.2.1.3] That the "vast majority of systems embrace the loser-pays principle ... reflects primarily an idea of basic fairness ...: it seems just that the loser must compensate the winner." [1.2.3.1] In the asserted justification for fee rules, the General Report advises, the United States stands apart: it is "the only country predicating its basic cost rule purely on instrumentalist grounds." [1.2.3.3][2] When it comes to fee agreements, according to the General Report, the United

They were drawn not to lambaste his work as a law reformer, but for his work for political and business interests. He represented "Boss" Tweed of Tammany Hall, and Fisk and Gould in the Erie railroad scandal. *See* Philip J. Bergan, *David Dudley Field: A Lawyer's Life*, *in* THE FIELDS AND THE LAW 21, 37–47 (1986). When Field died, Harper's Weekly noted his death by reprinting on the entire front page the painting of him by Robert Gordon Hardie in the Hall of the Court of Appeals in Albany. 38 HARPER'S WEEKLY 361 (April 21, 1894).

[2] The General Report observes that fairness arguments can be made in defense of American no-indemnity practice and singles out for mention the unpredictability of legal

States is not alone. Other systems allow lawyers and clients to agree on fees that are over and above fees shifted. Binding fee schedules are "on the decline." [1.3.2.2] The General Report speaks of "yet another 'Americanization' of law in many parts of the world." [1.3.2.2] The General Report observes three costs in freeing fees from regulation: it is incompatible with full fee shifting; it creates predictability and fairness issues; and it invites second-stage litigation about what is a reasonable fee. [1.3.2.2]

According to the United States National Report, at one time, many American states, including New York, were within today's worldwide norms. Fee shifting and fee schedules were parts of the American legal landscape.[3] According to David Dudley Field, Jr., the great reformer and lawyer satirized in the three illustrations in this article, in 1842 it was a proposition "which scarce anyone will object to ... that the losing party ought to indemnify the other so far as he can against his losses by the suit."[4] Only in the second half of the nineteenth century did no indemnity become the national norm and fee regulation and shifting disappeared.

The General Reporter invites the National Reporter to explain why the United States rejects loser pays and the simple justice that stands behind it. I accept the invitation. My explanation is subjective and tentative.

---

decisions. [1.2.3.3, Note 71] That argument rejects an underlying assumption of fee-shifting, that law is workably certain. That the argument has traction in the United States is attributable to the uncertainty of American law. In this conception, legal process is more of a method for divining an authoritative decision than an application of law to facts. On certainty and uncertainty, see James R. Maxeiner, *Legal Certainty and Legal Methods: A European Alternative to American Legal Indeterminacy?*, 15 TULANE J. INT'L & COMP. L. 541 (2007); James R. Maxeiner, *Legal Indeterminacy Made in America: American Legal Methods and the Rule of Law,* 41 VALPARAISO U.L. REV. 517 (2006).

[3] James R. Maxeiner, *Cost and Fee Allocation in Civil Procedure*, 58 AM. J. COMP. L. SUPP. 195, 216–219 (2010). *See* John Leubsdorf, *Toward a History of the American Rule on Attorney Fee Recovery*, 47 LAW & CONTEMP. PROBLEMS 9 (1984). Professor Leubsdorf's article remains the most insightful examination of fee and cost-shifting in the United States. Specifically on the presence of fee schedules in early America, see 1 ANTON-HERMANN CHOUST, THE RISE OF THE LEGAL PROFESSION IN AMERICA 85–89, 129–132, 159–160, 317–319 (1965). On the decline and occasional revival see WILLIAM G. ROSS, THE HONEST HOUR: THE ETHICS OF TIME-BASED BILLING BY ATTORNEYS 9–17 (1996).

[4] David Dudley Field, *Letter*, *printed as Appendix To the report of the Committee on the Judiciary, in relation to the more simple and speedy administration of justice*, STATE OF NEW-YORK, REPORT IN PART OF THE COMMITTEE ON THE JUDICIARY, IN RELATION TO THE ADMINISTRATION OF JUSTICE, DOCUMENT NO. 81 (1842), at 55 *collected in* 5 DOCUMENTS OF THE ASSEMBLY OF THE STATE OF NEW-YORK SIXTY-FOURTH [SIC, 65TH] SESSION (1842). [Bibliographic notes: the Appendix was sometimes distributed separately from the whole committee report. The committee report is collected in the documents series, in which each document is separately paginated. This volume is as of this writing available as a Google book.]

26.1.3 Lawyers Drive Civil Justice

> The machinery by which justice is wrought out has always been, and must forever remain, the creation of the profession. ... No one thinks of challenging the right of the bar to determine the methods of which the remedies affecting the profoundest concerns of life shall be administered.
>
> Charles M. Wilds
> *Address Before the Vermont State Bar Association* (1894)[5]

That private lawyers are the driving force behind civil justice explains the existence of the American practices of no indemnity for attorneys' fees and unregulated fee agreements. That lawyers are self-regulating explains why these practices continue. That lawyers control the conduct of litigation explains the great effect these practices have in the United States.

Self-regulating. Lawyers in the United States regulate themselves. With respect to fees they are little constrained by supervisory laws or authorities, even by those of their own making.[6] Moreover, there are no government bodies that have responsibility for the overall state of civil justice.[7]

Lawyers control litigation. Lawyers in the United States control the course of civil litigation. Judges are by and large passive observers. Lawyers, and not judges, define issues in disputed cases. They decide what evidence to take. They call witnesses and question them. Lawyers even write the first drafts of instructions that judges give to juries and of findings of fact and conclusions of law that judges use to decide cases without juries.[8]

The American "rule" was never legislated; it grew up as a practice. There is no rule; there is an absence of rules. In the absence of rules, practices are unguided by binding direction. It is not completely accurate to say that

---

[5] AN ADDRESS ON COMMON LAW PLEADINGS, BEFORE THE VERMONT BAR ASSOCIATION, OCTOBER 9, 1894 (1894).

[6] *See* LESTER BRICKMAN, LAWYER BARONS: WHAT THEIR CONTINGENCY FEES REALLY COST AMERICA 468–469 (2011) ("no profession is as exempt from societal control as is the legal profession. ... Lawyers' self-regulatory power largely flows from the judiciary's seizure of control over the practice of law ... to deprive legislatures of their historic authority to regulate lawyers. ...").

[7] The United States Department of Justice and the offices of the attorneys general of the several states do not have responsibilities comparable to German and other similar ministries of justice. Instead they function principally as lawyers for the government. The United States Supreme Court and the supreme courts of the several states have only limited oversight role over the state of civil justice and the regulation of lawyers. They do not have the extensive supervisory responsibilities characteristic of a supreme court with an administrative role such as that of the Supreme Court of Korea. They are composed principally of former lawyers. Not to be lost sight of is that in America judges are lawyers in judges' robes. *See generally* BENJAMIN H. BARTON, THE LAWYER-JUDGE BIAS IN THE AMERICAN LEGAL SYSTEM (2010).

[8] *See generally*, JAMES R. MAXEINER, GYOOHO LEE & ARMIN WEBER, FAILURES OF AMERICAN CIVIL JUSTICE IN INTERNATIONAL PERSPECTIVE (2011).

the United States has rejected loser pays, for rejection assumes a conscious choice. Better it is to say that American courts do not practice it.[9]

Practices do not need justification. The American practice of no indemnity, Professor Leubsdorf has shown, developed without one. "One of the most curious features of the American rule in the nineteenth century," he writes, "was its almost total absence of justification."[10] Today's justifications post-date the practices. They are practically apologies. The practices persist, because they suit the needs of lawyers, and because no one has legislated otherwise. Lawyers work in their world and in their world, it is "natural" to obtain their fees from their clients.[11] They would have to move out of that world to create a system of fee shifting. Of course, that lawyers remain in their world does not make them evil, it only makes them ordinary.

Despite witticisms to the contrary, lawyers are people. Historically they were, and today by-and-large still are, independent small businessmen. Like small businessmen everywhere who are dependent on their businesses for existence, they share two concerns: (1) that they have sufficient customers; and (2) that those customers pay promptly and well. There is nothing cynical in this observation: altruism has its limits where personal existence is at stake. Who would not steal bread if the alternative is to starve?[12]

The American practice of no indemnity responds to the first concern of lawyers as businessmen: getting customers. It helps them bring clients in. For lawyers' clients it cuts the risks of suing nearly in half. If they lose, they need pay only their own lawyers and not lawyers for opposing parties. For lawyers, it is easier to collect fees from their clients or from judgments subject to contingent fees, than to extract them from unwilling and possibly insolvent vanquished parties. Should they lose, they need not explain to clients the obligation to pay yet another lawyer's fee.[13]

Unregulated fee agreements let lawyers control their financial destinies. Lawyers take charge not only of the credit risks inherent in the choice of clients, but of the terms of those risks, namely reliability, timing and

---

[9] Cf. Acrambel v. Wiseman, 3 U.S. (Dall.) 306 (1796) ("The general practice of the United States is in opposition to [allowing attorneys' fees]; and even if that practice were not strictly correct in principle, it is entitled to the respect of the court, till it is changed, or modified, by statute.").

[10] Leubsdorf, *supra* note 3, at 28.

[11] Id.

[12] Salaried employees are no different than independent businessmen; only their concerns differ due to their different circumstances. They care (1) whether their employer is healthy, and (2) whether they continue to have a position with their employer. So too is it for politicians. They care (1) whether their government stays in power, and (2) whether they remain a part of that government. Lest we forget, it is true of law professors, too. Their concerns are those of salaried employees.

[13] Leubsdorf, *supra* note 3, at 17.

level of payment. They are not subject to outside constraints such as court decisions on costs or willingness or ability of vanquished parties to pay. At the outset of litigation lawyers can secure their investments through arrangements with their clients.

That the bar finds these practices congenial is suggested by their absence from the Federal Rules of Civil Procedure of 1938 and in the discussions that led up to the rules.[14] The organized bar's silence both before and since 1938 has been unbroken. None of the three principal national law reform organizations, the American Law Institute, the Uniform Laws Commission, and the American Judicature Society, seems ever to have substantially addressed the practice of no indemnity. Such proposals as there have been, have come from law reformers external to the bar.

In the Federal Rules of 1938, the bar achieved a long-sought goal: transfer of responsibility for civil procedure from legislators to judges. That meant, in practical effect, transfer to lawyers. Yet the rules have little to say about costs or attorneys' fees and nothing to say about fee regulation or fee-shifting. If the bar had been dissatisfied with those practices, they would have found place in the discussions. The bar did care in 1848 when New York adopted the other icon of American civil procedure history, the New York Code of Civil Procedure of 1848.

The New York Code of Civil Procedure of 1848 addressed both fee regulation and fee shifting directly. The Code repealed all fee regulations, but it retained fee shifting. The bar had long sought the former, while according to Field, everyone then still believed in the latter. The drafters of the 1848 Code, led by Field, justified abolition of fee regulation as necessary to protect freedom of contract between private parties. They rejected the idea that lawyers are public officers, chosen to do public duties, and that therefore their fees could be regulated.[15] The drafters justified retention of fee-shifting in the interest of justice. But compared to a proposal that Field alone had made earlier in the decade, the fee-shifting provisions of

---

[14] Neither issue seems to have come up substantively in the course of the drafting of the 1938 rules. There was a suggestion that they should: Philip M. Payne, *Costs in Common Law Actions in the Federal Courts*, 21 VA. L. REV. 397, 430 (1934). I do not know of any instance where these practices have come seriously under discussion in the establishment law reform organizations. Serious proposals have come from outside the bar. *See, e.g.*, MARIE GRYPHON, MANHATTAN INSTITUTE FOR POLICY RESEARCH, GREATER JUSTICE, LOWER COST: HOW A "LOSER PAYS" RULE WOULD IMPROVE THE AMERICAN LEGAL SYSTEM, CIVIL JUSTICE REPORT NO. 11 (December 2008).

[15] FIRST REPORT OF THE COMMISSIONERS ON PRACTICE AND PLEADING, CODE OF PROCEDURE 205 (1848). *Accord*, Field, *Letter*, *supra* note 4, at 55. In rejecting the characterization as officers of the court, Field may have been provocative, but not off the mark for the United States. *See* Eugene R. Gaetke, *Lawyers as Officers of the Court*, 42 VANDERBILT L. REV. 39 (1989) ("the characterization [is] vacuous and unduly self-laudatory. It confuses lawyers and misleads the public.").

the 1848 Code were substantially watered down, both as proposed by the three-member drafting committee, and still more so, as adopted by the legislature.[16] Leubsdorf senses a compromise, but how and by whom, remains unknown.[17] The fee-shifting provision was soon criticized as having "obviously failed" to achieve its objective.[18] Although the subsequent history remains to be written, it is one of neglect of fee-shifting.

26.1.4 Pernicious Products of American Practices

Lawyer control of litigation magnifies the effect of the no indemnity practice and extends its impact beyond reduction in value of valid claims. It destroys meritorious claims and promotes baseless ones. Through control of litigation, lawyers can force opposing parties to devote resources to litigation; thanks to the no indemnity practice, those resources are forever lost. In most cases the only substantial external check on lawyers' wreaking such havoc is the possibility that opposing parties retaliate.

At every step, parties must consider process costs. Even where there is no deliberate intention to create expenses, it has long been true that "unless the case involves a large amount of money [the] lawyer's bill eats up [the] judgment if obtained."[19] Every lawyer knows that in most cases, the other side, if so inclined, has the ability to render a victory Pyrrhic. A party

---

[16] Field's 1842 proposal had mandatory fee-shifting as fixed percentages of judgment amounts. The Commission's 1848 draft code made fee-shifting discretionary using "may" instead of "shall" and left percentage amounts blank for the legislature to fill in. The law as adopted by the legislature made the court's discretion explicit and limited its exercise to "difficult or extraordinary cases." Field's 1842 proposal is: Field, *Letter*, *supra* note 4. The Commission's 1848 Report on costs is FIRST REPORT, *supra* note 15, at 204–12 (1848). The law adopted is: An Act to Simplify and Abridge the Practice, Pleadings and Proceedings of the Courts of this State, ch. 379, 1848 N.Y. LAWS 544, § 258. [Bibliographic notes: 1842 Letter: The letter was sometimes distributed separately from the whole committee report and the volumes of documents. The committee report with the Appendix is collected in the documents series and is as of this writing available as a Google book. 1848 First Report: some electronic and print-on-demand editions to the First Report of the Commissions on Practice and Pleading are based on a hard copy in the New York Public Library where a contemporary user had pasted over the original sections relevant here §§ 262–263 the text of the law as adopted.]

[17] Leubsdorf, *supra* note 3, at 20.

[18] HENRY WHITAKER, PRACTICE AND PLEADING UNDER THE CODES, ORIGINAL AND AMENDED WITH AN APPENDIX OF FORMS 600 (1852).

[19] D.C., Letter to the Editor, *The Constitutional Convention, the Judiciary and the Bar*, NEW YORK TIMES, June 5, 1867. The General Report is misleading in suggesting that the American system does not ever eat up more than 50% of the amount in controversy, if that amount exceeds $100,000. I personally was involved in a second stage case over costs of $10,000 where the amount of attorneys' fees in the second stage for the $10,000 costs exceeded $100,000!

prepared to spend money may not be able to buy a victory, but it can deny the opposing party one.[20] Parties, of course, do not always engage their weapons of mass destruction. The practice is reminiscent of the Mutual Assured Destruction doctrine ("MAD") of Cold War days, where neither side attacked the other, because of fear of final retaliation. That reticence to use the weapon clouds the view of outside observers of a reality that is all too well-known to insiders.

The public seems resigned to destruction of meritorious claims; it may assume that litigation costs are inevitable. The public takes greater notice, however, of baseless claims that are enabled by no indemnity and lawyer control.[21] This combination permits weak parties with weak claims to extract settlements even from strong parties with strong defenses.[22] It enables strong parties with weak claims to bully weaker parties with strong defenses into surrendering their claims entirely.[23] While scholars may argue over the extent of the resulting distortions, about the totality of effect, or whether there are countervailing benefits, no one who has spent even a short time in litigation practice will reasonably deny that these distortions are routine features of American civil justice.

26.2 Exceptions and Variations: The Common Denominator

The General Report notes exceptions and variations to the American practice of no indemnity. No common theory supports them.[24] There is, however, one common denominator: helping lawyers get well-paying clients. Three variations – contingent fee, one-way fee shifting, and class action litigation – help lawyers gain clients who otherwise would be unable to

---

[20] Cf., id. ("A man is painted naked, with a large bundle of papers under his arm, and saying, 'I, who won the suit, am now stripped to the skin; what then, must be the fate of him who lost it?' It is unnecessary to enlarge upon this evil; it has been felt too keenly by everyone engaged in legal proceedings to be forgotten.").

[21] A notorious example is Pearson v. Chung, 961 A.2d 1067 (D.C. Ct. App. 2008) (lawsuit against dry cleaner claiming $67 million in damages for a lost pair of pants). A new documentary film, *Hot Coffee*, challenges the assertion that another notorious case, Liebeck v. McDonald's Restaurants, P.T.S., Inc., No. D-202 CV-93-02419, 1995 WL 360309 (Bernalillo County, N.M. Dist. Ct. August 18, 1994), is a baseless case taking advantage of the system. *See* http://hotcoffeethemovie.com/.

[22] According to the General Report, it is "the implicit encouragement of weak lawsuits (often with the sole goal to force the defendant to settle) – that sets the rule in the United States apart from pretty much the rest of the world." [1.2.3.3]

[23] In 2010 Congress directed the Patent and Trademark Office to study the issue of trademark bullying. The Trademark Technical and Conforming Amendment Act of 2010, Pub. L. No. 111–146, 124 Stat. 66 (2010).

[24] Leubsdorf sees "a bizarre variety of opinions, which might go far to justify the view that policy analysis is totally arbitrary and manipulable." Leubsdorf, *supra* note 3, at 28.

afford their services. Two variations – pro se representation and legal aid – help lawyers divert pressures to take on undesirable clients, i.e., free riders who would not pay well or at all. Finally, the exception to fee shifting – indemnity for costs – has been neutralized as a factor that might discourage clients by making costs trivial in most cases. We start with the exception of costs (26.2.1); we then proceed to variations that encourage desirable clients, i.e., business development (26.2.2); and we conclude with variations that help lawyers divert undesirable business to other providers, i.e., avoiding free riders (26.2.3).

26.2.1 Costs: Loser Pays (in Theory), as Elsewhere

For court costs, the rule (not a mere practice) in the United States is the same as elsewhere: loser-pays. The rule dates from the colonial era when lawyers were few and were not self-regulated. Costs discourage customers. While costs have never been abolished, lawyers have kept them low.[25]

Unlike in many countries, court costs in the United States are set without regard to amounts in dispute. For example, filing a lawsuit in federal court seeking $100,000 in damages requires that plaintiff pay $350.[26] In Germany, for a case of comparable magnitude, €75,000, plaintiff must pay €1,968 (or around $2,500) in costs.[27] Increase the claim ten-fold and the filing fee in Germany rises to €11,118 (around $15,000); in the United States, the filing fee is still $350. Moreover, thanks to inflation, sometimes what once were significant costs, now are trivial.[28] Although court costs are low, sometimes additional costs ancillary to the case, for example for court-appointed experts (rarely used) can be high.

Application after trial of the loser-pays costs rule is unusual because there are so few trials. More commonly it appears only after a pre-trial motion. Only about 2% of cases go to trial. Unlike elsewhere, the trial judge does not automatically calculate costs and include them in the judgment. Instead the winning party must apply for costs and complete itemized requests. Since total costs are low, often application is too burdensome to bother with. Other times, it is easier just to include a rough estimate in the discount usually given for prompt, voluntary payment of a judgment.

The original justification for shifting costs was the same as for attorneys' fees: it is just that parties in the right be made whole. Attorneys'

---

[25] *See* Leubsdorf, *supra* note 3, at 14.

[26] 28 U.S.C. § 1914(a).

[27] http://www.prozesskostenrechner.de/.

[28] For example, in 1853 the federal courts introduced a case fee of $20. It was originally intended as the attorney's fee. The federal courts still have the same case fee and it is still $20. *See* Leubsdorf, *supra* note 3, at 21–22.

fees were considered costs. Today, insofar as costs are discussed, the justification given for cost-shifting may just as well be the policy ground of discouraging litigation. When they are held low, on the other hand, the justification given likewise will be a policy one, but this time, to encourage litigation.

26.2.2 Business Development

They Do Each Other Honor
Mr. ***** (the *Most Ancient Fraud*). "Your fame has reached beyond this *cold world*, and I have come to ask you to defend *Me*."
Thomas Nast, HARPER'S WEEKLY MAGAZINE, 152 (Feb. 24, 1877)[29]

The American practice of no indemnity is not a complete solution to overcoming customer reluctance to buy into lawsuits. American lawsuits are expensive. The General Report finds that fact gathering in the United States is more expensive than anywhere else in the world. It reports:

---

[29]*See* ALEXANDER TABARROK, TWO CHEERS FOR CONTINGENT FEES (2006) (book description: "If America is a lawsuit hell, then contingent-fee lawyers are often considered its devils.").

> The practical impact of *not* shifting the lion's share of evidence costs (including expert witness fees) is tremendous: it entails a huge burden for the victor as well as a huge relief for the vanquished. In fact, not shifting the bulk of evidence costs is perhaps the defining feature that separates the United States from all other jurisdictions covered here.

Ordinary people cannot afford the huge burden.[30] At the outset of the lawsuit, they have to advance their lawyers a substantial part of the attorneys' fee. At the conclusion of the lawsuit, they have to turn over a substantial part of the award to their attorneys.

Once lawyers were freed to agree with their clients on fees, they could design contractual and other solutions to lift the burden from ordinary people and turn them into well-paying clients. The door was open to innovative arrangements designed by lawyers to turn ordinary people into paying customers. First came contingent fees designed for people with large open-ended claims. Then came one-way fee-shifting for ordinary people with claims newly created by statute. Then last came class actions for ordinary people with mundane claims too small to be handled alone profitably.

26.2.2.1 Contingent Fees

The General Report observes that contingent fee agreements are widely considered "a hallmark of the US-American legal system." The essence of a contingent fee agreement is that the lawyer's fee is due if, and only if, the lawyer achieves a favorable result. The fee is usually a percentage of the amount recovered. Typically that amount is 33%.[31] The contingent fee agreement may provide that the lawyer advances court costs and other expenses to the client to be paid or not paid later as the parties agree.

Ordinary people benefit at both key points of the lawsuit. At the outset, they do not have to advance fees that they do not have. At the conclusion, they do not have to pay at all if they lose; if they win, they do not have to pay more than they recover. The huge burden and risk are taken on by the lawyer. The downside for the client is that the lawyer's share is high, especially in those cases that do not incur the high costs of litigation.

Lawyers benefit from contingent fee arrangements by gaining clients that they would not otherwise have. They are compensated for taking on the process risk by being given a share of the recovery. In well-chosen cases, that recovery may vastly exceed the investment in services provided. They are able more surely and easily to collect their fees from judgments than from winning or losing parties.

---

30 *See* Leubsdorf, *supra* note 3, at 31.

31 Jeffrey D. Swett, *Determining a Reasonable Percentage in Establishing a Contingency Fee: A New Tool to Remedy and Old Problem*, 77 TENN. L. REV. 653, 655 (2010); *see generally*, HERBERT M. KRITZER, RISKS, REPUTATIONS, AND REWARDS: CONTINGENCY FEE LEGAL PRACTICE IN THE UNITED STATES 9–10 (2004).

Contingent fees became widely used in the second half of the nineteenth century after lawyers were freed to agree with their clients on fees. The practice of contingent fees was and is controversial, because it gives lawyers financial interests in their cases.[32] It is distasteful because it makes civil justice – which is about determining rights to resolve controversies – into cost/benefit risk decisions.[33] It is troubling because in large cases it can lead to enormous fees out of all proportion to time or risk invested – fees of $40 million have been reported.[34] Dissatisfaction with contingent fees has engendered spotty regulation with haphazard enforcement.[35]

The justification given for contingent fees is that they provide ordinary people with access to civil justice. Contingent fees, however, can only be a partial solution to access to justice. Contingent fees help only some clients. These are usually clients who as plaintiffs seek monetary relief and have large and open-ended claims.[36] Claims for fixed sums are less-desired, since they make transparent the costs of the contingent fee arrangement. Claims that are open-ended make the arrangement into a sharing of good fortune. This explains why tort claims are nearly all contingent fee based, but contract claims are not.

Contingent fees do not facilitate representation when claims are too small to generate sufficient revenues. Innovative Americans lawyers found solutions that helped them make representation in these cases possible and profitable as well. We turn now, first to one-way fee shifting statutes (Section 26.2.2.2 below), and then to aggregate or class action litigation (Section 26.2.2.3 below).

26.2.2.2 Only in America: One-Way Fee-Shifting[37]

What are lawyers to do with cases that do not lead to monetary recoveries or only to small ones insufficient to support their fees? One way would be to

---

[32] *Compare* EDWIN COUNTRYMAN, THE ETHICS OF COMPENSATION FOR PROFESSIONAL SERVICES: AN ADDRESS BEFORE THE ALBANY LAW SCHOOL AND AN ANSWER TO HOSTILE CRITIQUES (1882) *with* LESTER BRICKMAN, LAWYER BARONS: WHAT THEIR CONTINGENCY FEES REALLY COST AMERICA (2011). *See generally*, Peter Karsten, *Enabling the Poor to Have Their Day in Court: The Sanctioning of Contingency Fee Contracts, A History to 1940*, 47 DEPAUL L. REV. 231 (1997). Acceptance of contingent fees presupposes loosening or ending historic limitations on lawyers having financial interest in their cases.

[33] John A. Day, *Should you risk taking the case?*, TRIAL, January 2008, at 20.

[34] *See*, *e.g.*, Lawrence v. Miller, 48 A.D.3d 1, 853 N.Y.S.2d 1(2007) (upholding a $40 million dollar, 40% contingency fee, which in the view of the dissent amounted to a nearly 100% fee).

[35] *See* Swett, *supra note* 31, 659 *et seq*.

[36] *See* Maxeiner, *supra* note 3, at 207–209.

[37] It's not quite only in America; the General Report notes that there is also one-way fee-shifting in Japan in personal injury cases. [1.2.2.1]

abandon the American practice of no indemnity and adopt the global norm of loser-pays. That would, however, drive away customers who are unable to accept the risks posed by a loser pays rule.

The American legal system offers an ingenious solution: one-way fee shifting. If lawyers win for their clients, opposing parties pay their legal fees. On the other hand, if they lose for their clients, although they are not paid at all, at least their clients do not have to pay the attorneys' fees of the opposing parties. Used first in the last third of the nineteenth century to facilitate private enforcement of trade regulations,[38] the idea has been a hit. Hundreds of statutes direct that losing defendants pay fees of winning plaintiffs' lawyers, while leaving winning defendants to pay their own lawyers' fees.[39] One way fee-shifting remains concentrated in private enforcement of public law norms and does not extend to the historic private law.

One-way shifting is said to enlist private parties to act as "private attorneys general" in the enforcement of public law norms.[40] In a nation that is devoted to equality of treatment, in a profession that promotes fair contests, the challenges that such a "heads I win, tails you lose" rule poses to fairness are obvious. The challenges are not denied, but are confessed and avoided on instrumental grounds. Critics question the accuracy and the justice of the instrumental justification.

26.2.2.3 Class Actions: Where's the Agreement?

Most cases are not eligible for one-way fee-shifting. Many claims remain too small individually to support the high expenses of American litigation. American lawyers have an answer for that, too: aggregate or class-action litigation. Here a lawyer represents tens, hundreds or even thousands of parties with claims. Sometimes claims are large, but litigation expenses too high to handle them one-at-a-time. Sometimes claims are small, some as small as a few dollars each. In a legal system that prizes case-by-case consideration of each individual case, class action litigation seems strangely out-of-place. For a fee system of unregulated fee agreements, a valid agreement between one lawyer and a hundred or a thousand clients, each with a claim of few dollars, is hard to find. Since 2003, the Federal Rules of Civil Procedure have required that courts, as part of their approval of class action settlements, decide on the "reasonable attorneys' fee" to be allowed.[41]

---

[38] *See* Leubsdorf, *supra* note 3, at 25.

[39] *See* Harold J. Krent, *Explaining One-Way Fee Shifting*, 79 VA. L. REV. 2039, 2051 n.48 (1993) (citing examples).

[40] Alyeska Pipeline Service Co. v. The Wilderness Society, 421 U.S. 240, 261–263 (1975).

[41] Rule 23(h). *See generally* Jonathan R. Macey & Geoffrey P. Miller, *Judicial Settlement of Class Actions*, 1. J. LEGAL ANALYSIS 167 (2009).

26.2.3 *Diversion of Undesirable Business*

26.2.3.1 Self-Representation (Pro Se)

Self-representation (pro se) has been possible in the federal courts for as long as they have been in existence. Federal law, first adopted in 1789,[42] permits parties in federal court to "plead and conduct [their] own cases personally."[43] The reality is, of course, that few people can do that satisfactorily in any but the simplest of cases. This right is hardly meaningful except in courts where the unrepresented are helped to represent themselves.[44] That is true in some small claims courts. When proposals are made to increase the upper level jurisdictional amounts in small claims courts, litigation lawyers often lead the opposition.

The *possibility* of pro se representation, however, is essential to maintaining the present system. If there were a rule of mandatory representation, the denial of justice to those who could not afford counsel would be obvious and irrefutable. The American legal system would be compelled to offer legal aid as of right. That happened in Germany. There, where lawyers did not and do not regulate themselves, they were required to provide counsel for free for those who could not afford lawyers.[45]

26.2.3.2 Legal Aid

To represent oneself in court where the opposing side is represented by a lawyer takes special qualities which few people have. What are people who lack those qualities to do when they have litigation that does not qualify for contingent fee representation or one-way fee-shifting? Those claims account for the vast majority of legal claims. They include most defense cases, most cases for non-monetary relief, and most cases for amounts below $100,000. In the United States, people with such claims must beg for help. Unlike other legal systems, they have no claim of right to litigation

[42] § 35 of the Judiciary Act of 1789.

[43] 28 U.S.C. §1654.

[44] *See generally* THE FUTURE OF SELF-REPRESENTED LITIGATION: REPORT FROM THE MARCH 2005 SUMMIT (National Center for State Courts, 2005), available at www.ncsc.org; Tiffany Buxton, *Foreign Solutions to the U.S. Pro Se Phenomenon*, 34 CASE W. RES. J. INT'L L. 103 (2002); Drew Swank, *Note and Comment: The Pro Se Phenomenon*, 19 BYU J. PUB. L. 373 (2005); Nina Ingwer Van Wormer, *Note: Help at Your Fingertips: A Twenty-First Century Response to the Pro Se Phenomenon*, 60 VAND. L. REV. 983 (2007).

[45] *See* Heinrich Dittenberger, *Fünfzig Jahre Deutscher Anwaltverein 1871/1921, aus JW 1921, reprinted in* 125 JAHRE DEUTSCHER ANWALTVEREIN: EIN ÜBERBLICK (Deutscher Anwaltverein, ca. 1996); James R. Maxeiner, *A Right to Legal Aid: The ABA Model Access Act in International Perspective* (March 17, 2011) available at SSRN: http://ssrn.com/abstract=1791209.

help.[46] Many forego their legal rights simply because they cannot afford to pay for them.

Legal aid, or rather the lack of legal aid, in the United States, demonstrates the lawyer domination of the American system of costs and fees. Who can blame the lawyers? Bluntly put, why should small businessmen want customers who cannot pay for their products? Who in modern economies provides their goods or services to others for free?

At the beginning of the nineteenth century, in both the United States and Germany, lawyers represented the very poor without charge (in the United States, *in forma pauperis*). In the United States, lawyers and judges ran the system; they resisted requiring colleagues to work for free. When demand for representation grew, the bar ignored it; private parties outside the legal system had to provide the poor with legal services. In Germany, government officials ran the system; they drafted lawyers to provide free representation as their price for granting permission to practice. When demand for representation grew, the bar pleaded for relief; the government provided that it would pay for their work.[47]

26.3 The Shakespearean Question: Answers by Field, Nast, and Shakespeare, and Another Question

The General Report begins its first substantive section with what it calls a "Shakespearean Question": "To shift or not to shift." [1.2.1] It ends the report with a provocative answer: "one can perhaps say that at least among the common law jurisdictions, the United States has got it right after all: if lawyer fees are unregulated, unpredictable, and high, shifting them to the loser is so fraught with problems that it is better not to undertake it at all." [1.5.2] The answer assumes that fees are unregulated, unpredictable, and high. They are, but they should not be.

The United States does not have it right. No indemnity, unregulated fee agreements, and lawyer control of litigation, combine in a deadly cocktail that poisons civil justice in America. Civil justice fails in its stated goal of "just, speedy and inexpensive determination of every action and proceeding."[48] It is not a reliable instrument for applying law to facts to resolve disputes justly. Process considerations and party resources – rather than law and justice – determine too many cases.

David Dudley Field, Jr. knew that. In 1842 he made the case for fee shifting:

---

[46] Lassiter v. Dept. of Social Services, 452 U.S. 18 (1981).

[47] *See* James R. Maxeiner, *A Right to Legal Aid, supra* note 45.

[48] FED. R. CIV. P. 1. *See generally*, MAXEINER ET AL., *supra* note 8.

> The losing party ought to indemnify the other as far as possible against his losses by the suit. The former is in the wrong, the other is in the right; one ought not to lose by the wrong of another. All men we believe have equal rights. Their abilities to carry on lawsuits out of their own property are unequal. Unless then he who is in the wrong is made to pay the full amount of his adversary's expenses, just in that proportion has the rich man an advantage over the poor one, and the rights of the poor are unequally unprotected. If you would discourage unjust litigation, you must make the unjust litigant indemnify his adversary.[49]

Nast too understood the pernicious products of allowing one side to gain the upper hand through money. He reminded Field of that through an answer he found in Shakespeare:

> Plate sin with gold and the strong lance of justice hurtlessly breaks:
> Arm it in rags, a pigmy's straw doth pierce it.
>
> King Lear, act IV, scene 6

Principals not Men – A Lawyer Pleading for his "Client"
"The Bar of (Obstruction). Law."
Thomas Nast, HARPER'S WEEKLY MAGAZINE, August 7, 1875

[49] Letter, *supra* note 4, at 56.

26.4 Conclusion

The American experience is a lesson and a warning to other jurisdictions that may be considering the American model of no fee shifting and unregulated fee agreements.

The ultimate question that needs to be answered is not, "to shift or not to shift." It is, how can fee shifting and fee regulation be reconciled?

Deregulating fees, so notes the General Report, is intimately related to shifting them. Some regulation of attorneys' fees recoverable is essential to loser pays. Otherwise, richer parties could win by outspending poorer opponents and could compound the injustices of their victories by imposing their attorneys' fees as costs on the vanquished poor. Thus in New York in 1840, Theodore Sedgwick, Field's law office associate, in his loser-pays system, limited fees shifted to those fees for "a lawyer of respectability" and not those for a lawyer of "remarkable or extraordinary ability."[50] Field's preferred approach was a percentage of the amount of the recovery.[51]

If fees are shifted, however, clients expect that fees will be fully shifted and that they will be fully compensated when they win. The Virginia legislature saw that already in a statute of 1778: "it is, unreasonable that the party who prevails ... should be subject to the payment of a greater fee to his lawyer than he can recover from the adverse party."[52] That is a direct challenge to a lawyer of greater ability or, to a lawyer for a client with greater means to pay. In the United State the bar regulates itself and the lawyers that lead the bar are lawyers of greater ability who work for clients of greater means. Small wonder that they championed a market approach to fees while allowing fee shifting to disappear.

Although the American experience is a warning to the world, the dangers elsewhere are not great as in the United States, since legal fees elsewhere are not as unpredictable and usually also not as substantial. American fees are so substantial only partly because American lawyers are self-regulated. More important still is that American lawyers, through their control of litigation, determine what fees will be. So long as they drive the legal system, fees are likely to remain high.

---

[50] THEODORE SEDGWICK, HOW SHALL THE LAWYERS BE PAID? OR SOME REMARKS UPON TWO ACTS RECENTLY PASSED ON THE SUBJECT OF THE COSTS OF LEGAL PROCEEDINGS IN A LETTER TO JOHN ANTHON (1840).

[51] Field, *Letter*, *supra* note 4, at 57.

[52] 1778 Va. Acts, ch. 14, § 5, in A collection of all such public acts ... as are now in force 84 (Richmond 1785), *reprinted in* THE FIRST LAWS OF THE STATE OF VIRGINIA 84 (J. Cushing comp. 1982), as cited in Leubsdorf, *supra* note 3, at 11.

Author Biographies

Neela Badami received her first law degree (B.A., B.L (Hons.)) from the National Academy of Legal Studies and Research, University of Law, India, and her LL.M from the University of Michigan Law School, Ann Arbor, where she was a Hugo Grotius Fellow. She is currently a Senior Associate at *Narasappa, Doraswamy and Raja*, a Bangalore-based law firm. E-mail: neela@narasappa.com.

Alexandre Alcino de Barros is a Senior Associate at L.O. Baptista Advogados Associados, in Sao Paulo, Brazil. He received his law degree from the Mackenzie Presbyterian University in São Paulo. Mr. Barros obtained a Specialization in Civil Procedure at the Catholic University of Sao Paulo Law School, in São Paulo.

Nina Betetto has been a Justice of the Supreme Court of the Republic of Slovenia since 2006. From 2006 to 2008 she was the president of the Civil Law Study Commission of the International Association of Judges. She is the president of the Civil Section of the Slovenian Judges Association and the Slovenian delegate of the Consultative Council of the European Judges at the Council of Europe. She is also an international expert on various aspects of civil law and mediation, a regular lecturer and a leader of workshops and seminars for judges and mediators in Slovenia and abroad. She has published widely in the field of civil justice and mediation. In 2011 she was nominated the Vice-President of the Supreme Court of the Republic of Slovenia. E-mail: nina.betetto@sodisce.si.

Camille Cameron is a Professor in the Melbourne Law School, Australia. She was also the founder and is a co-Director of that law school's Civil Justice Research Group. She practiced law in Canada for 10 years, specializing in civil litigation, before becoming an academic. Her research and teaching interests are in Civil Procedure, Class Actions, Dispute Resolution and Court Reform in Transitional Legal Systems. In January 2012 Professor Cameron will take up the new position of Dean, Windsor Law School, Ontario, Canada. E-mail: c.cameron@unimelb.edu.au.

M. Reimann (ed.), *Cost and Fee Allocation in Civil Procedure*,
Ius Gentium: Comparative Perspectives on Law and Justice 11,
DOI 10.1007/978-94-007-2263-7, © Springer Science+Business Media B.V. 2012

Nicolas Cayrol Auteur d'une thèse intitulée «Les actes ayant pour objet l'action en justice» (Paris, Economica, 2001), agrégé des facultés de droit, Nicolas Cayrol enseigne la procédure civile à l'université Paris 8, Vincennes-St Denis et dirige l'Institut d'études Judiciaires François-Grua de l'Université de Tours. E-mail: nicolas.cayrol@univ-tours.fr.

Talia Fisher (LL.B., LL.M., LL.D., Hebrew University, 2004) is a Senior Lecturer at the Tel Aviv University Faculty of Law. She heads the Taubenschlag Institute of Criminal Law at Tel Aviv University. Her research interests include criminal law and private supply of legal institutions. E-mail: tafisher@post.tau.ac.il.

Greg Gordon, LL.B. (Hons), Dip. L.P. (Abdn), LL.M. (Cantab); Greg Gordon is a Lecturer in the School of Law at the University of Aberdeen. His teaching and research interests include oil and gas law, the law of obligations, adjectival law and professional responsibility. Prior to taking up his current appointment, he was a solicitor qualified to practice in Scotland and England and Wales. He specialized in litigation and his practice included commercial disputes, professional negligence as well as health and safety law. E-mail: law339@abdn.ac.uk.

Burkhard Hess is Professor of Private Law and Civil Procedure, International Private and Procedural Law at the University of Heidelberg Germany. He is a director of the University's Institute for Foreign and International Private and Commercial Law and serves as a part-time judge at the Court of Appeals in Karlsruhe. He has taught at various foreign universities as a visiting professor, served as the Dean of his faculty, and is Co-editor of several academic journals and series. E-mail: hess@ipr.uni-heidelberg.de.

Rudolf Huebner is a doctoral student and a research assistant at the Institute for Foreign and International Private and Commercial Law.

Jan Hurdík, DrSc., is professor of law and vice-head of the Civil Law Department of the Faculty of Law at the Masaryk University in Brno, Czech Republic. Since 2008, he has been a member of the Acquis Group of European Private Law, and since 2010, he has also belonged to the European Law Institute Association (ELIA). He is the author or a co-author of more than 80 books, textbooks, commentaries and articles on various issues concerning civil law and numerous articles and papers in specialized publications. In addition, he has been involved in a number of grant projects concerning legal education as well as in various research projects, as well as in government committee preparatory work on the new Civil Code. E-mail: jan.hurdik@law.muni.cz.

Gyooho Lee is professor of law at Chung-Ang University School of Law in Seoul, Republic of Korea. Besides being an active scholar, he serves as a director or vice president in various professional organizations, such as the Korean Civil Procedure Association and the Korea Private International

Law Association. He is a member of the International Association of Procedural Law and AIPPI Korea, and an associate member of American Society of Comparative Law. His special interests are intellectual property law, civil procedure, arbitration, private international law, law and economics, and comparative law. E-mail: ghlee@cau.ac.kr.

Marco B.M. Loos is professor of Private Law, in particular of European consumer law, at the Centre for the Study of European Contract Law of the University of Amsterdam as well as, inter alia, a member of the Study Group on a European Civil Code. He frequently publishes on Dutch and European contract law and consumer law, in particular with regard to sales law, service contract law, consumer protection and standard terms. E-mail: M.B.M.Loos@uva.nl.

Alessandra De Luca is researcher of comparative law, Faculty of Law, University of Florence, and lecturer of comparative law, Faculty of Economics, University of Florence. Her research areas are in comparative civil procedure, administration of justice, and access to justice. She is the author of *Accesso alla giustizia in Inghilterra fra stato e mercato* (Torino 2007). E-mail: adeluca@unifi.it.

Dr. Kalliopi Makridou is Professor of Civil Procedure and International Civil Procedure at the Law Faculty of the Aristotle University of Thessaloniki. Since 2008 she has also served as Vice-President of the Faculty. She has taught civil procedure at the Hellenic National School of judges (since 2000) and summer courses in "International Litigation" for the Tulane University School of Law, USA (2004–2007). She is a member of the Board of Directors of the Panhellenic Union of Civil Procedure Scholars, member of the International Association of Civil Procedure and of the I.C.C. She was recently appointed to the Committee to amend the Greek Code of Civil Procedure by the Ministry of Justice. Her academic interests are in the fields of Civil Procedure and International Litigation on which she has published various books and articles. E-mail: lioka2004@yahoo.gr.

Jarkko Männistö is a lawyer specializing in civil litigation. He works at his own law firm. Before starting his own firm, he worked as the secretary general of the Finnish Personal Injury Advisory Board. He is currently preparing his doctoral thesis on res judicata. E-mail: jarkko@jarkkomannisto.fi.

James R. Maxeiner is Associate Professor of Law at the University of Baltimore School of Law. Before becoming a professor of law, he was in international litigation practice in New York City with the law firms of Kaye Scholer and with Walter Conston (now Alston Bird), Vice President and Associate General Counsel of Dun & Bradstreet and Trial Attorney with the United States Department of Justice. In addition to law degrees from Cornell and Georgetown, he holds a doctorate in law (Dr. jur.) from the University of Munich obtained while he was Max Rheinstein Fellow of the Alexander von

Humboldt Foundation at the Max Planck Institute for Intellectual Property, Competition, and Tax Law. E-mail: jmaxeiner@ubalt.edu.

Sílvia Julio Bueno de Miranda is a Senior Associate at L.O.Baptista Advogados Associados, in Sao Paulo, Brazil. She received her law degree from the Catholic University of Sao Paulo Law School and her LL.M. from the University of Michigan Law School. Ms. Miranda obtained a Specialization in Corporate Law and another in Arbitration at the Fundação Getulio Vargas, in Sao Paulo. E-mail: sjbmiranda@gmail.com.

Richard Moorhead is a Professor of Law at Cardiff University. He has written extensively on lawyers, legal services and legal ethics. He is a former member of the Civil Justice Council in England and Wales. E-mail: moorheadr@cardiff.ac.uk.

H. Patrick Glenn is the Peter M. Laing Professor of Law, McGill University. He is a former Director of the McGill Institute of Comparative Law and a member of the Bars of British Columbia and Quebec. E-mail: patrick.glenn@mcgill.ca.

Cândida da Silva Antunes Pires, a former attorney and notary, is a professor at the University of Macau where she teaches, inter alia, civil procedure and comparative law. She was educated at the University of Lison, Portugal, but has lived in Macau since 1985. She has written widely on civil procedure and is a co-author of a commentary on the Code of Civil Procedure for Macau. She is also writing a commentary on the new Code of Civil Procedure of Cape Verde. Her further interests include commercial arbitration, labor law, family law, and environmental law. E-mail: csap@umac.mo.

Mathias Reimann is the Hessel E. Yntema Professor of Law at the University of Michigan. He is a titular member of the International Academy of Comparative Law and serves as the Editor-in-Chief of the American Journal of Comparative Law. His main interests are comparative law, international private law, and legal history.

Marianne Roth is professor of law and chairperson of the academic senate at Salzburg University, Austria. She is also practicing as an arbitrator under institutional and ad hoc rules, and has worked as a legal advisor and visiting professor for various institutions around the world (e.g. Thai Ministry of Justice, Ukrainian Cabinet of Ministers, University of the Pacific McGeorge School of Law, CA, University of Puerto Rico). In the past, Prof. Roth held chairs at Humboldt University Berlin and Christian Albrechts University Kiel, Germany. She completed her doctoral degree and habilitation at the Kepler University Linz, Austria, and holds an LL.M. from Harvard Law School. For her numerous writings Prof. Roth received several academic awards (e.g. the Albert S. Pergam Prize of the New York State Bar Association). E-mail: marianne.roth@sbg.ac.at.

Issi Rosen-Zvi teaches at the Tel Aviv University Faculty of Law. He obtained his LL.B. (magna cum laude) from Bar-Ilan University and his LL.M. in law and sociology from Tel Aviv University (summa cum laude). He continued his studies at Stanford Law School, where he received his J.S.D. in June, 2002. He clerked for the Honorable Chief Justice Aharon Barak of the Israeli Supreme Court and practiced law at Kirkland & Ellis, LLP in New York, before accepting his current appointment at Tel Aviv University in 2005. His research areas include environmental law, local government law and procedure. E-mail: issirz@post.tau.ac.il.

Vincent Sagaert is Professor of Private Law at the University of Leuven and Professor Property Law at the University of Antwerp. He has written numerous articles and books in the field of private law. He has been guest fellow at the University of Brussels, University of Hasselt, South African Research Chair Property Law, and the University of Utrecht. He is also an attorney at the Brussels Bar. E-mail: Vincent.sagaert@law.kuleuven.be.

Ilse Samoy is Professor Private Law at the University of Leuven and Hasselt. She teaches contract and tort law. Her research focuses on multiparty relationships. E-mail: ilse.samoy@law.kuleuven.be.

Francisco López Símo is full Professor of Procedural Law at the University of the Balearic Islands. He received his Ph.D. in law *summa cum laude* from the University of the Balearic Islands in 1990 and was a Lecturer in Procedural Law at the University Complutense of Madrid from 1991 to 1996. He is the author of almost 50 publications on a variety of topics of Spanish and European Procedural Law. He is a member of the *Instituto Iberoamericano de Derecho procesal*. E-mail: francisco.lopezsimo@uib.es.

Martin Sunnqvist is an Associate Judge of Appeal in the Scania and Blekinge Court of Appeal, Sweden. He is a graduate of the University of Lund Faculty of Law and has served as a co- organizer and active participants in comparative law conferences and workshops. E-mail: martin.sunnqvist@jur.lu.se.

José Ángel Torres Lana is full Professor of Civil Law at the University of the Balearic Islands. He received his Ph.D. in law *summa cum laude* from the University of Navarra in 1973 and was awarded the Extraordinary Prize for his doctoral thesis in 1974. He was a Lecturer in Civil Law at the Universities of Navarra and Granada and, since1985, at the University of Balearic Islands. He has been a member of the Spanish section of International Academy of Comparative Law since 1993. He is the author of more than 80 publications, including four books, on various topics of Spanish, European and American private law. E-mail: torres.lana@uib.es.

Manabu Wagatsuma is Professor of Law at the Tokyo Metropolitan Law Schoolin Japan. He specializes in civil procedure, bankruptcy and health law. He also serves as a judicial commissioner at the Tokyo Summary Court.

He was Fulbright visiting fellow at the Petrie-Flom Center at Harvard Law School from 2010 to 2011. E-mail: wagatsum@tmu.ac.jp.

Alena Zaytseva is the Deputy Chief of the Private Law Department at the Supreme Commercial Court of the Russian Federation. She is also a lecturer at the Faculty of Legal Provision for Market Economy Education of the Russian Academy of Civil Service under the President of the Russian Federation. E-mail: 7746817@mail.ru.

Caspar Zellweger is an attorney at law and partner in the firm of Flückiger, Mayer, Zellweger, Meyer, Hildbrand, in Basel, Switzerland. He holds a doctorate from the University of Basel and an LL.M. from the University of Michigan, USA. E-mail: zellweger@ballmer.ch.

Index

CPSIA information can be obtained at www.ICGtesting.com
Printed in the USA
LVOW100016040113
314313LV00007B/59/P